THE ARTIOS™ HOME COMPANY

"For I Know the Plans I Have For You"

CREATION TO THE FALL OF ROME

Elementary School

AUTHORS AND CONTRIBUTORS

LORI LANE

JOHN MICHAEL LANE

MARY E. HALL

JUDI PILLSBURY

PUBLISHED BY THE CREATED GROUP

Unless otherwise indicated, all Scripture quotations throughout this book are from The ESV® Bible (The Holy Bible, English Standard Version®) copyright © 2001 by Crossway Bibles, a publishing ministry of Good News Publishers. Used by permission. All rights reserved.

©CREATED GROUP 2023

Table of Contents

Curriculum Preface 1

Curriculum Details 6

Integration Chart 9

Unit 1: A Brand New World (4 lessons) 13

Unit 2: A Fallen World (4 lessons) 27

Unit 3: The Story of the Flood (2 lessons) 36

Unit 4: A Great Tower (2 lessons) 45

Unit 5: God Forms a New Nation (2 lessons) 52

Unit 6: Abraham and Isaac (2 lessons) 60

Unit 7: Jacob and Esau (3 lessons) 68

Unit 8: The Story of Joseph (4 lessons) 83

Unit 9: The Israelites in Egypt (3 lessons) 104

Unit 10: The Israelites in the Wilderness (4 lessons) 117

Unit 11: The Promised Land (5 lessons) 143

Unit 12: Great Kings and Prophets of Israel (4 lessons) 170

Unit 13: The Persian Empire (3 lessons) 189

Unit 14: Ancient India – "Land of Spice and Wonder" (4 lessons) 199

Unit 15: Ancient China – "Land of Legends" (3 lessons) 212

Unit 16: Ancient Japan – "Land of the Sunrise" (3 lessons) 225

Unit 17: Ancient Africa – "Land of Kingdoms (1 lessons) 236

Unit 18: Early People Groups of the Americas (3 lessons) 241

Unit 19: Ancient Greece (3 lessons) 256

Unit 20: Classical Greek History (3 lessons) 265

Unit 21: Classical Greek Culture (3 lessons) 283

Unit 22: Alexander the Great (1 lesson) 294

Unit 23: The Founding of Rome (4 lessons) 300

Unit 24: Making of an Empire (3 lessons) 318

Unit 25: The Culture of Ancient Rome (2 lessons) 330

Unit 26: Early Christian Life in the Roman World (2 lessons) 349

Unit 27: The Later Empire and the Christian Church (2 lessons) 361

Unit 28: The Fall of Rome (2 lessons) 373

The Artios Home Companion Series
Curriculum Preface

Welcome to The Artios Home Companion Series! The curriculum and resources in The Artios Home Companion Series are the same as those we use in our accredited academic program at our Artios Academies locations. Thus, you can know that it is a quality curriculum. However, The Artios Home Companion Series goes far beyond the usual tendency to promote the retention of facts and random pieces of information. A child is not educated by completing a particular curriculum or logging a certain number of hours. From God's viewpoint, "educated" is something you become.

As home educators, many of us desire to give our children a Biblical education grounded on Biblical principles. Many home educators apply Biblical principles to the content being taught. However, using Biblical principles in HOW you present the content is also essential. The reality is that many of us experienced education in a system with priorities, principles, and philosophies that, at their very core, were non-Biblical — or even worse, opposed to a Biblical perspective of education. Yet, we want to educate our children differently.

As a mom who home-educated her children for 23 years and a teacher of hundreds of home-educated students for more than 30 years, my search and study for a Biblical approach to education have been an ongoing journey. In many instances, I learned alongside my children while retraining my thoughts and methodology to fit what I saw in Scripture. I often wished I could buy one complete curriculum and finish my choices for the year. However, my heart told me that to meet the needs of each of my children individually, I needed to put much thought, prayer, and research into pulling together a unique curriculum that adapted to each of them. It wasn't easy and time-consuming to pull together pieces from various sources, knowing what to include and what to leave out.

Then, after going through this laborious process, it was even more daunting to realize the REAL work hadn't even begun. With materials selected and lesson plans ready, my job was just beginning. When it was time to execute the plan, I would need to be available to find those teachable "heart" moments with my children that would educate and stimulate so much more than just their minds. My goal with each of my children has been to graduate a well-rounded, heart-instructed student who knows the source of true knowledge and wisdom.

As my husband John and I began to envision how a Biblical approach to education would play out in the lives of each of our children and then in the life of our family, several key and core values began to surface. These core values formed a firm foundation to build our lives and family. They don't reflect methodology. Instead, they reflect a foundation upon which to base methodology. These values don't describe what we do. Instead, they reflect the foundation upon which we make strategic choices in fulfilling what God has called us to do.

These core values represent our worldview of education. "Exploring Christianity" quotes James Sire's definition of worldview as follows:
> "A world view is a set of presuppositions (assumptions which may be true, partially true or entirely false) which we hold (consciously or subconsciously, consistently or inconsistently) about the basic make-up of our world."

More simply put, worldview refers to the sum total of what we believe about the most important issues of life.[1]

As we began home-educating our children, we discussed what we felt were our God-given responsibilities and priorities in raising our children. The attempt to define and verbalize these priorities has been an ongoing process. However, I assure you that without these priorities, we will be tempted to make decisions based on fear, peer pressure, tradition, or other ungodly influences.

Throughout The Artios Home Companion curriculum, the choice of eclectic resources, the application of truths, the choice of emphasis, and the Heart Connections emphasized all reflect these core values. While developing The Artios Home Companion, we have tried to apply a Biblical worldview and the core values of Scripture. This curriculum will significantly help those parents wishing to reflect these core values to their children and will save them the time to pull together a myriad of resources.

What are these core values?
- God's Word reigns supreme and guides our thoughts and actions in every area of life.
- The heart is the focus of spiritual growth.
- God created man as a multi-faceted and unique individual.
- God's Word "equips" the children of God.
- Our lives and choices should reflect God's character to those around us.
- The family is a God-ordained institution through which the next generation is nurtured and discipled.

Let's look at each of these core values in more depth.

God's Word reigns supreme and guides our thoughts and actions in every area of life.
God's Word speaks to our issues, including questions regarding the world's origin, marriage, friends, entertainment, government, economics, and education. Because of this, God's Word and the principles found therein should be emphasized in the "teachable moments" found in every academic and arts-related topic. They should be discussed in every situation we face as we "walk along the way" with our students. More than throwing Scripture at a particular topic in arts and academics is required. Our goal should be to begin and end our study of each subject with God's Word as the foundation and the lens through which we view it.

2 Timothy 3:16 - 17 states this very plainly when it says, "All Scripture is breathed out by God and profitable for teaching, for reproof, for correction, and for training in righteousness, that the man of God may be complete, equipped for every good work." In Greek, this is the only instance of the word "Artios" appearing, and it means: competent, equipped, and thoroughly prepared. Isn't that what we want for our children? We want them to be competent, equipped, and prepared for whatever God has for them in the future. The answer to making sure they are equipped is not found in the perfect curriculum, the perfect methodology, or the perfect teacher. The source for preparing our children is God's Word. If we believe this is true, Scripture must reign in every aspect of life, instruction, and education. This belief should motivate us to ponder and consider the influence (or lack thereof) of God's Word in every academic and artistic subject.

In 2 Peter 1, Peter talks about the power of Scripture as including "all things that pertain to life and godliness." Thus, a Christian's worldview, including his approach to education, should be based on Biblical truth. To hurry through those teachable moments and opportunities, or to fail to see opportunities to teach our students how to apply God's truth as the guiding force behind their lives, is to miss a vital aspect of a truly Biblical approach to education. I love how Paul states this in I Corinthians 2:12-16 (ESV) when he says, "Now we have received not the spirit of the world, but the Spirit who is from God, that we might understand the things freely given us by God. And we impart this in words not taught by human wisdom but taught by the Spirit, interpreting spiritual truths to those who are spiritual. The natural person does not accept the things of the Spirit of God, for they are folly to him, and he is not able to understand them because they are spiritually discerned. The spiritual person judges all things, but is himself to be judged by no one. 'For who has understood the mind of the Lord so as to instruct him?' But we have the mind of Christ."

As I have journeyed through a study of Scripture to find what God says about the education of my children, I have realized time and time again that my thinking was "off" from what Scripture said was to be my priority. Colossians 2:8 gives a charge that many of us should take to heart: "See to it that no one takes you captive by

philosophy and empty deceit, according to human tradition, according to the elemental spirits of the world, and not according to Christ."

Many times, I have found myself influenced by a leader's personality, by peer pressure, by friends, by fear, and by tradition. Since my number-one core value and the guiding force behind my thoughts and actions is that God's Word reigns supreme, that should apply to my approach to education and the priorities for my children's education. It is to Scripture that I should first turn when making decisions in this and every area of my life.

In developing this curriculum, one of our goals has been to assist you in educating and equipping your children by providing you with a framework and specific help in finding those teachable moments, those times when God's Word can be applied to the topic at hand so that unique discussion and interaction can take place between you and your child as you "teach them in the way."

The heart is the focus of spiritual growth.

For a Christian educator, our primary focus should always be the instruction of the heart. In his 1828 dictionary, Webster defines the word heart as "the seat of affections and passions as of love, joy, grief, enmity, courage, pleasure." He defines "educate" in this way: "to bring up, as of a child; to instruct; to inform and enlighten the understanding; to instill into the mind principles of arts, science, morals, religion, and behavior. To educate children well is one of the most important duties of parents and guardians."

The heart is seen hundreds of times in Scripture. Its mention can be put into the following categories defined by Ruth Beechik, author of Heart and Mind: thought, emotion, motive, physical, spiritual, moral, general, or a combination. We instruct the heart of our students thoroughly and diligently. Deuteronomy 6:6-7 says, "And these words that I command you today shall be on your heart. You shall teach them diligently to your children, and shall talk of them when you sit in your house, and when you walk by the way, and when you lie down, and when you rise."

When we focus on the instruction of the heart, the things we find essential in education are forever altered. Although it is a noble aspiration to have your children do well in school, it is not a supreme priority. Although it is a noble aspiration to have them achieve high honors in various areas of life, it is not a top priority. More than a focus on outward performance and conformity is needed. Our goal should be the instruction of our child's heart. We must remember that the "fear of the Lord is the beginning of wisdom" — a wisdom that is much more than head knowledge but leads to a heart change.

Throughout this curriculum, we have found opportunities to assist you, not only with teaching the academic subjects but by pointing out those times when instruction of the heart is vital. Studying history, literature, science, the arts, and more, provides ample opportunities to demonstrate "heart matters."

God created man as a multi-faceted and unique individual.

Many of us have been educated in a secular system or private schools in which a secular philosophy of education has become prevalent. A secular philosophy of education views a student as a complex human organism just waiting to be filled by a learning process measured simply by the retention of facts and information.

In contrast, a Biblical view of education views education and learning as a personal process involving a student's heart, soul, and mind. With this view, education is measured by wisdom, understanding, and knowledge of the truth. Our children should be seen as "whole" and unique individuals whose whole being is addressed through the process we call education. Thus, our instructional approach throughout The Artios Home Companion Series is to implement a creative and integrative approach to learning. Just as each individual is unique and multi-faceted, life, in and of itself, is also multi-faceted. When a student is not guided to understand how his subject interacts with real life or other content areas, the motivation and enthusiasm for learning will not be strong. When

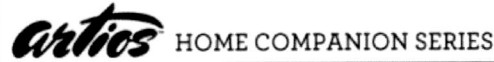

students realize that what they are studying is not alienated from other subjects or real life, there is a mental and emotional engagement. This is where real learning begins. At Artios, our subjects are integrated by time period, theme, and emphasis, referred to throughout the curriculum as "Heart Connections."

Not only is our approach to content and instruction creative, integrative, and multi-faceted, but throughout The Artios Home Companion Series, the learning activities and assessments are also creative, integrative, and multi-faceted, addressing various types of learning styles and teaching personalities.

Last, if you teach children of different ages within your home, we have integrated weekly topics at the appropriate age development level to allow for more family interaction, study, and discussion. This integration avoids having each student studying something different and the teacher (that's you) being pulled in numerous directions.

God's Word "equips" the children of God.

While traveling through this 23-year home education journey, I came across a book called *The Noah Plan* from The Foundation for American Education. Within that book, the authors contrast two historic worldviews of education. When we say that we have as a core value the fact that God's Word "equips" the children of God, it is essential to define the word "equip." To many, "equip" applies only to knowledge, academic competence, usefulness in society, and the ability to produce. However, the philosophy I found within this valuable resource, *The Noah Plan*, contrasted two very different views of someone "equipped" or "educated."

The authors contrasted a Hebrew philosophy with a Greek philosophy of education. I have included their chart:

	Hebrew Mindset	**Greek Mindset**
Education Begins:	Knowledge of God	Knowledge of Man
Essential Quality:	Holiness of God	Transference of Knowledge
Education is for:	All the people	Wealthy and leisure classes
Education is to develop:	The whole person	Aptitudes and talents
Why Learn:	To revere God	To comprehend
Object of Education	To know God and submit to the authority of His Word	To know thyself

While knowledge of man, a transference of knowledge, a knowledge of oneself, the ability to comprehend, and the development of specific aptitudes and talents may be essential, do you notice the difference in focus between the two columns? One column focuses on man, the other on God.

A few years ago, I wrote a book titled: *Beginning With the End in Mind*, which is a study of 2 Peter 1. In no uncertain terms, Peter tells us that our two highest priorities as Christians are to know God and to grow to become more like Him. If we "begin with the end in mind" in education, focusing on what God says is most important, then our approach and priorities in education will be transformed.

Our lives and choices should reflect God's character to those around us.

The study of history based on the lives and characters of individuals provides a superb means by which our focus on God's character helps us discern how the lives of significant historical figures did or did not portray

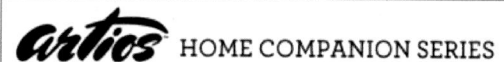

accurate reflections of their Creator. It has been said that studying history should prevent us from repeating past mistakes. However, it is one thing to study history. It is an entirely different approach to studying history through the study of individuals, studying the arts through the lens of historical events and their influences, and studying literature as a reflection of the time it was written. By studying these subjects and others in an integrative method, the subjects are given new meaning in the lives and minds of our children, and these individuals, events, actions, and products are all shown to be related. "No man is an island," and nothing could reveal this fact more accurately than studying subjects in an integrative and creative format.

It is all too common to study subjects in isolated and mindless file folders of information, never showing our students how life and LIVES interact. As children of the Most High God, we are to be a reflection of God to the world around us. But often, we think our actions and choices make little difference in the grand scheme of things. Nothing could be further from the truth. Our lives can influence for good or for evil, for positive action or negative apathy. Studying history, literature, the arts, and other subjects as they relate to each other helps students develop an integrated way of thinking and reasoning. On a spiritual level, it allows them to see their lives as a reflection of God in their unique spheres of influence.

The family is a God-ordained institution through which the next generation is nurtured and discipled.
The family is God's first institution shown in Scripture. By the very nature that God created it as a reflection of Christ and His church, it has essential meaning and an aspect of holiness and sanctity. Yet, each family is made up of individuals. Because of that, there are many variables in our approach to educating our children as individuals. We hope and pray that The Artios Home Companion Series will be able to come alongside you and assist you in your role as the God-ordained institution through which the next generation is nurtured and discipled. We hope that you will find contained within the pages of these resources the structure, guidance, and flexibility needed to approach the students within your family as individuals, all while you move together as a family unit to bring honor and glory to the One of whom we are to be a picture.

Faith and Courage,

Lori Lane
Artios Academies, Founder

---

1. Exploring Christianity - Truth, http://christianity.co.nz/2016/02/truth/

The Artios Home Companion Series
Curriculum Details

It has been said that methodology is nothing more than applied philosophy. All the core values I previously mentioned are now put into practical application through the logistics, choices, and options found within The Artios Home Companion Series. Each unit is divided into a teacher overview and one or more student lessons. For families with students at multiple grade levels, each level within the curriculum is color-coded: elementary, middle school, and high school.

Unit Overview

At the beginning of each unit, you will find a unit overview for you as the adult. On this page, you will find several important main headings: Topic Overview; Assignments and Activities; Key People, Places, and Events; Heart Connections; and, in some lessons, Vocabulary.

At the start of each unit, it will be essential for you to read through this overview. The information in this section will give you insight into the objectives for each unit. It will provide a broad overview of what you will be studying with your child throughout the unit and the emphasis suggested by The Artios Home Companion Series. Although middle school and high school students are becoming more independent than their elementary counterparts, it is still essential to stay abreast of what your student is studying even at these ages so that you can hold them accountable and keep them moving forward through the material and so that you can use the leading ideas and discussion questions as launching pads for discussions that lead to the discipleship of your children as you teach them "along the way."

Student Notebook

It is highly recommended that elementary and middle school students learn to set up a notebook based on their studies in The Artios Home Companion Series. This sets a wonderful foundation for the 4 R's of Research, Reason, Relate, and Record. You and your child's classroom teacher will determine the best means of organizing this notebook.

At the high school level, it is vitally important for students to conquer the skill of organization and to learn to set up a notebook of their own. These skills are crucial for college-level study in the future. This information will also prove helpful when your student is asked to research a particular topic at the college level. At that point, your student will find this notebook a beneficial resource.

History Section: In the case of history, the notebook serves as an excellent resource for portfolio review and a content-driven history timeline. This notebook can be set up based on the chronological sequence of the units in the curriculum, with a divider for each unit. It can be divided into seven-week sections or even one long line of notebook information. However you choose to use this notebook approach, be sure to place the information in the notebook in the order in which it is presented in the curriculum.

Literature Section: This section should be broken down by the book studied and contain information on the author, plot, literary elements, etc., pertaining to each literary piece studied.

Vocabulary Section: Last but not least, the student will be exposed to new vocabulary in both history and literature.

Lesson Contents

Teacher Overview: This section contains an overview of that unit's topic.

Assignments and Activities: Suggested reading, activities, and resources that correlate with the unit's topic and emphasis are included in this section. For elementary and middle school students, the assigned selection can be read aloud or independently, depending on the level and learning style of the student. For high school students, the assigned reading can be read independently. Still, during a week of a complicated topic or section of reading, the parent should be available for questions and discussion.

Heart Connections: These are ideas, principles, and lessons that can be taught based on the information contained in the unit and then reinforced through teachable moments and various activities. These principles are supported by Scripture that can be memorized to affirm this learning.

Key People, Places, and Events: Your student should give special attention to a list of important people, places, and events. The first significant instance of each of these in a lesson will be in a **bold** font.

Discussion Questions: It is suggested that following the reading for the day, the student "narrate" the information that has been read. At the elementary level, this can be done orally or in written form using one of the notebook pages provided in the student's notebook. Discussion questions serve as a guide to discern what information should be emphasized in that narration process. At the middle school and high school levels, the student should "narrate" in written form the information that has been read, including the answers to any discussion questions.

Vocabulary: In some lessons, vocabulary words will be listed. These should be written down, and a contextual or researched definition should also be written out. It is suggested that these be written in a separate divider section of the student's notebook and that one letter of the alphabet be assigned to each page. The first significant instance of each of these in a unit will be in a **bold** font.

Articles: Articles present one of our many opportunities as Christian parents and teachers to help students develop discernment. Some articles may present the myths and beliefs of various cultures and time periods. The articles sometimes present those beliefs as true (i.e., Greek and Roman Mythology). Occasionally an article may even present an invalid or incorrect view of an event or issue to challenge the student to research and search for the truth or do compare and contrast research. Please help your students to recognize those things that stand opposed to God's Truth as you go through each lesson together and contrast those beliefs with the Christian doctrines of monotheism and salvation by grace through faith.

Special Study: A student's interest or curiosity may be piqued by a person or historical event. Don't miss this opportunity to flex with the interest of your student. The Artios Home Companion Series provides suggested activities and a schedule outline.

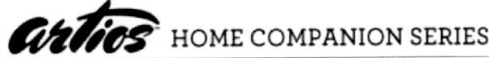

However, this should not be considered a constricting resource but a jumping-off point for interest-driven adventures!

Learning Styles: Each unit contains primary assignments and suggested activities. However, you may want to mix up activity types from time to time. This way, you will find optional or substitute activities for your student(s) to assess or reinforce their learning. These activities are made up of learning-style-specific activities designed to target different types of learners specifically.

Websites: Some units list websites and videos for a parent or student to access, either for suggested assignments or additional resources. Since websites are subject to being removed, instead of printing these in the textbook, they are provided on the ArtiosHCS curriculum website. Because of the dynamic nature of the Internet, any web addresses or links on the ArtiosHCS curriculum website may change or no longer be valid. As we become aware of these, we will attempt to find a replacement. **Note**: *The articles, websites, and videos selected for this curriculum represent various artistic and teaching styles to familiarize students with more than one style for conveying information. Also, while we benefit from the research involved in the production of each one, please be aware that some information presented within them, or values espoused by their producers, may not be entirely accurate or in agreement with Christian values. Please constantly be discerning while teaching.*

Unit #	History	Literature
Unit 1	EL: A Brand New World MS: In the Beginning . . . HS: Creation and the Fall	EL: *Hittite Warrior*, Joanne Williamson MS: *The Golden Fleece*, Padraic Colum HS: *Paradise Lost*, John Milton
Unit 2	EL: A Fallen World MS: The World's First Family HS: Effects of the Fall	EL: *Hittite Warrior*, Joanne Williamson MS: *The Golden Fleece*, Padraic Colum HS: *Paradise Lost*, John Milton
Unit 3	EL: The Story of the Flood MS: The Great Flood HS: The Deluge	EL: *Hittite Warrior*, Joanne Williamson MS: *The Golden Fleece*, Padraic Colum HS: *Paradise Lost*, John Milton
Unit 4	EL: A Great Tower MS: The Beginning of Post-Flood Civilization HS: Civilization Rises in Mesopotamia	EL: *Hittite Warrior*, Joanne Williamson MS: *The Golden Fleece*, Padraic Colum HS: *Paradise Lost*, John Milton
Unit 5	EL: God Forms a New Nation MS: The Ancient World and Israel HS: The Ancient World and Abraham	EL: *Hittite Warrior*, Joanne Williamson MS: *Mara, Daughter of the Nile*, Eloise Jarvis McGraw HS: *Oedipus Rex*, Sophocles
Unit 6	EL: Abraham and Isaac MS: God's Promise to Abraham HS: "Father of the Faithful"	EL: *The Golden Goblet*, Eloise Jarvis McGraw MS: *Mara, Daughter of the Nile*, Eloise Jarvis McGraw HS: *Oedipus Rex*, Sophocles
Unit 7	EL: Jacob and Esau MS: The Sons of Isaac HS: The Nations of Israel and Egypt	EL: *The Golden Goblet*, Eloise Jarvis McGraw MS: *Mara, Daughter of the Nile*, Eloise Jarvis McGraw HS: *Odyssey*, Homer

Unit #	History	Literature
Unit 8	EL: The Story of Joseph MS: Father Abraham Had Many Sons HS: Joseph in Egypt	EL: *The Golden Goblet,* Eloise Jarvis McGraw MS: *Iliad,* Homer HS: *Odyssey,* Homer
Unit 9	EL: The Israelites in Egypt MS: Many Sons Had Father Abraham HS: The Israelites in Egypt	EL: *The Golden Goblet,* Eloise Jarvis McGraw MS: *Iliad,* Homer HS: *Odyssey,* Homer
Unit 10	EL: The Israelites in the Wilderness MS: God's People Delivered HS: God Delivers the Israelites	EL: *The Golden Goblet,* Eloise Jarvis McGraw MS: *Iliad,* Homer HS: *Odyssey,* Homer
Unit 11	EL: The Promised Land MS: From the Desert to Israel's Golden Age HS: From Judges to Kings	EL: *Theras and His Town,* Caroline Dale Snedeker MS: *Iliad,* Homer HS: *Odyssey,* Homer
Unit 12	EL: Great Kings and Prophets of Israel MS: After Israel's Golden Age HS: Jewish Captivity and Restoration	EL: *Theras and His Town,* Caroline Dale Snedeker MS: *The Bronze Bow,* Elizabeth George Speare HS: Selected Scripture Passages
Unit 13	EL: The Persian Empire MS: Persia, Greece, and Israel HS: The Greco-Persian Wars	EL: *Theras and His Town,* Caroline Dale Snedeker MS: *The Bronze Bow,* Elizabeth George Speare HS: Selected Scripture Passages
Unit 14	EL: Ancient India – "Land of Spice and Wonder" MS: Ancient India – "Land of Contrasts" HS: Ancient India – "Land of the Tiger"	EL: *Theras and His Town,* Caroline Dale Snedeker MS: *The Bronze Bow,* Elizabeth George Speare HS: Selected Scripture Passages

Unit #	History	Literature
Unit 15	EL: Ancient China – "Land of Legends" MS: Ancient China – "Land of Mystery" HS: Ancient China – "Land of Dragons and Emperors"	EL: *The Samurai's Tale*, Erik C. Haugaard MS: *Masada: The Last Fortress*, Gloria D. Miklowitz HS: *Till We Have Faces*, C.S.Lewis
Unit 16	EL: Ancient Japan – "Land of the Sunrise" MS: Ancient Japan – "Land of the Sun's Origin" HS: Ancient Japan – "Land of the Rising Sun"	EL: *The Samurai's Tale*, Erik C. Haugaard MS: *Masada: The Last Fortress*, Gloria D. Miklowitz HS: *Till We Have Faces*, C.S.Lewis
Unit 17	EL: Ancient Africa – "Land of Kingdoms" MS: Early African History – "Land of Conquests" HS: Early Cultures of Africa – "Land of Gold"	EL: *The Samurai's Tale*, Erik C. Haugaard MS: *Masada: The Last Fortress*, Gloria D. Miklowitz HS: *Till We Have Faces*, C.S.Lewis
Unit 18	EL: Early People Groups of the Americas MS: Early Civilizations of the Americas HS: Early Cultures of the Americas	EL: *The Samurai's Tale*, Erik C. Haugaard MS: Research Paper/no literature HS: *Till We Have Faces*, C.S.Lewis
Unit 19	EL: Ancient Greece MS: Early Greek Cultures HS: Early Ancient Greece	EL: *The Samurai's Tale*, Erik C. Haugaard MS: Research Paper/no literature HS: *Aeneid*, Virgil
Unit 20	EL: Classical Greek History MS: History of Classical Greek HS: Classical Greek History	EL: *The Bronze Bow*, Elizabeth George Speare MS: Research Paper/no literature HS: *Aeneid*, Virgil
Unit 21	EL: Classical Greek Culture MS: Classical Greek Arts and Culture HS: Classical Greek Society and Arts	EL: *The Bronze Bow*, Elizabeth George Speare MS: *The Eagle of the Ninth*, Rosemary Sutcliff HS: *Aeneid*, Virgil

Unit #	History	Literature
Unit 22	EL: Alexander the Great MS: Alexander the Great and His Conquests HS: Alexander the Great and the Hellenistic Age	EL: *The Bronze Bow*, Elizabeth George Speare MS: *The Eagle of the Ninth*, Rosemary Sutcliff HS: *Aeneid*, Virgil
Unit 23	EL: The Founding of Rome MS: Early Roman History HS: The Rise of Rome	EL: *The Bronze Bow*, Elizabeth George Speare MS: *The Eagle of the Ninth*, Rosemary Sutcliff HS: *Quo Vadis*, Henryk Sienkiewicz
Unit 24	EL: Making of an Empire MS: Start of the Roman Empire HS: The Republic Becomes an Empire	EL: *The Bronze Bow*, Elizabeth George Speare MS: *The Eagle of the Ninth*, Rosemary Sutcliff HS: *Quo Vadis*, Henryk Sienkiewicz
Unit 25	EL: The Culture of Ancient Rome MS: Life and Culture in Ancient Rome HS: Ancient Roman Culture	EL: *The Martyr of the Catacombs,*v Author Unknown MS: Creative Writing / no literature HS: *Quo Vadis*, Henryk Sienkiewicz
Unit 26	EL: Early Christian Life in the Roman World MS: Start of the Pax Romana and the Christian Church HS: Start of the Pax Romana and Christianity	EL: *The Martyr of the Catacombs*, Author Unknown MS: Creative Writing / no literature HS: *Quo Vadis*, Henryk Sienkiewicz
Unit 27	EL: The Later Empire and the Christian Church MS: Rome's Later Empire HS: The Later Roman Empire: Church and State	EL: *The Martyr of the Catacombs*, Author Unknown MS: Creative Writing / no literature HS: *Quo Vadis*, Henryk Sienkiewicz
Unit 28	EL: The Fall of Rome MS: The End of the Ancient Story HS The Ancient Story Ends	EL: *The Martyr of the Catacombs*, Author Unknown MS: Creative Writing / no literature HS: Complete Essay / no literature

The Artios Home Companion Series
Unit 1: A Brand New World

Teacher Overview

GOD'S WORD TELLS us the story of the Creation of the world and the beginning of sin. This unit explores the story and man's disobedience and fall into sin. But it does not stop there. It also includes the promise of redemption for God's people through the person of His Son, Jesus Christ.

The Garden of Eden, by Izaak van Oosten (c.1655-1661)

Suggested Assignments

Based on your student's age and ability, the reading in this unit may be read aloud to the student, and journaling and notebook pages may be completed orally. Likewise, other assignments may be done with an appropriate combination of independent and guided study.

In this unit, students will:
- Complete four lessons in which they will learn about the **Creation of the world**, the **geography of the earth**, and the **Fall of Man**.
- Define vocabulary words.
- See the Additional Material section (below) for information about purchasing the **Ancient World map packet** that will be used throughout this year's curriculum.
- Please be sure to take note of extra map assignments in this unit to integrate geography with history.

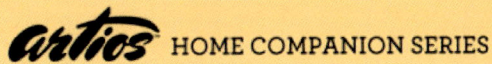 HOME COMPANION SERIES

Ancient: Elementary
Unit 1: A Brand New World

- On the **ArtiosHCS** curriculum website, you will find a link to a video with instructions on "How to Make a Mini-Book." Lesson One calls for a Mini-Book to be made.
- Visit the **ArtiosHCS** curriculum website at **www.ArtiosHCS.com** for additional resources and any videos and websites assigned for this unit.

NOTE: Throughout this volume, there are lessons where the article consists of a Scripture passage taken from the King James Version of the Bible (KJV). Students may read the Bible passage in the book or read it in another translation. Please use a translation, not a paraphrased version such as *The Message* or *The Living Bible*.

Also, please note that many of the readings in the lessons of this volume have been supplemented by the inclusion of text boxes that contain updated or additional information not included by the articles' original authors.

Heart Connections

God is our Creator.
>*In the beginning, God created the heavens and the earth.*
>   – Genesis 1:1

Man is fallen and in need of a Savior.
>*For all have sinned and fall short of the glory of God.*
>   – Romans 3:23

Vocabulary

Lesson 1:	Lesson 2:	Lesson 3:	Lesson 4:
firmament (or expanse)	none	beguile	elusive indulgence expulsion

Key People, Places, and Events

Six days of Creation Creation	Eve Adam	Garden of Eden Euphrates River	Tigris River

Additional Material For Parent or Teacher:

- See the link on the **ArtiosHCS** curriculum website to purchase the Ancient World map packet for use throughout this year's curriculum. You will receive instant access to the *Map Trek: Ancient World* e-book when you purchase it.
- A valuable resource to refer to during the Ancient time period is the book *Leading Little Ones to God* by Marian Schoolland and Paul Staub. This book takes many of the Biblical passages we are reading. It simplifies them so that even the youngest student will understand the passage's content, context, and Biblical principles.

Lesson One

History Overview and Assignments
God Creates the World

IN THE BEGINNING, God created the universe. Many history books teach that the universe developed by chance, but they don't explain how everything could have come from nothing or how it could have come together in the very special way it did. God's Word tells us the truth about how God, who has always existed, brought everything into being according to His wonderful plan.

When God made people, He created them, male and female, giving them the wonderful gift of marriage. Then He gave them the special job of cultivating the earth. Once He finished creating the world, He rested, blessing that day as a special day of rest.

The Creation, by James Tissot (c.1896–1902)

Suggested Reading and Assignments

- Read the article: *Genesis 1:1-2:3*.
- Define the vocabulary word in the context of the reading. Write the word and its definition in the vocabulary section of your notebook.
- After reading the article, summarize the story you read by either:
  - Retelling it out loud to your teacher or parent.
     OR
  - Completing an appropriate notebook page.

  Either way, be sure to include the answers to the discussion questions and an overview of key people, places, dates, and events in your summary.

Ancient: Elementary
Unit 1: A Brand New World

- Create a mini-book that features each of the six days of Creation and the one day of rest. You can draw what was created each day or find pictures to cut out and add to your mini-book. You will find a link to a video with instructions on your **ArtiosHCS** curriculum website.
- Be sure to visit your **ArtiosHCS** curriculum website for additional resources and any videos and websites assigned for this lesson.

Vocabulary

firmament (or expanse)

Key People, Places, and Events

Six days of Creation

Discussion Questions

1. What did God create on the first day of Creation?
2. What did God create on the second day of Creation?
3. What did God create on the third day of Creation?
4. What did God create on the fourth day of Creation?
5. What did God create on the fifth day of Creation?
6. What did God create on the sixth day of Creation?
7. What did God do on the seventh day?
8. What did God say at the end of each day of Creation?

Genesis 1:1 - 2:3

Genesis 1

1 In the beginning God created the heaven and the earth.

2 And the earth was without form, and void; and darkness was upon the face of the deep. And the Spirit of God moved upon the face of the waters.

3 And God said, Let there be light: and there was light.

4 And God saw the light, that it was good: and God divided the light from the darkness.

5 And God called the light Day, and the darkness he called Night. And the evening and the morning were the first day.

6 And God said, Let there be a **firmament** in the midst of the waters, and let it divide the waters from the waters.

7 And God made the firmament, and divided the waters which were under the firmament from the waters which were above the firmament: and it was so.

8 And God called the firmament Heaven. And the evening and the morning were the second day.

9 And God said, Let the waters under the heaven be gathered together unto one place, and let the dry land appear: and it was so.

10 And God called the dry land Earth; and the gathering together of the waters called the Seas: and God saw that it was good.

11 And God said, Let the earth bring forth grass, the herb yielding seed, and the fruit tree yielding fruit after his kind, whose seed is in itself, upon the earth: and it was so.

12 And the earth brought forth grass, and herb yielding seed after his kind, and the tree yielding fruit, whose seed was in itself, after his kind: and God saw that it was good.

13 And the evening and the morning were the third day.

14 And God said, Let there be lights in the firmament of the heaven to divide the day from the night; and let them be for signs, and for seasons, and for days, and years:

15 And let them be for lights in the firmament of the heaven to give light upon the earth: and it was so.

16 And God made two great lights; the greater light to rule the day, and the lesser light to rule the night: he made the stars also.

17 And God set them in the firmament of the heaven to give light upon the earth,

18 And to rule over the day and over the night, and to divide the light from the darkness: and God saw that it was good.

19 And the evening and the morning were the fourth day.

20 And God said, Let the waters bring forth abundantly the moving creature that hath life, and fowl that may fly above the earth in the open firmament of heaven.

21 And God created great whales, and every living creature that moveth, which the waters brought forth abundantly, after their kind, and every winged fowl after his kind: and God saw that it was good.

22 And God blessed them, saying, Be fruitful, and multiply, and fill the waters in the seas, and let fowl multiply in the earth.

23 And the evening and the morning were the fifth day.

24 And God said, Let the earth bring forth the living creature after his kind, cattle, and creeping thing, and beast of the earth after his kind: and it was so.

25 And God made the beast of the earth after his kind, and cattle after their kind, and every thing that creepeth upon the earth after his kind: and God saw that it was good.

26 And God said, Let us make man in our image, after our likeness: and let them have dominion over the fish of the sea, and over the fowl of the air, and over the cattle, and over all the earth, and over every creeping thing that creepeth upon the earth.

27 So God created man in his own image, in the image of God created he him; male and female created he them.

28 And God blessed them, and God said unto them, Be fruitful, and multiply, and replenish the earth, and subdue it: and have dominion over the fish of the sea, and over the fowl of the air, and over every living thing that moveth upon the earth.

29 And God said, Behold, I have given you every herb bearing seed, which is upon the face of all the earth, and every tree, in the which is the fruit of a tree yielding seed; to you it shall be for meat.

30 And to every beast of the earth, and to every fowl of the air, and to every thing that creepeth upon the earth, wherein there is life, I have given every green herb for meat: and it was so.

31 And God saw every thing that he had made, and, behold, it was very good. And the evening and the morning were the sixth day.

Genesis 2

1 Thus the heavens and the earth were finished, and all the host of them.

2 And on the seventh day God ended his work which he had made; and he rested on the seventh day from all his work which he had made.

3 And God blessed the seventh day, and sanctified it: because that in it he had rested from all his work which God created and made.

Lesson Two

History Overview and Assignments
God Planted a Garden

GOD DID NOT TOSS Creation together randomly but ordered and arranged everything He made according to His perfect plan and purpose.

The Garden of Eden With the Fall of Man, by Jan Brueghel the Elder (1612)

Suggested Reading and Assignments

- Read the article: *Genesis 2:8-14*.
- After reading the article, summarize the story you read by either:
    - Retelling it out loud to your teacher or parent.
        OR
    - Completing an appropriate notebook page.
    Either way, be sure to include the answers to the discussion questions and an overview of key people, places, dates, and events in your summary.
- Be sure to visit your **ArtiosHCS** curriculum website for additional resources and any videos and websites assigned for this lesson.

Discussion Questions

1. What were the ancient names of the four rivers that flowed out of Eden?

Genesis 2:8 - 14

Genesis 2

8 And the LORD God planted a garden eastward in Eden; and there he put the man whom he had formed.

9 And out of the ground made the LORD God to grow every tree that is pleasant to the sight, and good for food; the tree of life also in the midst of the garden, and the tree of knowledge of good and evil.

10 And a river went out of Eden to water the garden; and from thence it was parted, and became into four heads.

11 The name of the first is Pison: that is it which compasseth the whole land of Havilah, where there is gold;

12 And the gold of that land is good: there is bdellium and the onyx stone.

13 And the name of the second river is Gihon: the same is it that compasseth the whole land of Ethiopia.

14 And the name of the third river is Hiddekel: that is it which goeth toward the east of Assyria. And the fourth river is Euphrates.

The Garden of Eden,
by Thomas Cole (1828)

Lesson Three

History Overview and Assignments
Expelled

BECAUSE GOD is our Creator, He owns us, and we have a duty to obey Him in all things. Adam and Eve sinned against God when they disobeyed Him. Because of their sin, they were cast out of the Garden of Eden.

Adam and Eve in the Garden of Eden, by Johann Wenzel Peter (c.1800-1829)

Suggested Reading and Assignments

- Read the article: *Genesis 2:15-3:24*.
- After reading the article, summarize the story you read by either:
    - Retelling it out loud to your teacher or parent.
        OR
    - Completing an appropriate notebook page.
    Either way, be sure to include the answers to the discussion questions and an overview of key people, places, dates, and events in your summary.
- Define the vocabulary word in the context of the reading. Write the word and its definition in the vocabulary section of your notebook.
- Be sure to visit your **ArtiosHCS** curriculum website for additional resources and any videos and websites assigned for this lesson.

Vocabulary

beguile

Ancient: Elementary
Unit 1: A Brand New World

Discussion Questions

1. What job did God give the man when He put him into the Garden?
2. Did God have any rules in the Garden for Adam and Eve?
3. How did God create the woman, Eve?
4. What type of animal tempted Eve when she wandered near the tree they had been told not to eat from?
5. What did he say to her?
6. Did Eve obey God?
7. What happened after she and Adam disobeyed?
8. How were they punished?

Genesis 2:15 - 3:24

Genesis 2

15 And the LORD God took the man, and put him into the garden of Eden to dress it and to keep it.

16 And the LORD God commanded the man, saying, Of every tree of the garden thou mayest freely eat:

17 But of the tree of the knowledge of good and evil, thou shalt not eat of it: for in the day that thou eatest thereof thou shalt surely die.

18 And the LORD God said, It is not good that the man should be alone; I will make him an help meet for him.

19 And out of the ground the LORD God formed every beast of the field, and every fowl of the air; and brought them unto Adam to see what he would call them: and whatsoever Adam called every living creature, that was the name thereof.

20 And Adam gave names to all cattle, and to the fowl of the air, and to every beast of the field; but for Adam there was not found an help meet for him.

21 And the LORD God caused a deep sleep to fall upon Adam, and he slept: and he took one of his ribs, and closed up the flesh instead thereof;

22 And the rib, which the LORD God had taken from man, made he a woman, and brought her unto the man.

23 And Adam said, This is now bone of my bones, and flesh of my flesh: she shall be called Woman, because she was taken out of Man.

24 Therefore shall a man leave his father and his mother, and shall cleave unto his wife: and they shall be one flesh.

25 And they were both naked, the man and his wife, and were not ashamed.

Genesis 3

1 Now the serpent was more subtil than any beast of the field which the LORD God had made. And he said unto the woman, Yea, hath God said, Ye shall not eat of every tree of the garden?

2 And the woman said unto the serpent, We may eat of the fruit of the trees of the garden:

3 But of the fruit of the tree which is in the midst of the garden, God hath said, Ye shall not eat of it, neither shall ye touch it, lest ye die.

4 And the serpent said unto the woman, Ye shall not surely die:

5 For God doth know that in the day ye eat thereof, then your eyes shall be opened,

and ye shall be as gods, knowing good and evil.

6 And when the woman saw that the tree was good for food, and that it was pleasant to the eyes, and a tree to be desired to make one wise, she took of the fruit thereof, and did eat, and gave also unto her husband with her; and he did eat.

7 And the eyes of them both were opened, and they knew that they were naked; and they sewed fig leaves together, and made themselves aprons.

8 And they heard the voice of the LORD God walking in the garden in the cool of the day: and Adam and his wife hid themselves from the presence of the LORD God amongst the trees of the garden.

9 And the LORD God called unto Adam, and said unto him, Where art thou?

10 And he said, I heard thy voice in the garden, and I was afraid, because I was naked; and I hid myself.

11 And he said, Who told thee that thou wast naked? Hast thou eaten of the tree, whereof I commanded thee that thou shouldest not eat?

12 And the man said, The woman whom thou gavest to be with me, she gave me of the tree, and I did eat.

13 And the LORD God said unto the woman, What is this that thou hast done? And the woman said, The serpent **beguile**d me, and I did eat.

14 And the LORD God said unto the serpent, Because thou hast done this, thou art cursed above all cattle, and above every beast of the field; upon thy belly shalt thou go, and dust shalt thou eat all the days of thy life:

15 And I will put enmity between thee and the woman, and between thy seed and her seed; it shall bruise thy head, and thou shalt bruise his heel.

16 Unto the woman he said, I will greatly multiply thy sorrow and thy conception; in sorrow thou shalt bring forth children; and thy desire shall be to thy husband, and he shall rule over thee.

17 And unto Adam he said, Because thou hast hearkened unto the voice of thy wife, and hast eaten of the tree, of which I commanded thee, saying, Thou shalt not eat of it: cursed is the ground for thy sake; in sorrow shalt thou eat of it all the days of thy life;

18 Thorns also and thistles shall it bring forth to thee; and thou shalt eat the herb of the field;

19 In the sweat of thy face shalt thou eat bread, till thou return unto the ground; for out of it wast thou taken: for dust thou art, and unto dust shalt thou return.

20 And Adam called his wife's name Eve; because she was the mother of all living.

21 Unto Adam also and to his wife did the LORD God make coats of skins, and clothed them.

22 And the LORD God said, Behold, the man is become as one of us, to know good and evil: and now, lest he put forth his hand, and take also of the tree of life, and eat, and live for ever:

23 Therefore the LORD God sent him forth from the garden of Eden, to till the ground from whence he was taken.

24 So he drove out the man; and he placed at the east of the garden of Eden Cherubims, and a flaming sword which turned every way, to keep the way of the tree of life.

Lesson Four

History Overview and Assignments
Something From Nothing

"Man was expelled from Paradise and prevented from reentering it by cherubim's flaming sword. The only comfort in the sentence was that the 'seed' of the woman would eventually triumph over the 'seed' of the Serpent."

– from the adapted article below

Paradise, by Jan Brueghel the Younger (c.1650)

Suggested Reading and Assignments

- Read the article: *The History of the World Begins.*
- Define each vocabulary word in the context of the reading. Write the words and their definitions in the vocabulary section of your notebook.
- After reading the article, summarize the story you read by either:
    - Retelling it out loud to your teacher or parent.
        OR
    - Completing an appropriate notebook page.
  Either way, be sure to include the answers to the discussion questions and an overview of key people, places, dates, and events in your summary.

Ancient: Elementary
Unit 1: A Brand New World

- Using the map of Mesopotamia in the *Map Trek: Ancient World* eBook you purchased, identify the possible location for the Garden of Eden.
- Explore the website at the link found on your **ArtiosHCS** curriculum website.
  - Does the web article below agree with what we read in today's article about where the Garden of Eden may have been located?
- Be sure to visit your **ArtiosHCS** curriculum website for additional resources and any videos and websites assigned for this lesson.

Vocabulary

elusive
indulgence
expulsion

Key People, Places, and Events

Creation
Eve
Adam

Garden of Eden
Tigris River
Euphrates River

Discussion Questions

1. What was the original occupation (job) that God gave to man?
2. What were the three institutions that God established before the Fall?
3. Can we know where the Garden of Eden was?
4. What type of animal form did Satan take when he tempted Eve?
5. What great change did Adam and Eve experience once they disobeyed God?
6. Describe the woman's penalty for her disobedience.
7. Describe the man's penalty for his disobedience.
8. What was one of the remaining ways of achieving happiness for man after the Fall?

Adapted for Elementary School from the book:
Ancient States and Empires
by John Lord
The History of the World Begins

Creation

The history of our world begins with substance brought forth from nothing. In six days, God created light and darkness, day and night, the firmament and the continents in the midst of the waters; then fruits, grain, and herbs, moon and stars, fowl and fish, living creatures upon the face of the earth; and finally man, with dominion over the fish of the sea, and the birds of the air, and cattle, and all the earth, and every living thing that moves upon the earth.[1] He created man in His own image and blessed him with dominion over all created things. He formed him from the dust of the ground and breathed into his nostrils the breath of life. On the seventh day, God rested from this vast work of **creation**. He blessed the seventh day and sanctified it for a day of rest for all generations.

The Garden of Eden

He planted a garden eastward in Eden, with every tree pleasant to the sight and good for food, and there placed man to cultivate and keep it. The original occupation of man, and his destined happiness, were thus centered on farming work.

Adam and Eve

But man was alone, so God caused a

deep sleep to fall upon him, took one of his ribs, and made a woman, **Eve**. And **Adam** said, "This woman," which the Lord had brought to him, "is bone of my bone and flesh of my flesh. Therefore shall a man leave his father and mother and cleave unto his wife: and they shall be one flesh." Thus marriage was begun. We see three divine institutions established while man remained in a state of innocence and bliss— the Sabbath, farming employment, and marriage.

Primeval Paradise

We know not how long Adam and his wife lived in the **Garden of Eden**, with perfect innocence, bliss, and dominion. They did not even know what sin was. There were no other conditions imposed upon them than that they were not to eat of the fruit of the Tree of Knowledge of Good and Evil, which was in the midst of the garden— a beautiful tree, "pleasant to the eyes, and one to be desired."

Location of Eden

Where was this garden—this paradise— located? This isn't easy to answer. As far as we know, it lay at the headwaters of four rivers, two of which were the **Euphrates River** and the **Tigris River**. We might guess from this that it was situated somewhere among the mountains of Armenia, south of the Caucasus, a temperate region, in the latitude of Greece and Italy. But we cannot know for certain where it was.

Glory of Eden

We can only imagine how beautiful and fruitful this garden was, watered by mists from the earth and not by rains from the clouds, ever fresh and green. At the same time, its two noble occupants lived upon its produce, directly communing with God, in whose image they were made, moral and spiritual—free from all sin and misery, and, as we may imagine, able to speak with each other about great and lofty things.

But sin entered into this beautiful world, and death by sin.

The Temptation

The first of all people were tempted, and they did not resist the temptation. This was a devastating reality in view of its consequences.

The Devil

The tempter was the devil—the enemy of God—the evil power of the world which Scripture and all nations, in some form, have recognized. We do not know when rebellion against God began, but it certainly existed by the time Adam was placed in Eden.

His Taking of the Form of a Serpent

The form Satanic power assumed was that of a serpent—then the most **elusive** of the beasts of the field, and we may reasonably suppose not merely elusive but attractive, graceful, beautiful, and bewitching.

The Disobedience of Eve

The woman was first to feel the devil's evil fascination, and she was persuaded to disobey what she knew to be a direct command from God by the desire for knowledge and **indulgence** of the appetite. She placed her trust in the serpent. She believed his lie and was beguiled.

The Fall of Man

The man was not directly beguiled by the serpent. Why the serpent assailed woman rather than man, the Scriptures do not say. The man yielded to his wife. "She gave him the fruit, and he ate of it."

The Effect

Immediately a significant change came over both people. Their eyes were opened. They felt shame and remorse, for they had sinned. They hid themselves from the presence of the Lord and were afraid.

The Penalty

God pronounced the punishment—for the woman, the pains and sorrows of childbirth and being ruled over by her husband. For the man, labor, toil, sorrow—the curse of the ground which he was to till—thorns and thistles—lack of rest, and food obtained only by the sweat of the brow. All these pains and labors were inflicted upon both until they would return to the dust from which they were taken—an eternal decree, never changed, to last as long as man should till the earth or woman bring forth children.

Introduction of Sin

This is how sin came into the world, through the temptations introduced by Satan and man's weakness, with the penalty of labor, pain, sorrow, and death.

Expulsion From Paradise

Man was expelled from Paradise and prevented from reentering it by the flaming sword of cherubim, until the location of Eden, by thorns, briars, and the Deluge was lost. And man and woman were sent out into the world to reap the fruit of their folly and sin and to gain their food from severe toil amid the accumulated evils that sin introduced.

Adam and Eve Driven Out of Paradise, illustration from the 1890 Holman Bible

The Comfort After the Punishment

The only comfort in the sentence was that the "seed" (or offspring) of the woman would eventually triumph over the "seed" of the Serpent. The ritual of sacrifice, by killing an animal and clothing Adam and Eve with its skin, was introduced as a way of showing the payment for sin by the death of a substitute for the sinner, and thus a hope of final forgiveness held out for sin. Meanwhile, the miseries of life were eased by the fruits of labor.

Work—One of the Fundamental Conditions of Life

Upon being sent out from Eden, work became one of the remaining means of achieving human happiness. The rite of sacrifice held out hope of eternal life by the substitution which the sacrifice represented —the Savior who was in due time to appear.

With the **expulsion** from Eden also came the sad conflicts of mankind—conflicts with external wickedness, conflicts with the earth, and conflicts with evil passions in a man's soul.

---

1. Scripture references are paraphrased throughout the adapted articles in this book.

The Artios Home Companion Series
Unit 2: A Fallen World

Teacher Overview

AFTER CREATION and the fall of man into sin, the Bible next tells us about the children of Adam and Eve. Their first son, Cain, became terribly jealous of his brother Abel, and he killed him. This was the world's very first murder, and Cain was banished from his family. God gave Adam and Eve another son named Seth, and the human race continued to grow. Soon people developed specific skills, as seen in the individuals Jabal, Jubal, and Tubalcain.

The Story of Cain and Abel,
illustration from a Bible card published by the Providence Lithograph Company (1906)

Suggested Assignments

Based on your student's age and ability, the reading in this unit may be read aloud to the student, and journaling and notebook pages may be completed orally. Likewise, other assignments may be done with an appropriate combination of independent and guided study.

In this unit, students will:
- Complete four lessons in which they will learn about **Cain and Abel**, the **descendants of Cain**, the **development of society**, and **man's sinful nature**.
- Define vocabulary words.
- Visit the **ArtiosHCS** curriculum website at **www.ArtiosHCS.com** for additional resources and any videos and websites assigned for this unit.

Heart Connections

Man is fallen and in need of a Savior.
For all have sinned and fall short of the glory of God.
– Romans 3:23

Sin deserves death.
For the wages of sin is death, but the free gift of God is eternal life in Christ Jesus our Lord.
– Romans 6:23

Jealousy is sin.
But if you have bitter jealousy and selfish ambition in your hearts, do not boast and be false to the truth. This is not the wisdom that comes down from above, but is earthly, unspiritual, demonic.
– James 3:14-15

Vocabulary

Lesson 1:
tiller
sacrifice (offering)
countenance

Lesson 2:
expulsion
precarious

Lesson 3:
none

Lesson 4:
none

Key People and Events

Cain   Abel   Seth   Enoch   Jabal   Jubal   Tubalcain

Additional Material for Parent or Teacher:

There are two links on the **ArtiosHCS** curriculum website for Parents and Teachers to share with their student(s) at their discretion.

Cain and Abel

Lesson One

History Overview and Assignments
Am I My Brother's Keeper?

THE FIRST SON born to Adam and Eve became the world's first murderer. In a jealous rage, he killed his brother Abel, and then he lied about it to God. We all have sinful natures and must rely on the Holy Spirit and God's Word to avoid sinning against God and others.

Cain Slaying Abel, by Jacopo Palma (c.1590)
Palma il Vecchio, c.1480-July 1528, born Jacopo Palma or known as Jacopo Negretti, was an Italian painter of the Venetian school.

Suggested Reading and Assignments

- Read the article: *Genesis 4:1-16*.
- Define each vocabulary word in the context of the reading. Write the words and their definitions in the vocabulary section of your notebook.
- After reading the article, summarize the story you read by either:
    - Retelling it out loud to your teacher or parent.
        OR
    - Completing an appropriate notebook page.
    Either way, be sure to include the answers to the discussion questions and an overview of key people, places, dates, and events in your summary.
- Be sure to visit your **ArtiosHCS** curriculum website for additional resources and any videos and websites assigned for this lesson.

Vocabulary

tiller
countenance
sacrifice (offering)

Key People, Places, and Events

Cain
Abel

Ancient: Elementary
Unit 2: A Fallen World

Discussion Questions

1. Who were Cain and Abel?
2. What type of sacrifice did God require?
3. What type of sacrifice did Abel bring?
4. What type of sacrifice did Cain bring?
5. Why was God displeased with Cain's sacrifice?
6. Why was Cain angry with his brother?
7. What sin did Cain commit against his brother?
8. Cain committed another sin when God asked him where Abel was. What was it?
9. What was Cain's punishment?

Genesis 4:1 - 16

Genesis 4

1 And Adam knew Eve his wife; and she conceived, and bare **Cain**, and said, I have gotten a man from the LORD.

2 And she again bare his brother **Abel**. And Abel was a keeper of sheep, but Cain was a **tiller** of the ground.

3 And in process of time it came to pass, that Cain brought of the fruit of the ground an **offering** unto the LORD.

4 And Abel, he also brought of the firstlings of his flock and of the fat thereof. And the LORD had respect unto Abel and to his offering:

5 But unto Cain and to his offering he had not respect. And Cain was very wroth, and his **countenance** fell.

6 And the LORD said unto Cain, Why art thou wroth? and why is thy countenance fallen?

7 If thou doest well, shalt thou not be accepted? and if thou doest not well, sin lieth at the door. And unto thee shall be his desire, and thou shalt rule over him.

8 And Cain talked with Abel his brother: and it came to pass, when they were in the field, that Cain rose up against Abel his brother, and slew him.

9 And the LORD said unto Cain, Where is Abel thy brother? And he said, I know not: Am I my brother's keeper?

10 And he said, What hast thou done? the voice of thy brother's blood crieth unto me from the ground.

11 And now art thou cursed from the earth, which hath opened her mouth to receive thy brother's blood from thy hand;

12 When thou tillest the ground, it shall not henceforth yield unto thee her strength; a fugitive and a vagabond shalt thou be in the earth.

13 And Cain said unto the LORD, My punishment is greater than I can bear.

14 Behold, thou hast driven me out this day from the face of the earth; and from thy face shall I be hid; and I shall be a fugitive and a vagabond in the earth; and it shall come to pass, that every one that findeth me shall slay me.

15 And the LORD said unto him, Therefore whosoever slayeth Cain, vengeance shall be taken on him sevenfold. And the LORD set a mark upon Cain, lest any finding him should kill him.

16 And Cain went out from the presence of the LORD, and dwelt in the land of Nod, on the east of Eden.

Lesson Two

History Overview and Assignments
A Marked Man

"The first great conflict in history took place between Cain, the planter, and Abel, the shepherd—the representatives of two great divisions of the human family in the early ages."

– from the adapted article below

Cain and Abel, by Andrea Schiavone (1555)

Suggested Reading and Assignments

- Read the article: *Cain and Abel.*
- Define each vocabulary word in the context of the reading. Write the words and their definitions in the vocabulary section of your notebook.
- After reading the article, summarize the story you read by either:
  - Retelling it out loud to your teacher or parent.
    OR
  - Completing an appropriate notebook page.

  Either way, be sure to include the answers to the discussion questions and an overview of key people, places, dates, and events in your summary.
- Draw a picture of Cain's sacrifice.
- Draw a picture of Abel's sacrifice.
- Be sure to visit your **ArtiosHCS** curriculum website for additional resources and any videos and websites assigned for this lesson.

Ancient: Elementary
Unit 2: A Fallen World

Vocabulary

expulsion   precarious

Key People, Places, and Events

Cain   Abel   Seth

Discussion Questions

1. What was the name of Adam and Eve's third son?
2. What was the occupation (job) of Cain?
3. What was the occupation (job) of Abel?
4. What does the article say was Abel's virtue?
5. What does the article say was Cain's sin?
6. Describe Cain's punishment for his sin.
7. What did Cain's descendants do that brought about much sin in the world?
8. How did the Lord feel about this?
9. Do you ever struggle with the same sin that Cain struggled with?

Adapted for Elementary School from the book:
Ancient States and Empires
by John Lord
Cain and Abel

Cain and Abel

The first great conflict in history took place between **Cain**, the planter, and **Abel**, the shepherd—the representatives of two great divisions of the human family in the early ages. Cain killed Abel because the offering of Abel was preferred over Cain's. God knows what is in people's hearts, and He saw that Cain was not truly honoring Him with the offering he brought. The virtue of Abel was faith. The sins of Cain were jealousy, pride, resentment, and despair. The punishment of Cain was **expulsion** from his father's house, a greater curse of the land for him, and the hatred of the human family. He changed his occupation, became a wanderer, and scratched out a **precarious** living while his descendants invented arts and built cities.

The Descendants of Cain

Eve bore another son—**Seth**, among whose descendants the worship of God was preserved for a long time. But the descendants of Seth eventually intermarried with the descendants of Cain, from whom sprang a race of lawless men, so that the earth was filled with violence. The material civilization which the descendants of Cain introduced did not preserve them from moral wickedness. So great was the increasing sinfulness with the growth of the race that the Lord resolved to destroy the whole race—with the exception of one religious family—and change the whole surface of the earth by a mighty flood, which would destroy all animals and birds of the air, and all the early works of man.

Lesson Three

History Overview and Assignments
Industries

"And Adah bare Jabal: he was the father of such as dwell in tents, and of such as have cattle. And his brother's name was Jubal: he was the father of all such as handle the harp and organ."

– Genesis 4:20-21

Detail of stained glass window in Christ Church Cathedral in Dublin, Ireland, depicting Jubal, by John Hardman Powell
Photo by Andreas F. Borchert. CC BY-SA 3.0

Suggested Reading and Assignments

- Read the article: *Genesis 4:16-22*.
- After reading the article, summarize the story you read by either:
  - Retelling it out loud to your teacher or parent.
    OR
  - Completing an appropriate notebook page.

  Either way, be sure to include the answers to the discussion questions and an overview of key people, places, dates, and events in your summary.
- Be sure to visit your **ArtiosHCS** curriculum website for additional resources and any videos and websites assigned for this lesson.

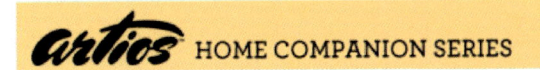

Ancient: Elementary
Unit 2: A Fallen World

Key People, Places, and Events

Enoch
Jabal
Jubal
Tubalcain

Discussion Questions

1. How does Scripture describe Jabal?
2. How does Scripture describe Jubal?
3. How does Scripture describe Tubalcain?
4. Based on the occupations of these three men, can you guess what the society of the time might have included?

Genesis 4:16 - 22

Genesis 4

16 And Cain went out from the presence of the LORD, and dwelt in the land of Nod, on the east of Eden.

17 And Cain knew his wife; and she conceived, and bare **Enoch**: and he builded a city, and called the name of the city, after the name of his son, Enoch.

18 And unto Enoch was born Irad: and Irad begat Mehujael: and Mehujael begat Methusael: and Methusael begat Lamech.

19 And Lamech took unto him two wives: the name of the one was Adah, and the name of the other Zillah.

20 And Adah bare **Jabal**: he was the father of such as dwell in tents, and of such as have cattle.

21 And his brother's name was **Jubal**: he was the father of all such as handle the harp and organ.

22 And Zillah, she also bare **Tubalcain**, an instructer of every artificer in brass and iron: and the sister of Tubalcain was Naamah.

Jabal the Shepherd

Jubal the Musician

Photos by Sailko. GNU Free Documentation License

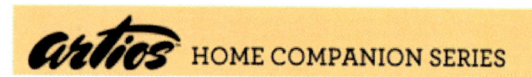

Ancient: Elementary
Unit 2: A Fallen World

Lesson Four

History Overview and Assignments
God's View

> "And the LORD said, 'I will destroy man whom I have created from the face of the earth; both man, and beast, and the creeping thing, and the fowls of the air; for it repenteth me that I have made them.'"
>
> – Genesis 6:7

God the Father, by Cima da Conegliano (c.1510–1517)

Suggested Reading and Assignments

- Read the article: *Genesis 6:5-7*.
- After reading the article, summarize the story you read by either:
    - Retelling it out loud to your teacher or parent.
      OR
    - Completing an appropriate notebook page.

  Either way, be sure to include the answers to the discussion questions and an overview of key people, places, dates, and events in your summary.
- Be sure to visit your **ArtiosHCS** curriculum website for additional resources and any videos and websites assigned for this lesson.

Discussion Questions

1. Why was God grieved by the people?
2. What did the people deserve because of their sin?

Genesis 6:5 - 7

Genesis 6

5 And God saw that the wickedness of man was great in the earth, and that every imagination of the thoughts of his heart was only evil continually.

6 And it repented the LORD that he had made man on the earth, and it grieved him at his heart.

7 And the LORD said, I will destroy man whom I have created from the face of the earth; both man, and beast, and the creeping thing, and the fowls of the air; for it repenteth me that I have made them.

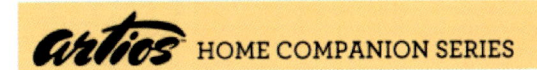

Ancient: Elementary
Unit 2: A Fallen World

The Artios Home Companion Series
Unit 3: The Story of the Flood

Teacher Overview

IN THE BIBLE STORY about the Great Flood, we see how God severely punished those who rejected His ways and insisted on living sinful lives. Our selfish, sinful nature doesn't always want to obey God, but He has the right as our Creator to rule over us, and we need to obey Him.

Noah tried to obey God's ways, and God honored him by rescuing Noah and his family from the great calamity of the Flood. From that family came all people who are now living.

Noah's Sacrifice, by Daniel Maclise (c.1850)

Heart Connections

Man is fallen and in need of a Savior.
For all have sinned and fall short of the glory of God.
– Romans 3:23

Sin deserves death.
For the wages of sin is death, but the free gift of God is eternal life in Christ Jesus our Lord.
– Romans 6:23

Jealousy is sin.
But if you have bitter jealousy and selfish ambition in your hearts, do not boast and be false to the truth. This is not the wisdom that comes down from above, but is earthly, unspiritual, demonic.
– James 3:14-15

Suggested Assignments

Based on your student's age and ability, the reading in this unit may be read aloud to the student, and journaling and notebook pages may be completed orally. Likewise, other assignments may be done with an appropriate combination of independent and guided study.

In this unit, students will:
- Complete two lessons in which they will learn about **Noah**, the **Great Flood**, and the **repopulation of the earth**.
- Define vocabulary words.

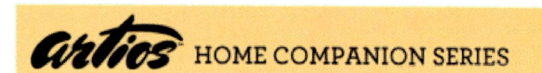

- Create a true-to-scale **model of Noah's ark.** *This will be due at the end of Unit 5.*
- Find as many pictures as possible of the animals that would have been on the ark.
- Visit the **ArtiosHCS** curriculum website at **www.ArtiosHCS.com** for additional resources and any videos and websites assigned for this unit.

Vocabulary

Lesson 1:
ark
pitch
cubit
covenant

Lesson 2:
deluge

Key People, Places, and Events

Noah

Additional Material for Parent or Teacher:

There are several links on the **ArtiosHCS** curriculum website that you may want to share one or more of with your student(s).

The Deluge, by John Martin (1834)

Ancient: Elementary
Unit 3: The Story of the Flood

Lesson One

History Overview and Assignments
"Make Thee an Ark"

"And God said unto Noah, 'The end of all flesh is come before me; for the earth is filled with violence through them; and, behold, I will destroy them with the earth.'"

– Genesis 6:13

Noah's Ark, by Edward Hicks (1846)

Suggested Reading and Assignments

- Read the article: *Genesis 6:13-8:20*.
- Define the vocabulary word in the context of the reading. Write the word and its definition in the vocabulary section of your notebook.
- After reading the article, summarize the story you read by either:
    - Retelling it out loud to your teacher or parent.
      OR
    - Completing an appropriate notebook page.

  Either way, be sure to include the answers to the discussion questions and an overview of key people, places, dates, and events in your summary.
- Be sure to visit your **ArtiosHCS** curriculum website for additional resources and any videos and websites assigned for this lesson.

Vocabulary

ark   cubit
pitch   covenant

Key People, Places, and Events

Noah

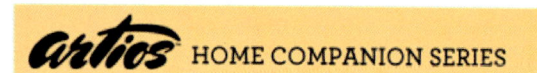

Discussion Questions

1. Why did God punish man?
2. Describe the ark that Noah built.
3. How old was Noah when the Flood occurred?
4. How long did the Flood last?
5. Where did the water come from?
6. Where did the ark come to rest as the flood waters went down?
7. How did Noah test to see how far the flood waters had gone down?
8. How did Noah thank God for preserving him and his family?

Genesis 6:13 - 8:20

Genesis 6

13 And God said unto **Noah**, The end of all flesh is come before me; for the earth is filled with violence through them; and, behold, I will destroy them with the earth.

14 Make thee an **ark** of gopher wood; rooms shalt thou make in the ark, and shalt pitch it within and without with **pitch**.

15 And this is the fashion which thou shalt make it of: The length of the ark shall be three hundred **cubit**s, the breadth of it fifty cubits, and the height of it thirty cubits.

16 A window shalt thou make to the ark, and in a cubit shalt thou finish it above; and the door of the ark shalt thou set in the side thereof; with lower, second, and third stories shalt thou make it.

17 And, behold, I, even I, do bring a flood of waters upon the earth, to destroy all flesh, wherein is the breath of life, from under heaven; and every thing that is in the earth shall die.

18 But with thee will I establish my **covenant**; and thou shalt come into the ark, thou, and thy sons, and thy wife, and thy sons' wives with thee.

19 And of every living thing of all flesh, two of every sort shalt thou bring into the ark, to keep them alive with thee; they shall be male and female.

20 Of fowls after their kind, and of cattle after their kind, of every creeping thing of the earth after his kind, two of every sort shall come unto thee, to keep them alive.

21 And take thou unto thee of all food that is eaten, and thou shalt gather it to thee; and it shall be for food for thee, and for them.

22 Thus did Noah; according to all that God commanded him, so did he.

Genesis 7

1 And the LORD said unto Noah, Come thou and all thy house into the ark; for thee have I seen righteous before me in this generation.

2 Of every clean beast thou shalt take to thee by sevens, the male and his female: and of beasts that are not clean by two, the male and his female.

3 Of fowls also of the air by sevens, the male and the female; to keep seed alive upon the face of all the earth.

4 For yet seven days, and I will cause it to rain upon the earth forty days and forty nights; and every living substance that I have made will I destroy from off the face of the earth.

5 And Noah did according unto all that the LORD commanded him.

6 And Noah was six hundred years old when the flood of waters was upon the earth.

7 And Noah went in, and his sons, and his wife, and his sons' wives with him, into the ark, because of the waters of the flood.

8 Of clean beasts, and of beasts that are not clean, and of fowls, and of every thing that creepeth upon the earth,

9 There went in two and two unto Noah into the ark, the male and the female, as God had commanded Noah.

10 And it came to pass after seven days, that the waters of the flood were upon the earth.

11 In the six hundredth year of Noah's life, in the second month, the seventeenth day of the month, the same day were all the fountains of the great deep broken up, and the windows of heaven were opened.

12 And the rain was upon the earth forty days and forty nights.

13 In the selfsame day entered Noah, and Shem, and Ham, and Japheth, the sons of Noah, and Noah's wife, and the three wives of his sons with them, into the ark;

14 They, and every beast after his kind, and all the cattle after their kind, and every creeping thing that creepeth upon the earth after his kind, and every fowl after his kind, every bird of every sort.

15 And they went in unto Noah into the ark, two and two of all flesh, wherein is the breath of life.

16 And they that went in, went in male and female of all flesh, as God had commanded him: and the LORD shut him in.

17 And the flood was forty days upon the earth; and the waters increased, and bare up the ark, and it was lift up above the earth.

18 And the waters prevailed, and were increased greatly upon the earth; and the ark went upon the face of the waters.

19 And the waters prevailed exceedingly upon the earth; and all the high hills, that were under the whole heaven, were covered.

20 Fifteen cubits upward did the waters prevail; and the mountains were covered.

21 And all flesh died that moved upon the earth, both of fowl, and of cattle, and of beast, and of every creeping thing that creepeth upon the earth, and every man:

22 All in whose nostrils was the breath of life, of all that was in the dry land, died.

23 And every living substance was destroyed which was upon the face of the ground, both man, and cattle, and the creeping things, and the fowl of the heaven; and they were destroyed from the earth: and Noah only remained alive, and they that were with him in the ark.

24 And the waters prevailed upon the earth an hundred and fifty days.

Genesis 8

1 And God remembered Noah, and every living thing, and all the cattle that was with him in the ark: and God made a wind to pass over the earth, and the waters assuaged;

2 The fountains also of the deep and the windows of heaven were stopped, and the rain from heaven was restrained;

3 And the waters returned from off the earth continually: and after the end of the hundred and fifty days the waters were abated.

4 And the ark rested in the seventh month, on the seventeenth day of the month, upon the mountains of Ararat.

5 And the waters decreased continually until the tenth month: in the tenth month, on the first day of the month, were the tops of the mountains seen.

6 And it came to pass at the end of forty days, that Noah opened the window of the ark which he had made:

7 And he sent forth a raven, which went forth to and fro, until the waters were dried up from off the earth.

8 Also he sent forth a dove from him, to see if the waters were abated from off the face of the ground;

9 But the dove found no rest for the sole of her foot, and she returned unto him into the ark, for the waters were on the face of the whole earth: then he put forth his hand, and took her, and pulled her in unto him into the ark.

10 And he stayed yet other seven days; and again he sent forth the dove out of the ark;

11 And the dove came in to him in the evening; and, lo, in her mouth was an olive leaf pluckt off: so Noah knew that the waters were abated from off the earth.

12 And he stayed yet other seven days; and sent forth the dove; which returned not again unto him any more.

13 And it came to pass in the six hundredth and first year, in the first month, the first day of the month, the waters were dried up from off the earth: and Noah removed the covering of the ark, and looked, and, behold, the face of the ground was dry.

14 And in the second month, on the seven and twentieth day of the month, was the earth dried.

15 And God spake unto Noah, saying,

16 Go forth of the ark, thou, and thy wife, and thy sons, and thy sons' wives with thee.

17 Bring forth with thee every living thing that is with thee, of all flesh, both of fowl, and of cattle, and of every creeping thing that creepeth upon the earth; that they may breed abundantly in the earth, and be fruitful, and multiply upon the earth.

18 And Noah went forth, and his sons, and his wife, and his sons' wives with him:

19 Every beast, every creeping thing, and every fowl, and whatsoever creepeth upon the earth, after their kinds, went forth out of the ark.

20 And Noah builded an altar unto the LORD; and took of every clean beast, and of every clean fowl, and offered burnt offerings on the altar.

Noah: The Eve of the Deluge,
by John Linnell (1848) ~ Photo by Wmpearl. CC0 1.0

Lesson Two

History Overview and Assignments
The Deluge

"The memory of the Deluge is preserved in the traditions of nearly all nations, as well as in the narrative of Moses, and most heathen mythologies mention some kind of sacred ark."
— from the adapted article below

The Subsiding of the Waters of the Deluge, by Thomas Cole (1829)

Suggested Reading and Assignments

- Read the article: *The Deluge*.
- Define the vocabulary word in the context of the reading. Write the word and its definition in the vocabulary section of your notebook.
- After reading the article, summarize the story you read by either:
    - Retelling it out loud to your teacher or parent.
        OR
    - Completing an appropriate notebook page.

  Either way, be sure to include the answers to the discussion questions and an overview of key people, places, dates, and events in your summary.
- Create a true-to-scale **model of Noah's ark**. *This will be due at the end of Unit 5.*

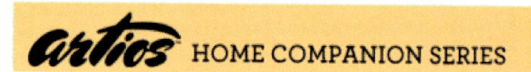

Ancient: Elementary
Unit 3: The Story of the Flood

- With your parent's help, find as many pictures as possible of the animals that would have been on the ark.
- Be sure to visit your **ArtiosHCS** curriculum website for additional resources and any videos and websites assigned for this lesson.

Vocabulary

deluge

Key People, Places, and Events

Noah

Discussion Questions

1. How does the author of today's article describe civilization at the time of Noah and the Flood?
2. How big was Noah's ark?
3. How long were Noah and his family on the ark?
4. What did Noah do when he and his family exited the ark?
5. What covenant did God make with Noah?
6. What was the sign God gave for this covenant?

Adapted for Elementary School from the book:
Ancient States and Empires
by John Lord
The Deluge

The Deluge

It is useless to ask whether the **Deluge** was universal or partial—whether it covered the whole earth or the existing habitations of men. All people were destroyed by it except **Noah**, his wife, their three sons, and their wives.

The Probable Condition of the World Before the Flood

This dreadful catastrophe took place in the 600th year of Noah's life, and there were probably more people destroyed than existed on the earth in the later time of Solomon. And as men lived longer in those primeval times than later and were larger and stronger, "for there were giants in those days," and early on had invented tents, the harp, and the organ, were skilled in working brass and iron, and built cities—as they were full of inventions as well as imaginations, it is not unreasonable to speculate, though we cannot know with certainty, that the world before the Flood may have been more splendid and luxurious than the world in the time of Solomon and Homer—the era of the Pyramids of Egypt.

The Ark

The art of building had undoubtedly been carried to considerable perfection by then, for the ark which Noah built was four hundred and fifty feet long, seventy-five wide, and forty-five deep, and was constructed so uniquely as to hold pairs of all known animals and birds, with provisions for them for more than ten months.

The Divine Covenant With Noah

This sacred ark or ship, built of gopher wood, floated on the world's waves until, in the seventh month, it rested upon the mountains of Ararat. It was nearly a year before Noah ventured from the ark. His first act, after he came forth, was to build an altar and offer sacrifice to the God who had preserved him and his family of the human race alone. And the Lord was well pleased and made a covenant with him that he would never again send like destruction upon the earth, and as a sign and seal of the covenant which he made with all flesh, he set his bow in the cloud.

The Tradition of the Deluge

The memory of the Deluge is preserved in the traditions of nearly all nations, and the narrative of Moses, and most heathen mythologies mention a sacred ark. Moreover, various geological phenomena in all parts of the world cannot be accounted for on any other ground than some violent disruption produced by a universal Deluge.

Cameo With Noah's Ark, possibly by Allessandro Masnago (c.1600)
This engraving, made from carved sardonyx and gold, features a line of animals on the gangway to Noah's ark. It is based on a woodcut by the French illustrator Bernard Salomon.
Photo courtesy of the Walters Art Museum. CC BY-SA 3.0

The Artios Home Companion Series
Unit 4: A Great Tower

Teacher Overview

AS PEOPLE BEGAN to multiply after the Flood, they began to think highly of themselves and their abilities. They wanted to build something grand that their descendants could be proud of, so they constructed a tall tower. It's possible they also did it to have a safe place to protect them in case of another great flood. Either way, they were disobeying God's command to spread out and fill the earth and were very prideful. God stopped their work by confusing their languages, which forced them to spread out into different people groups. Man's plans and actions never hinder God from achieving His purposes. This unit tells about this event and the rise of nations that took place afterward.

The Tower of Babel, by Abel Grimmer (1604)

Suggested Assignments

Based on your student's age and ability, the reading in this unit may be read aloud to the student, and journaling and notebook pages may be completed orally. Likewise, other assignments may be done with an appropriate combination of independent and guided study.

In this unit, students will:
- Complete two lessons in which they will learn about the **descendants of Noah**, the **Tower of Babel, and early Mesopotamian cultures**.
- Define vocabulary words.
- Explore the websites about Babel. The links may be found on the **ArtiosHCS** curriculum website.
- Draw or build their own **Tower of Babel**.
- Act out the story of the **Tower of Babel**.

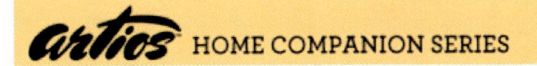

- Continue working on their true-to-scale model of **Noah's Ark**. *This will be due at the end of Unit 5.*
- Visit the **ArtiosHCS** curriculum website at **www.ArtiosHCS.com** for additional resources and any videos and websites assigned for this unit.

Heart Connections

Pride is one of the most harmful and destructive sins.

Pride goes before destruction, and a haughty spirit before a fall.
– Proverbs 16:18

God will accomplish His purpose.

Many are the plans in the mind of a man, but it is the purpose of the Lord that will stand.
– Proverbs 19:21

One's heart is revealed by one's words and actions.

The good person out of the good treasure of his heart produces good, and the evil person out of his evil treasure produces evil, for out of the abundance of the heart his mouth speaks.
– Luke 6:45

Vocabulary

Lesson 1:
restrain
confound

Lesson 2:
stupendous
civilization
ziggurat
cuneiform
empire

Key People, Places, and Events

Tower of Babel
Shem
Ham
Japheth
Nimrod

Mesopotamia
Sumer
Akkadians
Amorites
Babylonian Empire

A Summary account of silver for the governor written in Sumerian cuneiform on a clay tablet

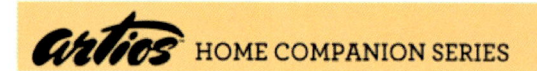

Lesson One

History Overview and Assignments
Reaching For Heaven

> *"And they said one to another, 'Go to, let us make brick, and burn them thoroughly.' And they had brick for stone, and slime had they for morter. And they said, 'Go to, let us build us a city and a tower, whose top may reach unto heaven; and let us make us a name, lest we be scattered abroad upon the face of the whole earth.'"*
>
> – Genesis 11:3-4

The Tower of Babel, by Marten van Valckenborch (c.1600)

Suggested Reading and Assignments

- Read the article: *Genesis 11:1-9*.
- Define each vocabulary word in the context of the reading. Write the words and their definitions in the vocabulary section of your notebook.
- After reading the article, summarize the story you read by either:
  - Retelling it out loud to your teacher or parent.
    OR
  - Completing an appropriate notebook page.

  Either way, be sure to include the answers to the discussion questions and an overview of key people, places, dates, and events in your summary.
- Explore the websites about the Tower of Babel that may be found on your **ArtiosHCS** curriculum website.
- Continue working on your true-to-scale model of Noah's Ark. *This will be due at the end of Unit 5.*
- Be sure to visit your **ArtiosHCS** curriculum website for additional resources and any videos and websites assigned for this lesson.

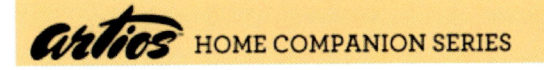

Ancient: Elementary
Unit 4: A Great Tower

Vocabulary

restrain
confound

Key People, Places, and Events

Tower of Babel

Discussion Questions

1. Why did the people decide to build the Tower of Babel?
2. How did God feel about the tower?
3. How did God make it impossible for the building of the tower to continue?

Genesis 11:1 - 9

Genesis 11

1 And the whole earth was of one language, and of one speech.

2 And it came to pass, as they journeyed from the east, that they found a plain in the land of Shinar; and they dwelt there.

3 And they said one to another, Go to, let us make brick, and burn them thoroughly. And they had brick for stone, and slime had they for morter.

4 And they said, Go to, let us build us a city and a tower, whose top may reach unto heaven; and let us make us a name, lest we be scattered abroad upon the face of the whole earth.

5 And the LORD came down to see the city and the tower, which the children of men builded.

6 And the LORD said, Behold, the people is one, and they have all one language; and this they begin to do: and now nothing will be **restrain**ed from them, which they have imagined to do.

7 Go to, let us go down, and there **confound** their language, that they may not understand one another's speech.

8 So the LORD scattered them abroad from thence upon the face of all the earth: and they left off to build the city.

9 Therefore is the name of it called **Babel**; because the LORD did there confound the language of all the earth: and from thence did the LORD scatter them abroad upon the face of all the earth.

Tower of Babel, by Leandro Bassano (c.1600)

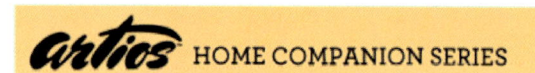

Lesson Two

History Overview and Assignments
The Tower of Babel

GOD HAD TOLD THE FIRST PEOPLE to multiply and fill the earth, but the early descendants of Noah did not wish to obey this command. They were skillful builders, and in their great pride, they decided to live together in one place and build an immensely tall tower as a monument to their greatness. God was displeased by this prideful work, and He soon put an end to it. This story teaches the great lesson of our need to depend upon God and submit to His will and laws.

The Construction of the Tower of Babel,
by Charles Gussin (1690)

Image of an unidentified cuneiform tablet in the British Museum, London

Suggested Reading and Assignments

- Read the article: *The Tower of Babel*.
- Define each vocabulary word in the context of the reading. Write the words and their definitions in the vocabulary section of your notebook.
- After reading the article, summarize the story you read by either:
  - Retelling it out loud to your teacher or parent.
    OR
  - Completing an appropriate notebook page.

  Either way, be sure to include the answers to the discussion questions and an overview of key people, places, dates, and events in your summary.
- Draw or build your own **Tower of Babel**.
- Act out the story of the **Tower of Babel**.
- Explore "The Story of the Tower of Babel" at the link found on your **ArtiosHCS** curriculum website.
  - Continue working on your true-to-scale model of Noah's Ark. *This will be due at the end of Unit 5.*
  - Be sure to visit your **ArtiosHCS** curriculum website for additional resources and any videos and websites assigned for this lesson.

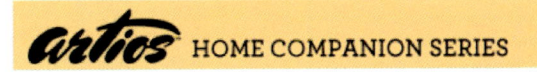

Ancient: Elementary
Unit 4: A Great Tower

Vocabulary

stupendous
civilization
cuneiform
ziggurat
empire

Key People, Places, and Events

Shem
Ham
Japheth
Nimrod
Tower of Babel
Mesopotamia
Sumer
Akkadians
Amorites
Babylonian Empire

Discussion Questions

1. What were the names of Noah's three sons?
2. Who was Nimrod?
3. Why did the people want to build a tower?
4. Before the Tower of Babel, how many languages did people speak?
5. Was God willing for men to exercise their gifts and skills?
6. What was it about the tower that God did not like?
7. What great lesson does this story teach?
8. What is a civilization?
9. What is the name of the earliest civilization that we know of?
10. What is an empire?
11. What is the name of the first empire that we know of?

Adapted for Elementary School from the book:
Wee Ones' Bible Stories
by Anonymous
The Tower of Babel

The sons of Noah were named **Shem**, **Ham**, and **Japheth**. These sons, in turn, became the fathers of children, so Noah's descendants were very numerous.

One of these descendants, named **Nimrod**, was a mighty hunter and a man of power and authority in the land, and it has even been said that the people worshiped him as a god.

In those days, men liked to build high towers reaching way up toward the heavens. Perhaps they were afraid of another flood, and perhaps they simply wished to show what they could do; however that may be, ruins of towers can still be seen in various parts of the world, one of the most noted of which is that of the "Tower of Nimrod." It is forty feet high and stands on the top of a hill near the Euphrates River in Asia.

In the time of Nimrod, the people said, "Let us build us a city and a tower, whose top may reach unto Heaven; and let us make us a name, lest we be scattered abroad upon the face of the whole earth." So they began to build the tower, and they made it very strong indeed and kept raising it higher and higher toward the heavens, possibly thinking, as Jewish tradition tells us, that they would have a shelter in which they would be perfectly safe from any flood which might come, or any fire. Some wished to use the tower as a temple for the idols they worshiped.

Six hundred thousand men worked upon this wonderful tower, so the story tradition goes on to say, and they kept up the work until the tower rose to a height of seventy miles, so that, toward the last, it took a year to get materials for the work up to the top where the laborers were employed. Of course, this story is exaggerated, but without a doubt, the tower rose to a great height and was a wondrous piece of work.

God was not pleased with what the people were doing, though, because they thought themselves so great and powerful that they did not need Him, so He put an end to their bold plans.

Up to this time, all the people of the world had spoken the same language, but now, when they were working upon this wonderful tower, God confused their speech so that they suddenly began to talk in different tongues. They could not understand each other, and there was great confusion. Owing to this, they were obliged to give up the tower building. They separated into groups or divisions, each speaking the same language and spreading worldwide, forming various nations.

The tower was called the **Tower of Babel** because of the "babel," or confusion, of tongues that had taken place there, and it was left unfinished to be a monument of God's power and man's weakness without Him.

These men were skillful in building, or they could never have gone as far as they did in their **stupendous** work, and God was willing that they should exercise their skill, just as He is willing that people shall do now, but when they thought themselves equal to Him, they learned how weak they were in comparison. The story teaches the great lesson of dependence upon God and submission to His will and laws.

Cultures in Mesopotamia

After the people spread out, they began to form **civilization**s, societies where many people lived in cities and had various jobs. The earliest of these we know about, from which we have artifacts from three to five thousand years before Christ lived, was called **Sumer**. This civilization grew up between the Tigris and Euphrates rivers in **Mesopotamia**, which means "land between the rivers," near where the Tower of Babel had been built. The Sumerian people rejected the idea of one creator god and worshiped many false gods instead. They built tremendous temples to these gods, called **ziggurat**s. These temples looked like pyramids made of steps.

The Sumerians developed the first form of writing that we know of. The words in this writing were formed by wedge-shaped tools made of reeds, which were pressed into wet clay. The writing is called **cuneiform**, which means "wedge-shaped."

The Sumerian people are known for several other developments as well, including the wheeled vehicle, advanced mathematics, and the division of hours and minutes into sixty units.

After the Sumerian people had lived in the Mesopotamian region for some time, the **Akkadian** people came into the northern part and gradually took over. They established a city called Akkad, and they called themselves Akkadians. This people group formed the first **empire**, a civilization where one nation ruled over others. Eventually, the Akkadian Empire was conquered by invaders called the **Amorites**. The resulting civilization eventually developed into the **Babylonian Empire**.

The Artios Home Companion Series
Unit 5: God Forms a New Nation

Teacher Overview

GOD MADE A PROMISE to Abraham to make of him a great nation. Abraham obeyed God's call to leave his country and traveled with his nephew Lot to a faraway country. However, when years passed and Abraham and his wife, Sarah, did not have children, Abraham took matters into his own hands and had a son with his wife's handmaid, Hagar. This led to jealousy between Sarah and Hagar, and eventually, Hagar was sent away from Abraham's camp when Abraham finally had a son with Sarah. God fulfilled his promise to Abraham but did so in His own timing.

Abraham Departs For Canaan, by Francesco da Ponte (c.1570)

Suggested Assignments

Based on your student's age and ability, the reading in this unit may be read aloud to the student, and journaling and notebook pages may be completed orally. Likewise, other assignments may be done with an appropriate combination of independent and guided study.

In this unit, students will:
- Complete two lessons in which they will learn about **Abraham**, **Lot**, **Sarah**, **Hagar,** and **ancient cultures**.
- Explore the website about "The Journey of Abraham" at the link found on the **ArtiosHCS** curriculum website.

- Complete their true-to-scale model of **Noah's Ark**. *This will be due at the end of this unit.*
- Visit the **ArtiosHCS** curriculum website at **www.ArtiosHCS.com** for additional resources and any videos and websites assigned for this unit.

Heart Connections

God will accomplish His purpose.
Many are the plans in the mind of a man, but it is the purpose of the Lord that will stand.
– Proverbs 19:21

One's heart is revealed by one's words and actions.
The good person out of the good treasure of his heart produces good, and the evil person out of his evil treasure produces evil, for out of the abundance of the heart his mouth speaks.
– Luke 6:45

Abraham trusted in God's promise.
No unbelief made him waver concerning the promise of God, but he grew strong in his faith as he gave glory to God, fully convinced that God was able to do what he had promised.
– Romans 4:20-21

Key People, Places, and Events

Abraham (Abram)
Lot
Babylonian Empire
India
Himalayan Mountains
Assyria
Minoan
Crete
Greece
Nile River
Egypt
Menes
Phoenicians
Sidon
Tyre
Sodom
Gomorrah
Sarah (Sarai)
Isaac
Hagar
Ishmael
Arabians
Hebrews

Abraham Serving the Three Angels, by Rembrandt (1646)

Lesson One

History Overview and Assignments
Abraham and Lot

"Then Abram said to Lot, 'Let there be no strife between you and me, and between your herdsmen and my herdsmen, for we are kinsmen. Is not the whole land before you? Separate yourself from me. I you take the left hand, then I will go to the right, or if you take the right hand, then I will go to the left.'"

– Genesis 13:8

The Caravan of Abraham, watercolor by James Tissot (before 1903)

Suggested Reading and Assignments

- Read the article:
  Genesis 13:2-11 & 17:1-5
- After reading the article, summarize the story you read by either:
  - Retelling it out loud to your teacher or parent.
    OR
  - Completing an appropriate notebook page.

  Either way, be sure to include the answers to the discussion questions and an overview of key people, places, dates, and events in your summary.
- In Unit 1, you were instructed to purchase a map packet. Using the map labeled *Called Out of Ur* or *Abraham's Journey*, trace Abraham's journeys and locate where he and his nephew Lot finally settled.
- Explore "The Journey of Abraham" at the link found on your **ArtiosHCS** curriculum website.
- Continue working on your true-to-scale model of **Noah's Ark**. *This will be due at the end of this unit.*
- Be sure to visit your **ArtiosHCS** curriculum website for additional resources and any videos and websites assigned for this lesson.

Key People, Places, and Events

Abraham (Abram)
Lot

Ancient: Elementary
Unit 5: God Forms a New Nation

Discussion Questions

1. What was the first thing Abraham did once he reached the end of his journey?
2. Whom did Abraham take with him?
3. What choice did Abraham give to his nephew Lot?
4. What did Lot choose?
5. Who changed Abram's name?
6. What did Abram's new name mean?

Genesis 13:2 - 11 & 17:1 - 5

Genesis 13

2 And **Abram** was very rich in cattle, in silver, and in gold.

3 And he went on his journeys from the south even to Bethel, unto the place where his tent had been at the beginning, between Bethel and Hai;

4 Unto the place of the altar, which he had make there at the first: and there Abram called on the name of the LORD.

5 And **Lot** also, which went with Abram, had flocks, and herds, and tents.

6 And the land was not able to bear them, that they might dwell together: for their substance was great, so that they could not dwell together.

7 And there was a strife between the herdmen of Abram's cattle and the herdmen of Lot's cattle: and the Canaanite and the Perizzite dwelled then in the land.

8 And Abram said unto Lot, Let there be no strife, I pray thee, between me and thee, and between my herdmen and thy herdmen; for we be brethren.

9 Is not the whole land before thee? separate thyself, I pray thee, from me: if thou wilt take the left hand, then I will go to the right; or if thou depart to the right hand, then I will go to the left.

10 And Lot lifted up his eyes, and beheld all the plain of Jordan, that it was well watered every where, before the LORD destroyed Sodom and Gomorrah, even as the garden of the LORD, like the land of Egypt, as thou comest unto Zoar.

11 Then Lot chose him all the plain of Jordan; and Lot journeyed east: and they separated themselves the one from the other.

Genesis 17

1 And when Abram was ninety years old and nine, the Lord appeared to Abram, and said unto him, I am the Almighty God; walk before me, and be thou perfect.

2 And I will make my covenant between me and thee, and will multiply thee exceedingly.

3 And Abram fell on his face: and God talked with him, saying,

4 As for me, behold, my covenant is with thee, and thou shalt be a father of many nations.

5 Neither shall thy name any more be called Abram, but thy name shall be **Abraham**; for a father of many nations have I made thee.

Lesson Two

History Overview and Assignments
A Special New Nation

AFTER THE GREAT FLOOD and the Tower of Babel, family groups of early people migrated to different areas. Some went west and founded cities in the land we now call India, while others moved south and started cultures in Canaan and Egypt; this was part of God's plan. It was also part of God's plan to form a special new group of people that He would call His own, which would later bless all the other family groups on the earth.

Hagar and Ishmael Banished by Abraham, by Pieter Jozef Verhaghen (1781)

Suggested Reading and Assignments

- Read the article: *The Story of Hagar and Ishmael*.
- After reading the article, summarize the story you read by either:
    - Retelling it out loud to your teacher or parent.
      OR
    - Completing an appropriate notebook page.

  Either way, be sure to include the answers to the discussion questions and an overview of key people, places, dates, and events in your summary.
- Complete your true-to-scale model of **Noah's Ark**.
- Be sure to visit your **ArtiosHCS** curriculum website for additional resources and any videos and websites assigned for this lesson.

Key People, Places, and Events

Babylonian Empire	Egypt	Abraham (Abram)
India	Menes	Sarah (Sarai)
Himalayan Mountains	Phoenicians	Isaac
Assyria	Sidon	Hagar
Minoan	Tyre	Ishmael
Crete	Sodom	Arabians
Greece	Gomorrah	Hebrews
Nile River		

Discussion Questions

1. What was one of the most significant differences between the people who had lived before the Flood and those who lived after it?
2. List some of the areas and cities to which people traveled and settled.
3. What book of the Bible takes place in the city of Nineveh?
4. Why were Sodom and Gomorrah destroyed?
5. What did Abraham and Sarah name their child?
6. What promise did the birth of Isaac fulfill?
7. Abraham had another son. What was his name, and who was his mother?
8. How did Sarah feel about Abraham's other son and her maid?
9. What happened to Hagar and Ishmael after they left Abraham's camp?
10. How did God provide for Hagar and Ishmael when they were in the desert?

Adapted for Elementary School from the book:
The Wonder Book of Bible Stories
arranged by Logan Marshall
The Story of Hagar and Ishmael

Early Nations

After the great Flood, the family of Noah and those who came after him grew in number until, as the years went on, the earth began to be full of people once more. But there was one significant difference between the people who had lived before the Flood and those who lived after it. Before the Flood, all the people stayed close together so that many lived in one land, and no one lived in other lands. But after the Flood and the Tower of Babel, families began to move from one place to another, seeking new homes. Some went one way and others another, so as the number of people grew, they covered much more of the earth than those who had lived before the Flood.

As we've already read, some people stayed nearby and developed the world's first great civilization, Sumer. The Sumerian people made significant developments in mathematics and written language. The Akkadians and other people groups eventually took them over, and the great Babylonian Empire developed from this mixture of cultures. This empire united the different people groups of the Mesopotamian region.

Relief detail of the Akkadian goddess Ishtar is shown on an Akkadian seal. She is equipped with weapons on her back, has a horned helmet, and tramples a lion on a leash (2350–2150 B.C.). Photo by Sailko. CC BY 3.0.

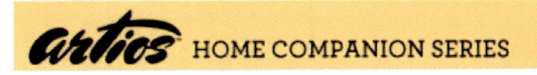

Some other people went east and founded cities in the land of **India**. They were a peaceful people, but their culture eventually declined, and in time they mixed with other people groups who came through the **Himalayan Mountains**.

Others went up north and built a city called Nineveh, which became the ruling city of the great nation called **Assyria**, whose people were called Assyrians.

Others ventured out across the Mediterranean Sea and started the **Minoan** culture on the island of **Crete** and then spread onto the mainland of **Greece**, forming city-states throughout the land.

Another company went away to the south, settled by the great Nile River, and founded the land of Egypt, with its strange temples and pyramids, sphinxes, and monuments. Egypt's civilization was first divided into two parts along the Nile River, called Upper Egypt and Lower Egypt. A ruler named **Menes** united the two regions, and a great empire developed to last for thousands of years.

Another group traveled northwest until they came to the shore of the great sea, which they called the Mediterranean Sea. The Phoenicians founded the cities of **Sidon** and **Tyre**, where the people were sailors, sailing to countries far away and bringing home many things from other lands to sell to the people of Babylon, Assyria, Egypt, and other countries.

A Special New Nation: The Hebrew People

All of these nations rejected God and chose to worship false gods instead, and God punished them for this, sometimes by wars and conquests by enemies and sometimes by other disasters. Among the many cities the people built were two that were exceedingly sinful: **Sodom** and **Gomorrah**. The people in these cities were very wicked and were nearly all destroyed. One good man named Lot and his family escaped.

Lot's uncle was another good man named **Abraham**, who did not live in those cities. He tried to do God's will, and God promised him a son to start a great and special nation.

After Sodom and Gomorrah were destroyed, Abraham moved his tent and camp away from that part of the land and lived near a place in the southwest, not far from the Great Sea. And there, at last, the child whom God had promised to Abraham and **Sarah**, his wife, was born when Abraham, his father, was a very old man.

They named this child **Isaac**, as the angel had told them he should be named. And Abraham and Sarah were so happy to have a little boy that after a time, they gave a great feast and invited all the people to come and rejoice with them, all in honor of little Isaac.

Edmonia Lewis's sculpture depicts Hagar, the biblical maidservant to Sarah and Abraham
Attribution: ©David Finn Archive, Department of Image Collections, National Gallery of Art Library, Washington, DC. CC BY-SA 4.0

Now Sarah had a maid named **Hagar**, an Egyptian woman. She already had a child with Abraham, and his name was **Ishmael**. So now there were two boys in Abraham's tent, the older boy, Ishmael, the son of Hagar, and the younger boy, Isaac, the son of Abraham and Sarah.

Ishmael did not like little Isaac and did not treat him kindly. This made his mother, Sarah, very angry, and she said to her husband, "I do not wish to have this boy Ishmael growing up with my son Isaac. Send Hagar and her boy away, for they trouble me."

And Abraham felt very sorry to have trouble come between Sarah and Hagar and between Isaac and Ishmael; for Abraham was a kind and good man and friend to them all.

But the Lord told Abraham, "Do not be troubled about Ishmael and his mother. Do as Sarah has asked you to do, and send them away. Isaac should be left alone in your tent, for he is to receive everything that is yours. I, the Lord, will take care of Ishmael and make a great people of his descendants, those who shall come from him."

So the following day, Abraham sent Hagar and her boy away. He gave them some food for the journey and a bottle of water to drink, by the way. The bottles in that country were not like ours, made of plastic or glass. They were made from the skin of a goat. One of these skin bottles Abraham filled with water and gave to Hagar.

And Hagar went away from Abraham's tent, leading her little boy. But somehow, she lost the road and wandered over the desert, not knowing where she was, until all the water in the bottle was used up, and her poor boy in the hot sun and the burning sand had nothing to drink. She thought he would die of his terrible thirst and laid him down under a bush. Then she went away, saying, "I cannot bear to look at my poor boy suffering and dying for want of water."

And just then, while Hagar was crying and her boy was moaning with thirst, she heard a voice saying to her: *"Hagar, what is your trouble? Do not be afraid. God has heard your cry and the cry of your child. God will take care of you both and make your boy a great nation of people."*

It was the voice of an angel from heaven. Hagar looked up, and there, close at hand, was a spring of water in the desert. How glad Hagar was as she filled the bottle with water and took it to her suffering boy under the bush!

After this, Hagar did not go down to Egypt. She found a place to live and brought up her son in the wilderness, far from other people. And Ishmael grew up in the desert and learned to shoot with a bow and arrow. He became a nomadic man (which means he moved from place to place), and his children after him grew up to be nomads, also. They were the **Arabians** of the desert. So Ishmael came to be the father of many people, and his descendants, the Arab people, live to this day in that land.

God began forming a special new people group called the **Hebrews** from Isaac, Abraham's second son.

Hagar and Ishmael in the Wilderness,
by Francesco Cozza (1665)

The Artios Home Companion Series
Unit 6: Abraham and Isaac

Teacher Overview

ABRAHAM HAD WAITED many years for a son—and then God asked him to prepare to offer his only son, Isaac, as a sacrifice to Him. What do you think went through the minds of Abraham and Isaac? Yet, Abraham humbly obeyed God's request, just like when God called him out of his homeland to a land that God promised him. Trusting God enough to obey Him is always important, even when we don't understand His request.

Abraham Receiving the Three Angels, by Bartolomé Esteban Murillo (1667)

Suggested Assignments

Based on your student's age and ability, the reading in this unit may be read aloud to the student, and journaling and notebook pages may be completed orally. Likewise, other assignments may be done with an appropriate combination of independent and guided study.

* Please note that for Lesson One, it might be wise to read the article yourself and then tell the story to your child in your own words due to some adult themes in a few verses. Or you might use the resource we mentioned in Unit 1 under 'Additional Materials' by reading the corresponding chapter in <u>Leading Little Ones to God</u>.

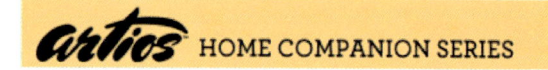

In this unit, students will:
- Complete two lessons in which they will learn about **Abraham**, **Lot**, and **Isaac**.
- Visit the **ArtiosHCS** curriculum website at **www.ArtiosHCS.com** for additional resources and any videos and websites assigned for this unit.

Heart Connections

God will accomplish His purpose.
Many are the plans in the mind of a man, but it is the purpose of the Lord that will stand.
– Proverbs 19:21

One's heart is revealed by one's words and actions.
The good person out of the good treasure of his heart produces good, and the evil person out of his evil treasure produces evil, for out of the abundance of the heart his mouth speaks.
– Luke 6:45

Abraham trusted in God's promise.
No unbelief made him waver concerning the promise of God, but he grew strong in his faith as he gave glory to God, fully convinced that God was able to do what he had promised.
– Romans 4:20-21

There is a certainty to God's promises.
For when God made a promise to Abraham, since He had no one greater by whom to swear, He swore by himself, saying, "Surely I will bless you and multiply you." And thus Abraham having patiently waited, obtained the promise.
– Hebrews 6:13-15

Key People, Places, and Events

Lot
Abraham
Isaac

Sodom's destruction, Lot and his daughters escape.
Monreale Cathedral mosaics

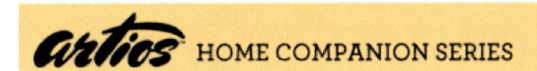

Lesson One

History Overview and Assignments
Raining Fire

> "Then the LORD rained upon Sodom and upon Gomorrah brimstone and fire from the LORD out of heaven; And he overthrew those cities, and all the plain, and all the inhabitants of the cities, and that which grew upon the ground."
>
> – Genesis 19:24-25

The Destruction of Sodom and Gomorrah, by John Martin (1852)

Suggested Reading and Assignments

- Read the article: *Genesis 19:1-28*.
- After reading the article, summarize the story you read by either:
    - Retelling it out loud to your teacher or parent.
        OR
    - Completing an appropriate notebook page.

    Either way, be sure to include the answers to the discussion questions and an overview of key people, places, dates, and events in your summary.
- Be sure to visit your **ArtiosHCS** curriculum website for additional resources and any videos and websites assigned for this lesson.

Key People, Places, and Events

Lot
Abraham

Discussion Questions

1. Why did God want to punish Sodom?
2. How did God punish Sodom?
3. What happened to Lot's wife?

Ancient: Elementary
Unit 6: Abraham and Isaac

Genesis 19:1 - 28

Genesis 19

1 And there came two angels to Sodom at even; and **Lot** sat in the gate of Sodom: and Lot seeing them rose up to meet them; and he bowed himself with his face toward the ground;

2 And he said, Behold now, my lords, turn in, I pray you, into your servant's house, and tarry all night, and wash your feet, and ye shall rise up early, and go on your ways. And they said, Nay; but we will abide in the street all night.

3 And he pressed upon them greatly; and they turned in unto him, and entered into his house; and he made them a feast, and did bake unleavened bread, and they did eat.

4 But before they lay down, the men of the city, even the men of Sodom, compassed the house round, both old and young, all the people from every quarter:

5 And they called unto Lot, and said unto him, Where are the men which came in to thee this night? bring them out unto us, that we may know them.

6 And Lot went out at the door unto them, and shut the door after him,

7 And said, I pray you, brethren, do not so wickedly.

8 Behold now, I have two daughters which have not known man; let me, I pray you, bring them out unto you, and do ye to them as is good in your eyes: only unto these men do nothing; for therefore came they under the shadow of my roof.

9 And they said, Stand back. And they said again, This one fellow came in to sojourn, and he will needs be a judge: now will we deal worse with thee, than with them. And they pressed sore upon the man, even Lot, and came near to break the door.

10 But the men put forth their hand, and pulled Lot into the house to them, and shut to the door.

11 And they smote the men that were at the door of the house with blindness, both small and great: so that they wearied themselves to find the door.

12 And the men said unto Lot, Hast thou here any besides? son in law, and thy sons, and thy daughters, and whatsoever thou hast in the city, bring them out of this place:

13 For we will destroy this place, because the cry of them is waxen great before the face of the LORD; and the LORD hath sent us to destroy it.

14 And Lot went out, and spake unto his sons in law, which married his daughters, and said, Up, get you out of this place; for the LORD will destroy this city. But he seemed as one that mocked unto his sons in law.

15 And when the morning arose, then the angels hastened Lot, saying, Arise, take thy wife, and thy two daughters, which are here; lest thou be consumed in the iniquity of the city.

16 And while he lingered, the men laid hold upon his hand, and upon the hand of his wife, and upon the hand of his two daughters; the LORD being merciful unto him: and they brought him forth, and set him without the city.

17 And it came to pass, when they had brought them forth abroad, that he said, Escape for thy life; look not behind thee, neither stay thou in all the plain; escape to the mountain, lest thou be consumed.

18 And Lot said unto them, Oh, not so, my LORD:

19 Behold now, thy servant hath found grace in thy sight, and thou hast magnified thy mercy, which thou hast shewed unto me in saving my life; and I cannot escape to the mountain, lest some evil take me, and I die:

20 Behold now, this city is near to flee unto, and it is a little one: Oh, let me escape thither, (is it not a little one?) and my soul shall live.

21 And he said unto him, See, I have accepted thee concerning this thing also, that I will not overthrow this city, for the which thou hast spoken.

22 Haste thee, escape thither; for I cannot do anything till thou be come thither. Therefore the name of the city was called Zoar.

23 The sun was risen upon the earth when Lot entered into Zoar.

24 Then the LORD rained upon Sodom and upon Gomorrah brimstone and fire from the LORD out of heaven;

25 And he overthrew those cities, and all the plain, and all the inhabitants of the cities, and that which grew upon the ground.

26 But his wife looked back from behind him, and she became a pillar of salt.

27 And **Abraham** gat up early in the morning to the place where he stood before the LORD:

28 And he looked toward Sodom and Gomorrah, and toward all the land of the plain, and beheld, and, lo, the smoke of the country went up as the smoke of a furnace.

The Flight of Lot and His Family From Sodom (after Rubens), by Jacob Jordaens (c.1618-20)

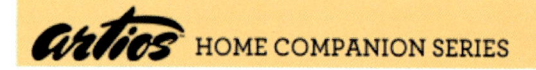

Lesson Two

History Overview and Assignments
"God Will Provide Himself a Lamb"

"God wished to show Abraham and all his descendants, those who should come after him, that He was not pleased with such offerings as those of living people, killed on the altars. And God chose a way to teach Abraham so that he and his children after him would never forget it."

– from the adapted article below

Key People, Places, and Events

Abraham   Isaac

Discussion Questions

1. What did God ask Abraham to do?
2. Was this an unusual request for that culture?
3. Why would this request have been especially difficult for Abraham to fulfill?
4. How did Isaac react to having no animal to sacrifice?
5. What is so remarkable about both the reaction of Abraham and the reaction of Isaac?
6. How do you think you would react if you were asked to sacrifice something very precious to you?

Abraham going up to offer Isaac as a sacrifice, as described in Genesis 22. Illustration from the 1890 Holman Bible

Suggested Reading and Assignments

- Read the article: *The Story of Abraham and Isaac*.
- After reading the article, summarize the story you read by either:
    - Retelling it out loud to your teacher or parent.
      OR
    - Completing an appropriate notebook page.

  Either way, be sure to include the answers to the discussion questions and an overview of key people, places, dates, and events in your summary.
- This is another great story for your students to illustrate and then orally tell back while showing or explaining their pictures. This is also an excellent article for showing God's priority on our obedience. This is a great discussion to have with your children.
- Be sure to visit your **ArtiosHCS** curriculum website for additional resources and any videos and websites assigned for this lesson.

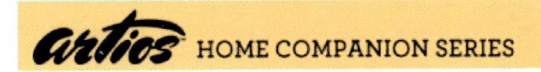

Ancient: Elementary
Unit 6: Abraham and Isaac

Adapted for Elementary School from the book:
The Wonder Book of Bible Stories
Arranged by Logan Marshall
The Story of Abraham and Isaac

You remember that in those times of which we are telling, when men worshiped God, they built an altar of earth or stone and laid an offering upon it as a gift to God, to atone for their sins. The offering was generally a sheep, a goat, or a young ox—some animal used for food. Such an offering was called a "sacrifice."

But the people who worshiped idols often did what seems strange and terrible to us. They thought that it would please their gods if they would offer as a sacrifice the most precious living things that were their own—they would take their little children and kill them upon their altars as offerings to the gods of wood and stone, which were no real gods, but only images.

God wished to show **Abraham** and all his descendants, those who should come after him, that He was not pleased with such offerings as those of living people killed on the altars. And God chose a way to teach Abraham so that he and his children after him would never forget it. Then at the same time, He wished to show how faithful and obedient Abraham would be to His commands, how fully Abraham would trust in God, or, as we would say, how great Abraham's faith in God was. In addition to these things, God wanted most of all to demonstrate to His people that someday a precious son would be sacrificed for the people—but it would be His own Son.

So God gave Abraham a command which He did not mean to have obeyed, though He did not tell Abraham. He said, *"Take now your son, your only son **Isaac**, whom you love so greatly, and go to the land of Moriah, and there on a mountain that I will show you, offer him for a burnt offering to Me."*

Though this command filled Abraham's heart with pain, he would not be as surprised to receive it as a father would in our day; for such offerings were very common among all those people in the land where Abraham lived. Abraham never for one moment doubted or disobeyed God's Word. He knew that Isaac was the child God had promised and that, too, Isaac should have children and that those coming from Isaac should be a great nation. He did not see how God could keep His promise concerning Isaac if Isaac should be killed as an offering—unless God should raise him from the dead afterward.

But Abraham undertook at once to obey God's command. He took two young men with him and a donkey laden with wood for the fire, and he went toward the mountain in the north, Isaac, his son, walking by his side. For two days they walked, sleeping under the trees at night in the open country. And on the third day, Abraham saw the mountain far away. And as they drew near the mountain, Abraham said to the young men, "Stay here with the donkey, while I go up yonder mountain with Isaac to worship; and when we have worshiped, we will come back to you." Abraham may have believed that, in some way, God would bring Isaac back to life. He took the wood from the donkey and placed it on Isaac, and they two walked up the mountain together.

Ancient: Elementary
Unit 6: Abraham and Isaac

As they walked, Isaac said, "Father, here is the wood, but where is the lamb for the offering?"

And Abraham said, "My son, God will provide Himself a lamb for a burnt offering."

And they came to the place on the top of the mountain. Abraham built an altar of stones and earth, heaped it up, and placed the wood on it. Then he tied Isaac's hands and feet and laid him on the altar, on the wood. And Abraham lifted his hand, holding a knife to kill his son. Another moment longer, Isaac would be slain by his father's hand.

But just at that moment, the angel of the Lord out of heaven called to Abraham, saying, "Abraham! Abraham!"

And Abraham answered, "Here I am, Lord."

Then the angel of the Lord said, "Do not lay your hand upon your son. Do not harm him. Now I know that you love God more than you love your only son and are obedient to God since you are ready to give up your son, your only son, to God."

What a relief and a joy these words from heaven brought to the heart of Abraham! How glad he was to know that it was not God's will for him to kill his son! Then Abraham looked around, and there in the thicket was a ram caught by his horns. And Abraham took the ram and offered him up for a burnt offering in place of his son. So Abraham's words came true when he said that God would provide for Himself a lamb.

Abraham named the place where this altar was built *Jehovah Jireh*, words in the language that Abraham spoke meaning, "The Lord will provide."

This offering, which seems so strange, did much good. It showed to Abraham and Isaac also that Isaac belonged to God, for to God he had been offered; and through Isaac all those who should come from him, his descendants, had been given to God. Then it showed to Abraham and to all the people after him that God did not wish for children or men to be killed as offerings for worship; and while all the people around offered such sacrifices, the Israelites, who came from Abraham and from Isaac, never offered them, but offered oxen and sheep and goats instead.

These gifts, which cost so much toil, they felt must be pleasing to God, because they expressed their thankfulness to Him. But they were glad to be taught that God does not desire men's lives to be taken—except for that of His own beloved Son in the final sacrifice that paid for the sins of all His people—but He loves our living gifts of love and kindness.

Abraham embraces his son Isaac after receiving him back from God. Early 1900s Bible illustration by Otto Adolph Stemier

Ancient: Elementary
Unit 6: Abraham and Isaac

The Artios Home Companion Series
Unit 7: Jacob and Esau

Teacher Overview

THE LIFE OF JACOB is a vivid picture of Luke 6:45, which says, "Out of the abundance of the heart his mouth speaks." This is seen in Jacob's deception of his father and brother Esau. But God used the sin of Jacob to weave together His plan for the nation of Israel. The meaning of "what goes around, comes around" is shown when Laban later deceives Jacob regarding his marriage to Rachel, just as Jacob had deceived Isaac regarding receiving the birthright.

Jacob Leading the Flocks of Laban,
by Giovanni Benedetto Castiglione (c.1632)

Suggested Assignments

Based on your student's age and ability, the reading in this unit may be read aloud to the student, and journaling and notebook pages may be completed orally. Likewise, other assignments may be done with an appropriate combination of independent and guided study.

In this unit, students will:
- Complete three lessons in which they will learn about **Isaac**, **Rebekah**, **Jacob**, **Esau**, **Rachel**, and **Leah**.
- Define vocabulary words.
- Explore websites with the lyrics and performance of "We Are Climbing Jacob's Ladder."
- Create their own Jacob's Ladder using the website with the link on the **ArtiosHCS** curriculum website.
- Visit the **ArtiosHCS** curriculum website at **www.ArtiosHCS.com** for additional resources and any videos and websites assigned for this unit.

Heart Connections

God will accomplish His purpose.
Many are the plans in the mind of a man, but it is the purpose of the Lord that will stand.
– Proverbs 19:21

One's heart is revealed by one's words and actions.
The good person out of the good treasure of his heart produces good, and the evil person out of his evil treasure produces evil, for out of the abundance of the heart his mouth speaks.
– Luke 6:45

Abraham trusted in God's promise.
No unbelief made him waver concerning the promise of God, but he grew strong in his faith as he gave glory to God, fully convinced that God was able to do what he had promised.
– Romans 4:20-21

There is a certainty to God's promises.
For when God made a promise to Abraham, since He had no one greater by whom to swear, He swore by himself, saying, "Surely I will bless you and multiply you." And thus Abraham having patiently waited, obtained the promise.
– Hebrews 6:13-15

Vocabulary

Lesson 1:
savoury (savory)
peradventure (perhaps)
subtilty (subtle)
birthright

Lesson 2:
none

Lesson 3:
none

Key People, Places, and Events

Isaac
Esau
Rebekah
Jacob
Laban
Rachel
Leah
Joseph

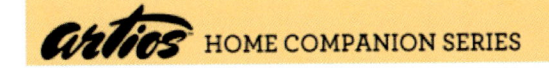

Lesson One

History Overview and Assignments
Stealing the Birthright

"And Jacob said unto his father, 'I am Esau thy first born; I have done according as thou badest me: arise, I pray thee, sit and eat of my venison, that thy soul may bless me.'"

– Genesis 27:19

The Mess of Pottage, by James Tissot (c.1896-1902)

Suggested Reading and Assignments

- Read the article: *Genesis 27:1-28:22*.
- Define each vocabulary word in the context of the reading. Write the words and their definitions in the vocabulary section of your notebook.
- After reading the article, summarize the story you read by either:
    - Retelling it out loud to your teacher or parent.
      OR
    - Completing an appropriate notebook page.

  Either way, be sure to include the answers to the discussion questions and an overview of key people, places, dates, and events in your summary.
- Be sure to visit your **ArtiosHCS** curriculum website for additional resources and any videos and websites assigned for this lesson.

Vocabulary

savoury (savory)
peradventure (perhaps)
subtilty (subtle)
birthright

Key People, Places, and Events

Isaac
Esau
Rebekah
Jacob

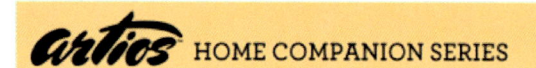

Discussion Questions

1. What did Isaac ask Esau to prepare for him?
2. Who overheard Isaac's request?
3. What did Rebekah instruct Jacob to do? Why?
4. How did Jacob trick Isaac?
5. How did Esau react to Jacob's deceit?
6. To where did Jacob flee?

Esau and Jacob Presented to Isaac, by Benjamin West (c.1779-1801)

Genesis 27:1 - 28:22

Genesis 27

1 And it came to pass, that when **Isaac** was old, and his eyes were dim, so that he could not see, he called **Esau** his eldest son, and said unto him, My son: and he said unto him, Behold, here am I.

2 And he said, Behold now, I am old, I know not the day of my death:

3 Now therefore take, I pray thee, thy weapons, thy quiver and thy bow, and go out to the field, and take me some venison;

4 And make me **savoury** meat, such as I love, and bring it to me, that I may eat; that my soul may bless thee before I die.

5 And **Rebekah** heard when Isaac spake to Esau his son. And Esau went to the field to hunt for venison, and to bring it.

6 And Rebekah spake unto **Jacob** her son, saying, Behold, I heard thy father speak unto Esau thy brother, saying,

7 Bring me venison, and make me savoury meat, that I may eat, and bless thee before the LORD before my death.

8 Now therefore, my son, obey my voice according to that which I command thee.

9 Go now to the flock, and fetch me from thence two good kids of the goats; and I will make them savoury meat for thy father, such as he loveth:

10 And thou shalt bring it to thy father, that he may eat, and that he may bless thee before his death.

11 And Jacob said to Rebekah his mother, Behold, Esau my brother is a hairy man, and I am a smooth man:

12 My father **peradventure** will feel me, and I shall seem to him as a deceiver; and I shall bring a curse upon me, and not a blessing.

13 And his mother said unto him, Upon

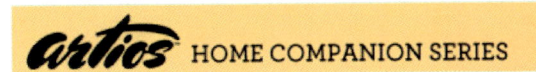

me be thy curse, my son: only obey my voice, and go fetch me them.

14 And he went, and fetched, and brought them to his mother: and his mother made savoury meat, such as his father loved.

15 And Rebekah took goodly raiment of her eldest son Esau, which were with her in the house, and put them upon Jacob her younger son:

16 And she put the skins of the kids of the goats upon his hands, and upon the smooth of his neck:

17 And she gave the savoury meat and the bread, which she had prepared, into the hand of her son Jacob.

18 And he came unto his father, and said, My father: and he said, Here am I; who art thou, my son?

19 And Jacob said unto his father, I am Esau thy first born; I have done according as thou badest me: arise, I pray thee, sit and eat of my venison, that thy soul may bless me.

20 And Isaac said unto his son, How is it that thou hast found it so quickly, my son? And he said, Because the LORD thy God brought it to me.

21 And Isaac said unto Jacob, Come near, I pray thee, that I may feel thee, my son, whether thou be my very son Esau or not.

22 And Jacob went near unto Isaac his father; and he felt him, and said, The voice is Jacob's voice, but the hands are the hands of Esau.

23 And he discerned him not, because his hands were hairy, as his brother Esau's hands: so he blessed him.

24 And he said, Art thou my very son Esau? And he said, I am.

25 And he said, Bring it near to me, and I will eat of my son's venison, that my soul may bless thee. And he brought it near to him, and he did eat: and he brought him wine and he drank.

26 And his father Isaac said unto him, Come near now, and kiss me, my son.

27 And he came near, and kissed him: and he smelled the smell of his raiment, and blessed him, and said, See, the smell of my son is as the smell of a field which the LORD hath blessed:

28 Therefore God give thee of the dew of heaven, and the fatness of the earth, and plenty of corn and wine:

29 Let people serve thee, and nations bow down to thee: be lord over thy brethren, and let thy mother's sons bow down to thee: cursed be every one that curseth thee, and blessed be he that blesseth thee.

30 And it came to pass, as soon as Isaac had made an end of blessing Jacob, and Jacob was yet scarce gone out from the presence of Isaac his father, that Esau his brother came in from his hunting.

31 And he also had made savoury meat, and brought it unto his father, and said unto his father, Let my father arise, and eat of his son's venison, that thy soul may bless me.

32 And Isaac his father said unto him, Who art thou? And he said, I am thy son, thy firstborn Esau.

33 And Isaac trembled very exceedingly, and said, Who? where is he that hath taken venison, and brought it me, and I have eaten of all before thou camest, and have blessed him? yea, and he shall be blessed.

34 And when Esau heard the words of his father, he cried with a great and exceeding bitter cry, and said unto his father, Bless me, even me also, O my father.

35 And he said, Thy brother came with **subtilty**, and hath taken away thy blessing.

36 And he said, Is not he rightly named Jacob? for he hath supplanted me these two times: he took away my **birthright**; and, behold, now he hath taken away my blessing. And he said, Hast thou not reserved a blessing for me?

37 And Isaac answered and said unto Esau, Behold, I have made him thy lord, and all his brethren have I given to him for servants; and with corn and wine have I sustained him: and what shall I do now unto thee, my son?

38 And Esau said unto his father, Hast thou but one blessing, my father? bless me, even me also, O my father. And Esau lifted up his voice, and wept.

39 And Isaac his father answered and said unto him, Behold, thy dwelling shall be the fatness of the earth, and of the dew of heaven from above;

40 And by thy sword shalt thou live, and shalt serve thy brother; and it shall come to pass when thou shalt have the dominion, that thou shalt break his yoke from off thy neck.

41 And Esau hated Jacob because of the blessing wherewith his father blessed him: and Esau said in his heart, The days of mourning for my father are at hand; then will I slay my brother Jacob.

42 And these words of Esau her elder son were told to Rebekah: and she sent and called Jacob her younger son, and said unto him, Behold, thy brother Esau, as touching thee, doth comfort himself, purposing to kill thee.

43 Now therefore, my son, obey my voice; arise, flee thou to Laban my brother to Haran;

44 And tarry with him a few days, until thy brother's fury turn away;

45 Until thy brother's anger turn away from thee, and he forget that which thou hast done to him: then I will send, and fetch thee from thence: why should I be deprived also of you both in one day?

46 And Rebekah said to Isaac, I am weary of my life because of the daughters of Heth: if Jacob take a wife of the daughters of Heth, such as these which are of the daughters of the land, what good shall my life do me?

Genesis 28

1 And Isaac called Jacob, and blessed him, and charged him, and said unto him, Thou shalt not take a wife of the daughters of Canaan.

2 Arise, go to Padanaram, to the house of Bethuel thy mother's father; and take thee a wife from thence of the daughters of Laban thy mother's brother.

3 And God Almighty bless thee, and make thee fruitful, and multiply thee, that thou mayest be a multitude of people;

4 And give thee the blessing of Abraham, to thee, and to thy seed with thee; that thou mayest inherit the land wherein thou art a stranger, which God gave unto Abraham.

5 And Isaac sent away Jacob: and he went to Padanaram unto Laban, son of Bethuel the Syrian, the brother of Rebekah, Jacob's and Esau's mother.

6 When Esau saw that Isaac had blessed Jacob, and sent him away to Padanaram, to take him a wife from thence; and that as he blessed him he gave him a charge, saying, Thou shalt not take a wife of the daughters of Canaan;

7 And that Jacob obeyed his father and his mother, and was gone to Padanaram;

8 And Esau seeing that the daughters of Canaan pleased not Isaac his father;

9 Then went Esau unto Ishmael, and

took unto the wives which he had Mahalath the daughter of Ishmael Abraham's son, the sister of Nebajoth, to be his wife.

10 And Jacob went out from Beersheba, and went toward Haran.

11 And he lighted upon a certain place, and tarried there all night, because the sun was set; and he took of the stones of that place, and put them for his pillows, and lay down in that place to sleep.

12 And he dreamed, and behold a ladder set up on the earth, and the top of it reached to heaven: and behold the angels of God ascending and descending on it.

13 And, behold, the LORD stood above it, and said, I am the LORD God of Abraham thy father, and the God of Isaac: the land whereon thou liest, to thee will I give it, and to thy seed;

14 And thy seed shall be as the dust of the earth, and thou shalt spread abroad to the west, and to the east, and to the north, and to the south: and in thee and in thy seed shall all the families of the earth be blessed.

15 And, behold, I am with thee, and will keep thee in all places whither thou goest, and will bring thee again into this land; for I will not leave thee, until I have done that which I have spoken to thee of.

16 And Jacob awaked out of his sleep, and he said, Surely the LORD is in this place; and I knew it not.

17 And he was afraid, and said, How dreadful is this place! this is none other but the house of God, and this is the gate of heaven.

18 And Jacob rose up early in the morning, and took the stone that he had put for his pillows, and set it up for a pillar, and poured oil upon the top of it.

19 And he called the name of that place Bethel: but the name of that city was called Luz at the first.

20 And Jacob vowed a vow, saying, If God will be with me, and will keep me in this way that I go, and will give me bread to eat, and raiment to put on,

21 So that I come again to my father's house in peace; then shall the LORD be my God:

22 And this stone, which I have set for a pillar, shall be God's house: and of all that thou shalt give me I will surely give the tenth unto thee.

Esau Selling His Birthright to Jacob or *The Lentil Stew,* by circle of Matthias Stom (17th century)

Lesson Two

History Overview and Assignments
Jacob and Esau

"Now Esau, when he grew up, did not care much for his birthright or the blessing God had promised. But Jacob, a wise man, wished greatly to have the birthright which would come to Esau when his father died."

– from the adapted article below

Isaac Blessing Jacob, by José de Riberia (1637)

Suggested Reading and Assignments

- Read the article: *Jacob and Esau.*
- After reading the article, summarize the story you read by either:
    - Retelling it out loud to your teacher or parent.
      OR
    - Completing an appropriate notebook page.

  Either way, be sure to include the answers to the discussion questions and an overview of key people, places, dates, and events in your summary.
- Be sure to visit your **ArtiosHCS** curriculum website for additional resources and any videos and websites assigned for this lesson.

Key People, Places, and Events

Isaac
Rebekah
Esau
Jacob

Discussion Questions

1. Why was receiving the birthright so important in a Jewish family?
2. Describe Esau.
3. Describe Jacob
4. Which of the twins did Isaac prefer?
5. Which of the twins did Rebekah prefer?
6. How did the "heart" of Jacob reveal itself when he deceived his father?
7. How did the descendants of Esau fall away from the Lord?
8. Where did the descendants of Esau settle?

Ancient: Elementary
Unit 7: Jacob and Esau

Adapted for Elementary School from the book:
The Wonder Book of Bible Stories
Arranged by Logan Marshall
Jacob and Esau

After Abraham died, his son **Isaac** lived in the land of Canaan. Like his father, Isaac had his home in a tent. Around him were the tents of his people and many flocks of sheep and herds of cattle feeding wherever they could find grass to eat and water to drink.

Isaac and his wife, **Rebekah,** had two children. The older was named **Esau**, which meant "red," and the younger's name was **Jacob**, which meant "deceiver."

Esau was a man of the woods and very fond of hunting, and he was rough and covered with reddish hair.

Jacob was quiet and thoughtful, staying at home, dwelling in a tent, and caring for his father's flocks.

Isaac loved Esau more than Jacob because Esau brought to his father what he had killed while hunting. But Rebekah liked Jacob because she saw he was wise and careful in his work.

Among the people in those lands, when a man dies, his older son receives twice as much as the younger of what the father has owned. This was called his "birthright," for it was his right as the oldest born. So Esau, as the older, had a "birthright" to more of Isaac's possessions than Jacob. And besides this, God had promised that the family of Isaac should receive great blessings.

Now Esau, when he grew up, did not care much for his birthright or the blessing which God had promised. But Jacob, a wise man, wished greatly to have the birthright which would come to Esau when his father died. Once, when Esau came home, hungry and tired from hunting in the fields, he saw that Jacob had a bowl of something he had just cooked for dinner. And Esau said:

"Give me some of that red stuff in the dish. Will you not give me some? I am hungry."

And Jacob answered, "I will give it to you if you will first sell me your birthright."

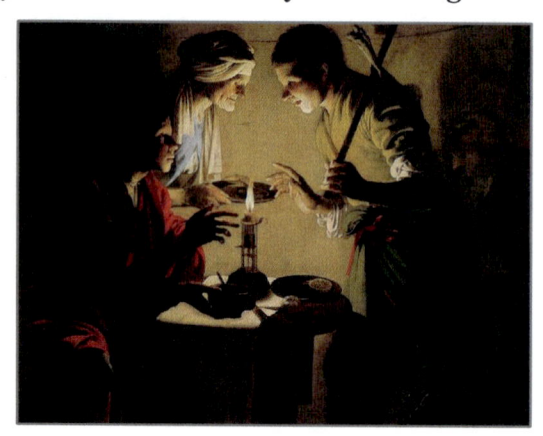

Esau Selling His Birthright,
by Hendrick ter Brugghen (c.1625)

And Esau said, "What is the use of the birthright to me now when I am almost starving to death? You can have my birthright if you give me something to eat."

Then Esau made Jacob a promise to give Jacob his birthright, all for a bowl of food. It was not right for Jacob to deal so selfishly with his brother, but it was very wrong of Esau to care so little for his birthright and God's blessing.

Sometime after this, when Esau was forty years old, he married two wives. Many men in those days married more than one woman, even though that was not God's way. Even worse, Esau's two wives were women from the people of Canaan who worshiped idols and not the true God. And they taught their children also to pray to idols. In this way, Esau's descendants lost all knowledge of God and became very wicked. But that was long after this time.

Isaac and Rebekah were very sorry to have their son Esau marry women who prayed to idols, not God. But Isaac still loved his energetic son Esau more than his quiet son Jacob. And Rebekah loved Jacob more than Esau.

Isaac became very old, feeble, and so blind that he could see scarcely anything. One day he said to Esau:

"My son, I am very old and do not know how soon I must die. But before I die, I wish to give to you, as my older son, God's blessing upon you and your children and your descendants. Go out into the fields, and with your bow and arrows, shoot some animal that is good for food, and make me a dish of cooked meat such as you know I love, and after I have eaten it, I will give you the blessing."

Now Esau ought to have told his father that the blessing did not belong to him, for he had sold it to his brother Jacob. But he did not tell his father. He went out into the fields hunting to find the kind of meat which his father liked the most.

Now Rebekah was listening and heard all that Isaac had said to Esau. She wanted Jacob to have the blessing rather than Esau because she loved Jacob more than Esau. So she called to Jacob and told him what Isaac had said to Esau, saying:

"Now, my son, do what I tell you, and you will get the blessing instead of your brother. Go to the flocks and bring me two young goats, and I will cook them just like the meat Esau cooks for your father. And you will bring it to your father, and he will think that you are Esau and will give you the blessing."

But Jacob answered, "Esau and I are not alike. His neck and arms are covered with hair, while mine are smooth. My father will feel me and will find that I am not Esau. Then, instead of blessing me, I am afraid he will curse me."

But Rebekah answered her son, "Never mind, just do as I have told you, and I will take care of you. If any harm comes, it will come to me, so do not be afraid but go and bring the meat."

Then Jacob brought a pair of young goats from the flocks, and his mother made a food dish just as Isaac liked it. Then Rebekah found some of Esau's clothes and dressed Jacob in them, and she placed some of the goats' skins on his neck and hands so that his neck and hands would feel rough and hairy to the touch.

Then Jacob came into his father's tent, bringing the dinner, and speaking as much like Esau as he could, he said:

"Here I am, my father."

And Isaac said, "Who are you, my son?"

And Jacob answered, "I am Esau, your oldest son. I have done as you bade me. Now sit up and eat the dinner that I have made, and then give me your blessing as you promised me."

And Isaac said, "How did you find it so quickly?"

Jacob answered, "Because the Lord your God showed me where to go and gave me success."

Isaac did not feel confident that it was his son Esau, and he said, "Come near and let me feel you so that I may know that you are my son Esau."

And Jacob went up close to Isaac's bed, and Isaac felt his face, and then his neck and his hands, and he said:

"The voice sounds like Jacob, but the

hands are the hands of Esau. Are you my son Esau?"

And Jacob told a lie to his father, saying, "I am."

Then the old man ate the food Jacob had brought him, and he kissed Jacob. Then, believing him to be Esau, he gave him the blessing, saying:

"May God give you the dew of heaven, the earth's richness, and plenty of grain and wine. May nations bow down to you and peoples become your servants. May you be the master over your brother, and may your family and descendants rule over his family and descendants. Blessed be those that bless you, and cursed be those that curse you."

Just as soon as Jacob had received the blessing, he rose and hastened away. He had scarcely gone out when Esau came in from hunting with the dish of food that he had cooked. And he said to Isaac:

"Let my father arise, eat the food I have brought, and give me the blessing."

And Isaac answered, "Why, who are you?"

Esau replied, "I am your son. Your oldest son, Esau."

And Isaac trembled and said, "Who then is the one that came in and brought me food? I have eaten his food and have blessed him. Yes, and he shall be blessed."

When Esau heard this, he knew he had been cheated, and he cried aloud with a bitter cry, "O, my father, my brother has taken away my blessing, just as he took away my birthright! But can you not give me a blessing too? Have you given everything to my brother?"

And Isaac told him everything he had said to Jacob, making him the ruler over his brother.

But Esau begged for another blessing, so Isaac said:

"My son, your dwelling shall be of the earth's riches and the dew of heaven. You shall live by your sword, and your descendants shall serve your brother's descendants. But in time to come, they shall break loose, shake off the yoke of your brother's rule, and be free."

All these things came to pass many years afterward. Esau's descendants lived in Edom, in the southern part of the land of Israel, near where Jacob's descendants lived. And after a time, the Israelites became rulers over the Edomites. Eventually, the Edomites freed themselves from the Israelites. But all this took place hundreds of years afterward.

It was better that Jacob's descendants, those who came after him, should have the blessing than that Esau's people should have it, for Jacob's people worshiped God, while Esau's people walked in the way of the idols and became wicked.

The Mess of Pottage,
by James Jacques Joseph Tissot (C/1907=10-2

Ancient: Elementary
Unit 7: Jacob and Esau

Lesson Three

History Overview and Assignments
The Ladder That Reached to Heaven

"And God said to Jacob: 'I am the Lord, the God of Abraham, and the God of Isaac your father, and I will be your God, too. The land where you are lying all alone shall belong to you and your children after you, and your children shall spread abroad over the lands, east, and west, and north and south like the dust of the earth, and through your family all the world shall receive a blessing. And I am with you in your journey, and I will keep you where you are going and bring you back to this land. I will never leave you and will surely keep my promise to you.'"

– from the adapted article below

Jacob's Ladder, illustration in the *American Book of Bible Stories for Children*,
By O. A. Stemler and Bess Bruce Cleveland

Suggested Reading and Assignments

- Read the article: *The Story of the Ladder That Reached to Heaven*.
- After reading the article, summarize the story you read by either:
    - Retelling it out loud to your teacher or parent.
      OR
    - Completing an appropriate notebook page.

  Either way, be sure to include the answers to the discussion questions and an overview of key people, places, dates, and events in your summary.
- Listen to the performance of the spiritual "We Are Climbing Jacob's Ladder" at the YouTube link found on your **ArtiosHCS** curriculum website. What do you think the words mean?
- Create your own Jacob's Ladder. Instructions may be found at the link on your **ArtiosHCS** curriculum website.
- Visit the link on your **ArtiosHCS** curriculum website to the lyrics to "Jacob's Ladder."
- Be sure to visit your **ArtiosHCS** curriculum website for additional resources and any videos and websites assigned for this lesson.

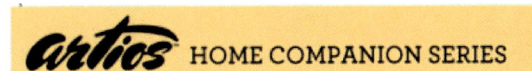

Ancient: Elementary
Unit 7: Jacob and Esau

Key People, Places, and Events

Esau
Jacob
Isaac
Rebekah
Laban
Rachel
Leah
Joseph

Discussion Questions

1. Who lived in Haran?
2. Why was Jacob sent to visit these relatives?
3. Describe the dream Jacob had on his journey.
4. What did God promise Jacob?
5. How did Jacob respond to this dream and promise?
6. What did he name this place?
7. Who did Jacob love and want to marry?
8. What did he have to do to marry her?
9. How did Laban deceive Jacob?
10. Of what does this deception remind you?

Adapted for Elementary School from the book:
The Wonder Book of Bible Stories
Arranged by Logan Marshall
The Story of the Ladder That Reached to Heaven

After **Esau** found that he had lost his birthright and his blessing, he was very angry with his brother **Jacob**. He said to himself and told others:

"My father **Isaac** is very old and cannot live long. As soon as he dies, I shall kill Jacob for having robbed me of my right."

When **Rebekah** heard this, she told Jacob, "Before it is too late, go away from home and get out of Esau's sight. Perhaps when Esau sees you no longer, he will forget his anger, and you can return home. Visit my brother Laban in Haran and stay with him for a while."

We must remember that Rebekah came from the family of Nahor, Abraham's younger brother, who lived in Haran, a long distance northeast of Canaan, and that Laban was Rebekah's brother.

So Jacob went out of Beersheba, on the border of the desert, and walked alone, carrying his staff in his hand. One evening, just about sunset, he came to a place among the mountains, more than sixty miles distant from his home. And as he had no bed to lie down upon, he took a stone, rested his head upon it for a pillow, and lay down to sleep.

And on that night, Jacob had a wonderful dream. In his dream, he saw stairs leading from the earth where he lay up to heaven, and angels were going up and coming down upon the stairs. And above the stairs, he saw the Lord God standing. And God said to Jacob:

"I am the Lord, the God of Abraham, and the God of Isaac, your father, and I will be your God, too. The land where you are lying all alone shall belong to you and your children after you, and your children shall spread abroad over the lands, east, west, north, and south like the dust of the earth, and through your family, all the world shall receive a blessing. And I am with you in your journey, and I will keep you where you are going and bring you back to this land. I will never leave you and will surely keep my promise to you."

And in the morning, Jacob awakened from his sleep and said: *"Surely, the Lord is in this place, and I did not know it! I thought I was alone, but God has been with me. This place is God's house— the gate of heaven!"*

And Jacob took the stone on which his head rested and set it up as a pillar, and poured oil on it as an offering to God. And Jacob named that place Bethel, which in the language Jacob spoke means "The House of God."

And Jacob made a promise to God at that time, saying:

"If God really will go with me and keep me, and will give me bread to eat and will bring me to my father's house in peace, then the Lord shall be my God, and this stone which I have set up as a pillar shall be the house of God, and of all that God gives me I will give back to God one-tenth as an offering."

Jacob Talks With Laban, from illustrators of the 1897 *Bible Pictures and What They Teach Us,* by Charles Foster

Then Jacob went onward in his long journey. He walked across the river Jordan in a shallow place, feeling his way with his staff. He climbed mountains and journeyed beside the great desert on the east and finally came to Haran. Beside the city was the well where Abraham's servant had met Jacob's mother, Rebekah. After Jacob had waited a while, he saw a young woman coming with her sheep to give them water.

Then Jacob took off the flat stone over the mouth of the well, drew water, and gave it to the sheep. And when he found that this young woman was his cousin **Rachel**, the daughter of Laban, he was so glad that he wept for joy. And at that moment, he began to love Rachel and longed to have her as his wife.

Rachel's father, Laban, who was Jacob's uncle, welcomed Jacob and took him into his home.

And Jacob asked Laban if he would give his daughter Rachel to him as his wife, saying, "If you give me Rachel, I will work for you seven years."

And Laban said, "It is better that you should have her than that a stranger should marry her."

So Jacob lived seven years in Laban's house, caring for his sheep, oxen, and camels, but his love for Rachel made the time seem short.

At last, the wedding day came, and the bride was brought in. After the manner of that land, she was covered with a thick veil so that her face could not be seen. And she was married to Jacob. But the following day, he found that he had not married Rachel, but her older sister **Leah**, who was not beautiful, and whom Jacob did not love at all!

Jacob was furious that he had been deceived, although that was just how Jacob himself had deceived his father and cheated his brother Esau. But his uncle Laban said, "In our land, we never allow the younger daughter to be married before the older daughter. Keep Leah for your wife and work for me seven years longer, and you shall have Rachel also."

In those times, as we have seen, men

often had two wives or even more than two. So Jacob was given Rachel as a second wife in exchange for agreeing to serve seven years more.

While Jacob was living in Haran, eleven sons were born to him. But only one of these was the child of Rachel, whom Jacob loved. This son was **Joseph**, who was dearer to Jacob than any other of his children, partly because he was the youngest and partly because he was the child of his beloved Rachel.

Jacob and Rachel at the Well, by François Lemoyne (1720)

The Artios Home Companion Series
Unit 8: The Story of Joseph

Teacher Overview

SINS ARE OFTEN REPEATED in family lines, and the sins of jealousy and deception came down through Jacob's. Just as Isaac had favored Jacob over Esau, Jacob favored his son Joseph. Joseph dreamed that his brothers would bow down before him, and this provoked jealousy in their hearts. The frightful way they responded showed the depth of wickedness in their hearts. The story of these brothers stands as a warning to us of the dangers of harboring jealous and spiteful feelings in our hearts. Their story also shows us how God took deeds meant for evil purposes and used them in the end to bring great blessing to the entire nation.

Joseph's Dream of Stars, illustration by Owen Jones from *The History of Joseph and His Brethren* (1869)

Suggested Assignments

Based on your student's age and ability, the reading in this unit may be read aloud to the student, and journaling and notebook pages may be completed orally. Likewise, other assignments may be done with an appropriate combination of independent and guided study.

In this unit, students will:
- Complete four lessons in which they will learn about the **life of Joseph** and **Egyptian culture during this time**.
- Define vocabulary words.
- Visit the **ArtiosHCS** curriculum website at **www.ArtiosHCS.com** for additional resources and any videos and websites assigned for this unit.

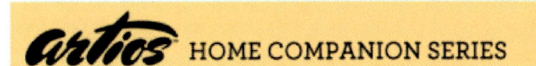

Heart Connections

God will accomplish His purpose.
> *Many are the plans in the mind of a man, but it is the purpose of the Lord that will stand.*
> – Proverbs 19:21

One's heart is revealed by one's words and actions.
> *The good person out of the good treasure of his heart produces good, and the evil person out of his evil treasure produces evil, for out of the abundance of the heart his mouth speaks.*
> – Luke 6:45

God works all things for our good and His glory.
> *"As for you, you meant evil against me, but God meant it for good, to bring it about that many people should be kept alive, as they are today."*
> – Genesis 50:20

Vocabulary

Lesson 1:
obeisance
conspire

Lesson 2, 3 & 4:
none

Key People, Places, and Events

Jacob/Israel
Joseph
Reuben
Judah
Pharaoh
Pharaoh's chief butler
Pharaoh's chief baker
Benjamin
Judah

Joseph and His Brethren Welcomed by Pharaoh,
watercolor by James Tissot (before 1903)

Ancient: Elementary
Unit 8: The Story of Joseph

Lesson One

History Overview and Assignments
A Dreaming Lad

"Now Israel loved Joseph more than all his children, because he was the son of his old age: and he made him a coat of many colours. And when his brethren saw that their father loved him more than all his brethren, they hated him, and could not speak peaceably unto him. And Joseph dreamed a dream, and he told it his brethren: and they hated him yet the more."
— Genesis 37:3-5

Joseph's brothers selling him as a slave

Suggested Reading and Assignments

- Read the article: *Genesis 37*.
- Define each vocabulary word in the context of the reading. Write the words and their definitions in the vocabulary section of your notebook.
- After reading the article, summarize the story you read by either:
  - Retelling it out loud to your teacher or parent.
    OR
  - Completing an appropriate notebook page.

  Either way, be sure to include the answers to the discussion questions and an overview of key people, places, dates, and events in your summary.
- Be sure to visit your **ArtiosHCS** curriculum website for additional resources and any videos and websites assigned for this lesson.

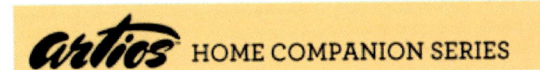

Ancient: Elementary
Unit 8: The Story of Joseph

Vocabulary

obeisance
conspire

Key People, Places, and Events

Jacob/Israel
Joseph
Reuben
Judah

Discussion Questions

1. Which of his sons did Jacob/Israel favor?
2. Describe the dreams Joseph had.
3. What did these dreams mean?
4. Why did Jacob send Joseph to find his brothers?
5. What did his brothers do to Joseph, and why?
6. What did their actions show was in their hearts?
7. How did the brothers explain Joseph's disappearance to their father?

Genesis 37

Genesis 37

1 And **Jacob** dwelt in the land wherein his father was a stranger, in the land of Canaan.

2 These are the generations of Jacob. **Joseph**, being seventeen years old, was feeding the flock with his brethren; and the lad was with the sons of Bilhah, and with the sons of Zilpah, his father's wives: and Joseph brought unto his father their evil report.

3 Now **Israel** loved Joseph more than all his children, because he was the son of his old age: and he made him a coat of many colours.

4 And when his brethren saw that their father loved him more than all his brethren, they hated him, and could not speak peaceably unto him.

5 And Joseph dreamed a dream, and he told it his brethren: and they hated him yet the more.

6 And he said unto them, Hear, I pray you, this dream which I have dreamed:

7 For, behold, we were binding sheaves in the field, and, lo, my sheaf arose, and also stood upright; and, behold, your sheaves stood round about, and made **obeisance** to my sheaf.

8 And his brethren said to him, Shalt thou indeed reign over us? or shalt thou indeed have dominion over us? And they hated him yet the more for his dreams, and for his words.

9 And he dreamed yet another dream, and told it his brethren, and said, Behold, I have dreamed a dream more; and, behold, the sun and the moon and the eleven stars made obeisance to me.

10 And he told it to his father, and to his brethren: and his father rebuked him, and said unto him, What is this dream that thou hast dreamed? Shall I and thy mother and thy brethren indeed come to bow down ourselves to thee to the earth?

11 And his brethren envied him; but his father observed the saying.

12 And his brethren went to feed their father's flock in Shechem.

13 And Israel said unto Joseph, Do not thy brethren feed the flock in Shechem? come, and I will send thee unto them. And he said to him, Here am I.

14 And he said to him, Go, I pray thee,

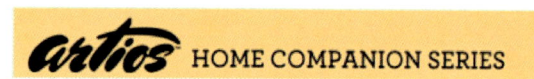

see whether it be well with thy brethren, and well with the flocks; and bring me word again. So he sent him out of the vale of Hebron, and he came to Shechem.

15 And a certain man found him, and, behold, he was wandering in the field: and the man asked him, saying, What seekest thou?

16 And he said, I seek my brethren: tell me, I pray thee, where they feed their flocks.

17 And the man said, They are departed hence; for I heard them say, Let us go to Dothan. And Joseph went after his brethren, and found them in Dothan.

18 And when they saw him afar off, even before he came near unto them, they **conspire**d against him to slay him.

19 And they said one to another, Behold, this dreamer cometh.

20 Come now therefore, and let us slay him, and cast him into some pit, and we will say, Some evil beast hath devoured him: and we shall see what will become of his dreams.

21 And **Reuben** heard it, and he delivered him out of their hands; and said, Let us not kill him.

22 And Reuben said unto them, Shed no blood, but cast him into this pit that is in the wilderness, and lay no hand upon him; that he might rid him out of their hands, to deliver him to his father again.

23 And it came to pass, when Joseph was come unto his brethren, that they stript Joseph out of his coat, his coat of many colours that was on him;

24 And they took him, and cast him into a pit: and the pit was empty, there was no water in it.

25 And they sat down to eat bread: and they lifted up their eyes and looked, and, behold, a company of Ishmeelites came from Gilead with their camels bearing spicery and balm and myrrh, going to carry it down to Egypt.

26 And **Judah** said unto his brethren, What profit is it if we slay our brother, and conceal his blood?

27 Come, and let us sell him to the Ishmeelites, and let not our hand be upon him; for he is our brother and our flesh. And his brethren were content.

28 Then there passed by Midianites merchantmen; and they drew and lifted up Joseph out of the pit, and sold Joseph to the Ishmeelites for twenty pieces of silver: and they brought Joseph into Egypt.

29 And Reuben returned unto the pit; and, behold, Joseph was not in the pit; and he rent his clothes.

30 And he returned unto his brethren, and said, The child is not; and I, whither shall I go?

31 And they took Joseph's coat, and killed a kid of the goats, and dipped the coat in the blood;

32 And they sent the coat of many colours, and they brought it to their father; and said, This have we found: know now whether it be thy son's coat or no.

33 And he knew it, and said, It is my son's coat; an evil beast hath devoured him; Joseph is without doubt rent in pieces.

34 And Jacob rent his clothes, and put sackcloth upon his loins, and mourned for his son many days.

35 And all his sons and all his daughters rose up to comfort him; but he refused to be comforted; and he said, For I will go down into the grave unto my son mourning. Thus his father wept for him.

36 And the Midianites sold him into Egypt unto Potiphar, an officer of Pharaoh's, and captain of the guard.

Lesson Two

History Overview and Assignments
A Dreaming Monarch

"And Pharaoh said unto Joseph, 'Forasmuch as God hath shewed thee all this, there is none so discreet and wise as thou art: Thou shalt be over my house, and according unto thy word shall all my people be ruled: only in the throne will I be greater than thou.'"

– Genesis 41:39-40

Key People, Places, and Events

Pharaoh
Pharaoh's chief butler
Pharaoh's chief baker
Joseph

Joseph Interpreting Pharaoh's Dream, by Peter von Cornelius
(between 1816 and 1817)

Suggested Reading and Assignments

- Read the article: *Genesis 41*.
- After reading the article, summarize the story you read by either:
    - Retelling it out loud to your teacher or parent.
        OR
    - Completing an appropriate notebook page.

    Either way, be sure to include the answers to the discussion questions and an overview of key people, places, dates, and events in your summary.
- Be sure to visit your **ArtiosHCS** curriculum website for additional resources and any videos and websites assigned for this lesson.

Discussion Questions

1. Describe the dream Pharaoh had.
2. How did Joseph interpret that dream?
3. Why did Pharaoh make Joseph the overseer of the kingdom?
4. What were the names of the two sons of Joseph?

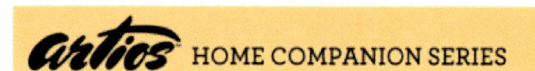

Genesis 41

Genesis 41

1 And it came to pass at the end of two full years, that **Pharaoh** dreamed: and, behold, he stood by the river.

2 And, behold, there came up out of the river seven well favoured kine and fatfleshed; and they fed in a meadow.

3 And, behold, seven other kine came up after them out of the river, ill favoured and leanfleshed; and stood by the other kine upon the brink of the river.

4 And the ill favoured and leanfleshed kine did eat up the seven well favoured and fat kine. So Pharaoh awoke.

5 And he slept and dreamed the second time: and, behold, seven ears of corn came up upon one stalk, rank and good.

6 And, behold, seven thin ears and blasted with the east wind sprung up after them.

7 And the seven thin ears devoured the seven rank and full ears. And Pharaoh awoke, and, behold, it was a dream.

8 And it came to pass in the morning that his spirit was troubled; and he sent and called for all the magicians of Egypt, and all the wise men thereof: and Pharaoh told them his dream; but there was none that could interpret them unto Pharaoh.

9 Then spake the **chief butler** unto Pharaoh, saying, I do remember my faults this day:

10 Pharaoh was wroth with his servants, and put me in ward in the captain of the guard's house, both me and the **chief baker**:

11 And we dreamed a dream in one night, I and he; we dreamed each man according to the interpretation of his dream.

12 And there was there with us a young man, an Hebrew, servant to the captain of the guard; and we told him, and he interpreted to us our dreams; to each man according to his dream he did interpret.

13 And it came to pass, as he interpreted to us, so it was; me he restored unto mine office, and him he hanged.

14 Then Pharaoh sent and called **Joseph**, and they brought him hastily out of the dungeon: and he shaved himself, and changed his raiment, and came in unto Pharaoh.

15 And Pharaoh said unto Joseph, I have dreamed a dream, and there is none that can interpret it: and I have heard say of thee, that thou canst understand a dream to interpret it.

16 And Joseph answered Pharaoh, saying, It is not in me: God shall give Pharaoh an answer of peace.

17 And Pharaoh said unto Joseph, In my dream, behold, I stood upon the bank of the river:

18 And, behold, there came up out of the river seven kine, fatfleshed and well favoured; and they fed in a meadow:

19 And, behold, seven other kine came up after them, poor and very ill favoured and leanfleshed, such as I never saw in all the land of Egypt for badness:

20 And the lean and the ill favoured kine did eat up the first seven fat kine:

21 And when they had eaten them up, it could not be known that they had eaten them; but they were still ill favoured, as at the beginning. So I awoke.

22 And I saw in my dream, and, behold, seven ears came up in one stalk, full and good:

23 And, behold, seven ears, withered, thin, and blasted with the east wind, sprung up after them:

24 And the thin ears devoured the seven good ears: and I told this unto the magicians; but there was none that could declare it to me.

Biblical illustration by Jim Padgett, Sweet Publishing, Ft. Worth, TX, and Gospel Light, Ventura, CA. Copyright 1984. Released under new license, CC-BY-SA 3.0

25 And Joseph said unto Pharaoh, The dream of Pharaoh is one: God hath shewed Pharaoh what he is about to do.

26 The seven good kine are seven years; and the seven good ears are seven years: the dream is one.

27 And the seven thin and ill favoured kine that came up after them are seven years; and the seven empty ears blasted with the east wind shall be seven years of famine.

28 This is the thing which I have spoken unto Pharaoh: What God is about to do he sheweth unto Pharaoh.

29 Behold, there come seven years of great plenty throughout all the land of Egypt:

30 And there shall arise after them seven years of famine; and all the plenty shall be forgotten in the land of Egypt; and the famine shall consume the land;

31 And the plenty shall not be known in the land by reason of that famine following; for it shall be very grievous.

32 And for that the dream was doubled unto Pharaoh twice; it is because the thing is established by God, and God will shortly bring it to pass.

33 Now therefore let Pharaoh look out a man discreet and wise, and set him over the land of Egypt.

34 Let Pharaoh do this, and let him appoint officers over the land, and take up the fifth part of the land of Egypt in the seven plenteous years.

35 And let them gather all the food of those good years that come, and lay up corn under the hand of Pharaoh, and let them keep food in the cities.

36 And that food shall be for store to the land against the seven years of famine, which shall be in the land of Egypt; that the land perish not through the famine.

37 And the thing was good in the eyes of Pharaoh, and in the eyes of all his servants.

38 And Pharaoh said unto his servants, Can we find such a one as this is, a man in whom the Spirit of God is?

39 And Pharaoh said unto Joseph, Forasmuch as God hath shewed thee all this, there is none so discreet and wise as thou art:

40 Thou shalt be over my house, and according unto thy word shall all my people be ruled: only in the throne will I be greater than thou.

41 And Pharaoh said unto Joseph, See, I have set thee over all the land of Egypt.

42 And Pharaoh took off his ring from his hand, and put it upon Joseph's hand, and arrayed him in vestures of fine linen, and put a gold chain about his neck;

43 And he made him to ride in the

second chariot which he had; and they cried before him, Bow the knee: and he made him ruler over all the land of Egypt.

44 And Pharaoh said unto Joseph, I am Pharaoh, and without thee shall no man lift up his hand or foot in all the land of Egypt.

45 And Pharaoh called Joseph's name Zaphnathpaaneah; and he gave him to wife Asenath the daughter of Potipherah priest of On. And Joseph went out over all the land of Egypt.

46 And Joseph was thirty years old when he stood before Pharaoh king of Egypt. And Joseph went out from the presence of Pharaoh, and went throughout all the land of Egypt.

47 And in the seven plenteous years the earth brought forth by handfuls.

48 And he gathered up all the food of the seven years, which were in the land of Egypt, and laid up the food in the cities: the food of the field, which was round about every city, laid he up in the same.

49 And Joseph gathered corn as the sand of the sea, very much, until he left numbering; for it was without number.

50 And unto Joseph were born two sons before the years of famine came, which Asenath the daughter of Potipherah priest of On bare unto him.

51 And Joseph called the name of the firstborn Manasseh: For God, said he, hath made me forget all my toil, and all my father's house.

52 And the name of the second called he Ephraim: For God hath caused me to be fruitful in the land of my affliction.

53 And the seven years of plenteousness, that was in the land of Egypt, were ended.

54 And the seven years of dearth began to come, according as Joseph had said: and the dearth was in all lands; but in all the land of Egypt there was bread.

55 And when all the land of Egypt was famished, the people cried to Pharaoh for bread: and Pharaoh said unto all the Egyptians, Go unto Joseph; what he saith to you, do.

56 And the famine was over all the face of the earth: and Joseph opened all the storehouses, and sold unto the Egyptians; and the famine waxed sore in the land of Egypt.

57 And all countries came into Egypt to Joseph for to buy corn; because that the famine was so sore in all lands.

Pharoah's Dream, by anonymous (c.1640-1677)

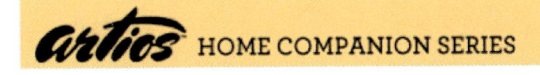

Lesson Three

History Overview and Assignments
The Lad Becomes a Ruler

"And Pharaoh took from his hand the ring which held his seal and put it on Joseph's hand so that he could sign for the King, and seal in the King's place. And he dressed Joseph in robes of fine linen and put around his neck a gold chain. And he made Joseph ride in a chariot next in rank to his own. And the people cried out before Joseph, 'Bow the knee!' And thus Joseph was made ruler over all the land of Egypt."

– from the adapted article below

Joseph, as ruler of Egypt, welcomes his brothers.

Discussion Questions

1. To whom did Joseph's brothers sell him?
2. Who bought Joseph once he was in Egypt?
3. Describe the chief butler's dream and Joseph's interpretation.
4. Describe the chief baker's dream and Joseph's interpretation.
5. What character qualities do we see in Joseph regardless of his circumstances?

Suggested Reading and Assignments

- Read the article: *The Dreams of a King*.
- After reading the article, summarize the story you read by either:
    - Retelling it out loud to your teacher or parent.
        OR
    - Completing an appropriate notebook page.

  Either way, be sure to include the answers to the discussion questions and an overview of key people, places, dates, and events in your summary.
- Be sure to visit your **ArtiosHCS** curriculum website for additional resources and any videos and websites assigned for this lesson.

Key People, Places, and Events

Joseph
Pharaoh
Pharaoh's chief butler
Pharaoh's chief baker

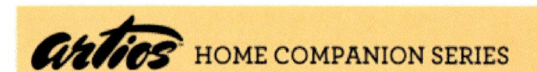

Adapted for Elementary School from the book:
The Wonder Book of Bible Stories
Arranged by Logan Marshall
The Dreams of a King

The men who bought **Joseph** from his brothers were called Ishmaelites because they belonged to the family of Ishmael, who, you remember, was the son of Hagar, the servant of Sarah. These men carried Joseph southward over the plain beside the great sea west of Canaan. After many days they brought Joseph to Egypt. How strange it must have seemed to the boy who had lived in tents to see the great river, Nile, the cities thronged with people, the temples, and the mighty pyramids!

The Ishmaelites sold Joseph as a slave to a man named Potiphar, an officer in the army of **Pharaoh**, the King of Egypt. Joseph was a fine-looking young man capable of all he undertook, so his master Potiphar regarded him highly. After a time, he placed Joseph in charge of his house and everything in it. For some years, Joseph continued in the house of Potiphar, a slave in name but in reality the master of all his affairs and ruler over his fellow servants.

But Potiphar's wife became his enemy because Joseph would not do wrong to please her. She told her husband falsely that Joseph had done a wicked deed. Her husband believed her and was very angry at Joseph, putting him in prison with those sent there for breaking the laws of the land. How hard it must have been for Joseph to be charged with a crime when he had done no wrong and was thrust into a dark prison among wicked people!

But Joseph had faith in God that all would come out right at some time, so he was cheerful and helpful in prison, as he had always been. The prison keeper saw that Joseph was not like the other men around him, and he was kind to Joseph. Before long, Joseph was in charge of all his fellow prisoners and watched over them just as he had taken care of everything in Potiphar's house. The prison keeper scarcely looked into the prison at all, for he had confidence in Joseph that he would be faithful and wise in doing the work given to him. Joseph did right and served God, and God blessed Joseph in everything.

While Joseph was in prison, two men were sent there by the King of Egypt because he was displeased with them. One was the King's **chief butler**, who served the King with wine. The other was the **chief baker**, who served him with bread. These two men were under Joseph's care, and Joseph waited on them, for they were men of rank.

One morning, when Joseph came into the room where the butler and the baker were kept, he found them looking quite sad. Joseph asked them, "Why do you look so sad today?"

And one of them said, "Each of us dreamed last night a very strange dream, and there is no one to tell us what our dreams mean."

In those times, before God gave the Bible to men, He often spoke to men in dreams, and some wise men could sometimes tell what the dreams meant.

"Tell me," said Joseph, "what your dreams are. Perhaps my God will help me understand them."

Then the chief butler told his dream. He

said, "In my dream, I saw a grapevine with three branches, and as I looked, the branches shot out buds. The buds became blossoms, and the blossoms turned into clusters of ripe grapes. And I picked the grapes and squeezed their juice into King Pharaoh's cup, and it became wine, and I gave it to King Pharaoh to drink, just as I used to do when I was beside his table."

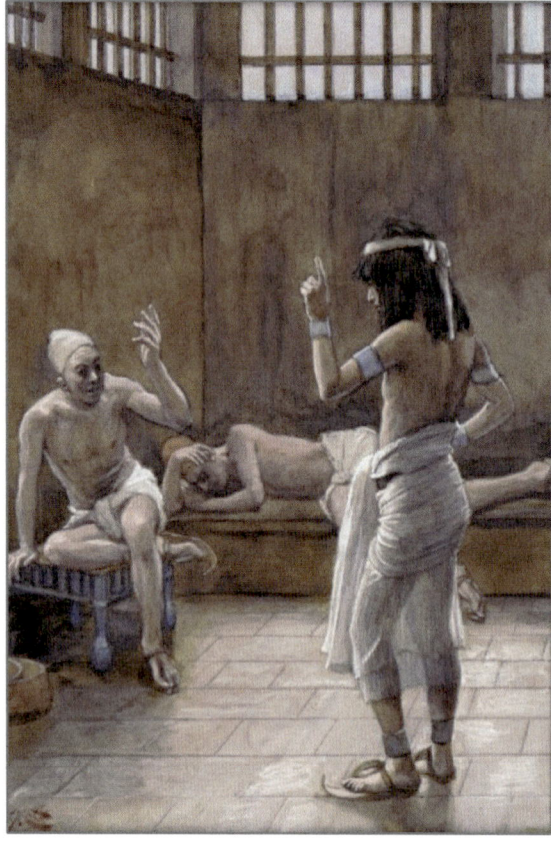

Joseph Interprets the Dreams While in Prison,
by James Tissot (c.1896-1920)

Then Joseph said, "This is what your dream means. The three branches mean three days. In three days, Pharaoh shall call you out of prison and put you back in your place, and you shall stand at his table and give him his wine, as you have given it before. But when you leave prison, please remember me and try to find some way to get me out of this prison. For I was stolen out of the land of Canaan and sold as a slave, and I have done nothing wrong to deserve being put in this prison. Do speak to the King for me, that I may be set free."

Of course, the chief butler felt very happy to hear that his dream had so pleasant a meaning. And the chief baker spoke next, hoping to receive an answer as good.

"In my dream," said the baker, "there were three baskets of white bread on my head, one above another, and in the topmost basket were all kinds of roasted meat and food for Pharaoh. Birds came and ate the food from the baskets on my head."

And Joseph said to the baker, "This is the meaning of your dream, and I am sorry to tell it to you. The three baskets are three days. In three days, by order of the King, you shall be lifted up and hanged upon a tree, and the birds shall eat your flesh from your bones as you hang in the air."

And these things came to pass just as Joseph had said. Three days later, Pharaoh sent his officers to the prison. They came and took out both the chief butler and the chief baker. They hung the baker up by his neck to die and left his body for the birds to pick in pieces. The chief butler they brought back to his old place, where he waited at the King's table and handed him his wine to drink.

You would have supposed that the butler would remember Joseph, who had given him the promise of freedom and had shown such wisdom. But in his gladness, he forgot all about Joseph. And two whole years passed while Joseph was still in prison until he was a man thirty years old.

But one night, Pharaoh himself dreamed a dream—two dreams in one. And in the morning, he sent for all the wise men of Egypt and described his dreams to them, but there was no man among them who could give them the meaning. And the King was troubled, for he felt the dreams had some significant meaning.

Then suddenly, the chief butler by the King's table remembered his dream in the prison two years before and the young man who had told its meaning so exactly. And he said, "I do remember my faults this day. Two years ago, Pharaoh was angry with his servants, the chief baker and me, and sent us to the prison. While we were in prison, one night, each of us dreamed a dream, and the next day a young man in the prison, a Hebrew from the land of Canaan, told us what our dreams meant. Three days later, they came true, just as the young Hebrew had said. If this young man is still in prison, he could tell the King the meaning of his dreams."

You notice that the butler spoke of Joseph as "a Hebrew." The people of Israel, to whom Joseph belonged, were called Hebrews and Israelites. The word Hebrew means "one who crossed over," It was given to the Israelites because Abraham, their father, had come from a land on the other side of the great Euphrates River and had crossed over the river on his way to Canaan.

Then Pharaoh sent in haste to the prison for Joseph, who was immediately taken out and dressed in new garments, then was led into Pharaoh in the palace. And Pharaoh said, "I have dreamed a dream, and no one can tell what it means. And I have been told that you have the power to understand dreams and what they mean."

And Joseph answered Pharaoh, "The power is not in me, but God will give Pharaoh a good answer. What is the dream that the King has dreamed?"

"In my first dream," said Pharaoh, "I was standing by the river and saw seven fat and handsome cows come up from the river to feed in the grass. And while they were feeding, seven other cows followed them up from the river, very thin, poor, and lean—such miserable creatures as I had never seen before. And the seven lean cows ate up the seven fat cows, and after they had eaten them up, they were as lean and miserable as before. Then I awoke.

"And I fell asleep again and dreamed again. In my second dream, I saw seven heads of grain growing up on one stalk, large, strong, and sound. And then seven heads came up after them that were thin, and poor, and withered. And the seven thin heads swallowed up the seven good heads and afterward were as poor and withered as before.

"And I told these two dreams to all the wise men, and no one can explain them. Can you tell me what these dreams mean?"

And Joseph said to the King, "The two dreams have the same meaning. God is showing Pharaoh what He will do in this land. The seven good cows mean seven years, and the seven good heads of grain mean the same seven years. The seven lean cows and the seven thin heads of grain also mean seven years. The good cows and the good grain mean seven years of plenty, and the seven thin cows and thin heads of grain mean seven poor years. There are coming upon the land of Egypt seven years of such plenty as have never been seen when the fields shall bring greater crops than ever before. But after those years shall come seven years in which the fields shall bring no crops. And then, for seven years, there shall be such need that the years of plenty will be forgotten, for the people will have nothing to eat. The two dreams have the same meaning.

"Now, let Pharaoh find some man who is able and wise, and let him set this man to rule over the land. And during the seven years of plenty, let a part of the crops be put away for the years of need. If this shall be done, then when the years of need come, there will be plenty of food for all the people, and no one will suffer, for all will have enough."

And Pharaoh said to Joseph, "Since God has shown you all this, no other man is as wise as you. I will appoint you to do this work and to rule over the land of Egypt. All the people shall be under you, and only on the throne of Egypt I will be above you."

And Pharaoh took from his hand the ring which held his seal and put it on Joseph's hand so that he could sign for the King, and seal in the King's place. And he dressed Joseph in robes of fine linen and put around his neck a gold chain. And he made Joseph ride in a chariot next in rank to his own. And the people cried out before Joseph, "Bow the knee!" And thus, Joseph was made ruler over all the land of Egypt.

Joseph Explains Pharaoh's Dream to Him, illustration from the 1728 *Figures de la Bible*; illustrated by Gerard Hoet (1648–1733) and others

Lesson Four

History Overview and Assignments
Money in the Bags

"Then Joseph placed his arms around Benjamin's neck, and kissed him, and wept upon him. And Benjamin wept on his neck. And Joseph kissed all his brothers, to show them that he had fully forgiven them. Then his brothers began to lose their fear of Joseph and talked with him more freely."

– from the adapted article below

The Cup is Found, by James Tissot (c.1896-1902)

Suggested Reading and Assignments

- Read the article: *The Story of the Money in the Sacks*.
- After reading the article, summarize the story you read by either:
    - Retelling it out loud to your teacher or parent.
        OR
    - Completing an appropriate notebook page.
  Either way, be sure to include the answers to the discussion questions and an overview of key people, places, dates, and events in your summary.
- Be sure to visit your **ArtiosHCS** curriculum website for additional resources and any videos and websites assigned for this lesson.

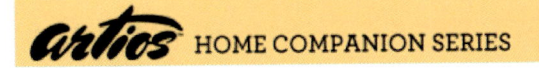

Ancient: Elementary
Unit 8: The Story of Joseph

Key People, Places, and Events

Joseph
Jacob
Benjamin
Judah

Discussion Questions

1. Why did Joseph's brothers come to Egypt?
2. How did Joseph treat them?
3. Why did Joseph test his brothers by putting their money and a silver cup back in the bag?
4. Why did Joseph ask his brothers to bring Benjamin to see him?
5. How did Joseph's brothers react to seeing him again once they recognized him?

Adapted for Elementary School from the book:
The Wonder Book of Bible Stories
Arranged by Logan Marshall
The Story of the Money in the Sacks

When **Joseph** was made ruler over the land of Egypt, he did just as he had always done. It was not Joseph's way to sit down, to rest and enjoy himself and make others wait on him. He found his work at once and began to do it faithfully and thoroughly. He went out over all the land of Egypt and saw how rich and abundant the fields of grain were, giving much more than the people could use for their own needs. He told the people not to waste it but to save it for the coming time of need.

And he called upon the people to give him for the King one bushel of grain out of every five, to be stored up. The people brought their grain, after taking for themselves as much as they needed, and Joseph stored it up in great storehouses in the cities, so much at last that no one could keep account of it.

The King of Egypt gave a wife to Joseph from the noble young women of his kingdom. Her name was Asenath, and to Joseph and his wife God gave two sons. The oldest son he named Manasseh, a word which means "making to forget."

"For," said Joseph, "God has made me to forget all my troubles and my toil as a slave."

The second son he named Ephraim, a word that means "fruitful." "Because," declared Joseph, "God has not only made the land fruitful, but he has made me fruitful in the land of my troubles."

The seven years of plenty soon passed by, and then came the years of need. In all the lands around people were hungry and there was no food for them to eat, but in the land of Egypt everybody had enough. Most of the people soon used up the grain that they had saved. Many had saved none at all, and they all cried to the King to help them.

"Go to Joseph!" replied Pharaoh, "and do whatever he tells you to do."

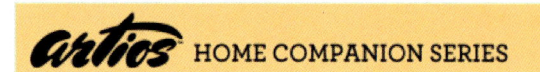

Then the people came to Joseph, and Joseph opened the storehouses and sold to the people all the grain that they wished to buy. And not only did the people of Egypt came to buy grain, but people of all the lands around as well, for there was great need and famine everywhere. And the need was as great in the land of Canaan, where **Jacob** lived, as in other lands. Now Jacob was rich in flocks and cattle, and gold and silver, but his fields gave no grain, and there was danger that his family and his people would starve. And Jacob—who was now called Israel—heard that there was food in Egypt. So he said to his sons, "Why do you look at each other, asking what to do to find food? I have been told there is grain in Egypt. Go down to that land. Take money with you and bring grain, so that we may have bread and live."

Then the ten older brothers of Joseph went down to the land of Egypt. They rode upon donkeys, for horses were not much used in those times, and they brought money with them. But Jacob would not let **Benjamin**, Joseph's younger brother, go with them, for he was all the more dear to his father now that Joseph was no longer with him, and Jacob feared that harm might come to him.

Then Joseph's brothers came to Joseph to buy food. They did not recognize him, grown up to be a man, dressed as a prince, and seated on a throne. Joseph was now nearly forty years old, and it had been almost twenty-three years since they had sold him. But Joseph knew them all as soon as he saw them. He was stern with them, not because he hated them, but because he wished to see what their spirit was like and whether they were as selfish and cruel and wicked as they had been in earlier days.

They came before him and bowed with their faces to the ground. Then, no doubt, Joseph remembered the dream that had come to him while he was a boy, of his brothers' sheaves bending down around his sheaf. He spoke to them as a stranger, as if he did not understand their language, and he had their words translated to him in the language of Egypt.

"Who are you? And from what place do you come?" demanded Joseph in a harsh, stern manner.

They answered him very meekly, "We have come from the land of Canaan to buy food."

"No," refuted Joseph, "I know what you have come for. You have come as spies, to see how helpless the land is, so that you can bring an army against us and make war on us."

"No, no," cried Joseph's ten brothers. "We are no spies. We are the sons of one man who lives in the land of Canaan, and we have come for food because we have none at home."

Joseph Selling Grain in Egypt,
by Bartholomeus Breenbergh or workshop (after 1644)

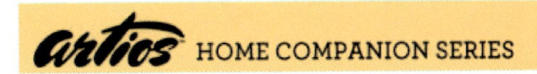

And they said: "Our father is an old man in Canaan. We did have a younger brother, but he was lost. We have one brother still, who is the youngest of all, but his father could not spare him to come with us."

"No," refuted Joseph. "You are not good, honest men. You are spies. I shall put you all in prison—all except one—and he shall go and bring that youngest brother of yours. Then, when I see him, I will believe that you tell the truth."

So Joseph put all the ten men in prison and kept them under guard for three days. Then he sent for them again.

They did not know that he could understand their language, and they said to each other in Joseph's hearing, "This has come upon us because of the wrong that we did to our brother Joseph, more than twenty years ago. We heard him cry and plead with us when we threw him into the pit, and we would not have mercy on him. God is giving us only what we have deserved."

Reuben, who had tried to save Joseph, said, "Did I not tell you not to harm the boy? But you would not listen to me. God is bringing our brother's blood upon us all."

When Joseph heard this, his heart was wrenched with grief, for he saw that his brothers were truly sorry for the wrong they had done to him. He turned away from them so that they could not see his face, and he wept. Then he turned again to them and spoke roughly as before, saying, "This I will do, for I serve God. I will let you all go home, except one man. One of you I will shut up in prison, but the rest of you can go home and take food for your people. And you must come back and bring your youngest brother with you, and I shall know then that you have spoken the truth."

Then Joseph gave orders, and his servants seized one of his brothers, whose name was Simeon, and bound him in their sight and took him away to prison. And he ordered his servants to fill the men's sacks with grain and to put every man's money back into the sack before it was tied up, so that they would find the money as soon as they opened the sack. Then the men loaded their donkeys with the sacks of grain and started to go home, leaving their brother Simeon a prisoner.

When they stopped on the way to feed their donkeys, one of the brothers opened his sack, and there he found his money lying on the top of the grain. He called out to his brothers: "See, here is my money given again to me!" And they were frightened, but they did not dare to go back to Egypt and meet the stern ruler of the land. They went home and told their old father all that had happened to them, and how their brother Simeon was in prison and must stay there until they should return, bringing Benjamin with them.

When they opened their sacks of grain, there in the mouth of each sack was the money that they had given, and they were filled with fear. Then they spoke of going again to Egypt and taking Benjamin with them, but Jacob said to them, "You are taking my sons away from me. Joseph is gone, and Simeon is gone, and now you would take Benjamin away. All these things are against me!"

Reuben replied, "Here are my own two boys. You may kill them, if you wish, if I do not bring Benjamin back to you."

But Jacob said, "My youngest son shall not go with you. His brother is dead, and he alone is left to me. If harm should come to him, it would bring down my gray hairs with sorrow to the grave."

Mystery of the Lost Brother

The food which Jacob's sons had brought from Egypt did not last long, for Jacob's family was large. Most of his sons were married and had children of their own, so that the children and grandchildren were sixty-six, besides the servants who waited on them and the men who cared for Jacob's flocks. So around the tent of Jacob was quite a camp of other tents and an army of people.

When the food that had come from Egypt was nearly eaten up, Jacob said to his sons, "Go down to Egypt again, and buy some food for us."

And **Judah**, the son who years before had urged his brothers to sell Joseph to the Ishmaelites, said to his father, "It is of no use for us to go to Egypt unless we take Benjamin with us. The man who rules in that land said to us, 'You shall not see my face unless your youngest brother returns with you.'"

And Israel said, "Why did you tell the man that you had a brother? You did me great harm when you told him."

"Why," said Jacob's sons, "we could not help telling him. The man asked us all about our family, 'Is your father yet living? Have you any more brothers?' And we had to tell him, his questions were so direct. How should we know that he would say, 'Bring your brother here, for me to see him'?"

And Judah said, "Send Benjamin with me, and I will take care of him. I promise you that I will bring him safely home. If he does not come back, let me bear the blame forever. He must go, or we shall die for lack of food. By now we could have gone down to Egypt and come home again, if we had not been kept back."

And Jacob answered, "If he must go, then he must. But take a gift to the man, some of the choicest fruits of the land, some spices and perfumes, and nuts and almonds. And take twice as much money, besides the money that was in your sacks. Perhaps that was a mistake, when the money was given back to you. And take your brother Benjamin, and may the Lord God make the man kind to you, so that he will set Simeon free and let you bring Benjamin back. But if it is God's will that I lose my children, then so be it."

So ten brothers of Joseph went down a second time to Egypt, Benjamin going in place of Simeon. They came to Joseph's office, the place where he sold grain to the people, and they bowed before their brother as before.

Joseph saw that Benjamin was with them, and he said to his steward, the man who was over his house, "Make ready a dinner, for all these men shall dine with me today."

When Joseph's brothers found that they were to be taken into Joseph's house, they were filled with fear. They said to each other, "We have been taken here on account of the money in our sacks. They will say that we have stolen it, and then they will sell us all for slaves."

But Joseph's steward, the man who was over his house, treated the men kindly, and when they spoke of the money in their sacks, he would not take it again, saying, "Never fear, for your God must have sent you this as a gift. I had your money."

The stewards received the men into Joseph's house and washed their feet, according to the custom of the land. And at noon, Joseph came in to meet them. They brought him the gift from their father, and again they bowed before him, with their faces on the ground.

And Joseph asked them if they were well, saying, "Is your father still living, the old man of whom you spoke? Is he well?"

And they answered, "Our father is well, and he is living." And again they bowed to Joseph.

And Joseph looked at his younger brother Benjamin, the child of his own mother Rachel, and said, "Is this your youngest brother, of whom you spoke to me? God be gracious unto you, my son."

And Joseph's heart was so full that he could not keep back his tears. He went in haste to his own room and wept there. Then he washed his face and came out again, and ordered the table to be set for dinner. They set Joseph's table for himself, as the ruler, and another table for his Egyptian officers, and another for the eleven men from Canaan, for Joseph had brought Simeon out of the prison and had given him a place with his brothers.

Joseph himself arranged the order of the seats for his brothers, the oldest at the head, and all in order of age down to the youngest. The men wondered at this, and could not see how the ruler of Egypt could know the order of their ages. And Joseph sent dishes from his table to his brothers, and he gave to Benjamin five times as much as to the others. Perhaps he wished to see whether they were as jealous of Benjamin as in other days they had been toward him.

After dinner, Joseph said to his steward, "Fill the men's sacks with grain, as much as they can carry, and put each man's money in his sack. And put my silver cup in the sack of the youngest, with his money."

The steward did as Joseph had said, and early in the morning the brothers started to go home. A little while afterward, Joseph said to his steward, "Hasten, follow after the men from Canaan, and say, 'Why have you wronged me, after I had treated you kindly? You have stolen my master's silver cup, out of which he drinks'."

The steward followed the men and overtook them, and charged them with stealing.

And they said to him, "Why do you speak to us in this manner? We have stolen nothing. Why, we brought back to you the money that we found in our sacks. Is it likely that we would steal from your lord his silver or gold? You may search us, and if you find your master's cup on any of us, let him die, and the rest of us may be sold as slaves."

Then they took down the sacks from the donkeys and opened them, and in each man's sack was his money, for the second time. And when they came to Benjamin's sack, there was the ruler's silver cup! Then, in the greatest sorrow, they tied up their bags again and laid them on the donkeys, and they came back to Joseph's palace.

And Joseph accused them, saying, "What wicked thing is this that you have done? Did you not know that I would surely find out your deeds?"

Then Judah said, "O, my lord, what can we say? God has punished us for our sins, and now we must all be slaves, both we that are older, and the younger in whose sack the cup was found."

"No," replied Joseph. "Only one of you is guilty—the one who has taken away my cup. I will hold him as a slave, and the rest of you can go home to your father."

Joseph wished to see whether his brothers were still selfish, willing to let Benjamin suffer if they could escape.

Then Judah, the very man who had urged his brothers to sell Joseph as a slave, came forward, fell at Joseph's feet, and pleaded with him to let Benjamin go. He told again the whole story—how Benjamin was the one whom his father loved the most of all his children, now that his brother was lost. He said, "I promised to bear the blame if this boy was not brought home in safety. If he does not go back it will kill my poor old father, who has seen much trouble. Now let my youngest brother go home to his father, and I will stay here as a slave in his place!"

Joseph knew now what he had longed to know, that his brothers were no longer cruel or selfish, but one of them was willing to suffer so that his brother might be spared. And Joseph could not any longer keep his secret, for his heart longed after his brothers and he was ready to weep again, with tears of love and joy. He sent all of his Egyptian servants out of the room, so that he might be alone with his brothers, and then he said, "Come near to me. I wish to speak with you."

And they came near, wondering. Then Joseph said, "I am Joseph. Does my father truly still live?"

How frightened his brothers were as they heard these words spoken in their own language by the ruler of Egypt—and for the first time they knew that this stern man, who held their lives in his hand, was their own brother whom they had wronged!

Then Joseph said again, "I am Joseph, your brother, whom you sold into Egypt. But be not troubled because of what you did. For God sent me before you to save your lives. There have been two years of need and famine so far, and there are to be five years more, when there shall neither be plowing of fields nor harvest. It was not you who sent me here, but God, and He sent me to save your lives. God has made me like a father to Pharaoh and ruler over all the land of Egypt. Now I wish you to go home, and to bring down to me my father and all his family."

Then Joseph placed his arms around Benjamin's neck, and kissed him, and wept upon him. And Benjamin wept on his neck. And Joseph kissed all his brothers, to show them that he had fully forgiven them. Then his brothers began to lose their fear of Joseph and talked with him more freely.

Afterward Joseph sent his brothers home with good news, and rich gifts, and abundant food. He sent also wagons in which Jacob and his sons' wives and the little ones of their families might ride from Canaan down to Egypt. And Joseph's brothers went home happier than they had been for many years.

Joseph Reveals Himself to His Brothers, by Peter von Cornelius (c.1816)

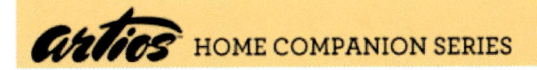

The Artios Home Companion Series
Unit 9: The Israelites in Egypt

Teacher Overview

WHEN LATER RULERS came into power in Egypt, they were frightened by how many Israelites lived in their country. The pharaohs enslaved them to weaken the power of this large nation of people. But despite all that they did to harm the Jews, God continued to lead His people. In this unit, we will follow the story of the Israelites in Egypt after the time of Joseph and will explore what life was like in Egypt under the pharaohs.

Jacob Blessing the Sons of Joseph, by Rembrandt (1656)

Suggested Assignments

Based on your student's age and ability, the reading in this unit may be read aloud to the student, and journaling and notebook pages may be completed orally. Likewise, other assignments may be done with an appropriate combination of independent and guided study.

In this unit, students will:
- Complete three lessons in which they will learn about **how the Israelites came to be enslaved in Egypt** and **what life was like in Egypt under the pharaohs**.
- Define vocabulary words.
- Visit the **ArtiosHCS** curriculum website at **www.ArtiosHCS.com** for additional resources and any videos and websites assigned for this unit.

Heart Connections

God will accomplish His purpose.
Many are the plans in the mind of a man, but it is the purpose of the Lord that will stand.
– Proverbs 19:21

One's heart is revealed by one's words and actions.
The good person out of the good treasure of his heart produces good, and the evil person out of his evil treasure produces evil, for out of the abundance of the heart his mouth speaks.
– Luke 6:45

God works all things for our good and His glory.
"As for you, you meant evil against me, but God meant it for good, to bring it about that many people should be kept alive, as they are today."
– Genesis 50:20

God controls world leaders.
The king's heart is a stream of water in the hand of the Lord; he turns it wherever he will.
– Proverbs 21:1

Vocabulary

Lessons 1 & 2: /~~~~~~~~~~~~~~~Lesson 3:~~~~~~~~~~~~~~~~~\
none

hieroglyphic	emblem	hospitable
labyrinth	papyrus	contemplative
migrate	frugal	

Key People, Places, and Events

Joseph	Menes	Amun
Israelites (children of Israel)	Old Kingdom period	Ra
Moses	Pyramids of Giza	Osiris
Aaron	Senusret I	Isis
Egypt	Middle Kingdom period	Set
Hebrew	Hyksos	Joseph
Abraham	New Kingdom period	Moses
Lower Egypt	Amhose I	Zipporah
Upper Egypt	Rameses I	
Nile River	Rameses II	

Lesson One

History Overview and Assignments
Israel Moves to Egypt

"And God sent me before you to preserve you a posterity in the earth, and to save your lives by a great deliverance."

– Genesis 45:7

Joseph and Jacob Reunited, by Owen Jones.
Illustration from *The History of Joseph and His Brethren* (1869)

Suggested Reading and Assignments

- Read the article: *Genesis 45-Genesis 46*.
- After reading the article, summarize the story you read by either:
    - Retelling it out loud to your teacher or parent.
        OR
    - Completing an appropriate notebook page.
  Either way, be sure to include the answer to the discussion questions and an overview of key people, places, dates, and events in your summary.
- Be sure to visit your **ArtiosHCS** curriculum website for additional resources and any videos and websites assigned for this lesson.

Key People, Places, and Events

Joseph

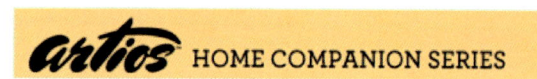

Discussion Question

1. Describe how and why the Israelites came to be in Egypt.
2. How did Joseph arrange for the Israelites to live separately from the Egyptians?

Genesis 45 - Genesis 46

Genesis 45

1 Then **Joseph** could not refrain himself before all them that stood by him; and he cried, Cause every man to go out from me. And there stood no man with him, while Joseph made himself known unto his brethren.

2 And he wept aloud: and the Egyptians and the house of Pharaoh heard.

3 And Joseph said unto his brethren, I am Joseph; doth my father yet live? And his brethren could not answer him; for they were troubled at his presence.

4 And Joseph said unto his brethren, Come near to me, I pray you. And they came near. And he said, I am Joseph your brother, whom ye sold into Egypt.

5 Now therefore be not grieved, nor angry with yourselves, that ye sold me hither: for God did send me before you to preserve life.

6 For these two years hath the famine been in the land: and yet there are five years, in the which there shall neither be earing nor harvest.

7 And God sent me before you to preserve you a posterity in the earth, and to save your lives by a great deliverance.

8 So now it was not you that sent me hither, but God: and he hath made me a father to Pharaoh, and lord of all his house, and a ruler throughout all the land of Egypt.

9 Haste ye, and go up to my father, and say unto him, Thus saith thy son Joseph, God hath made me lord of all Egypt: come down unto me, tarry not:

10 And thou shalt dwell in the land of Goshen, and thou shalt be near unto me, thou, and thy children, and thy children's children, and thy flocks, and thy herds, and all that thou hast:

11 And there will I nourish thee; for yet there are five years of famine; lest thou, and thy household, and all that thou hast, come to poverty.

12 And, behold, your eyes see, and the eyes of my brother Benjamin, that it is my mouth that speaketh unto you.

13 And ye shall tell my father of all my glory in Egypt, and of all that ye have seen; and ye shall haste and bring down my father hither.

14 And he fell upon his brother Benjamin's neck, and wept; and Benjamin wept upon his neck.

15 Moreover he kissed all his brethren, and wept upon them: and after that his brethren talked with him.

16 And the fame thereof was heard in Pharaoh's house, saying, Joseph's brethren are come: and it pleased Pharaoh well, and his servants.

17 And Pharaoh said unto Joseph, Say unto thy brethren, This do ye; lade your beasts, and go, get you unto the land of Canaan;

18 And take your father and your households, and come unto me: and I will give you the good of the land of Egypt, and ye shall eat the fat of the land.

19 Now thou art commanded, this do ye; take you wagons out of the land of Egypt for your little ones, and for your wives, and bring your father, and come.

20 Also regard not your stuff; for the good of all the land of Egypt is yours.

21 And the children of Israel did so: and Joseph gave them wagons, according to the

commandment of Pharaoh, and gave them provision for the way.

22 To all of them he gave each man changes of raiment; but to Benjamin he gave three hundred pieces of silver, and five changes of raiment.

23 And to his father he sent after this manner; ten asses laden with the good things of Egypt, and ten she asses laden with corn and bread and meat for his father by the way.

24 So he sent his brethren away, and they departed: and he said unto them, See that ye fall not out by the way.

25 And they went up out of Egypt, and came into the land of Canaan unto Jacob their father,

26 And told him, saying, Joseph is yet alive, and he is governor over all the land of Egypt. And Jacob's heart fainted, for he believed them not.

27 And they told him all the words of Joseph, which he had said unto them: and when he saw the wagons which Joseph had sent to carry him, the spirit of Jacob their father revived:

28 And Israel said, It is enough; Joseph my son is yet alive: I will go and see him before I die.

Genesis 46

1 And Israel took his journey with all that he had, and came to Beersheba, and offered sacrifices unto the God of his father Isaac.

2 And God spake unto Israel in the visions of the night, and said, Jacob, Jacob. And he said, Here am I.

3 And he said, I am God, the God of thy father: fear not to go down into Egypt; for I will there make of thee a great nation:

4 I will go down with thee into Egypt; and I will also surely bring thee up again: and Joseph shall put his hand upon thine eyes.

5 And Jacob rose up from Beersheba: and the sons of Israel carried Jacob their father, and their little ones, and their wives, in the wagons which Pharaoh had sent to carry him.

6 And they took their cattle, and their goods, which they had gotten in the land of Canaan, and came into Egypt, Jacob, and all his seed with him:

7 His sons, and his sons' sons with him, his daughters, and his sons' daughters, and all his seed brought he with him into Egypt.

Joseph and His Brethren Welcomed by Pharaoh,
watercolor by James Tissot (before 1903)

8 And these are the names of the children of Israel, which came into Egypt, Jacob and his sons: Reuben, Jacob's firstborn.

9 And the sons of Reuben; Hanoch, and Phallu, and Hezron, and Carmi.

10 And the sons of Simeon; Jemuel, and

Jamin, and Ohad, and Jachin, and Zohar, and Shaul the son of a Canaanitish woman.

11 And the sons of Levi; Gershon, Kohath, and Merari.

12 And the sons of Judah; Er, and Onan, and Shelah, and Pharez, and Zarah: but Er and Onan died in the land of Canaan. And the sons of Pharez were Hezron and Hamul.

13 And the sons of Issachar; Tola, and Phuvah, and Job, and Shimron.

14 And the sons of Zebulun; Sered, and Elon, and Jahleel.

15 These be the sons of Leah, which she bare unto Jacob in Padanaram, with his daughter Dinah: all the souls of his sons and his daughters were thirty and three.

16 And the sons of Gad; Ziphion, and Haggi, Shuni, and Ezbon, Eri, and Arodi, and Areli.

17 And the sons of Asher; Jimnah, and Ishuah, and Isui, and Beriah, and Serah their sister: and the sons of Beriah; Heber, and Malchiel.

18 These are the sons of Zilpah, whom Laban gave to Leah his daughter, and these she bare unto Jacob, even sixteen souls.

19 The sons of Rachel Jacob's wife; Joseph, and Benjamin.

20 And unto Joseph in the land of Egypt were born Manasseh and Ephraim, which Asenath the daughter of Potipherah priest of On bare unto him.

21 And the sons of Benjamin were Belah, and Becher, and Ashbel, Gera, and Naaman, Ehi, and Rosh, Muppim, and Huppim, and Ard.

22 These are the sons of Rachel, which were born to Jacob: all the souls were fourteen.

23 And the sons of Dan; Hushim.

24 And the sons of Naphtali; Jahzeel, and Guni, and Jezer, and Shillem.

25 These are the sons of Bilhah, which Laban gave unto Rachel his daughter, and she bare these unto Jacob: all the souls were seven.

26 All the souls that came with Jacob into Egypt, which came out of his loins, besides Jacob's sons' wives, all the souls were threescore and six;

27 And the sons of Joseph, which were born him in Egypt, were two souls: all the souls of the house of Jacob, which came into Egypt, were threescore and ten.

28 And he sent Judah before him unto Joseph, to direct his face unto Goshen; and they came into the land of Goshen.

29 And Joseph made ready his chariot, and went up to meet Israel his father, to Goshen, and presented himself unto him; and he fell on his neck, and wept on his neck a good while.

30 And Israel said unto Joseph, Now let me die, since I have seen thy face, because thou art yet alive.

31 And Joseph said unto his brethren, and unto his father's house, I will go up, and shew Pharaoh, and say unto him, My brethren, and my father's house, which were in the land of Canaan, are come unto me;

32 And the men are shepherds, for their trade hath been to feed cattle; and they have brought their flocks, and their herds, and all that they have.

33 And it shall come to pass, when Pharaoh shall call you, and shall say, What is your occupation?

34 That ye shall say, Thy servants' trade hath been about cattle from our youth even until now, both we, and also our fathers: that ye may dwell in the land of Goshen; for every shepherd is an abomination unto the Egyptians.

Lesson Two

History Overview and Assignments
The Israelites Become Slaves

"Now there arose up a new king over Egypt, which knew not Joseph. And he said unto his people, 'Behold, the people of the children of Israel are more and mightier than we.'"

– Exodus 1:8-9

Israel in Egypt, by Edward Poynter (1867)

Suggested Reading and Assignments

- Read the article: *Exodus 1*.
- After reading the article, summarize the story you read by either:
  - Retelling it out loud to your teacher or parent.
    OR
  - Completing an appropriate notebook page.

  Either way, be sure to include the answers to the discussion questions and an overview of key people, places, dates, and events in your summary.
- Be sure to visit your **ArtiosHCS** curriculum website for additional resources and any videos and websites assigned for this lesson.

Key People, Places, and Events

Israelites (children of Israel)

Discussion Questions

1. Name the sons of Jacob/Israel that moved to Egypt.
2. Why was the new pharaoh afraid of the Israelites?
3. What two things did he do to prevent them from rising up in rebellion?

Exodus 1

Exodus 1

1 Now these are the names of the **children of Israel**, which came into Egypt; every man and his household came with Jacob.

2 Reuben, Simeon, Levi, and Judah,

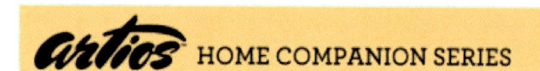

3 Issachar, Zebulun, and Benjamin,

4 Dan, and Naphtali, Gad, and Asher.

5 And all the souls that came out of the loins of Jacob were seventy souls: for Joseph was in Egypt already.

6 And Joseph died, and all his brethren, and all that generation.

7 And the children of Israel were fruitful, and increased abundantly, and multiplied, and waxed exceeding mighty; and the land was filled with them.

8 Now there arose up a new king over Egypt, which knew not Joseph.

9 And he said unto his people, Behold, the people of the children of Israel are more and mightier than we:

10 Come on, let us deal wisely with them; lest they multiply, and it come to pass, that, when there falleth out any war, they join also unto our enemies, and fight against us, and so get them up out of the land.

11 Therefore they did set over them taskmasters to afflict them with their burdens. And they built for Pharaoh treasure cities, Pithom and Raamses.

12 But the more they afflicted them, the more they multiplied and grew. And they were grieved because of the children of Israel.

13 And the Egyptians made the children of Israel to serve with rigour:

14 And they made their lives bitter with hard bondage, in morter, and in brick, and in all manner of service in the field: all their service, wherein they made them serve, was with rigour.

15 And the king of Egypt spake to the Hebrew midwives, of which the name of the one was Shiphrah, and the name of the other Puah:

16 And he said, When ye do the office of a midwife to the Hebrew women, and see them upon the stools; if it be a son, then ye shall kill him: but if it be a daughter, then she shall live.

17 But the midwives feared God, and did not as the king of Egypt commanded them, but saved the men children alive.

18 And the king of Egypt called for the midwives, and said unto them, Why have ye done this thing, and have saved the men children alive?

19 And the midwives said unto Pharaoh, Because the Hebrew women are not as the Egyptian women; for they are lively, and are delivered ere the midwives come in unto them.

20 Therefore God dealt well with the midwives: and the people multiplied, and waxed very mighty.

21 And it came to pass, because the midwives feared God, that he made them houses.

22 And Pharaoh charged all his people, saying, Every son that is born ye shall cast into the river, and every daughter ye shall save alive.

A tomb relief depicts workers plowing the fields, harvesting the crops, and threshing the grain under the direction of an overseer. Copy of a 15th-century B.C. painting in the tomb of Nakht

Lesson Three

History Overview and Assignments
Egypt and the Pharaohs

"The glories of the monarchy, now decidedly military, reached their height with Rameses II. He extended his rule as far as Scythia and Thrace while his naval expeditions penetrated to the Indian Ocean. The captives he brought from his wars were set to work digging canals, which crossed the country for purposes of irrigation. The Ramesseum, his memorial temple, was his greatest architectural work. Behind an avenue of sphinxes and obelisks stands a great statue of Rameses himself, sixty-two feet high, carved from a single stone of red granite."

– from the adapted article below

Color reproduction of the relief depicting Ramesses II storming the Hittite fortress of Dapur, German lithograph (1879)

Suggested Reading and Assignments

- Read the article: *Egypt and the Pharaohs*.
- Define each vocabulary word in the context of the reading. Write the words and their definitions in the vocabulary section of your notebook.
- After reading the article, summarize the story you read by either:
  - Retelling it out loud to your teacher or parent.
    OR
  - Completing an appropriate notebook page.

  Either way, be sure to include the answers to the discussion questions and an overview of key people, places, dates, and events in your summary.
- Be sure to visit your **ArtiosHCS** curriculum website for additional resources and any videos and websites assigned for this lesson.

Ancient: Elementary
Unit 9: The Israelites in Egypt

Vocabulary

hieroglyphic
labyrinth
migrate
emblem
papyrus
frugal
hospitable
contemplative

Key People, Places, and Events

Egypt
Hebrew
Abraham
Lower Egypt
Upper Egypt
Nile River
Menes
Old Kingdom period
Pyramids of Giza
Senusret I
Middle Kingdom period
Hyksos

New Kingdom period
Amhose I
Rameses I
Rameses II
Amun
Ra
Osiris
Isis
Set
Joseph
Moses
Zipporah

Discussion Questions

1. From whose descendants was the nation of Egypt primarily formed?
2. What very long river runs through Egypt?
3. What did that river do every year that made the land fertile?
4. What is the name of the man that historians believe was the founding ruler of Egypt's First Dynasty?
5. Who were the Hyksos people, and what did they do when they migrated to Egypt?
6. Who expelled the Hyksos from Egypt, and when?
7. What was the religion of the ancient Egyptians like?
8. List some of the accomplishments of the ancient Egyptians.

Adapted for Elementary School from the book:
Ancient States and Empires
by John Lord
Egypt and the Pharaohs

Ancient Egypt

Egypt was one of the early cultures formed mainly by the descendants of Ham. With a more powerful kingdom than any existing on the earth by the time of the great **Hebrew** forefather **Abraham**, Egypt had a language, traditions, and monuments that pointed to the early development of a high level of culture.

Some of Egypt's early inhabitants settled in the northern delta area, where the Nile splits into numerous rivulets and runs into the Mediterranean Sea. This region became known as **Lower Egypt**. Others ventured further south along the Nile and settled in what became known as **Upper Egypt**.

The Fertility of Egypt

The **Nile River**, issuing from Lake Victoria below the equator, runs more than 4,000 miles, nearly due north to the Mediterranean. Its annual floods covered the valley with rich soil brought down from the mountains, making it the most fertile in the world.

In Egypt's early days, a significant part of the country was irrigated and abounded in orchards, gardens, and vineyards. Every kind of vegetable was cultivated, and grain was raised in abundance so that the people lived in luxury and plenty. At the same time, other nations were subject to occasional famines.

In old times the horses of Egypt were famous, as well as cattle, sheep, and poultry. Quail were abundant, while the marshes afforded every kind of web-footed fowl. Fish, too, abounded in the Nile and the lakes. Bees were kept, and honey was produced, though inferior to Greece's.

The climate of this fruitful land was wholesome without being wearying, and the soil could support a large population.

On the banks of the Nile were great cities whose ruins still astonish travelers. The land, except that owned by the priests, belonged to the ruler, called a *pharaoh*, who was supreme and unlimited in power.

Egyptian Dynasties

Most historians agree that **Menes**, having united Upper Egypt in the south and Lower Egypt in the north, was the founding ruler of the First Dynasty of Egypt's **Old Kingdom period**. **Hieroglyphic** writing, which used pictures to represent words, may have been invented during this time.

The Pyramids

During the Fourth Dynasty of kings, the **Pyramids of Giza** were built. These were the tombs of the pharaohs, who believed in the immortality of the soul and its final reunion with the body. These beliefs led to a desire to preserve the body as well as possible in some enduring monuments.

The Middle Kingdom Period

The first notable name among the Egyptian pharaohs was **Senusret I**, who reigned with his father, the founder of the Twelfth Dynasty of pharaohs during Egypt's **Middle Kingdom period**. Senusret was a great conqueror, and by the kings of this dynasty, Ethiopia was conquered. An incredible **labyrinth** was said to be built, and an impressive canal was dug to control the Nile floods. Under these rulers, Thebes became a great city.

The dynasty lasted 100 years, and it was probably during this Middle Kingdom time period that the Israelites came by way of Joseph to Egypt. These early Egyptian pharaohs were fond of peace, and their subjects enjoyed prosperity. But in their love of peace, they failed to build up effective defensive forces, so they were taken over by the **Hyksos** people, who **migrate**d into Lower Egypt and gradually brought native rule to an end.

The "Rulers of Foreign Lands"

The Hyksos took over Egypt in about 1650 B.C. They left no monuments and were very different from the conquered race in language and habits. They settled mainly in Lower Egypt, where the land was most fertile. The name Hyksos means "rulers of foreign lands."

Expulsion of the Hyksos Kings

Meanwhile, the descendants of the old pharaohs lived in Thebes. They were allowed to reign during five dynasties but only as subjects to the Hyksos, oppressed and forced to pay tribute.

The first king of the Eighteenth Dynasty, which marked the beginning of Egypt's **New Kingdom period**, seems to have been a remarkable man—the deliverer of his nation. His name was **Amhose I**, and he gathered strength and expelled the Hyksos from the greater part of Egypt sometime during the mid-sixteenth century B.C. Chariots and horses can be found on monuments from his reign. He built temples in Thebes and Memphis and established a navy. His successors continued the conquest, extended their dominion from Ethiopia to Mesopotamia, and seized that part of Western Asia formerly held by the Chaldeans.

A scene from Egyptian mythology: The deities Seth (left) and Horus (right) adoring Pharaoh Ramesses in the small temple at Abu Simbel

The Greatness of Rameses II

The grandest period of Egyptian history began with the Nineteenth Dynasty, founded by **Rameses I**. The famous Hypostyle Hall in the Temple of Karnak was built during this dynasty, along with the finest tombs of the Theban kings. On the walls of the great temple are depicted the conquests of Seti I, especially over the Hittites.

But the glories of the monarchy, now decidedly military, reached their height with **Rameses II**. He extended his rule as far as Scythia and Thrace while his naval expeditions penetrated the Indian Ocean. The captives he brought from his wars were set to work digging canals, which crossed the country for purposes of irrigation. The Ramesseum, his memorial temple, was his greatest architectural work. Behind an avenue of sphinxes and obelisks stands a great statue of Rameses himself, sixty-two feet high, carved from a single stone of red granite.

Religion

The religion of the ancient Egyptians was idolatrous. They worshiped various divinities, such as **Amun** (said to be king of the gods, one of the creators and later combined with Ra), Khnum (another creator as well as the god of the Nile flood), Ptah (god of craftsmen), **Ra** (the sun god), Thoth (patron of letters), **Osiris** (god of the dead and personification of good), **Isis** (a protective goddess who presided over funeral rites), and **Set** (god of chaos and personification of evil).

These deities were worshiped through sacred animals as **emblem**s of divinity, including the bull, crocodile, asp, cat, and beetle. The worship of these and other animals was conducted with great ceremony, and sacrifices were made to them of other animals, fruits, and vegetables.

According to their religious teachings, man was held accountable for his actions and to be judged according to them. He was said to be brought before Osiris at death and receive future rewards or punishments.

Lifestyle

The rich were hospitable and delighted to give feasts at which dancers and musicians performed. They possessed chariots and horses and lived lives filled with pleasure-seeking activities. In the upper classes, women were treated with great respect. They ruled their households. The poor people toiled with scanty clothing and poor fare.

Drawing of a Greater Bird of Paradise and the papyrus plant

Egyptian Science and Art

Hieroglyphic writing was used from early times. The **papyrus**, an early form of paper made from Nile papyrus reeds, was used for writing, and wonderfully creative stories have come down to us from early Egyptian days. Priests cultivated astronomy and developed it to an impressive degree without modern instruments. Math also reached considerable complexity. Mechanics must have been developed greatly when we remember that vast blocks of stone were transported 500 miles and elevated to enormous heights. Ancient Egyptians also produced intricate works of metal.

But architecture was the great art in which the Egyptians excelled, as we can see from the ruins of temples and palaces, and their beautiful walls were ornamented with paintings, some of which have preserved their color to this day. The architecture was massive, grand, and imposing. The industry reached great excellence, especially in weaving linen, pottery, and household furniture.

Ancient Egyptian hieroglyphic inscriptions on a column in the Karnak Temple complex, Egypt

The Egyptians were great musicians, using harps, flutes, cymbals, and drums. They also excelled as gardeners. In their dress, they were simple, **frugal** in diet (though given to occasional excess), fond of war but not cruel like the Assyrians, **hospitable** among themselves, wary of strangers, patriotic in feeling, and **contemplative** in character.

Punishment in Ancient Egypt. Wall painting from a 15th century B.C. Egyptian tomb

The Artios Home Companion Series
Unit 10: The Israelites in the Wilderness

Teacher Overview

IN TIME GOD raised a leader who would confront the reigning pharaoh and lead His people out of slavery in the land of Egypt toward the Promised Land. Once again, through this story, God demonstrated that He is in control of the hearts and affairs of men and uses everything to bring honor and glory to Himself.

God then used the forty years the Israelites were in the wilderness, from the time they were released from Egypt until their entrance into the land of Canaan, to build them into a strong and godly nation. During these years, He taught them how He wanted them to live and worship Him.

Baby Moses Rescued From the Nile, by Nicolas Poussin (1638)

Vocabulary

Lessons 1-3:
none

Lesson 4:
commandment
tabernacle
consecration
tablet
magistrate
convene
elders
oracle
tithe
trustee

Suggested Assignments

Based on your student's age and ability, the reading in this unit may be read aloud to the student, and journaling and notebook pages may be completed orally. Likewise, other assignments may be done with an appropriate combination of independent and guided study.

In this unit, students will:
- Complete four lessons in which they will learn **how Moses rose to leadership to help deliver the Israelites**, **their wanderings in the wilderness**, and the **receiving of God's law**.
- Define vocabulary words.

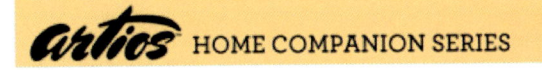

- Using *The Exodus From Egypt* map from the map packet you were instructed to purchase in Unit 1, trace the route of the Israelites as they left Egypt and headed toward Mt. Sinai.
- Visit the **ArtiosHCS** curriculum website at www.ArtiosHCS.com for additional resources and any videos and websites assigned for this unit.

Heart Connections

God will accomplish His purpose.

Many are the plans in the mind of a man, but it is the purpose of the Lord that will stand.
– Proverbs 19:21

One's heart is revealed by one's words and actions.

The good person out of the good treasure of his heart produces good, and the evil person out of his evil treasure produces evil, for out of the abundance of the heart his mouth speaks.
– Luke 6:45

God works all things for our good and His glory.

"As for you, you meant evil against me, but God meant it for good, to bring it about that many people should be kept alive, as they are today."
– Genesis 50:20

God controls world leaders.

The king's heart is a stream of water in the hand of the Lord; he turns it wherever he will.
– Proverbs 21:1

Key People, Places, and Events

| Moses | Aaron | Joseph | Zipporah | Sinai |

Additional Material for Parent or Teacher:

For an alternate way to introduce this story to your student, visit the 'Additional Material...' link on the **ArtiosHCS** curriculum website. It features an interactive map and a read-aloud recorded account.

Detail image of Olive Deering, Edward G. Robinson, and Charlton Heston in the **1956** trailer for the film *The Ten Commandments*

Lesson One

History Overview and Assignments
Plagued

"And Pharaoh rose up in the night, he, and all his servants, and all the Egyptians; and there was a great cry in Egypt; for there was not a house where there was not one dead. And he called for Moses and Aaron by night, and said, 'Rise up, and get you forth from among my people, both ye and the children of Israel; and go, serve the Lord, as ye have said.'"
— Exodus 12:30-31

Massacre of the Firstborn and Egyptian Darkness (c.1490)

Suggested Reading and Assignments

- Read the article: *Exodus 5 – Exodus 12*.
- After reading the article, summarize the story you read by either:
  - Retelling it out loud to your teacher or parent.
     OR
  - Completing an appropriate notebook page.

  Either way, be sure to include the answers to the discussion questions and an overview of key people, places, dates, and events in your summary.
- As an alternative to answering the discussion questions dealing with the ten plagues, students may make a booklet with drawings or pictures describing the ten plagues and then present it as a story to the class.
- Be sure to visit your **ArtiosHCS** curriculum website for additional resources and any videos and websites assigned for this lesson.

Key People, Places, and Events

Moses
Aaron

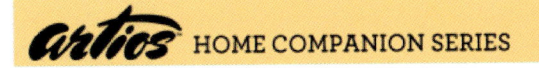

Ancient: Elementary
Unit 10: The Israelites in the Wilderness

Discussion Questions

1. How did Pharaoh punish the Israelites after Moses visited him?
2. Why did Moses think he was a poor choice to lead the Israelites?
3. Describe what happened to the staff of Moses when he threw it on the ground.
4. How long had the Israelites been in Egypt when Pharaoh decided to let them go?
5. Describe the plague of the Passover.
6. Can you see any similarities between the Passover and the sacrifice of Christ for us?

Exodus 5 – Exodus 12

Chapter 5

1 And afterward **Moses** and **Aaron** went in, and told Pharaoh, Thus saith the LORD God of Israel, Let my people go, that they may hold a feast unto me in the wilderness.

2 And Pharaoh said, Who is the LORD, that I should obey his voice to let Israel go? I know not the LORD, neither will I let Israel go.

3 And they said, The God of the Hebrews hath met with us: let us go, we pray thee, three days' journey into the desert, and sacrifice unto the LORD our God; lest he fall upon us with pestilence, or with the sword.

4 And the king of Egypt said unto them, Wherefore do ye, Moses and Aaron, let the people from their works? get you unto your burdens.

5 And Pharaoh said, Behold, the people of the land now are many, and ye make them rest from their burdens.

6 And Pharaoh commanded the same day the taskmasters of the people, and their officers, saying,

7 Ye shall no more give the people straw to make brick, as heretofore: let them go and gather straw for themselves.

8 And the tale of the bricks, which they did make heretofore, ye shall lay upon them; ye shall not diminish ought thereof: for they be idle; therefore they cry, saying, Let us go and sacrifice to our God.

9 Let there more work be laid upon the men, that they may labour therein; and let them not regard vain words.

10 And the taskmasters of the people went out, and their officers, and they spake to the people, saying, Thus saith Pharaoh, I will not give you straw.

11 Go ye, get you straw where ye can find it: yet not ought of your work shall be diminished.

12 So the people were scattered abroad throughout all the land of Egypt to gather stubble instead of straw.

13 And the taskmasters hasted them, saying, Fulfil your works, your daily tasks, as when there was straw.

14 And the officers of the children of Israel, which Pharaoh's taskmasters had set over them, were beaten, and demanded, Wherefore have ye not fulfilled your task in making brick both yesterday and to day, as heretofore?

15 Then the officers of the children of Israel came and cried unto Pharaoh, saying, Wherefore dealest thou thus with thy servants?

16 There is no straw given unto thy

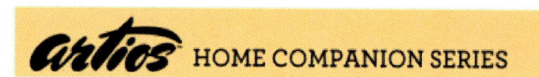

servants, and they say to us, Make brick: and, behold, thy servants are beaten; but the fault is in thine own people.

17 But he said, Ye are idle, ye are idle: therefore ye say, Let us go and do sacrifice to the LORD.

18 Go therefore now, and work; for there shall no straw be given you, yet shall ye deliver the tale of bricks.

19 And the officers of the children of Israel did see that they were in evil case, after it was said, Ye shall not minish ought from your bricks of your daily task.

20 And they met Moses and Aaron, who stood in the way, as they came forth from Pharaoh:

21 And they said unto them, The LORD look upon you, and judge; because ye have made our savour to be abhorred in the eyes of Pharaoh, and in the eyes of his servants, to put a sword in their hand to slay us.

22 And Moses returned unto the LORD, and said, Lord, wherefore hast thou so evil entreated this people? why is it that thou hast sent me?

23 For since I came to Pharaoh to speak in thy name, he hath done evil to this people; neither hast thou delivered thy people at all.

Chapter 6

1 Then the LORD said unto Moses, Now shalt thou see what I will do to Pharaoh: for with a strong hand shall he let them go, and with a strong hand shall he drive them out of his land.

2 And God spake unto Moses, and said unto him, I am the LORD:

3 And I appeared unto Abraham, unto Isaac, and unto Jacob, by the name of God Almighty, but by my name JEHOVAH was I not known to them.

4 And I have also established my covenant with them, to give them the land of Canaan, the land of their pilgrimage, wherein they were strangers.

5 And I have also heard the groaning of the children of Israel, whom the Egyptians keep in bondage; and I have remembered my covenant.

6 Wherefore say unto the children of Israel, I am the LORD, and I will bring you out from under the burdens of the Egyptians, and I will rid you out of their bondage, and I will redeem you with a stretched out arm, and with great judgments:

7 And I will take you to me for a people, and I will be to you a God: and ye shall know that I am the LORD your God, which bringeth you out from under the burdens of the Egyptians.

8 And I will bring you in unto the land, concerning the which I did swear to give it to Abraham, to Isaac, and to Jacob; and I will give it you for an heritage: I am the LORD.

9 And Moses spake so unto the children of Israel: but they hearkened not unto Moses for anguish of spirit, and for cruel bondage.

10 And the LORD spake unto Moses, saying,

11 Go in, speak unto Pharaoh king of Egypt, that he let the children of Israel go out of his land.

12 And Moses spake before the LORD, saying, Behold, the children of Israel have not hearkened unto me; how then shall Pharaoh hear me, who am of uncircumcised lips?

13 And the LORD spake unto Moses and unto Aaron, and gave them a charge unto the children of Israel, and unto Pharaoh

king of Egypt, to bring the children of Israel out of the land of Egypt.

14 These be the heads of their fathers' houses: The sons of Reuben the firstborn of Israel; Hanoch, and Pallu, Hezron, and Carmi: these be the families of Reuben.

15 And the sons of Simeon; Jemuel, and Jamin, and Ohad, and Jachin, and Zohar, and Shaul the son of a Canaanitish woman: these are the families of Simeon.

16 And these are the names of the sons of Levi according to their generations; Gershon, and Kohath, and Merari: and the years of the life of Levi were an hundred thirty and seven years.

17 The sons of Gershon; Libni, and Shimi, according to their families.

18 And the sons of Kohath; Amram, and Izhar, and Hebron, and Uzziel: and the years of the life of Kohath were an hundred thirty and three years.

19 And the sons of Merari; Mahali and Mushi: these are the families of Levi according to their generations.

20 And Amram took him Jochebed his father's sister to wife; and she bare him Aaron and Moses: and the years of the life of Amram were an hundred and thirty and seven years.

21 And the sons of Izhar; Korah, and Nepheg, and Zichri.

22 And the sons of Uzziel; Mishael, and Elzaphan, and Zithri.

23 And Aaron took him Elisheba, daughter of Amminadab, sister of Naashon, to wife; and she bare him Nadab, and Abihu, Eleazar, and Ithamar.

24 And the sons of Korah; Assir, and Elkanah, and Abiasaph: these are the families of the Korhites.

25 And Eleazar Aaron's son took him one of the daughters of Putiel to wife; and she bare him Phinehas: these are the heads of the fathers of the Levites according to their families.

26 These are that Aaron and Moses, to whom the LORD said, Bring out the children of Israel from the land of Egypt according to their armies.

27 These are they which spake to Pharaoh king of Egypt, to bring out the children of Israel from Egypt: these are that Moses and Aaron.

28 And it came to pass on the day when the LORD spake unto Moses in the land of Egypt,

29 That the LORD spake unto Moses, saying, I am the LORD: speak thou unto Pharaoh king of Egypt all that I say unto thee.

30 And Moses said before the LORD, Behold, I am of uncircumcised lips, and how shall Pharaoh hearken unto me?

Chapter 7

1 And the LORD said unto Moses, See, I have made thee a god to Pharaoh: and Aaron thy brother shall be thy prophet.

2 Thou shalt speak all that I command thee: and Aaron thy brother shall speak unto Pharaoh, that he send the children of Israel out of his land.

3 And I will harden Pharaoh's heart, and multiply my signs and my wonders in the land of Egypt.

4 But Pharaoh shall not hearken unto you, that I may lay my hand upon Egypt, and bring forth mine armies, and my people the children of Israel, out of the land of Egypt by great judgments.

5 And the Egyptians shall know that I am the LORD, when I stretch forth mine hand upon Egypt, and bring out the children of Israel from among them.

6 And Moses and Aaron did as the LORD commanded them, so did they.

7 And Moses was fourscore years old, and Aaron fourscore and three years old, when they spake unto Pharaoh.

8 And the LORD spake unto Moses and unto Aaron, saying,

9 When Pharaoh shall speak unto you, saying, Shew a miracle for you: then thou shalt say unto Aaron, Take thy rod, and cast it before Pharaoh, and it shall become a serpent.

10 And Moses and Aaron went in unto Pharaoh, and they did so as the LORD had commanded: and Aaron cast down his rod before Pharaoh, and before his servants, and it became a serpent.

11 Then Pharaoh also called the wise men and the sorcerers: now the magicians of Egypt, they also did in like manner with their enchantments.

12 For they cast down every man his rod, and they became serpents: but Aaron's rod swallowed up their rods.

13 And he hardened Pharaoh's heart, that he hearkened not unto them; as the LORD had said.

14 And the LORD said unto Moses, Pharaoh's heart is hardened, he refuseth to let the people go.

15 Get thee unto Pharaoh in the morning; lo, he goeth out unto the water; and thou shalt stand by the river's brink against he come; and the rod which was turned to a serpent shalt thou take in thine hand.

16 And thou shalt say unto him, The LORD God of the Hebrews hath sent me unto thee, saying, Let my people go, that they may serve me in the wilderness: and, behold, hitherto thou wouldest not hear.

17 Thus saith the LORD, In this thou shalt know that I am the LORD: behold, I will smite with the rod that is in mine hand upon the waters which are in the river, and they shall be turned to blood.

The First Plague: Water Is Changed into Blood,
by James Tissot (before 1903)

18 And the fish that is in the river shall die, and the river shall stink; and the Egyptians shall loathe to drink of the water of the river.

19 And the LORD spake unto Moses, Say unto Aaron, Take thy rod, and stretch out thine hand upon the waters of Egypt, upon their streams, upon their rivers, and upon their ponds, and upon all their pools of water, that they may become blood; and that there may be blood throughout all the land of Egypt, both in vessels of wood, and in vessels of stone.

20 And Moses and Aaron did so, as the LORD commanded; and he lifted up the rod, and smote the waters that were in the river, in the sight of Pharaoh, and in the sight of

his servants; and all the waters that were in the river were turned to blood.

21 And the fish that was in the river died; and the river stank, and the Egyptians could not drink of the water of the river; and there was blood throughout all the land of Egypt.

22 And the magicians of Egypt did so with their enchantments: and Pharaoh's heart was hardened, neither did he hearken unto them; as the LORD had said.

23 And Pharaoh turned and went into his house, neither did he set his heart to this also.

24 And all the Egyptians digged round about the river for water to drink; for they could not drink of the water of the river.

25 And seven days were fulfilled, after that the LORD had smitten the river.

Chapter 8

1 And the LORD spake unto Moses, Go unto Pharaoh, and say unto him, Thus saith the LORD, Let my people go, that they may serve me.

2 And if thou refuse to let them go, behold, I will smite all thy borders with frogs:

3 And the river shall bring forth frogs abundantly, which shall go up and come into thine house, and into thy bedchamber, and upon thy bed, and into the house of thy servants, and upon thy people, and into thine ovens, and into thy kneadingtroughs:

4 And the frogs shall come up both on thee, and upon thy people, and upon all thy servants.

5 And the LORD spake unto Moses, Say unto Aaron, Stretch forth thine hand with thy rod over the streams, over the rivers, and over the ponds, and cause frogs to come up upon the land of Egypt.

6 And Aaron stretched out his hand over the waters of Egypt; and the frogs came up, and covered the land of Egypt.

7 And the magicians did so with their enchantments, and brought up frogs upon the land of Egypt.

8 Then Pharaoh called for Moses and Aaron, and said, Intreat the LORD, that he may take away the frogs from me, and from my people; and I will let the people go, that they may do sacrifice unto the LORD.

9 And Moses said unto Pharaoh, Glory over me: when shall I intreat for thee, and for thy servants, and for thy people, to destroy the frogs from thee and thy houses, that they may remain in the river only?

10 And he said, To morrow. And he said, Be it according to thy word: that thou mayest know that there is none like unto the LORD our God.

11 And the frogs shall depart from thee, and from thy houses, and from thy servants, and from thy people; they shall remain in the river only.

12 And Moses and Aaron went out from Pharaoh: and Moses cried unto the LORD because of the frogs which he had brought against Pharaoh.

13 And the LORD did according to the word of Moses; and the frogs died out of the houses, out of the villages, and out of the fields.

14 And they gathered them together upon heaps: and the land stank.

15 But when Pharaoh saw that there was respite, he hardened his heart, and hearkened not unto them; as the LORD had said.

16 And the LORD said unto Moses, Say unto Aaron, Stretch out thy rod, and smite the dust of the land, that it may become lice throughout all the land of Egypt.

17 And they did so; for Aaron stretched

out his hand with his rod, and smote the dust of the earth, and it became lice in man, and in beast; all the dust of the land became lice throughout all the land of Egypt.

18 And the magicians did so with their enchantments to bring forth lice, but they could not: so there were lice upon man, and upon beast.

19 Then the magicians said unto Pharaoh, This is the finger of God: and Pharaoh's heart was hardened, and he hearkened not unto them; as the LORD had said.

20 And the LORD said unto Moses, Rise up early in the morning, and stand before Pharaoh; lo, he cometh forth to the water; and say unto him, Thus saith the LORD, Let my people go, that they may serve me.

21 Else, if thou wilt not let my people go, behold, I will send swarms of flies upon thee, and upon thy servants, and upon thy people, and into thy houses: and the houses of the Egyptians shall be full of swarms of flies, and also the ground whereon they are.

22 And I will sever in that day the land of Goshen, in which my people dwell, that no swarms of flies shall be there; to the end thou mayest know that I am the LORD in the midst of the earth.

23 And I will put a division between my people and thy people: to morrow shall this sign be.

24 And the LORD did so; and there came a grievous swarm of flies into the house of Pharaoh, and into his servants' houses, and into all the land of Egypt: the land was corrupted by reason of the swarm of flies.

25 And Pharaoh called for Moses and for Aaron, and said, Go ye, sacrifice to your God in the land.

26 And Moses said, It is not meet so to do; for we shall sacrifice the abomination of the Egyptians to the LORD our God: lo, shall we sacrifice the abomination of the Egyptians before their eyes, and will they not stone us?

27 We will go three days' journey into the wilderness, and sacrifice to the LORD our God, as he shall command us.

28 And Pharaoh said, I will let you go, that ye may sacrifice to the LORD your God in the wilderness; only ye shall not go very far away: intreat for me.

29 And Moses said, Behold, I go out from thee, and I will intreat the LORD that the swarms of flies may depart from Pharaoh, from his servants, and from his people, to morrow: but let not Pharaoh deal deceitfully any more in not letting the people go to sacrifice to the LORD.

30 And Moses went out from Pharaoh, and intreated the LORD.

31 And the LORD did according to the word of Moses; and he removed the swarms of flies from Pharaoh, from his servants, and from his people; there remained not one.

32 And Pharaoh hardened his heart at this time also, neither would he let the people go.

The Plague of Flies, by James Tissot (c.1806-1902)

Chapter 9

1 Then the LORD said unto Moses, Go in unto Pharaoh, and tell him, Thus saith the LORD God of the Hebrews, Let my people go, that they may serve me.

2 For if thou refuse to let them go, and wilt hold them still,

3 Behold, the hand of the LORD is upon thy cattle which is in the field, upon the horses, upon the asses, upon the camels, upon the oxen, and upon the sheep: there shall be a very grievous murrain.

4 And the LORD shall sever between the cattle of Israel and the cattle of Egypt: and there shall nothing die of all that is the children's of Israel.

5 And the LORD appointed a set time, saying, To morrow the LORD shall do this thing in the land.

6 And the LORD did that thing on the morrow, and all the cattle of Egypt died: but of the cattle of the children of Israel died not one.

7 And Pharaoh sent, and, behold, there was not one of the cattle of the Israelites dead. And the heart of Pharaoh was hardened, and he did not let the people go.

8 And the LORD said unto Moses and unto Aaron, Take to you handfuls of ashes of the furnace, and let Moses sprinkle it toward the heaven in the sight of Pharaoh.

9 And it shall become small dust in all the land of Egypt, and shall be a boil breaking forth with blains upon man, and upon beast, throughout all the land of Egypt.

10 And they took ashes of the furnace, and stood before Pharaoh; and Moses sprinkled it up toward heaven; and it became a boil breaking forth with blains upon man, and upon beast.

11 And the magicians could not stand before Moses because of the boils; for the boil was upon the magicians, and upon all the Egyptians.

12 And the LORD hardened the heart of Pharaoh, and he hearkened not unto them; as the LORD had spoken unto Moses.

13 And the LORD said unto Moses, Rise up early in the morning, and stand before Pharaoh, and say unto him, Thus saith the LORD God of the Hebrews, Let my people go, that they may serve me.

14 For I will at this time send all my plagues upon thine heart, and upon thy servants, and upon thy people; that thou mayest know that there is none like me in all the earth.

15 For now I will stretch out my hand, that I may smite thee and thy people with pestilence; and thou shalt be cut off from the earth.

16 And in very deed for this cause have I raised thee up, for to shew in thee my power; and that my name may be declared throughout all the earth.

17 As yet exaltest thou thyself against my people, that thou wilt not let them go?

18 Behold, to morrow about this time I will cause it to rain a very grievous hail, such as hath not been in Egypt since the foundation thereof even until now.

19 Send therefore now, and gather thy cattle, and all that thou hast in the field; for upon every man and beast which shall be found in the field, and shall not be brought home, the hail shall come down upon them, and they shall die.

20 He that feared the word of the LORD among the servants of Pharaoh made his servants and his cattle flee into the houses:

21 And he that regarded not the word of the LORD left his servants and his cattle in the field.

22 And the LORD said unto Moses, Stretch forth thine hand toward heaven, that there may be hail in all the land of Egypt, upon man, and upon beast, and upon every herb of the field, throughout the land of Egypt.

23 And Moses stretched forth his rod toward heaven: and the LORD sent thunder and hail, and the fire ran along upon the ground; and the LORD rained hail upon the land of Egypt.

24 So there was hail, and fire mingled with the hail, very grievous, such as there was none like it in all the land of Egypt since it became a nation.

25 And the hail smote throughout all the land of Egypt all that was in the field, both man and beast; and the hail smote every herb of the field, and brake every tree of the field.

Seventh Plague of Egypt, by John Martin (1823)

26 Only in the land of Goshen, where the children of Israel were, was there no hail.

27 And Pharaoh sent, and called for Moses and Aaron, and said unto them, I have sinned this time: the LORD is righteous, and I and my people are wicked.

28 Intreat the LORD (for it is enough) that there be no more mighty thunderings and hail; and I will let you go, and ye shall stay no longer.

29 And Moses said unto him, As soon as I am gone out of the city, I will spread abroad my hands unto the LORD; and the thunder shall cease, neither shall there be any more hail; that thou mayest know how that the earth is the LORD's.

30 But as for thee and thy servants, I know that ye will not yet fear the LORD God.

31 And the flax and the barley was smitten: for the barley was in the ear, and the flax was bolled.

32 But the wheat and the rie were not smitten: for they were not grown up.

33 And Moses went out of the city from Pharaoh, and spread abroad his hands unto the LORD: and the thunders and hail ceased, and the rain was not poured upon the earth.

34 And when Pharaoh saw that the rain and the hail and the thunders were ceased, he sinned yet more, and hardened his heart, he and his servants.

35 The heart of Pharaoh was hardened, neither would he let the children of Israel go; as the LORD had spoken by Moses.

Chapter 10

1 And the LORD said unto Moses, Go in unto Pharaoh: for I have hardened his heart, and the heart of his servants, that I might shew these my signs before him:

2 And that thou mayest tell in the ears of thy son, and of thy son's son, what things I have wrought in Egypt, and my signs which I have done among them; that ye may know how that I am the LORD.

3 And Moses and Aaron came in unto Pharaoh, and said unto him, Thus saith the LORD God of the Hebrews, How long wilt thou refuse to humble thyself before me? let my people go, that they may serve me.

4 Else, if thou refuse to let my people go, behold, to morrow will I bring the locusts into thy coast:

5 And they shall cover the face of the earth, that one cannot be able to see the earth: and they shall eat the residue of that which is escaped, which remaineth unto you from the hail, and shall eat every tree which groweth for you out of the field:

6 And they shall fill thy houses, and the houses of all thy servants, and the houses of all the Egyptians; which neither thy fathers, nor thy fathers' fathers have seen, since the day that they were upon the earth unto this day. And he turned himself, and went out from Pharaoh.

7 And Pharaoh's servants said unto him, How long shall this man be a snare unto us? let the men go, that they may serve the LORD their God: knowest thou not yet that Egypt is destroyed?

8 And Moses and Aaron were brought again unto Pharaoh: and he said unto them, Go, serve the LORD your God: but who are they that shall go?

9 And Moses said, We will go with our young and with our old, with our sons and with our daughters, with our flocks and with our herds will we go; for we must hold a feast unto the LORD.

10 And he said unto them, Let the LORD be so with you, as I will let you go, and your little ones: look to it; for evil is before you.

11 Not so: go now ye that are men, and serve the LORD; for that ye did desire. And they were driven out from Pharaoh's presence.

12 And the LORD said unto Moses, Stretch out thine hand over the land of Egypt for the locusts, that they may come up upon the land of Egypt, and eat every herb of the land, even all that the hail hath left.

13 And Moses stretched forth his rod over the land of Egypt, and the LORD brought an east wind upon the land all that day, and all that night; and when it was morning, the east wind brought the locusts.

14 And the locust went up over all the land of Egypt, and rested in all the coasts of Egypt: very grievous were they; before them there were no such locusts as they, neither after them shall be such.

15 For they covered the face of the whole earth, so that the land was darkened; and they did eat every herb of the land, and all the fruit of the trees which the hail had left: and there remained not any green thing in the trees, or in the herbs of the field, through all the land of Egypt.

16 Then Pharaoh called for Moses and Aaron in haste; and he said, I have sinned against the LORD your God, and against you.

17 Now therefore forgive, I pray thee, my sin only this once, and intreat the LORD your God, that he may take away from me this death only.

18 And he went out from Pharaoh, and intreated the LORD.

19 And the LORD turned a mighty strong west wind, which took away the locusts, and cast them into the Red sea; there remained not one locust in all the coasts of Egypt.

20 But the LORD hardened Pharaoh's heart, so that he would not let the children of Israel go.

21 And the LORD said unto Moses, Stretch out thine hand toward heaven, that there may be darkness over the land of Egypt, even darkness which may be felt.

22 And Moses stretched forth his hand toward heaven; and there was a thick darkness in all the land of Egypt three days:

23 They saw not one another, neither rose any from his place for three days: but all the children of Israel had light in their dwellings.

24 And Pharaoh called unto Moses, and

said, Go ye, serve the LORD; only let your flocks and your herds be stayed: let your little ones also go with you.

25 And Moses said, Thou must give us also sacrifices and burnt offerings, that we may sacrifice unto the LORD our God.

26 Our cattle also shall go with us; there shall not an hoof be left behind; for thereof must we take to serve the LORD our God; and we know not with what we must serve the LORD, until we come thither.

27 But the LORD hardened Pharaoh's heart, and he would not let them go.

28 And Pharaoh said unto him, Get thee from me, take heed to thyself, see my face no more; for in that day thou seest my face thou shalt die.

29 And Moses said, Thou hast spoken well, I will see thy face again no more.

Chapter 11

1 And the LORD said unto Moses, Yet will I bring one plague more upon Pharaoh, and upon Egypt; afterwards he will let you go hence: when he shall let you go, he shall surely thrust you out hence altogether.

2 Speak now in the ears of the people, and let every man borrow of his neighbour, and every woman of her neighbour, jewels of silver and jewels of gold.

3 And the LORD gave the people favour in the sight of the Egyptians. Moreover the man Moses was very great in the land of Egypt, in the sight of Pharaoh's servants, and in the sight of the people.

4 And Moses said, Thus saith the LORD, About midnight will I go out into the midst of Egypt:

5 And all the firstborn in the land of Egypt shall die, from the first born of Pharaoh that sitteth upon his throne, even unto the firstborn of the maidservant that is behind the mill; and all the firstborn of beasts.

6 And there shall be a great cry throughout all the land of Egypt, such as there was none like it, nor shall be like it any more.

7 But against any of the children of Israel shall not a dog move his tongue, against man or beast: that ye may know how that the LORD doth put a difference between the Egyptians and Israel.

8 And all these thy servants shall come down unto me, and bow down themselves unto me, saying, Get thee out, and all the people that follow thee: and after that I will go out. And he went out from Pharaoh in a great anger.

9 And the LORD said unto Moses, Pharaoh shall not hearken unto you; that my wonders may be multiplied in the land of Egypt.

10 And Moses and Aaron did all these wonders before Pharaoh: and the LORD hardened Pharaoh's heart, so that he would not let the children of Israel go out of his land.

Chapter 12

1 And the LORD spake unto Moses and Aaron in the land of Egypt saying,

2 This month shall be unto you the beginning of months: it shall be the first month of the year to you.

3 Speak ye unto all the congregation of Israel, saying, In the tenth day of this month they shall take to them every man a lamb, according to the house of their fathers, a lamb for an house:

4 And if the household be too little for the lamb, let him and his neighbour next unto his house take it according to the number of the souls; every man according to

his eating shall make your count for the lamb.

5 Your lamb shall be without blemish, a male of the first year: ye shall take it out from the sheep, or from the goats:

6 And ye shall keep it up until the fourteenth day of the same month: and the whole assembly of the congregation of Israel shall kill it in the evening.

7 And they shall take of the blood, and strike it on the two side posts and on the upper door post of the houses, wherein they shall eat it.

8 And they shall eat the flesh in that night, roast with fire, and unleavened bread; and with bitter herbs they shall eat it.

9 Eat not of it raw, nor sodden at all with water, but roast with fire; his head with his legs, and with the purtenance thereof.

10 And ye shall let nothing of it remain until the morning; and that which remaineth of it until the morning ye shall burn with fire.

11 And thus shall ye eat it; with your loins girded, your shoes on your feet, and your staff in your hand; and ye shall eat it in haste: it is the LORD's passover.

12 For I will pass through the land of Egypt this night, and will smite all the firstborn in the land of Egypt, both man and beast; and against all the gods of Egypt I will execute judgment: I am the LORD.

13 And the blood shall be to you for a token upon the houses where ye are: and when I see the blood, I will pass over you, and the plague shall not be upon you to destroy you, when I smite the land of Egypt.

14 And this day shall be unto you for a memorial; and ye shall keep it a feast to the LORD throughout your generations; ye shall keep it a feast by an ordinance for ever.

15 Seven days shall ye eat unleavened bread; even the first day ye shall put away leaven out of your houses: for whosoever eateth leavened bread from the first day until the seventh day, that soul shall be cut off from Israel.

16 And in the first day there shall be an holy convocation, and in the seventh day there shall be an holy convocation to you; no manner of work shall be done in them, save that which every man must eat, that only may be done of you.

17 And ye shall observe the feast of unleavened bread; for in this selfsame day have I brought your armies out of the land of Egypt: therefore shall ye observe this day in your generations by an ordinance for ever.

18 In the first month, on the fourteenth day of the month at even, ye shall eat unleavened bread, until the one and twentieth day of the month at even.

19 Seven days shall there be no leaven found in your houses: for whosoever eateth that which is leavened, even that soul shall be cut off from the congregation of Israel, whether he be a stranger, or born in the land.

20 Ye shall eat nothing leavened; in all your habitations shall ye eat unleavened bread.

21 Then Moses called for all the elders of Israel, and said unto them, Draw out and take you a lamb according to your families, and kill the passover.

22 And ye shall take a bunch of hyssop, and dip it in the blood that is in the bason, and strike the lintel and the two side posts with the blood that is in the bason; and none of you shall go out at the door of his house until the morning.

23 For the LORD will pass through to smite the Egyptians; and when he seeth the

blood upon the lintel, and on the two side posts, the LORD will pass over the door, and will not suffer the destroyer to come in unto your houses to smite you.

24 And ye shall observe this thing for an ordinance to thee and to thy sons for ever.

25 And it shall come to pass, when ye be come to the land which the LORD will give you, according as he hath promised, that ye shall keep this service.

26 And it shall come to pass, when your children shall say unto you, What mean ye by this service?

27 That ye shall say, It is the sacrifice of the LORD's passover, who passed over the houses of the children of Israel in Egypt, when he smote the Egyptians, and delivered our houses. And the people bowed the head and worshipped.

28 And the children of Israel went away, and did as the LORD had commanded Moses and Aaron, so did they.

29 And it came to pass, that at midnight the LORD smote all the firstborn in the land of Egypt, from the firstborn of Pharaoh that sat on his throne unto the firstborn of the captive that was in the dungeon; and all the firstborn of cattle.

30 And Pharaoh rose up in the night, he, and all his servants, and all the Egyptians; and there was a great cry in Egypt; for there was not a house where there was not one dead.

31 And he called for Moses and Aaron by night, and said, Rise up, and get you forth from among my people, both ye and the children of Israel; and go, serve the LORD, as ye have said.

32 Also take your flocks and your herds, as ye have said, and be gone; and bless me also.

33 And the Egyptians were urgent upon the people, that they might send them out of the land in haste; for they said, We be all dead men.

34 And the people took their dough before it was leavened, their kneadingtroughs being bound up in their clothes upon their shoulders.

35 And the children of Israel did according to the word of Moses; and they borrowed of the Egyptians jewels of silver, and jewels of gold, and raiment:

36 And the LORD gave the people favour in the sight of the Egyptians, so that they lent unto them such things as they required. And they spoiled the Egyptians.

37 And the children of Israel journeyed from Rameses to Succoth, about six hundred thousand on foot that were men, beside children.

38 And a mixed multitude went up also with them; and flocks, and herds, even very much cattle.

39 And they baked unleavened cakes of the dough which they brought forth out of Egypt, for it was not leavened; because they were thrust out of Egypt, and could not tarry, neither had they prepared for themselves any victual.

40 Now the sojourning of the children of Israel, who dwelt in Egypt, was four hundred and thirty years.

41 And it came to pass at the end of the four hundred and thirty years, even the selfsame day it came to pass, that all the hosts of the LORD went out from the land of Egypt.

42 It is a night to be much observed unto the LORD for bringing them out from the land of Egypt: this is that night of the LORD to be observed of all the children of Israel in their generations.

43 And the LORD said unto Moses and

Aaron, This is the ordinance of the passover: There shall no stranger eat thereof:

44 But every man's servant that is bought for money, when thou hast circumcised him, then shall he eat thereof.

45 A foreigner and an hired servant shall not eat thereof.

46 In one house shall it be eaten; thou shalt not carry forth ought of the flesh abroad out of the house; neither shall ye break a bone thereof.

47 All the congregation of Israel shall keep it.

48 And when a stranger shall sojourn with thee, and will keep the passover to the LORD, let all his males be circumcised, and then let him come near and keep it; and he shall be as one that is born in the land: for no uncircumcised person shall eat thereof.

49 One law shall be to him that is homeborn, and unto the stranger that sojourneth among you.

50 Thus did all the children of Israel; as the LORD commanded Moses and Aaron, so did they.

51 And it came to pass the selfsame day, that the LORD did bring the children of Israel out of the land of Egypt by their armies.

The Israelites Leaving Egypt, by David Roberts (1829)

Lesson Two

History Overview and Assignments
Cloud by Day, Fire by Night

"And Moses said unto the people, 'Fear ye not, stand still, and see the salvation of the Lord, which he will shew to you to day: for the Egyptians whom ye have seen to day, ye shall see them again no more for ever.'"

– Exodus 14:13

Israel's Escape From Egypt, illustration from a Bible card published 1907 by Providence Lithograph Company

Suggested Reading and Assignments

- Read the article: *Exodus 14*.
- After reading the article, summarize the story you read by either:
  - Retelling it out loud to your teacher or parent.
    OR
  - Completing an appropriate notebook page.

  Either way, be sure to include an overview of key people, places, dates, and events in your summary.
- The events of these chapters of Exodus may be very familiar, so familiar that sometimes we don't stop to think about how God truly saved the nation of Israel. Choose a person from this great event. It could be Moses, the wife of Moses, Aaron, a child, or even Pharaoh. Retell the story found in Exodus 14, but do so through the eyes of the person that you chose.
- Be sure to visit your **ArtiosHCS** curriculum website for additional resources and any videos and websites assigned for this lesson.

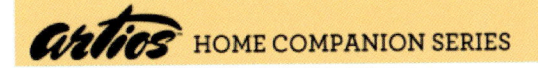

Key People, Places, and Events

Moses

Ancient: Elementary
Unit 10: The Israelites in the Wilderness

Exodus 14

Chapter 14

1 And the Lord spake unto **Moses**, saying,

2 Speak unto the children of Israel, that they turn and encamp before Pihahiroth, between Migdol and the sea, over against Baalzephon: before it shall ye encamp by the sea.

3 For Pharaoh will say of the children of Israel, They are entangled in the land, the wilderness hath shut them in.

4 And I will harden Pharaoh's heart, that he shall follow after them; and I will be honoured upon Pharaoh, and upon all his host; that the Egyptians may know that I am the Lord. And they did so.

5 And it was told the king of Egypt that the people fled: and the heart of Pharaoh and of his servants was turned against the people, and they said, Why have we done this, that we have let Israel go from serving us?

6 And he made ready his chariot, and took his people with him:

7 And he took six hundred chosen chariots, and all the chariots of Egypt, and captains over every one of them.

8 And the Lord hardened the heart of Pharaoh king of Egypt, and he pursued after the children of Israel: and the children of Israel went out with an high hand.

9 But the Egyptians pursued after them, all the horses and chariots of Pharaoh, and his horsemen, and his army, and overtook them encamping by the sea, beside Pihahiroth, before Baalzephon.

10 And when Pharaoh drew nigh, the children of Israel lifted up their eyes, and, behold, the Egyptians marched after them; and they were sore afraid: and the children of Israel cried out unto the Lord.

11 And they said unto Moses, Because there were no graves in Egypt, hast thou taken us away to die in the wilderness? wherefore hast thou dealt thus with us, to carry us forth out of Egypt?

12 Is not this the word that we did tell thee in Egypt, saying, Let us alone, that we may serve the Egyptians? For it had been better for us to serve the Egyptians, than that we should die in the wilderness.

13 And Moses said unto the people, Fear ye not, stand still, and see the salvation of the Lord, which he will shew to you to day: for the Egyptians whom ye have seen to day, ye shall see them again no more for ever.

14 The Lord shall fight for you, and ye shall hold your peace.

15 And the Lord said unto Moses, Wherefore criest thou unto me? speak unto the children of Israel, that they go forward:

16 But lift thou up thy rod, and stretch out thine hand over the sea, and divide it: and the children of Israel shall go on dry ground through the midst of the sea.

17 And I, behold, I will harden the hearts of the Egyptians, and they shall follow them: and I will get me honour upon Pharaoh, and upon all his host, upon his chariots, and upon his horsemen.

18 And the Egyptians shall know that I am the Lord, when I have gotten me honour upon Pharaoh, upon his chariots, and upon his horsemen.

19 And the angel of God, which went before the camp of Israel, removed and went behind them; and the pillar of the cloud went from before their face, and stood behind them:

20 And it came between the camp of the Egyptians and the camp of Israel; and it was a cloud and darkness to them, but it gave light by night to these: so that the one came not near the other all the night.

21 And Moses stretched out his hand over the sea; and the Lord caused the sea to go back by a strong east wind all that night, and made the sea dry land, and the waters were divided.

22 And the children of Israel went into the midst of the sea upon the dry ground: and the waters were a wall unto them on their right hand, and on their left.

23 And the Egyptians pursued, and went in after them to the midst of the sea, even all Pharaoh's horses, his chariots, and his horsemen.

24 And it came to pass, that in the morning watch the Lord looked unto the host of the Egyptians through the pillar of fire and of the cloud, and troubled the host of the Egyptians,

25 And took off their chariot wheels, that they drave them heavily: so that the Egyptians said, Let us flee from the face of Israel; for the Lord fighteth for them against the Egyptians.

26 And the Lord said unto Moses, Stretch out thine hand over the sea, that the waters may come again upon the Egyptians, upon their chariots, and upon their horsemen.

27 And Moses stretched forth his hand over the sea, and the sea returned to his strength when the morning appeared; and the Egyptians fled against it; and the Lord overthrew the Egyptians in the midst of the sea.

28 And the waters returned, and covered the chariots, and the horsemen, and all the host of Pharaoh that came into the sea after them; there remained not so much as one of them.

29 But the children of Israel walked upon dry land in the midst of the sea; and the waters were a wall unto them on their right hand, and on their left.

30 Thus the Lord saved Israel that day out of the hand of the Egyptians; and Israel saw the Egyptians dead upon the sea shore.

31 And Israel saw that great work which the Lord did upon the Egyptians: and the people feared the Lord, and believed the Lord, and his servant Moses.

The Israelites Crossing the Red Sea, by Circle of Juan de la Corte (between 1630 and 1660)

Lesson Three

History Overview and Assignments
The Story of Moses

"Finally free, they moved eastward into the waste places at the foot of Mount Sinai, the peak named after Sin, the Babylonian God of the Moon. There Moses became the head of the Jewish people and taught them according to the commandments given to him by God upon the mountain."

– from the adapted article below

Moses as a Baby, illustration from a Bible card published by the Providence Lithograph Company

Suggested Reading and Assignments

- Read the article: *This Is the Story of Moses*.
- After reading the article, summarize the story you read by either:
  - Retelling it out loud to your teacher or parent.
    OR
  - Completing an appropriate notebook page.

  Either way, be sure to include the answers to the discussion questions and an overview of key people, places, dates, and events in your summary.
- Be sure to visit your **ArtiosHCS** curriculum website for additional resources and any videos and websites assigned for this lesson.

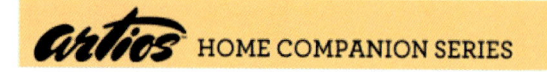

Ancient: Elementary
Unit 10: The Israelites in the Wilderness

Key People, Places, and Events

Joseph   Moses   Zipporah

Discussion Questions

1. Do you remember the story of baby Moses and the basket in the river? If not, read the story in Exodus 2. Can you retell it?

2. Why did Moses have to flee into the desert?

3. Where was Moses to lead his people once they left Egypt?

Adapted for Elementary School from the book:
Ancient Man: The Beginning of Civilizations
by Hendrik Willem van Loon
This Is the Story of Moses

The Jews in Egypt

For many years after Joseph brought the Israelites (also known as the Jews or the Hebrews) down to Egypt, they lived in the eastern part of their adopted country, and all was well with them.

Then a significant change took place.

A sudden revolution among the Egyptians overthrew their rulers, the Hyksos. The Egyptians deprived them of power and forced them to leave the country. Once more, the Egyptians were masters within their own country. They had never liked foreigners very much, and three hundred years of oppression by the Hyksos had significantly increased this feeling of loathing for everything foreign.

The Jews, on the other hand, had been on friendly terms with the Hyksos, who were related to them by blood and race. This was enough to make them traitors in the eyes of the Egyptians.

Joseph was no longer alive to protect his people.

After a short struggle, the Jews were taken away from their old homes, driven into the heart of the country, and made into slaves.

For many years they were subjected to hard labor, made to carry stones for building pyramids, bake bricks for public buildings, construct roads, and dig canals to carry the water of the Nile to distant Egyptian farms.

Though their suffering was great, they never lost courage—and help was near.

There lived a certain young Jewish man whose name was **Moses**. He was knowledgeable and received a good education. This was because the Pharaoh's daughter adopted him out of pity during a time when male Jewish babies were being killed to prevent the Jews' numbers from growing. The Egyptians decided Moses should enter the service of Pharaoh.

If nothing had happened to arouse his anger, Moses might have ended his days peacefully as the governor of a small province or the collector of taxes of an outlying district.

But the Egyptians, as I have told you before, despised those who did not look like themselves or dress in true Egyptian fashion, and they were apt to insult such people because they were "different."

And because the foreigners were in the minority, they could not defend themselves well. Nor did it serve any good purpose to carry their complaints before a tribunal, for the judge would not smile upon the grievances of a man who refused to worship the Egyptian gods and pleaded his case with a strong foreign accent.

Now it occurred one day when Moses saw an Egyptian beating a Hebrew Moses, who was a hot-headed youth, hit him. The blow was severe, and the Egyptian fell dead.

To kill a native was a terrible thing, and the Egyptian laws were not as wise as those of Hammurabi, the early Babylonian king who recognized the difference between premeditated murder and the killing of a man in defense of another.

Moses fled.

He escaped into the land of his ancestors, into the Midian desert, along the eastern bank of the Red Sea, where his tribe had tended their sheep several hundred years before.

A kind priest named Jethro received him into his house and gave him one of his seven daughters, **Zipporah**, as his wife.

Moses lived there for a long time, and God spoke to him there. One day while he was out pasturing the flock, the angel of the Lord appeared to him in the midst of a burning bush and told him to return to Egypt to bring his people out of the oppressive land. Moses obeyed the voice of God and went back to confront Pharaoh.

During the following time, Pharaoh repeatedly refused to let the Jews go, increasing their hardships each time Moses approached him. In response, God inflicted the land of Egypt with ten plagues—the last of which killed the firstborn of Egyptian families.

Amidst the confusion and the panic which followed this silent death, the Jews packed their belongings and hastily fled from the land.

As soon as the flight became known, the Egyptians tried to follow them with their armies, but their soldiers met with disaster in the Red Sea, and the Jews escaped.

Finally free, they moved eastward into the waste places at the foot of Mount Sinai, the peak named after Sin, the Babylonian God of the Moon.

There Moses became the head of the Jewish people and taught them according to the commandments God gave him upon the mountain.

For many years they lived amidst the trackless hills of the desert. They suffered great hardships and almost perished from a lack of food and water.

But Moses kept high their hopes of a Promised Land, which would offer a lasting home to the faithful followers of Jehovah.

At last, they reached a more fertile region.

They crossed the Jordan River and, carrying the Holy Tablets of Law given to Moses on Mount Sinai, made ready to occupy the pastures which stretch from Dan to Beersheba.

But as for Moses, he would no longer be their leader. He had grown old and was very tired. He had been allowed to see the distant ridges of the Palestine Mountains, among which the Jews were to find a homeland. Then he had closed his wise eyes for all time.

He had accomplished the task which God had set for him. He had led his people out of foreign slavery and brought them to a new land where they could live and worship God without oppression.

Lesson Four

History Overview and Assignments
In the Wilderness

THE ISRAELITE PEOPLE lived in Egypt for hundreds of years, surrounded by Egyptian idolatry. When God removed them from that culture, He gave them new laws and values to live by. Separated from other people groups because they lived in the wilderness, the Israelite people were able to develop into a special nation governed by God.

Vocabulary

commandment
tabernacle
consecration
tablet
magistrate
convene
elders
oracle
tithe
trustee

Key People, Places, and Events

Sinai
Moses
Aaron

Moses and the Ten Commandments,
by James Tissot (c.1896-1902)

Suggested Reading and Assignments

- Read the article: *The Jews Until the Death of Moses*.
- Define each vocabulary word in the context of the reading. Write the words and their definitions in the vocabulary section of your notebook.
- For younger elementary students, this lesson's article may be challenging to comprehend, but the parent/teacher needs to read it as background information for the units that follow. A parent/teacher might also choose to share this information with the student via the resource mentioned earlier, *Leading Little Ones to God*.

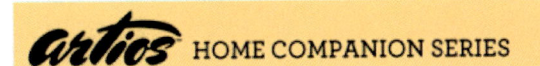

Ancient: Elementary
Unit 10: The Israelites in the Wilderness

- After reading the article, summarize the story you read by either:
  - Retelling it out loud to your teacher or parent.
    OR
  - Completing an appropriate notebook page.

  Either way, be sure to include an overview of key people, places, dates, and events in your summary.
- Using *The Exodus From Egypt* map from the map packet you were instructed to purchase in Unit 1, trace the route of the Israelites as they left Egypt and headed toward Mt. Sinai.
- Be sure to visit your **ArtiosHCS** curriculum website for additional resources and any videos and websites assigned for this lesson.

Adapted for Elementary School from the book:
Ancient Civilizations and Empire
by John Lord
The Jews Until the Death of Moses

The Jewish Law

During their various wanderings in the wilderness of Sinai—forty years of training and discipline—God gave the Israelites the rules they were to live by. These made up a great system of law that has entered, more or less, into the law codes of all nations.

The great foundational principle of the Jewish code was that the God of Abraham, Isaac, and Jacob was the supreme head of the Jewish state, and the people were required, first and last, to honor Him and obey His laws. He had spoken to the patriarchs, brought them into the land of Egypt, and delivered them when they were oppressed. Hence, they were to have no other gods than the God of Abraham—this supreme, personal, loving God. Any violation of this fundamental law would earn the severest penalties. So **Moses** restored the worship of the Supreme Deity. The spiritual idea of God as the supreme object of all obedience and faith was impressed upon the minds of the Israelites.

The Ten Commandments

The way this came about was that Moses ascended the mountain of Sinai and remained there forty days and forty nights, receiving the **commandment**s of God. He then received directions concerning the **Tabernacle**, the special tent where the people were to worship God. And then the priesthood of **Aaron** was ordained, as well as the ceremonies which pertained to the **consecration** of priests, the altar of incense, and the bronze laver.

After renewed commands to observe the Sabbath, Moses received the two tablets of stone from the Lord, "written by the finger of God." But as he descended the mountain with these tablets after the forty days and came near the camp, he saw the golden calf which Aaron had made from the Egyptian earrings and jewelry they had brought with them—made to please the complaining people, so soon did they forget the faithful God who brought them out of Egypt. And Moses, in anger, cast down the tablets and broke them, and then destroyed the calf and ordered the slaughter of three thousand of the people by the hands of the children of Levi.

But God forgave the people's sin, renewed the tablets, and made a new covenant with Moses, telling him to destroy the Canaanites and rid the land of idolatry. Moses again gathered together the people of

Israel and renewed the command to observe the Sabbath. Then they began preparations for building the Tabernacle, as the Lord directed, and also for making the sacred vessels, holy garments, and the various ceremonial aspects of worship. He then consecrated Aaron and his sons as priests, laid down the law for them in their sacred functions, and established other diverse rules for the nation to govern their social and political relations.

The Jewish Law

The main points of these civil laws concerned the equality of the people, the distribution of the land among the citizens, which were to remain in the families to which they were given, and the sacredness of life and family relations. These were fundamental principles, and they were much more just and fair than the laws of other nations.

The tribe of Levi was assigned the duties of the priesthood, as well as the general oversight of education and the laws. The members of this favored tribe were thus to be the priests, lawyers, and teachers of the people.

Moses remained the highest **magistrate** until his death when the command was given to Joshua. Moses and Joshua **convene**d the assemblies, presided over their deliberations, commanded the army, and decided all appeals in civil questions. The office of the chief magistrate was elected and held for life—no salary was attached to it. This chief ruler had no outward badges of authority, did not wear a crown, nor was he surrounded by a court. His power was great as the commander of the armies and president of the assemblies, but he did not make laws or impose taxes.

He was assisted by a body of seventy **elders**—a council or senate, whose decisions were submitted to the general body of citizens for confirmation. These "senators" were elected. The office was not hereditary, nor was any salary attached to it.

It was impossible for the elders or Moses to address two million people, so they spoke to a select assembly. This assembly made the laws that the executive officers carried out.

He Led Them by a Pillar of Cloud. Illustration from a Bible card published between 1896 and 1913 by the Providence Lithograph Company

The Pillars of Cloud and Fire

The pillars of cloud and fire directed the wanderings of the people in the wilderness. Appearing amid the thunders of Sinai, this **oracle** decided all final questions and difficult points of justice. It could not be consulted by private persons, only by the High Priest himself, clad in his pontifical vestments and with the sacred insignia of his office. Inside the most sacred recesses of the Tabernacle, in the Holy of Holies, God made known His will to the most sacred person of the nation. This oracle of the Hebrew God was a wise provision that preserved a continual sense of the principal design of their law code—to keep the Hebrews from idolatry and for the worship of the only true God as their immediate protector so that their security and prosperity rested solely upon adhering to His counsels and commands.

Aaron, depicted by Jacques Bergé
CC BY-SA 4.0

The Priesthood

The priests belonged to the tribe of Levi, which was set apart to God, the King of the country. They were, therefore, not merely a religious body appointed to the service of the altar, but they also had essential civil and political functions, primarily to teach the people the laws.

As head of the hierarchy and supreme interpreter of the laws, the high priest had his seat in the nation's capital, while the priests of his tribe were scattered among the other tribes and were hereditary. The Hebrew priests only interpreted the laws—unlike the priests of Egypt, who made theirs. The **tithe**s granted to the Levites cannot be called excessive compared to what the Egyptian priesthood received, especially when we remember that all the expenses connected with sacrifice and worship were taken from them. The treasures that flowed into the sacred treasury belonged to the Lord; of these, the priests were **trustee**s rather than owners.

Such, in general terms, briefly presented was the Hebrew law code framed by Moses under the direction of God. It was representative in spirit, and the power of the people through their representatives was great and controlling. Property rights were most sacredly guarded, and crime was severely punished.

We look in vain to the ancient constitutions of Greece and Rome for the wisdom we see in the Mosaic code. Under no ancient government were men so free or the laws so just. The Puritans derived much from the Hebrew constitution in building the government of New England.

The Wanderings of the Israelites

We cannot recount all the details of the wanderings under the leadership of Moses, guided by the pillars of fire and cloud. After forty years, they marched to the hilly country east of Jordan, inhabited by the Amorites. After a conflict with this nation, they gained possession of the whole territory, from Mount Hermon to the river Anton, which runs into the Dead Sea. The hills south of this river were inhabited by pastoral Moabites—descendants of Lot, and beyond them to the Great Desert lived the Ammonites, descendants of Lot.

Here Moses delivered his farewell instructions, appointed his successor, and passed away on Mount Pisgah, where he could see the Promised Land but which he was not permitted to conquer. That task was reserved for Joshua, but the complete conquest of the Canaanites did not take place until the reign of David.

The Artios Home Companion Series
Unit 11: The Promised Land

Teacher Overview

DURING THE GENERATIONS following the Israelites' years in the wilderness, God continued working to mold and shape them into a special people group of His own, which He would later use to bless all the other groups of the world. During these years and through special men and women such as Gideon, Samson, Ruth, Boaz, Saul, and David, He taught the Israelites how important it is to trust and obey Him, even when everyone else refuses to do so—and He showed the surrounding nations over and over again that He is the Supreme God.

Joshua Passing the River Jordan With the Ark of the Covenant, by Benjamin West (1800)

Suggested Assignments

Based on your student's age and ability, the reading in this unit may be read aloud to the student, and journaling and notebook pages may be completed orally. Likewise, other assignments may be done with an appropriate combination of independent and guided study.

In this unit, students will:
- Complete five lessons in which they will learn about **Joshua**, **Gideon**, **Samson**, **Ruth and Boaz**, and **David**.
- Define vocabulary words.
- As a review, use the map called *The Promised Land* found in the map packet and retrace the wanderings and travels of the nation of Israel after they left the land of Egypt.

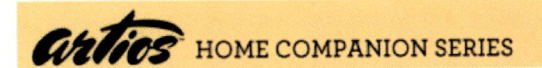

- Using the map *12 Tribes of Israel* found in the map packet, show the students where each one of the twelve tribes of Israel was assigned to live in Canaan.
- Explore the websites found at the URLs on the **ArtiosHCS** curriculum website about Gideon and Ruth.
- Visit the **ArtiosHCS** curriculum website at www.ArtiosHCS.com for additional resources and any videos and websites assigned for this unit.

Heart Connections

God will accomplish His purpose.
Many are the plans in the mind of a man, but it is the purpose of the Lord that will stand.
– Proverbs 19:21

One's heart is revealed by one's words and actions.
The good person out of the good treasure of his heart produces good, and the evil person out of his evil treasure produces evil, for out of the abundance of the heart his mouth speaks.
– Luke 6:45

God works all things for our good and His glory.
"As for you, you meant evil against me, but God meant it for good, to bring it about that many people should be kept alive, as they are today."
– Genesis 50:20

God controls world leaders.
The king's heart is a stream of water in the hand of the Lord; he turns it wherever he will.
– Proverbs 21:1

Vocabulary

Lesson 1:	Lesson 3:	Lesson 4:	Lesson 5:
none	none	reaper	none
		sickle	
Lesson 2:		sheave	
none			

Key People, Places, and Events

Mt. Sinai	Ephraim	Naomi	Saul
Moses	Manasseh	Orpah	David
Joshua	Gideon	Ruth	Goliath
Caleb	Samson	Boaz	
Baal	Elimelech	Samuel	

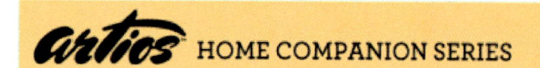

Ancient: Elementary
Unit 11: The Promised Land

Lesson One

History Overview and Assignments
Forgetting How God Led

"And the Lord, out of this glory, spoke to Moses and said, 'How long will this people disobey Me and despise Me? They shall not go into the good land that I have promised them. Not one of them shall enter except Caleb and Joshua, who have been faithful to Me.'"

– from the adapted article below

The Two Reports of the Spies: Numbers 13:17-20, 23-33.
Illustration from a Bible card published in 1907 by Providence Lithograph Company

Suggested Reading and Assignments

- Read the article: *The Story of the Grapes of Canaan*.
- After reading the article, summarize the story you read by either:
  - Retelling it out loud to your teacher or parent.
    OR
  - Completing an appropriate notebook page.

  Either way, be sure to include the answers to the discussion questions and an overview of key people, places, dates, and events in your summary.
- As a review, use the map called *The Promised Land* found in the map packet and retrace the wanderings and travels of the nation of Israel after they left the land of Egypt.
- Using the map *12 Tribes of Israel* found in the map packet, see where each of the twelve tribes of Israel was assigned to live in Canaan.
- Be sure to visit your **ArtiosHCS** curriculum website for additional resources and any videos and websites assigned for this lesson.

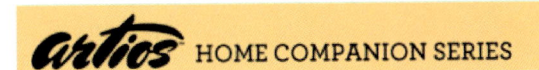

Ancient: Elementary
Unit 11: The Promised Land

Key People, Places, and Events

Mt. Sinai
Moses
Joshua
Caleb

Discussion Questions

1. After the events on Mt. Sinai, where did the Israelites travel?
2. Why did Moses send men ahead into Canaan before all the people entered?
3. What did the men find there? Describe the land they saw.
4. How many spies were afraid to enter the land?
5. What were the names of the two spies who believed they should enter Canaan?
6. How did the Israelites react to what Joshua and Caleb said?
7. How did God punish the Israelites for their disobedience?
8. Did the Israelites initially submit to that punishment?
9. Why do you think the Israelites were so stubborn?

Adapted for Elementary School from the book:
The Wonder Book of Bible Stories
Arranged by Logan Marshall
The Story of the Grapes of Canaan

The Israelites stayed in their camp at the base of **Mount Sinai** for almost a year while they built the Tabernacle and learned God's laws given through **Moses**. At last, the cloud over the Tabernacle rose up, and the people knew that this was the sign for them to move. They took down the Tabernacle and their own tents, and they journeyed toward the land of Canaan for many days.

Moses Comes Down from Mount Sinai,
by Gustave Doré (1866)

At last, they came to a place on the border between the desert and Canaan called Kadesh. Here they stopped to rest, for there were many springs of water and some grass for their cattle. While they were waiting at Kadesh and were expecting soon to march into the land which was to be their home, God told Moses to send ahead some men who should walk through the land and look it over and then come back and tell what they had found—what kind of a land it was, and what fruits grew in it, and what people were living in it. The Israelites could more easily win the land if, after walking through it, these men could act as their guides and point out the best places and plans for making war upon it. God wanted the Israelites to conquer the people who lived in these lands because they were idolatrous.

So Moses chose some men of high rank among the people, one ruler from each tribe, twelve men in all. One of these was **Joshua**, who was the helper of Moses in caring for the people, and another was

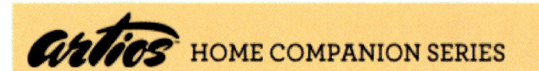

Caleb, who belonged to the tribe of Judah. These twelve men went out and walked over the mountains of Canaan and looked at the cities and saw the fields.

In one place, just before they came back to the camp, they cut down a cluster of ripe grapes so large that two men carried it between them, hanging from a staff. They named the place where they found this bunch of grapes Eshcol, a word that means "a cluster." These twelve men were called "spies" because they went "to spy out the land"; after forty days, they returned to the camp. This was what they said:

"We walked all over the land and found it a rich land. There is grass for all our flocks, fields where we can raise grain, trees bearing fruits, and streams running down the sides of the hills. But we found that the people living there are powerful men of war. They have cities with walls almost reaching the sky, and some men are so tall that we felt like grasshoppers beside them."

Joshua and Caleb Carrying Fruit of the Promised Land, by Albrecht Altdorfer (before 1538)

But Caleb, one of the spies, said, "All that is true, yet we need not be afraid to go up and take the land. It is a good land, well worth fighting for. God is on our side and will help us overcome those people."

But all the other spies—except Joshua—said, "No, there is no use in trying to make war upon such strong people. We can never take those walled cities and dare not fight those tall giants."

And the people, who had journeyed through the wilderness to find this very land, were so frightened by the words of the ten spies that now, on the very border of Canaan, they dared not enter it. They forgot that God had led them out of Egypt, that He had kept them safe in the dangers of the desert, that He had given them water out of the rock, bread from the sky, and His law from the mountain.

All that night, after the spies had returned with their report, the people were so frightened that they could not sleep. They cried out against Moses and blamed him for bringing them out of the land of Egypt. They forgot all their troubles in Egypt, their toil, and their slavery and resolved to go back to that land. They said:

"Let us choose a ruler in place of Moses, who has brought us into all these evils, and let us turn back to the land of Egypt!"

But Caleb and Joshua said, "Why should we fear? The land of Canaan is good. It is rich with milk and honey. If God is our friend and with us, we can easily conquer the people there. Above all things, let us not rebel against the Lord or disobey Him and make Him our enemy."

But the people were so angry with Caleb and Joshua that they were ready to stone them and kill them. Then suddenly the people saw a strange sight. The glory of the

Lord, which stayed in the Holy of Holies, the inner room of the Tabernacle, now flashed out and shone from the door of the Tabernacle.

And the Lord spoke to Moses out of this glory and said, "How long will this people disobey Me and despise Me? They shall not go into the good land that I have promised them. Not one of them shall enter except Caleb and Joshua, who have been faithful to Me. All the people who are twenty years old and over shall die in the desert, but their little children shall grow up in the wilderness, and when they become men, they shall enter in and own the land that I promised to their fathers. You, people, are not worthy of the land I have kept for you. Now turn back into the desert and stay there until you die. After you are dead, Joshua shall lead your children into the land of Canaan. And because Caleb showed another spirit, was true to me, and followed my will fully, Caleb shall live to go into the land and have his choice of a home there. Tomorrow, turn back into the desert by way of the Red Sea."

And God told Moses that for every day the spies had spent in Canaan looking at the land, the people would spend a year in the wilderness so that they would live in the desert for forty years instead of going at once into the Promised Land.

When Moses told all God's words to the people, they felt worse than before. They changed their minds as suddenly as they had made up their minds.

"No," they said, "we will not return to the wilderness. We will go straight into the land and see if we can take it, as Joshua and Caleb have said."

"You must not go into the land," said Moses.

But the people would not obey. They marched up the mountain and tried to march at once into the land. But they were without leaders and order—a mob of men, untrained and confused. And the people in that part of the land, the Canaanites and the Amorites came down upon them, killed many of them, and drove them away. Then, discouraged and beaten, they obeyed the Lord and Moses and went again into the desert.

And in the desert of Paran, on the south of the land of Canaan, the children of Israel stayed nearly forty years, all because they had refused to trust in the Lord.

The Grapes of Canaan,
by James Tissot (c.1896-1902)

Lesson Two

History Overview and Assignments
An Army of Three Hundred

"One day, a man named Gideon was threshing wheat in a hidden place when he saw an angel sitting under an oak tree. The angel said, 'You are a brave man, Gideon, and the Lord is with you. Go out boldly, and save your people from the power of the Midianites.'

Gideon answered the angel, 'O, Lord, how can I save Israel? Mine is a poor family in Manasseh, and I am the least in my father's house.'

The angel said to him, 'Surely I will be with you, and I will help you drive out the Midianites.'"

– from the adapted article below

Gideon and His Three Hundred, as in Judges 7:9-23.
Illustration from a Bible card published by the Providence Lithograph Company in 1907

Suggested Reading and Assignments

- Read the article: *The Story of Gideon and His Three Hundred Soldiers*.
- After reading the article, summarize the story you read by either:
    - Retelling it out loud to your teacher or parent.
        OR
    - Completing an appropriate notebook page.

  Either way, be sure to include the answers to the discussion questions and an overview of key people, places, dates, and events in your summary.

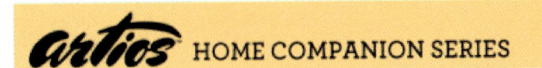

Ancient: Elementary
Unit 11: The Promised Land

- Explore the websites about Gideon found at the URLs on your **ArtiosHCS** curriculum website.
- Be sure to visit your **ArtiosHCS** curriculum website for additional resources and any videos and websites assigned for this lesson.

Key People, Places, and Events

Baal   Ephraim   Manasseh   Gideon

Discussion Questions

1. After the Israelites came into Canaan, how did they worship? Did they worship the true God?
2. How did God judge their disobedience?
3. Who was Gideon, and how did God speak to him?
4. How did Gideon respond?
5. What was the difference between Gideon's response and how most of Israel responded to God?
6. What did the people of Gideon's village want to do to Gideon because he had destroyed the image of Baal? Who was Baal?
7. What was the response of Joash?
8. Why did God want Gideon's army to be smaller?
9. How did he reduce its size?
10. Describe how Gideon and his army won the battle.

Adapted for Elementary School from the book:
The Wonder Book of Bible Stories
Arranged by Logan Marshall
The Story of Gideon and His Three Hundred Soldiers

At last, the people of Israel came into the Promised Land, where God granted them miraculous victories over Jericho and other idolatrous cultures. The land was divided among the Israelite tribes. But the people did evil in the sight of the Lord by adopting the worship of **Baal**, and the Lord left them to suffer for their sins. In time the Midianites, living near the desert in the east of Israel, came against the tribes. The two tribes that suffered the hardest fate were **Ephraim** and the part of **Manasseh** that lived west of Jordan. For seven years, the Midianites swept over their land every year, just at the time of harvest, and carried away all their grain crops until the Israelites had no food for themselves or their sheep and cattle. The Midianites also brought their flocks and camels without number, which ate all the grass of the field.

The people of Israel were driven away from their villages and farms and were compelled to hide in the caves of the mountains. And if any Israelite could raise any grain, he buried it in pits covered with earth or empty winepress pits, where the Midianites could not find it.

One day, a man named **Gideon** was threshing wheat in a hidden place when he saw an angel sitting under an oak tree. The angel said to him, "You are a brave man, Gideon, and the Lord is with you. Go out boldly, and save your people from the power of the Midianites."

Gideon answered the angel, "O, Lord, how can I save Israel? Mine is a poor family in Manasseh, and I am the least in my father's house."

The angel said to him, "Surely I will be with you, and I will help you drive out the Midianites."

Gideon felt that the Lord was talking with him in the form of an angel. He brought an offering and laid it on a rock before the angel. Then the angel touched the offering with his staff. At once a fire leaped up and burned the offering, and the angel vanished from his sight. Gideon was afraid when he saw this, but the Lord said, "Peace be unto you, Gideon, do not fear, for I am with you."

The angel of the Lord appears to Gideon, from *The Story of the Bible From Genesis to Revelation* (1873)

On the spot where the Lord appeared to Gideon, under an oak tree, near the village of Ophrah, in the tribe land of Manasseh, Gideon built an altar and called it by a name that means: "The Lord is peace." This altar was standing long afterward in that place.

Then the Lord told Gideon that before setting his people free from the Midianites, he must first set them free from the service of Baal and Asherah, the two idols most worshiped among them. Near the house of Gideon's father stood an altar to Baal and the image of Asherah.

That night, Gideon went out with ten men and threw down the image of Baal, cut the wooden image of Asherah in pieces, and destroyed the altar before these idols. And in its place, he built an altar to the God of Israel, and on it, he laid the broken pieces of the idols for wood, and with them offered a young ox as a burnt offering.

On the following day, when the people of the village went out to worship their idols, they found them cut in pieces, the altar taken away; in its place, an altar of the Lord, and on it, the pieces of the Asherah were burning as wood under a sacrifice to the Lord. The people looked at the broken and burning idols and said, "Who has done this?"

Someone said, "Gideon, the son of Joash, did this last night."

Then they came to Joash, Gideon's father, and said, "We are going to kill your son because he has destroyed the image of Baal, who is our god."

And Joash, Gideon's father, said, "If Baal is a god, he can take care of himself and punish the man who has destroyed his image. Why should you help Baal? Let Baal help himself."

And when they saw that Baal could not harm the man who had broken down his altar and his image, the people turned from Baal to their Lord God.

Gideon sent messengers through all of Manasseh on the west of Jordan, and the tribes near on the north, and the men of the tribes gathered around him with a few swords and spears, but very few, for the Israelites were not ready for war. They met beside a great spring on Mount Gilboa, called "the fountain of Harod." Mount Gilboa is one of the three mountains on the east of the Plain of Esdraelon, or the Plain of Jezreel, where once there had been a great battle. On the plain, stretching up the side of another of these mountains, called "the Hill of Moreh," was the camp of a vast Midianite army. For as soon as the Midianites heard that Gideon had undertaken to set his people free, they came against him with a mighty host.

Gideon was a man of faith. He wished to be sure that God was leading him, and he prayed to God and said, "O Lord God, give me some sign that Thou wilt save Israel through me. Here is a fleece of wool on this threshing floor. If tomorrow morning the fleece is wet with dew, while the grass around it is dry, then I shall know that Thou art with me and that Thou wilt give me victory over the Midianites."

Very early the following day, Gideon came to look at the fleece. He found it wringing wet with dew while all around the grass was dry. But Gideon was not yet satisfied. He said to the Lord, "O Lord, be not angry with me; give me just one more sign. Tomorrow morning let the fleece be dry and let the dew fall all around it, and then I will doubt no more."

The next morning, Gideon found the grass and the bushes wet with dew while the fleece of wool was dry. And Gideon was now sure that God had called him and would give him victory over the enemies of Israel.

The Lord said to Gideon, "Your army is too large. If Israel won, they would say, 'We won it by our might.' Send home all those who are afraid to fight."

Many of the people were frightened as they looked at the host of their enemies, and the Lord knew that these men would only hinder the rest in the battle. So Gideon sent word through the camp:

"Whoever is afraid of the enemy may go home." And twenty-two thousand people went away, leaving only ten thousand in Gideon's army. But the army was stronger though smaller, for the cowards had gone, and only the brave men were left.

But the Lord said to Gideon, "The people are yet too many. You need only a few of the bravest and best men to fight in this battle. Bring the men down the mountain, past the water, and I will show you how to find the men you need."

In the morning, by God's command, Gideon called his ten thousand men out and made them march down the hill, just as though they were going to attack the enemy. And as they were beside the water, he noticed how they drank and set them apart in two companies, according to their way of drinking.

When they came to the water, most men threw aside their shields and spears, knelt, and scooped up a draft of the water with both hands like a cup—these men Gideon commanded to stand in one company.

A few men did not stop to take a large draft of water. Holding a spear and shield in the right hand to be ready for the enemy if one should suddenly appear, they merely caught up a handful of the water in passing and marched on, lapping it from one hand. God said to Gideon:

"Set by themselves these men who lapped up the water. These are the men whom I have chosen to set Israel free."

Gideon counted these men and found only three hundred of them while all the rest bowed down on their faces to drink. The difference between them may have been that the three hundred were earnest men of one purpose, not turning aside from their aim even to drink as the others did. Then, too, they were watchful men, always ready to meet their enemies.

So Gideon, at God's command, sent back to the camp on Mount Gilboa all the rest of his army, nearly ten thousand men, keeping with himself only his little band of three hundred.

Gideon's plan did not need a large army, but it required a small number of careful, bold men who should do exactly as their leader commanded them. He gave each man a lamp, pitcher, and trumpet and told the men what was to be done with them. The lamp was lighted but placed inside the pitcher so it could not be seen. He divided his men into three companies, very quietly led them down the mountain in the middle of the night, and arranged them all in order around the camp of the Midianites.

Then at one moment, a great shout rang out in the darkness, "The sword of the Lord and of Gideon," After it came a crash of breaking pitchers and a flash of light in every direction. The three hundred men had shouted, and broken their pitchers, so lights shone on every side. The men blew their trumpets with a mighty noise; the Midianites were roused from sleep to see enemies all around them, lights beaming and swords flashing, while the sharp sound of the trumpets was heard everywhere.

They were filled with sudden terror and thought only of escape, not of fighting. But wherever they turned, their enemies stood with swords drawn. They trampled each other down to death, flying from the Israelites. Their land was in the east, across the river Jordan, and they fled in that direction, down one of the valleys between the mountains.

Gideon had thought that the Midianites would turn toward their land if they should be beaten in the battle, and he had already planned to cut off their flight. He had placed the ten thousand men in the camp on the sides of the valley leading to the Jordan. They slew many Midianites as they fled down the steep pass toward the river. And Gideon had also sent to the men of the tribe of Ephraim, who had thus far taken no part in the war, to hold the only place at the river where men could wade through the water. Those of the Midianites who had escaped from Gideon's men on either side of the valley were now met by the Ephraimites at the river, and many more of them were slain. Among the slain were two of the Midianites princes, Oreb and Zeeb.

A part of the Midianite army was able to get across the river and continue its flight toward the desert. Still, Gideon and his brave three hundred men followed closely after them, fought another battle with them, destroyed them utterly, and took their two kings, Zebah and Zalmunna, whom he killed. After this great victory, the Israelites were freed forever from the Midianites. They never again ventured to leave their home in the desert to make war on the tribes of Israel.

After this, as long as Gideon lived, he ruled as Judge in Israel. The people wished him to make himself a king.

"Rule over us as king," they said, "and let your son be king after you and his son king after him."

But Gideon said, "No, you have a king already; for the Lord God is the King of Israel. No one but God shall be king over these tribes."

Of all the fifteen men who ruled as Judges of Israel, Gideon, the fifth judge, was the greatest in courage, wisdom, and faith in God.

Lesson Three

History Overview and Assignments
Made Weak by a Haircut

"Samson did much to set his people free, but he might have done much more if he had led his people under God's direction instead of trusting in his own strength and if he had lived more earnestly and not done his deeds as though he was playing pranks. Samson had deep faults, but in the end, he sought God's help and found it, and God used Samson to set His people free."

— from the adapted article below

Samson and Delilah, by Lucas Cranach the Younger (1537)

Suggested Reading and Assignments

- Read the article: *The Story of Samson, the Strong Man*.
- After reading the article, summarize the story you read by either:
  - Retelling it out loud to your teacher or parent.
    OR
  - Completing an appropriate notebook page.

  Either way, be sure to include the answers to the discussion questions and an overview of key people, places, dates, and events in your summary.
- Be sure to visit your **ArtiosHCS** curriculum website for additional resources and any videos and websites assigned for this lesson.

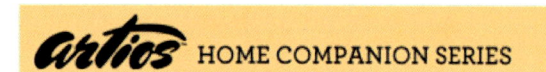

Key People, Places, and Events

Samson

Discussion Questions

1. At this time, Israel did not have a king. How did God rule Israel through people during these years?
2. What sin did the Israelites return to once again?
3. Describe what God told Samson's mother about his life.
4. What riddle did Samson tell at his wedding celebration?
5. Whom did Samson marry? Why were his parents unhappy about this?
6. Who was the second woman Samson loved? How did she betray him?
7. List the steps of disobedience that Samson followed that led to his destruction.

Adapted for Elementary School from the book:
The Wonder Book of Bible Stories
Arranged by Logan Marshall
The Story of Samson, the Strong Man

Three judges who led Israel were named Ibzan, Elon, and Abdon. None of these were men of war, and the land was quiet in their days.

But the people of Israel again began to worship idols. As a punishment, God allowed them once more to fall under the power of their enemies. The seventh oppression which now fell upon Israel was by far the hardest, the longest, and the most widely spread of any, for it was over all the tribes. It came from the Philistines, a strong and warlike people living west of Israel on the plain beside the Great Sea. They worshiped an idol called Dagon, made as a fish's head on a man's body.

These people, the Philistines, sent their armies up from the plain beside the sea to the mountains of Israel and overran all the land. They took away from the Israelites all their swords and spears so they could not fight, and they robbed their land of all the crops, so the people suffered for lack of food. And as before, the Israelites in their trouble cried out to the Lord, and the Lord heard their prayer.

In the tribe land of Dan, next to the country of the Philistines, there was a man named Manoah. One day an angel came to his wife and said, "You shall have a son, and when he grows up, he will begin to save Israel from the hand of the Philistines. But your son must never drink wine or strong drinks as long as he lives. And his hair must be allowed to grow long and must never be cut, for he shall be a Nazarite under a vow to the Lord."

When a child was given especially to God, or when a man presented himself to some work for God, he was forbidden to drink wine, and as a sign, his hair was left to grow long while the vow or promise to God was upon him. Such a person as this was called a Nazarite, a word which means "one who has a vow,"; and Manoah's child was to be a Nazarite, and under a vow, as long as he lived.

The child was born and was named

Samson. He grew up to become the strongest man whom the Bible tells about. Samson was no general, like Gideon or Jephthah, to call out his people and lead them into war. He did much to free his people, but all he did was by his own strength.

When Samson became a young man, he went down to Timnath, in the land of the Philistines. There he saw a young Philistine woman he loved and wished to have as his wife. His father and mother were not pleased that he should marry among the enemies of his people. They did not know that God would make this marriage the means of bringing harm upon the Philistines and of helping the Israelites.

Samson Rending the Lion, by Albrecht Dürer (c.1497)

As Samson was going down to Timnath to see this young woman, a hungry lion came out of the mountain, roaring against him. Samson seized the lion and tore him in pieces as easily as another man would have killed a little kid of the goats and then went on his way. He visited and came home but said nothing to anyone about the lion.

After a time, Samson returned to Timnath for his marriage to the Philistine woman. On his way, he stopped to look at the dead lion, and in its body, he found a swarm of bees and honey which they had made. He took some of the honey and ate it as he walked but told no one of it.

Many Philistine young men amused each other with questions and riddles at the wedding feast, which lasted a whole week.

"I will give you a riddle," said Samson. "If you answer it during the feast, I will give you thirty suits of clothing; and if you cannot answer it, you must give me the thirty suits of clothing."

"Let us hear your riddle," they said.

And this was Samson's riddle: "Out of the eater came forth meat, and out of the strong came something sweet."

They could not find the answer, though they tried all that day and the following days. And at last, they came to Samson's wife and said, "Coax your husband to tell you the answer. If you do not find it out, we will set your house on fire and burn you and all your people."

And Samson's wife urged him to tell her the answer. She cried and pleaded with him and said, "If you really loved me, you would not keep this a secret from me."

At last, Samson yielded, told his wife how he had killed the lion, and found the honey in its body. She told her people, and just before the end of the feast, they came to Samson with the answer. They said, "What is sweeter than honey? And what is stronger than a lion?"

And Samson said to them, "If you had

not plowed with my heifer, you would not have found out my riddle."

By his "heifer"— a young cow—of course, Samson meant his wife. Then Samson was required to give them thirty suits of clothing. He went out among the Philistines, killed the first thirty men he found, took off their clothes, and gave them to the guests at the feast. But all this made Samson very angry. He left his wife and went home to his father's house. Then the parents of his wife gave her to another man.

But after a time, Samson's anger passed away, and he returned to Timnath to see his wife. But her father told him, "You went away angry, and I supposed you cared nothing for her. I gave her to another man, and now she is his wife. But here is her younger sister; you can have her for your wife instead."

But Samson would not take his wife's sister. He went out very angry, determined to harm the Philistines because they had cheated him. Samson caught all the wild foxes he could find until he had three hundred of them. Then he tied them together in pairs, by their tails, and between each pair of foxes, he secured a piece of dry wood to their tails which he set on fire and turned them loose among the fields of the Philistines when the grain was ripe. They ran wildly over the fields, set the grain on fire, and burned it, and with the grain, the olive trees in the fields.

When the Philistines saw their harvests destroyed, they said, "Who has done this?"

And the people said, "Samson did this because his wife was given by her father to another man."

The Philistines looked at Samson's father-in-law as the cause of their loss, and they came and set his home on fire and burned the man and his daughter whom Samson had married. Then Samson came down again and alone fought a company of Philistines and killed them all as a punishment for burning his wife.

After this, Samson lived in a hollow place in a split rock called the Rock of Etam. The Philistines came up in a great army and overran the fields in the tribal land of Judah.

"Why do you come against us?" asked the men of Judah. "What do you want from us?"

"We have come," they said, "to bind Samson and to deal with him as he has dealt with us."

The men of Judah said to Samson, "Do you not know that the Philistines are ruling over us? Why do you make them angry by killing their people? You see that we suffer through your pranks. Now we must bind you and give you to the Philistines, or they will ruin us all."

And Samson said, "I will let you bind me if you promise not to kill me yourselves, but only to give me safely into the hands of the Philistines."

They made the promise, and Samson gave himself up to them and allowed them to tie him up fast with new ropes. The Philistines shouted for joy as they saw their enemy brought to them, led in bonds by his people. But as soon as Samson came among them, he burst the bonds as though they had been light strings; he picked up a donkey's jawbone from the ground and struck right and left with it as with a sword. He killed almost a thousand of the Philistines with this strange weapon.

Afterward, he sang a song about it:
*"With the jawbone of a donkey,
heaps upon heaps,
With the jawbone of a donkey,
have I slain a thousand men."*

After this, Samson went down to the chief city of the Philistines, which was named Gaza. It was a large city; like all large cities, it was surrounded by a high wall. When the men of Gaza found Samson in their city, they shut the gates, thinking they could now hold him as a prisoner. But in the night, Samson rose, went to the gates, pulled their posts out of the ground, and put the gates with their posts upon his shoulder. He carried off the gates of the city and left them on the top of a hill not far from the city of Hebron.

After this, Samson saw another woman among the Philistines and loved her. The name of this woman was Delilah. The rulers of the Philistines came to Delilah and said to her:

"Find out what makes Samson so strong, and tell us. If you help us control him to have him in our power, we will give you a great sum of money."

And Delilah coaxed and pleaded with Samson to tell her what made him so strong. Samson told her, "If they tie me with seven green twigs from a tree, then I shall not be strong anymore."

They brought her seven green twigs, like those of a willow tree, and she bound Samson with them while he was asleep. Then she called him, "Wake up, Samson, the Philistines are coming against you!"

And Samson rose up, broke the twigs as easily as if they had been charred in the fire, and went away easily.

And Delilah tried again to find his secret. She said, "You are only making fun of me. Now tell me truly how you can be bound."

And Samson said, "Let them bind me with new ropes that have never been used before, and then I cannot get away."

While Samson was asleep again, Delilah bound him with new ropes. Then she called out as before, "Get up, Samson, for the Philistines are coming!" And when Samson rose, the ropes broke as if they were thread.

And Delilah again urged him to tell her, and he said, "You notice that my long hair is in seven locks. Weave it together in the loom as if it were the threads in a piece of cloth."

Then, while he was asleep, she wove his hair in the loom and fastened it with a large pin to the weaving frame. But when he awoke, he rose and carried away the pin and the beam of the weaving frame, for he was as strong as before.

And Delilah, who was anxious to serve her people, said, "Why do you tell me that you love me, as long as you deceive me and keep from me your secret?"

And she pleaded with him day after day until, at last, he yielded to her and told her the real secret of his strength. He said, "I am a Nazarite, under a vow to the Lord not to drink wine and not to allow my hair to be cut. If I should let my hair be cut short, then the Lord would forsake me, and my strength would go from me, and I would be like other men."

Then Delilah knew that she had found the truth at last. She sent for the rulers of the Philistines, saying, "Come up this once, and you shall have your enemy; for he has told me all that is in his heart."

Then, while the Philistines watched outside, Delilah let Samson sleep with his head on her knees. While he was sound asleep, they took a razor and shaved off all his hair. Then she called out as at other times, "Rise, Samson, the Philistines are upon you."

He awoke and rose, expecting to find himself strong as before; for he did not at first know that his long hair had been cut off. But the vow to the Lord was broken, and the Lord had left him. He was now as weak as other men and helpless in the hands of his enemies. The Philistines quickly made him their prisoner, and that he might never do them more harm, they put out his eyes. Then they chained him with fetters and sent him to prison in Gaza. And in prison, they made Samson turn a heavy millstone to grind grain, just as though he were a beast of burden.

But while Samson was in prison, his hair grew long again; with his hair, his strength returned to him; for Samson renewed his vow to the Lord.

One day, the Philistines held a great feast in the temple of their fish god, Dagon. For they said:

"Our god has given Samson, our enemy, into our hand. Let us be glad together and praise Dagon."

And the temple was thronged with people, and the roof over it was also crowded with more than three thousand men and women. They sent for Samson to rejoice over him, and Samson was led into the temple court before all the people to amuse them. After a time, Samson said to the boy who was leading him:

"Take me up to the front of the temple so I may stand by one of the pillars and lean against it."

And while Samson stood between the two pillars, he prayed, "O Lord God, remember me, I pray thee, and give me strength, only this once, O God, and help me, that I may obtain vengeance upon the Philistines for my two eyes!"

Then he placed one arm around the pillar on one side and the other arm around the pillar on the other and said, "Let me die with the Philistines."

And he bowed forward with all his might, and pulled the pillars over with him, bringing down the roof and all upon it upon those under it. Samson himself was among the dead, but in his death, he killed more of the Philistines than he had killed during his life.

An etching of Samson, from an 1882 German Bible

Then in the terror which came upon the Philistines, the men of Samson's tribe came down, found his dead body, and buried it in their land. After that, it was years before the Philistines tried again to rule over the Israelites.

Samson did much to set his people free, but he might have done much more if he had led his people under God's direction instead of trusting in his own strength and if he had lived more earnestly and not done his deeds as though he was playing pranks. There were deep faults in Samson, but in the end, he sought God's help and found it, and God used Samson to set His people free.

Lesson Four

History Overview and Assignments
"Entreat Me Not to Leave Thee"

"Then Orpah kissed Naomi and returned to her people, but Ruth would not leave her. She said, 'Do not ask me to leave you, for I never will. Where you go, I will go; where you live, I will live; your people shall be my people; and your God shall be my God. Where you die, I will die and be buried. Nothing but death itself shall part you and me.'"

– from the adapted article below

Gleaners, as in Deuteronomy 24:19-21, watercolor by James Tissot (c.1896-1902)

Suggested Reading and Assignments

- Read the article: *The Story of Ruth, the Gleaner*.
- Define each vocabulary word in the context of the reading. Write the words and their definitions in the vocabulary section of your notebook.
- After reading the article, summarize the story you read by either:
    - Retelling it out loud to your teacher or parent.
        OR
    - Completing an appropriate notebook page.

    Either way, be sure to include the answers to the discussion questions and an overview of key people, places, dates, and events in your summary.
- Watch the video about Ruth on your **ArtiosHCS** curriculum website.
- Be sure to visit your **ArtiosHCS** curriculum website for additional resources and any videos and websites assigned for this lesson.

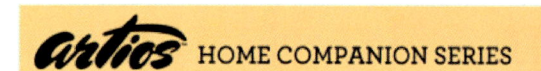

Ancient: Elementary
Unit 11: The Promised Land

Vocabulary

reaper
sickle
sheave

Key People, Places, and Events

Elimelech
Naomi
Orpah
Ruth
Boaz

Discussion Questions

1. Where were Naomi and her family living when her husband Elimelech died?
2. Why did Naomi decide to return to Judah?
3. What did Naomi encourage Orpah and Ruth to do?
4. Describe the relationship between Ruth and Boaz.
5. How did Ruth show her faith and trust in Naomi during these events?

Adapted for Elementary School from the book:
The Wonder Book of Bible Stories
Arranged by Logan Marshall
The Story of Ruth, the Gleaner

In the time of the Judges in Israel, a man named **Elimelech** was living in the town of Bethlehem, in the tribe of Judah, about six miles south of Jerusalem. His wife's name was **Naomi**, and his two sons were Mahlon and Chilion. For some years, the crops were poor, and food was scarce in Judah; and Elimelech, with his family, went to live in the land of Moab, which was on the east of the Dead Sea, as Judah was on the west.

They stayed there for ten years, and Elimelech died at that time. His two sons married women of the country of Moab, one named **Orpah**, the other named **Ruth**. But the two young men also died in the land of Moab, so Naomi and her two daughters-in-law were all left widows.

Naomi heard that God had again given good harvests and bread to the land of Judah, and she rose to go from Moab back to her land and her town of Bethlehem. The two daughters-in-law loved her, and both would have gone with her, though the land of Judah was a strange land to them, for they were of the Moabite people.

Naomi said to them, "Go back, my daughters, to your own mothers' homes. May the Lord deal kindly with you, as you have been kind to your husbands and me. May the Lord grant that each of you may yet find another husband and a happy home."

Then Naomi kissed them in farewell, and the three women wept together. The two young widows said to her, "You have been a good mother to us, and we will go with you and live among your people."

"No, no," said Naomi. "You are young, and I am old. Go back and be happy among your people."

Then Orpah kissed Naomi and returned to her people, but Ruth would not leave her. She said, "Do not ask me to leave you, for I never will. Where you go, I will go; where you live, I will live; your people shall be my people; and your God shall be my God. Where you die, I will die and be buried.

Nothing but death itself shall part you and me."

When Naomi saw that Ruth was firm in her purpose, she ceased trying to persuade her, so the two women went on together. They walked around the Dead Sea, crossed the river Jordan, climbed the mountains of Judah, and came to Bethlehem.

Naomi had been absent from Bethlehem for ten years, but her friends were glad to see her again. They said, "Is this Naomi, whom we knew years ago?"

Now the name Naomi means "pleasant." And Naomi said, "Call me not Naomi; call me Mara, for the Lord has made my life bitter. I went out full with my husband and two sons; now I come home empty, without them."

The name "Mara," by which Naomi wished to be called, means "bitter." But Naomi later learned that "Pleasant" was the right name.

There was a wealthy man named Boaz living in Bethlehem at that time. He owned large fields that were abundant in their harvests, and he was related to the family of Elimelech, Naomi's husband, who had died.

It was the custom in Israel when they reaped the grain not to gather all the stalks but to leave some for the poor people, who followed the **reaper**s with their **sickle**s and gathered what was left. When Naomi and Ruth came to Bethlehem, it was the time of the barley harvest; Ruth went out into the fields to glean the grain the reapers had left. It so happened that she was gleaning in the field that belonged to Boaz, this rich man.

Boaz came out from the town to see his men reaping, and he said to them, "The Lord be with you," and they answered him, "The Lord bless you."

And Boaz said to his master of the reapers, "Who is this young woman that I see gleaning in the field?"

The man answered, "It is the young woman from the land of Moab who came with Naomi. She asked to glean after the reapers and has been here gathering grain since yesterday."

Then Boaz said to Ruth: "Listen to me, my daughter. Do not go to any other field, but stay here with my young women. No one shall harm you, and when you are thirsty, drink at our water vessels."

So Ruth went out into the fields to glean the grain. Then she bowed to Boaz and thanked him for his kindness, all the more kind because she was a stranger in Israel.

Boaz said, "I have heard how true you have been to your mother-in-law Naomi in leaving your land and coming with her to this land. May the Lord, under whose wings you have come, reward you!"

And at noon, when they sat down to rest and eat, Boaz gave her some food. And he said to the reapers, "When you are reaping, leave some of the **sheave**s for her, and drop out some sheaves from the bundles, where she may gather them."

That evening, Ruth showed Naomi how much she had gleaned and told her of the rich man Boaz, who had been so kind to her.

And Naomi said, "This man is a near relation of ours. Stay in his fields as long as the harvest lasts." And so Ruth gleaned in the fields of Boaz until the harvest had been gathered.

At the end of the harvest, Boaz held a feast on the threshing floor. And after the feast, by the advice of Naomi, Ruth went to him and said to him, "You are a near relation of my husband and his father,

Elimelech. Now will you not do good to us for his sake?"

And when Boaz saw Ruth, he loved her. Soon after this, he took her as his wife. And Naomi and Ruth went to live in his home so that Naomi's life was no more bitter but pleasant. And Boaz and Ruth had a son, whom they named Obed. Obed had a son named Jesse, and Jesse was the father of David, the shepherd boy who became king. So Ruth, the young woman of Moab, who chose the people and the God of Israel, became the mother of kings.

Ruth Decides to Go to Bethlehem With Naomi, by Jacob Pynas (by 1650)

Lesson Five

History Overview and Assignments
A Shepherd Boy Faces a Giant

"Seven young men came, and Samuel said, 'None of these is the man whom God has chosen. Are these all your children?'

'There is one more,' said Jesse. 'The youngest of all. He is a boy in the field caring for the sheep.'

And Samuel said, 'Send for him; we will not sit down until he comes.' So after a time, the youngest son was brought in. His name was David, a word that means 'darling,' He was a handsome boy, perhaps fifteen years old, with fresh cheeks and bright eyes.

As soon as the young David came, the Lord said to Samuel, 'Arise, anoint him, for this is the one whom I have chosen.'"

– from the adapted article below

The Triumphant David, by Matteo Rosselli. (1620)

Suggested Reading and Assignments

- Read the article: *The Story of David the Shepherd Boy.*
- After reading the article, summarize the story you read by either:
    - Retelling it out loud to your teacher or parent.
        OR
    - Completing an appropriate notebook page.

  Either way, be sure to include the answers to the discussion questions and an overview of key people, places, dates, and events in your summary.
- Draw a picture of David's encounter with the giant, Goliath.
- Be sure to visit your **ArtiosHCS** curriculum website for additional resources and any videos and websites assigned for this lesson.

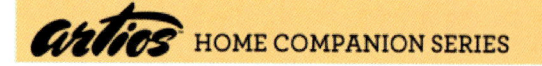

Ancient: Elementary
Unit 11: The Promised Land

Key People, Places, and Events

Samuel
Saul
David
Goliath

Discussion Questions

1. Describe the birth of Samuel.
2. What type of government did Israel desire?
3. Whom did Samuel choose as king?
4. Why did God remove Saul as king?
5. Whom did He choose in his stead?
6. How and why did David come to meet Saul?

Adapted for Elementary School from the book:
The Wonder Book of Bible Stories
Arranged by Logan Marshall
The Story of David, the Shepherd Boy

Living at Ramah, in the mountains of Ephraim, there was a man named Elkanah. He had two wives, as did many men at that time. One of these wives had children, but the other wife, Hannah, had no child.

Every year, Elkanah and his family went up to worship at the Lord's house in Shiloh, about fifteen miles from his home. And at one of these visits, Hannah prayed to the Lord, saying:

"O Lord, if thou wilt look upon me and give me a son, he shall be given to the Lord as long as he lives."

The Lord heard Hannah's prayer and gave her a little boy, and she called his name **Samuel**, which means "Asked of God," because he had been given in answer to her prayer.

Samuel grew up to be a good man and a wise judge, and he made his sons judges in Israel to help him in the care of the people. But Samuel's sons did not walk in his ways. They did not always try to do justly.

The elders of all the tribes of Israel came to Samuel at his home in Ramah and said to him: "You are growing old, and your sons do not rule as well as you ruled. All the lands around us have kings. Let us have a king also; you choose the king for us."

This was not pleasing to Samuel. He tried to make the people change their minds and showed them what trouble a king would bring them.

But they would not follow his advice. They said, "No; we will have a king to reign over us."

So Samuel chose as their king a tall young man named **Saul**, a farmer's son of the tribe of Benjamin. When Saul was brought before the people, he stood head and shoulders above them all. And Samuel said, "Look at the man the Lord has chosen! There is not another like him among all the people!"

And all the people shouted, "God save the King! Long live the King!"

Then Samuel told the people what the laws should be for the King and the people to obey. He wrote them down in a book and placed the book before the Lord. Then Samuel sent the people home, and Saul returned to his own house at Gibeah. With Saul went a company of men to whose hearts God had given a love for the King.

So after three hundred years under the fifteen judges, Israel now had a king. But among the people, some were not pleased with the new king because he was an unknown man from a farm. They said, "Can such a man as this save us?"

They showed no respect to the King and looked down upon him in their hearts. But Saul said nothing and showed his wisdom by not noticing them. But in another thing, he was not so wise. He forgot to heed the old prophet's advice and instructions about ruling wisely and doing as the Lord said. It was not long before Samuel told him he had disobeyed God and would lose his kingdom.

When Samuel told Saul that the Lord would take the kingdom from him, he did not mean that Saul would lose the kingdom immediately. He was no longer God's king; as soon as the right man in God's sight should be found and trained for his duty as king, God would take Saul's power and give it to the man God had chosen. But it was years before this came to pass.

The Lord told Samuel, "Do not weep and mourn any longer over Saul, for I have refused him as king. Fill the horn with oil and go to Bethlehem in Judah. Find a man named Jesse there, for I have chosen a king among his sons."

But Samuel knew that Saul would be outraged if he should learn that Samuel had named any other man as king. He said to the Lord, "How can I go? If Saul hears of it, he will kill me."

The Lord told Samuel, "Take a young cow with you and tell the people that you have come to make an offering to the Lord. And call Jesse and his sons to the sacrifice. I will tell you what to do, and you shall anoint the one whom I name to you."

Samuel went over the mountains southward from Ramah to Bethlehem, about ten miles, leading a cow. The rulers of the town were alarmed at his coming, for they feared that he had come to judge the people for some evildoing. But Samuel said, "I have come in peace to make an offering and to hold a feast to the Lord. Prepare yourselves and come to the sacrifice."

And he invited Jesse and his sons to the service. When they came, he looked at the sons of Jesse very closely. The oldest was named Eliab, and he was so tall and noble-looking that Samuel thought, "Surely this young man must be the one whom God has chosen."

But the Lord said to Samuel, "Do not look on his face, nor the height of his body, for I have not chosen him. Man judges by the outward looks, but God looks at the heart."

Then Jesse's second son, named Abinadab, passed by. And the Lord said, "I have not chosen this one."

The Shepherd David,
by Elizabeth Jane Gardner (c.1895)

Seven young men came, and Samuel

said, "None of these is the man whom God has chosen. Are these all your children?"

"There is one more," said Jesse. "The youngest of all. He is a boy in the field caring for the sheep."

And Samuel said, "Send for him; we will not sit down until he comes." So after a time, the youngest son was brought in. His name was **David**, a word that means "darling," He was a handsome boy, perhaps fifteen years old, with fresh cheeks and bright eyes.

As soon as the young David came, the Lord said to Samuel, "Arise, anoint him, for this is the one whom I have chosen."

Then Samuel poured oil on David's head in the presence of all his brothers. But no one knew the anointing meant that David was to be king. Perhaps they thought that David was chosen to be a prophet like Samuel.

From that time, the Spirit of God came upon David, and he began to show signs of coming greatness. He returned to his sheep on the hillsides around Bethlehem, but God was with him.

David grew up strong and brave, not afraid of the wild beasts which prowled around and tried to carry away his sheep. More than once, he fought with lions and bears and killed them when they seized the lambs of his flock. And David, alone all day, practiced throwing stones in a sling until he could strike exactly the place for which he aimed. When he swung his sling, he knew the stone would go to the very spot he was throwing it.

And young as he was, David thought of God and talked with God, and God spoke with David and showed David His will.

After Saul had disobeyed the voice of the Lord, the Spirit of the Lord left Saul and no longer spoke to him. And Saul became very sad of heart. At times a madness would come upon him, and he was always very unhappy. The servants of Saul noticed that when someone played on the harp and sang, Saul's spirit was more cheerful, and the sadness of his soul left him. Saul once said: "Find someone who can play well, and bring him to me. Let me listen to music; for it drives away my sadness."

One of the young men said, "I have seen a young man, a son of Jesse in Bethlehem, who can play well. He is handsome in his looks and agreeable to talking. I have also heard that he is a brave young man who can fight as well as play, and the Lord is with him."

Then Saul sent a message to Jesse, David's father. He said, "Send me your son David, who is with the sheep. Let him come and play before me."

Then David came to Saul, bringing a present for the King from Jesse. When Saul saw him, he loved him, as did everybody who saw the young David. And David played on the harp and sang before Saul. And David's music cheered Saul's heart and drove away his sad feelings.

Saul liked David so well that he made him his armor-bearer, and David carried the shield, spear, and sword for Saul when the King was before his army. But Saul did not know that Samuel had anointed David.

After a time, Saul seemed well; and David returned to Bethlehem and was once more among his sheep in the field. Perhaps it was at this time that David sang his shepherd song, or it may have been long afterward when David looked back in thought to those days when he was leading his sheep. This is the song that you may have heard often:

"The Lord is my shepherd; I shall not

want. He maketh me to lie down in green pastures; He leadeth me beside the still waters; He restoreth my soul; He leadeth me in the paths of righteousness for his name's sake. Yea, though I walk through the valley of the shadow of death, I will fear no evil; for thou art with me; Thy rod and thy staff, they comfort me. Thou preparest a table before me in the presence of mine enemies; Thou anointest my head with oil; my cup runneth over. Surely goodness and mercy shall follow me all the days of my life: And I will dwell in the house of the Lord forever" (Psalm 23, KJV).

David and Goliath, by Osmar Schindler (1888)

The Story of the Fight With the Giant

All through the reign of Saul, there was constant war with the Philistines, who lived in the lowlands west of Israel. At one time, when David was still with his sheep, a few years after he had been anointed by Samuel, the camps of the Philistines and the Israelites were set against each other on opposite sides of the valley of Elah. In the army of Israel were the three oldest brothers of David.

Every day a giant came out of the camp of the Philistines and dared someone to come from the Israelites' camp and fight with him. The giant's name was **Goliath**. He was nine feet tall. He wore armor from head to foot and carried a spear twice as long and as heavy as any other man could hold, and his shield-bearer walked before him. He came every day and called out across the little valley, "I am a Philistine, and you are servants of Saul. Now choose one of your men and let him come out and fight with me. If I kill him; then you shall submit to us; and if he kills me, then we will give up to you. Come, now, send out your man!"

But no man in the army, not even King Saul, dared to go out and fight with the giant. The camps stood against each other for forty days, and the Philistine giant continued his call.

One day, old Jesse, the father of David, sent David from Bethlehem to visit his three brothers in the army. David came and spoke to his brothers, and while he was talking with them, Goliath, the giant, came out as before in front of the camp, calling for someone to fight with him.

They said one to another, "If any man will go out and kill this Philistine, the King will give him a great reward and a high rank; and the King's daughter shall be his wife."

And David said, "Who is this man that speaks in this proud manner against the armies of the living God? Why does not someone go out and kill him?"

David's brother Eliab said, "What are you doing here, leaving your sheep in the field? I know that you have come down to see the battle."

But David did not care for his brother's words. He thought he saw a way to kill this boasting giant, and he said, "If no one else will go, I will go out and fight with this enemy of the Lord's people."

They brought David before King Saul. Some years had passed since Saul had met David, and he had grown from a boy to a man so that Saul did not know him as the shepherd who had played on the harp before him in earlier days.

Saul said to David, "You cannot fight with this great giant. You are very young, and he is a man of war, trained from his youth."

And David answered King Saul, "I am only a shepherd, but I have fought with lions and bears when they have tried to steal my sheep. And I am not afraid to fight with this Philistine."

Then Saul put his own armor on David—a helmet on his head, a coat of mail on his body, and a sword at his waist. But Saul was almost a giant, and his armor was far too large for David. David said, "I am not used to fighting with such weapons as these. Let me fight in my way."

So David took off Saul's armor. While everybody in the army had been looking at the giant with fear, David had been thinking out the best way to fight him; God had given David a plan. It was to throw the giant off his guard by appearing weak and helpless, and while so far away that the giant could not reach him with a sword or spear, to strike him down with a weapon that the giant would not expect and would not be prepared for.

David took his shepherd's staff in his hand as though that were to be his weapon. But out of sight, in a bag under his mantle, he had five carefully chosen smooth stones and a sling—the weapon he knew how to use. Then he came out to meet the Philistine.

The giant looked down on the youth and despised him - and laughed.

"Am I a dog?" he said, "that this boy comes to me with a staff? I will give his body to the birds of the air and the beasts of the field."

And the Philistine cursed David by the gods of his people. And David answered him, "You come against me with a sword, and a spear, and a dart; but I come to you in the name of the Lord of hosts, the God of the armies of Israel. This day will the Lord give you into my hand. I will strike you down, and take off your head, and the host of the Philistines shall be dead bodies, to be eaten by the birds and the beasts; so that all may know that there is a God in Israel and that He can save in other ways besides with sword and spear."

And David ran toward the Philistine as if to fight him with his shepherd's staff. But when he was near enough for a good aim, he took out his sling and hurled a stone at the giant's forehead. David's aim was good; the stone struck the Philistine in his forehead. It stunned him, and he fell to the ground.

While the two armies stood wondering and scarcely knowing what had caused the giant to fall so suddenly, David ran forward, drew out the giant's sword, and cut off his head. Then the Philistines knew their great warrior, whom they trusted, was dead. They turned to flee to their own land; the Israelites followed after them, killing them by the hundred and the thousand, even to the gates of their own city of Gath.

So by God's hand, David won a great victory on that day, and he stood before all the land as the one who had saved his people from their enemies.

Artios Home Companion Series
Unit 12: Great Kings and Prophets of Israel

Teacher Overview

AFTER THE DEATH of King Saul, David became King of Israel. Said to be "a man after God's own heart," King David tried to please and honor God throughout his life. Although he was sinful like others, David repented with great remorse over his sins, and God blessed him by making him a great and mighty king. His son Solomon, who ruled after him, was granted the great honor of building God's Temple.

After Solomon's death, the nation of Israel split into two kingdoms. The Kingdom of Judah in the south made up of the descendants of David and Solomon in the tribes of Judah and Benjamin, continued to follow God. The Kingdom of Israel in the north, comprised of the other tribes and ruled by ambitious men, kept turning away from God even though God sent prophet after prophet to warn them against this. One of the prophets, named Jonah, was sent by God during this time to preach to the people of Nineveh. Jonah resisted the call, but in the end, he learned a great lesson in obedience.

The Kingdom of Judah was more obedient to God than the Kingdom of Israel, but they were sometimes lured into idolatry and other sins. God allowed them to be invaded by Babylon, and many Jewish people were taken captive. One of them was Daniel, who honored God in the palace of that foreign land despite significant threats of harm.

The Flight of the Prisoners, by James Tissot (c.1896-1902)

Suggested Assignments

Based on your student's age and ability, the reading in this unit may be read aloud to the student, and journaling and notebook pages may be completed orally. Likewise, other assignments may be done with an appropriate combination of independent and guided study.

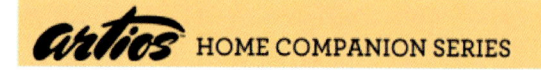

Ancient: Elementary
Unit 12 : Great Kings and Prophets of Israel

In this unit, students will:
- Complete four lessons in which they will learn about **Kings David and Solomon, the Babylonian Empire, Jonah**, and **Daniel**.
- Define vocabulary words.
- Explore the following websites at the URLs found on the **ArtiosHCS** curriculum website.
    - All About Ancient Babylon
    - Interactive website and map about the ancient city of Babylon
    - Read some more about Hammurabi on the websites below
    - Interactive Seven Wonders of the World: Hanging Gardens of Babylon
    - "Story of Jonah" and "Dare to Be a Daniel"
- Visit the **ArtiosHCS** curriculum website at **www.ArtiosHCS.com** for additional resources and any videos and websites assigned for this unit.

Heart Connections

In order to be obedient to God, we must understand his character.

"I prayed to the LORD my God and made confession, saying, 'O Lord, the great and awesome God, who keeps covenant and steadfast love with those who love him and keep his commandments . . .'"

– Daniel 9:4

The testimony of each individual can make a difference in the lives of those around him.

"You are the light of the world. A city set on a hill cannot be hidden; nor does anyone light a lamp and put it under a basket, but on the lampstand, and it gives light to all who are in the house. Let your light shine before men in such a way that they may see your good works, and glorify your Father who is in heaven."

– Matthew 5:14-16

Vocabulary

Lessons 1:	**Lesson 2:**	**Lessons 3:**	**Lessons 4:**
none	decipher	none	none
	squalor		
	maim		

Key People, Places, and Events

Saul	Amorite	Cimmerian	Nineveh
Jonathan	Hammurabi	Scythian	Jehoiakim
David	Babylonian Empire	Chaldean	Daniel
Solomon's Temple	Code of Hammurabi	Ur	Shadrach
Solomon	Hittite	Nebuchadnezzar	Meshach
Adonijah	Assyrian	Persia	Abednego
Sargon the Great	Tiglath Pileser	Jonah	

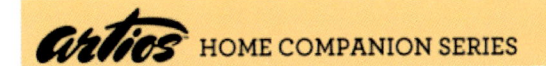

Lesson One

History Overview and Assignments
David and Solomon

"When Saul died, he was followed as king by David, the shepherd boy, now grown to manhood and greatly loved by the people. King David had many battles to fight with the Philistines and was nearly always victorious. He was a warrior king, but he was more than a warrior. He played his harp and composed many beautiful hymns and songs collected in the Book of Psalms. He was a good king and tried to obey God's commands. He had a long reign, and his people were happy and prosperous."

– from the adapted article below

Statue of King David,
by Nicolas Cordier in the Borghese Chapel of the
Basilica di Santa Maria Maggiore

Suggested Reading and Assignments

- Read the combined article: *The Story of the Cave of Adullam* and *The Story of Solomon and His Temple.*
- After reading the article, summarize the story you read by either:
    - Retelling it out loud to your teacher or parent.
      OR
    - Completing an appropriate notebook page.

  Either way, be sure to include the answers to the discussion questions and an overview of key people, places, dates, and events in your summary.
- Be sure to visit your **ArtiosHCS** curriculum website for additional resources and any videos and websites assigned for this lesson.

Key People, Places, and Events

Saul
Jonathan
David
Solomon's Temple
Solomon
Adonijah

Ancient: Elementary
Unit 12 : Great Kings and Prophets of Israel

Discussion Questions

1. Why did David hide in a cave?
2. What cruel act did King Saul commit while trying to find David?
3. Briefly describe King David's reign.
4. Why didn't God permit David to build His Temple?
5. What difficulty did his son Solomon have in becoming king after David?
6. What was King Solomon like?

Adapted for Elementary School from the book:
The Wonder Book of Bible Stories
arranged by Logan Marshall
The Story of the Cave of Adullam ~ and ~
The Story of Solomon and His Temple

King David

Now King **Saul** had a son, **Jonathan**, near David's age. He and David became fast friends and loved one another as brothers. Saul, the king, became very jealous of **David** because the people praised him after his fight with Goliath. He even threatened to take David's life. He tried to catch him in his own house, but David's wife let him down from a window by a rope, and he escaped. He met his friend Jonathan, who told him that he should flee. They renewed their promises of friendship, which they kept ever afterward.

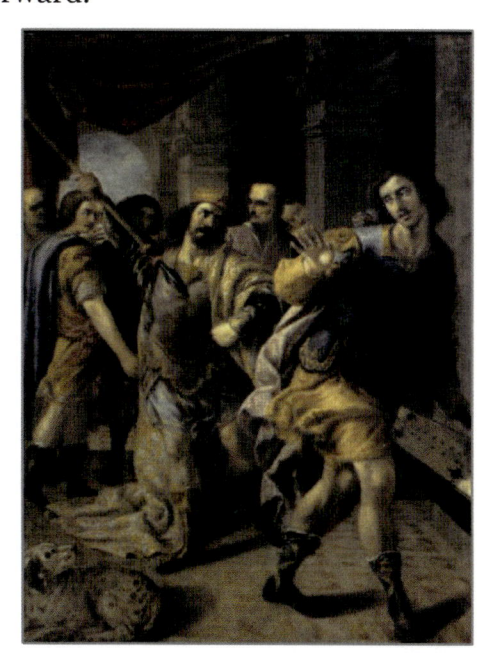

Saul Threatening David, by José Leonardo (1640s)

From his meeting with Jonathan, David went forth to be a wanderer, having no home as long as Saul lived. He found a great cave called the Cave of Adullam and hid in it. Soon people heard where he was, and from all parts of the land, especially from his tribe of Judah, men who were not satisfied with the rule of King Saul gathered around David.

Saul soon heard that David, with a band of men, was hiding among the mountains of Judah and that certain priests were among those who aided him.

This enraged King Saul, and he ordered his guards to kill all the priests. The guards would not obey him, for they felt it was wicked to lay hands upon the priests of the Lord.

But he found one man named Doeg, an Edomite, willing to obey the king. And Doeg the Edomite killed eighty-five men who wore priestly garments.

All through the land went the news of Saul's dreadful deed, and everywhere the people began to turn from Saul and look toward David as the nation's only hope.

When Saul died, he was followed as king by David, the shepherd boy, now grown to manhood and greatly loved by the people.

Ancient: Elementary
Unit 12 : Great Kings and Prophets of Israel

King David had many battles to fight with the Philistines and was nearly always victorious. He was a warrior king, but he was more than a warrior. He played his harp and composed many beautiful hymns and songs collected in the Book of Psalms. He was a good king and tried to obey God's commands. He had a long reign, and his people were happy and prosperous. He had many sons and daughters and beautiful palaces for them to live in.

Solomon and the Plan for the Temple, from a Bible card published by the Providence Lithograph Company

Solomon and His Temple For God

During the later years of David's reign, he laid up great treasures of gold and silver, brass, and iron to build a house to the Lord on Mount Moriah. This house came to be called **Solomon's Temple**, and it was to be made very beautiful, the most beautiful building, and the richest in all the land. David had greatly desired to build this house while he was king of Israel, but God said to him:

"You have been a man of war, fought many battles, and shed much blood. A man of peace shall build my house. When you die, your son **Solomon** shall reign, and he shall have peace and build my house."

So David made ready a great store of precious things for the temple, also stone and cedar to be used in the building. And David said to Solomon, his son: "God has promised that there shall be rest and peace to the land while you are king, and the Lord will be with you, and you shall build a house, where God shall live among His people."

But David had other sons who were older than Solomon, and one of these sons, whose name was **Adonijah**, formed a plan to make himself king. David was now very old and could no longer leave his palace and be seen among the people.

Adonijah gathered his friends; among them were Joab, the army general, and Abiathar, one of the two high priests. They met outside the wall, had a great feast, and were about to crown Adonijah as king when word came to David in the palace. David, though old and feeble, was still wise. He said:

"Let us make Solomon king at once and thus put an end to the plans of these men."

So at David's command, they brought out the mule on which no one but the King was allowed to ride; and they placed Solomon upon it; and with the King's guards, and the nobles, and the great men, they brought the young Solomon down to the valley of Gihon, south of the city.

And Zadok, the priest, took from the Tabernacle the horn filled with holy oil, which was used for anointing or pouring oil on the head of the priests when they were set apart for their work. He poured oil from this horn on the head of Solomon, and then the priests blew the trumpets, and all the people cried aloud, "God save King Solomon!"

All this time, Adonijah, Joab, and their friends were not far away, almost in the same valley, feasting and making merry, intending to make Adonijah king. They heard the sound of the trumpets and the shouting of the people. Joab said: "What is the cause of all this noise and uproar?"

A moment later, Jonathan, the son of Abiathar, came running in. Jonathan said to the men who were feasting:

"Our lord King David has made Solomon king, and he has just been anointed in Gihon; and all the princes, and the heads of the army, are with him, and the people are shouting, 'God save King Solomon!' And David has sent a message to Solomon from his bed, saying, 'May the Lord make your name greater than mine has been! Blessed be the Lord, who has given me a son to sit this day on my throne!'"

When Adonijah and his friends heard this, they were filled with fear. Every man went at once to his house except Adonijah. He hastened to the altar of the Lord, knelt before it, and took hold of the horns on its corners in front. This was a holy place, and he hoped Solomon might have mercy on him. And Solomon said, "If Adonijah will do right and be faithful to me as the king of Israel, no harm shall come to him; but if he does wrong, he shall die."

Then Adonijah came and bowed down before King Solomon and promised to obey him, and Solomon said, "Go to your own house."

David sent for Solomon not long after this, and from his bed, David gave his last advice to Solomon. And soon after that, David died, an old man, having reigned in all forty years, seven years over the tribe of Judah, at Hebron, and thirty-three years over all Israel, in Jerusalem. He was buried in great honor on Mount Zion, and his tomb remained standing for many years.

The outstanding work of Solomon's reign was building the House of God. It was generally called the Temple. It was built on Mount Moriah, one of the hills of Jerusalem. King David had prepared for it by gathering great stores of silver, stone, and cedar wood. The walls were made of stone, and the roof of cedar. Solomon had great ships which visited other lands and brought precious stones and fine wood for the building. Seven years were spent building the Temple, and it was set apart to the worship of God with beautiful ceremonies in which Solomon took part in his robes of state.

King Solomon dedicating the Temple at Jerusalem. Painting by James Tissot or follower (c.1896–1902)

Solomon was indeed a great king, and it was said that he was also the wisest man in all the world. He wrote many wise sayings in the Book of Proverbs and many more that have been lost.

Lesson Two

History Overview and Assignments
Wonder of the World

"This Hammurabi, who lived twenty-one centuries before the birth of Christ, was a fascinating man. He made Babylon the most important town of the ancient world, where learned priests governed using the Code of Hammurabi, a set of laws their great ruler said he had received from the sun god himself, and merchants loved to trade because they treated fairly and honorably."

– from the adapted article below

The Hanging Gardens of Babylon, by Ferdinand Knab (1886)

Suggested Reading and Assignments

- Read the article: *Assyria and Babylonia, the Great Melting Pot.*
- Define each vocabulary word in the context of the reading. Write the words and their definitions in the vocabulary section of your notebook.
- After reading the article, summarize the story you read by either:
    - Retelling it out loud to your teacher or parent.
        OR
    - Completing an appropriate notebook page.
  Either way, be sure to include the answers to the discussion questions and an overview of key people, places, dates, and events in your summary.
- Explore the websites about Babylon and Hammurabi at the URLs found on your **ArtiosHCS** curriculum website.
- Be sure to visit your **ArtiosHCS** curriculum website for additional resources and any videos and websites assigned for this lesson.

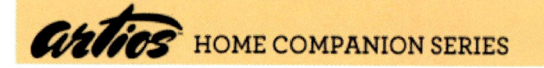

Vocabulary

decipher　　　　　　squalor　　　　　　maim

Key People, Places, and Events

Akkadian
Sargon the Great
Amorite
Hammurabi
Babylonian Empire

Code of Hammurabi
Hittite
Assyrian
Tiglath Pileser
Cimmerian

Scythian
Chaldean
Ur
Nebuchadnezzar
Persia

Discussion Questions

1. Where is Babylonia located on a modern map?
2. List some of the accomplishments of the Babylonians.
3. Which people group conquered Mesopotamia, and who was their ruler?
4. Who was the first ruler of the Babylonian Empire, and for what is he primarily known?
5. Who conquered the region next?
6. Name three things Nebuchadnezzar accomplished during his reign.

Adapted for Elementary School from the book:
Ancient Man: The Beginning of Civilizations
by: Hendrik Willem Van Loon
Assyria and Babylonia, the Great Melting Pot

We often call America the "Melting-pot." When we use this term, we mean that many races from all over the earth have gathered along the banks of the Atlantic and the Pacific Oceans to find a new home and begin new lives. Mesopotamia was indeed much smaller than America. But the fertile valley was the most remarkable "melting pot" the world has ever seen, and it continued to absorb new tribes for almost two thousand years. The story of each new person clamoring for homesteads along the banks of the Tigris and the Euphrates is interesting, but we can only give you a very short record of their adventures.

Hammurabi

The Sumerians we met before, scratching their history upon rocks and bits of clay, were the first nomads to wander into Mesopotamia. Nomads are people who have no settled homes, grain fields, or vegetable gardens but who live in tents, keep sheep and goats and cows, and move from pasture to pasture, taking their flocks and tents wherever the grass is green and the water abundant.

Far and wide, their mud huts had covered the plains. They were good fighters, and for a long time, they could hold their own against all invaders.

But four thousand years ago, a tribe of desert people called the **Akkadian**s left Arabia, defeated the Sumerians, and conquered Mesopotamia. The most famous king of these Akkadians was called **Sargon the Great**.

He taught his people how to write their Semitic language in the alphabet of the Sumerians whose territory they had just occupied. He ruled so wisely that the differences between the original settlers and the invaders soon disappeared, and they became fast friends and lived together in peace and harmony.

The fame of his empire spread rapidly throughout western Asia, and others, hearing of this success, were tempted to try their luck.

A new tribe of desert nomads called the **Amorite**s, broke up camp and moved northward. The valley became the scene of great turmoil until an Amorite chieftain by the name of **Hammurabi** established himself in the town of Bav-Illi (which means the Gate of the God) and made himself the ruler of a great Bav-Illian or **Babylonian Empire**.

Inscription of Hammurabi, King of Babylon,
Source: *A Guide to the Babylonian and Assyrian Antiquities* (Published in 1908)

Hammurabi, who lived twenty-one centuries before the birth of Christ, was a fascinating man. He made Babylon the most crucial town of the ancient world, where learned priests governed using the **Code of Hammurabi**, a set of laws that their great ruler said he had received from the sun god himself, and where merchants loved to trade because they were treated fairly and honorably.

Indeed, if it were not for the lack of space (these laws of Hammurabi would cover fully forty of these pages if I were to give them to you in detail), I would be able to show you that this ancient Babylonian state was in many ways better managed. That law and order were maintained more carefully, and there was greater freedom of speech and thought than in many modern countries.

But our world was never meant to be perfect, and soon other hordes of rough and murderous men descended from the northern mountains and destroyed the work of Hammurabi's genius.

The name of these new invaders was the **Hittite**s. I can tell you even less about these Hittites than the Sumerians. The Bible mentions them. Ruins of their civilization have been found far and wide. They used strange hieroglyphics, but no one has yet been able to **decipher** these and read their meaning. They were not greatly gifted as governors. They ruled for a few years, and then their domains fell to pieces.

Of all their glory, there remains nothing but a mysterious name and the reputation of having destroyed many things which other people had built up with great pain and care.

Then came another very different invasion.

A fierce tribe of desert wanderers, who murdered and pillaged in the name of their chief god Assur, left Arabia and marched northward until they reached the slopes of the mountains. Then they turned eastward, and along the banks of the Euphrates, they built a city called Ninua, a name which has come down to us in the Greek form of Nineveh. At once, these newcomers, generally known as the **Assyrian**s, began a slow but terrible warfare upon all the other inhabitants of Mesopotamia.

In the twelfth century before Christ, they made a first attempt to destroy Babylon, but after a first success on the part of their king,

Tiglath Pileser, they were defeated and forced to return to their own country.

Five hundred years later, they tried again. An adventurous general named Bulu made himself master of the Assyrian throne. He assumed the name of old Tiglath Pileser, who was considered the national hero of the Assyrians, and announced his intention of conquering the whole world.

He was as good as his word.

Asia Minor, Armenia, Egypt, Northern Arabia, Western Persia, and Babylonia became Assyrian provinces. They were ruled by Assyrian governors, who collected taxes and forced all the young men to serve as soldiers in the Assyrian armies. They made themselves thoroughly hated and despised for their greed and cruelty.

Fortunately, the Assyrian Empire at its greatest height did not last very long. It was like a ship with too many masts, sails, and a small hull. There were too many soldiers and not enough farmers.

The King and the nobles grew very rich, but the masses lived in **squalor** and poverty. Never for a moment was the country at peace. It was forever fighting someone, somewhere, for causes that did not interest the subjects at all. Until, through this continuous warfare, most of the Assyrian soldiers had been killed or **maim**ed, and it became necessary to allow foreigners to enter the army. These foreigners had little love for their brutal masters who had destroyed their homes and stolen their children, so they fought badly.

Life along the Assyrian frontier was no longer safe.

Strange new tribes were constantly attacking the northern boundaries. One of these was called the **Cimmerian**s. When we first hear of them, the Cimmerians inhabited the vast plain beyond the northern mountains. The ancient Greek poet Homer describes their country in his account of the voyage of Odysseus and tells us that it was a place "forever steeped in darkness." They had been driven out of their former homes by another group of Asiatic wanderers, the **Scythian**s.

The Scythians were the ancestors of the modern Cossacks who lived in Ukraine and Russia, and even in those remote days, they were famous for their horsemanship.

Nineveh Destroyed

The Cimmerians, hard pressed by the Scythians, crossed from Europe into Asia and conquered the land of the Hittites. Then they left the mountains of Asia Minor and descended into the valley of Mesopotamia, where they made terrible **havoc** among the impoverished people of the Assyrian Empire.

Nineveh called for volunteers to stop this invasion. Her worn-out regiments were marching northward when news of a more immediate danger came.

For many years a small tribe of Semitic nomads called the **Chaldean**s, had been living peacefully in the southeastern part of the fertile valley in the country called **Ur**. Suddenly these Chaldeans had gone upon the warpath and had begun a campaign against the Assyrians.

Attacked from all sides, the Assyrian state, which had never gained the goodwill of a single neighbor, was doomed.

When Nineveh fell and this forbidding treasure house, filled with the plunder of centuries, was destroyed, there was joy in every hut and hamlet from the Persian Gulf to the Nile.

When the Greeks visited the Euphrates a

few generations later and asked what these vast ruins, covered with shrubs and trees, might be, there was no one to tell them.

The people had hastened to forget the very name of the city that had been such a cruel master and had so miserably oppressed them.

Babylon, on the other hand, which had ruled its subjects in a very different way, came back to life.

The ancient temples were rebuilt during the long reign of the wise King Nebuchadnezzar. Vast palaces were built within a short space of time. New canals were dug all over the valley to help irrigate the fields. Quarrelsome neighbors were severely punished.

Egypt was reduced to a mere frontier province, and Jerusalem, the capital of the Jews, was destroyed. The holy books of Moses were taken to Babylon, and several thousand Jews were forced to follow the Babylonian king to his capital as hostages to ensure good behavior among those who remained behind in Palestine.

Wonder of the Ancient World

But Babylon was made into one of the seven wonders of the ancient world. Trees were planted along the banks of the Euphrates. Flowers were made to grow upon the many walls of the city, and after a few years, it seemed that a thousand gardens were hanging from the roofs of the ancient town.

As soon as the Chaldeans had made their capital the showplace of the world, they devoted their attention to matters of the mind and spirit. Like all desert folk, they were deeply interested in the stars which had guided them safely through the trackless desert at night. They studied the heavens and named the twelve signs of the Zodiac.

They made maps of the sky, and they discovered the first five planets. To these, they gave the names of their gods. When the Romans conquered Mesopotamia, they translated the Chaldean names into Latin, which explains why today we talk of Jupiter, Venus, Mars, Mercury, and Saturn.

They divided the equator into three hundred and sixty degrees, the day into twenty-four hours, and the hour into sixty minutes—and no modern man has ever been able to improve upon this old Babylonian invention. They possessed no watches, but they measured time by the sundial's shadow.

They learned to use the decimal (based on the number ten) and the duodecimal (based on twelve) systems. The duodecimal system accounts for the sixty minutes, sixty seconds, and twenty-four hours into which our days are divided.

The Chaldeans also saw the need for a regular day of rest. When they divided the year into weeks, they ordered six days of labor to be followed by one day devoted to the "peace of the soul."

The Persians

It was a pity that the center of so much intelligence and industry could not exist forever. But not even the genius of some wise kings could save the ancient people of Mesopotamia from their ultimate fate.

It was time for a new civilization.

In the fifth century before Christ, an Indo-European people called the **Persian**s left their pastures amidst the high mountains of Iran and conquered the fertile valley.

The city of Babylon was captured

without a struggle. Nabonidus, the last Babylonian king, who had been more interested in religious problems than defending his own country, fled. A few days later, his small son, who had remained behind, died.

Cyrus, the Persian king, buried the child with great honor and then proclaimed himself the legitimate successor of the old rulers of Babylonia.

Mesopotamia ceased to be an independent state. It became a Persian province ruled by a Persian "satrap," or governor.

As for Babylon, when the kings no longer used the city as their residence, it soon lost all importance and became a mere country village.

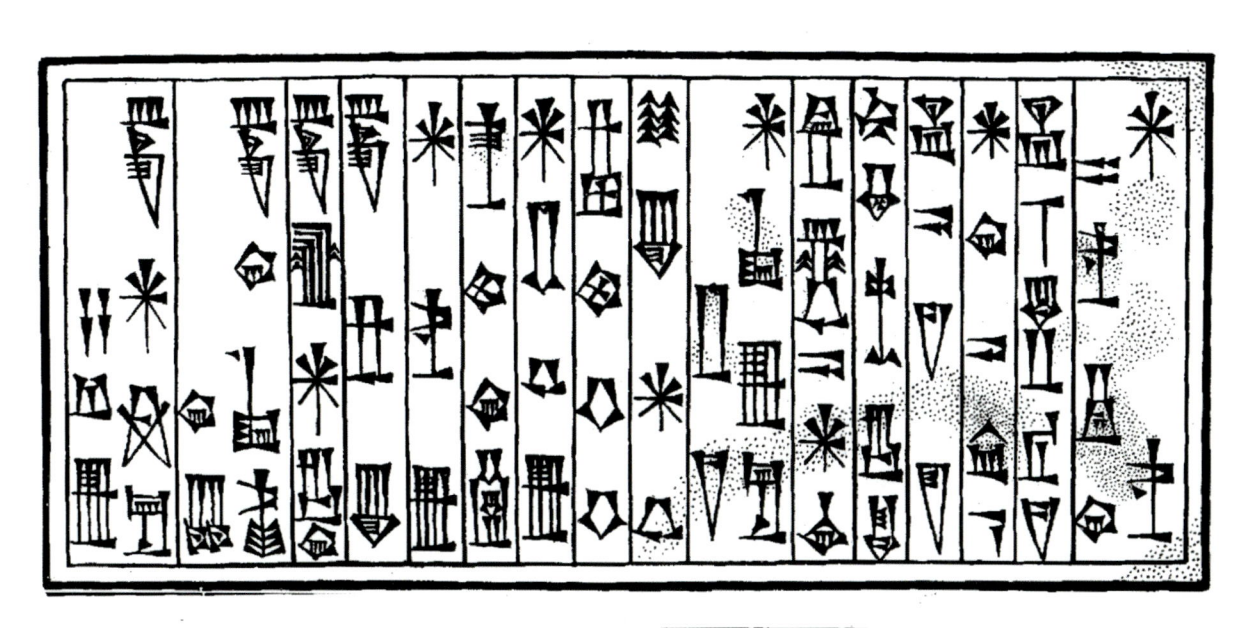

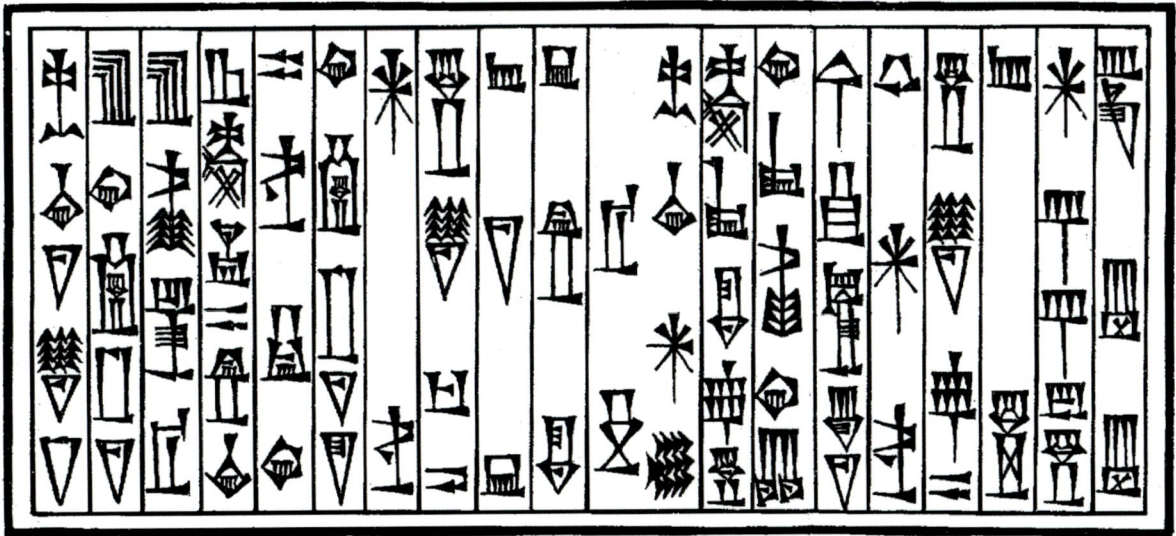

Hammurabi tablet, British Museum 90939. Complete transcription of the obverse and reverse of the tablet, with the name of Hammurabi appearing in the 5th column from the start (top right corner)

Lesson Three

History Overview and Assignments
A Whale of a Tale

"They asked him, 'What shall we do to you, that the storm may cease?' Then said Jonah, 'Take me up and throw me into the sea. Then the storm will cease, and the waters will be calm, for I know that for my sake, this great tempest is upon you.'"

– from the adapted article below

Suggested Reading and Assignments

- Read the article: *The Story of Jonah*.
- After reading the article, summarize the story you read by either:
    - Retelling it out loud to your teacher or parent.
        OR
    - Completing an appropriate notebook page.

    Either way, be sure to include an overview of key people, places, dates, and events in your summary.
- Draw a series of pictures telling the story of Jonah.
- Watch the video about Jonah found on your ArtiosHCS curriculum website
- Be sure to visit your **ArtiosHCS** curriculum website for additional resources and any videos and websites assigned for this lesson.

Key People, Places, and Events

Jonah
Nineveh

Jonah, as in Jonah 2:10,
"And the Lord commanded the fish, and it vomited Jonah onto dry land."
Watercolor by James Tissot (c.1896–1902)

Ancient: Elementary
Unit 12 : Great Kings and Prophets of Israel

Adapted for Elementary School from the book:
The Wonder Book of Bible Stories
Arranged by Logan Marshall
The Story of Jonah and the Whale

A prophet named **Jonah** was called to give the word of the Lord to the Israelites. The Israelites were hardhearted and resisted the calls to repent. The Lord then spoke to Jonah, saying, "Go to **Nineveh**, that great city, and preach to it, for its wickedness rises before Me."

But Jonah did not wish to preach to the people of Nineveh. This may have been because they were Assyrians, enemies of his land, the land of Israel. He may have wished Nineveh to die in its sins and not to turn to God and live. So Jonah tried to escape going to the city where God had sent him. He went down to Joppa and took a ship for Tarshish.

But the Lord had plans for some of the people from idolatrous lands. He also knew that Nineveh would repent and give a good example to the stubborn Israelites. He saw Jonah on the ship and sent a great storm upon the sea so that the ship seemed as though it would go to pieces. The sailors threw overboard everything on board the vessel. And when they could do no more, every man prayed to his god to save the ship and themselves. Jonah was fast asleep, and the ship's captain came to him and said, "What do you mean by sleeping in such a time as this? Awake, rise up, and call upon your God. Perhaps He will hear you and save our lives."

But the storm continued to rage around the ship, and the sailors said, "There is some man on this ship who has brought upon us this trouble. Let us cast lots and find who it is."

Then they cast lots, and the lot fell on Jonah. They asked him all at once, "Tell us, who are you? From what country do you come? What is your business? To what people do you belong? Why have you brought all this trouble upon us?"

Then Jonah told them the whole story, how he came from the land of Israel and had fled away from the presence of the Lord.

They asked him, "What shall we do to you that the storm may cease?"

Then said Jonah, "Take me up and throw me into the sea. Then the storm will cease, and the waters will be calm, for I know that for my sake, this great tempest is upon you."

But the men were not willing to throw Jonah into the sea. They rowed hard to bring the ship to the land but could not. Then they cried unto the Lord and said, "We pray Thee, O Lord, we pray Thee, let us not die for this man's life. For thou, O Lord, hast done as it pleased Thee."

At last, they threw Jonah into the sea when they could do nothing else to save themselves.

At once, the storm ceased, and the waves became still. Then the men on the ship feared the Lord greatly. They offered a sacrifice to the Lord and made promises to serve Him.

The Lord caused a great fish to swallow up Jonah, and Jonah was alive within the fish for three days and three nights. In the fish, Jonah cried to the Lord; and the Lord caused the great fish to throw up Jonah upon the dry land.

Notice throughout this story that, although Jonah was God's servant, he was always thinking about himself. God protected Jonah and saved him, not because he was such a good man, but because he wanted to teach him a great lesson.

By this time, Jonah had learned that some men who worshiped idols were kind in their hearts and were dear to the Lord. This was part of the lesson that God meant Jonah to learn, and now the call of the Lord came to Jonah a second time, "Arise, go to Nineveh, that great city, and preach to it what I command you."

So Jonah went to the city of Nineveh. As he entered it, he called out to the people, "Within forty days shall Nineveh be destroyed."

He walked through the city all day, crying only this, "Within forty days shall Nineveh be destroyed."

The people of Nineveh believed the word of the Lord as spoken by Jonah. They turned away from their sins, fasted, and sought the Lord from the greatest of them, even to the least. The King of Nineveh arose from his throne, laid aside his royal robes, covered himself with sackcloth, and sat in ashes as a sign of his sorrow. And the King commanded his people that they should fast and seek the Lord, and turn from sin.

God saw that the people of Nineveh were sorry for their wickedness, and He forgave them and did not destroy their city. But this made Jonah very angry. He did not wish to have Nineveh spared. He also feared that men would call him a false prophet when his word did not come to pass.

So Jonah said to the Lord, "O Lord, I was sure that it would be thus, that Thou wouldest spare the city, and for that reason, I tried to flee away, for I know that Thou wast a gracious God, full of pity, slow to anger, and rich in mercy. Now, O Lord, take away my life, for it is better for me to die than to live."

Jonah, under his booth, from *The Story of the Bible From Genesis to Revelation* (1873), author unknown

Jonah went out of the city, built a little hut on the east side of it, and sat under its roof to see whether God would keep the word that He had spoken. Then the Lord caused a plant with thick leaves to grow up and shade Jonah from the sun, and Jonah was glad and sat under its shadow. But a worm destroyed the plant; the next day, a hot wind blew, and Jonah suffered from the heat; again, he wished he might die. And the Lord said to Jonah:

"You were sorry to see the plant die, though you did not make it grow, and though it came up in a night and died in a night. And should I not pity Nineveh, that great city, where there are more than a hundred thousand little children and many cattle, all helpless and knowing nothing?"

Then Jonah learned that men, women, and little children are all precious in the sight of the Lord, even though they know not God, for He can turn their hearts toward Him.

Lesson Four

History Overview and Assignments
Standing Firm

"Then the soldiers of the King's army seized the three young Jews as they stood in their loose robes, with their turbans on their heads. They tied them with ropes, dragged them to the mouth of the furnace, and threw them into the fire. The flames rushed from the open door with such fury that they burned to death even the soldiers who were holding these men, while the Jews themselves fell bound into the middle of the fiery furnace."

– from the adapted article below

Daniel and his three friends refusing the King's wine. Early 1900s Bible illustration by Otto Adolph Stemler

Key People, Places, and Events

Jehoiakim
Nebuchadnezzar
Daniel
Shadrach
Meshach
Abednego

Suggested Reading and Assignments

- Read the article: *The Story of the Fiery Furnace*.
- After reading the article, summarize the story you read by either:
    - Retelling it out loud to your teacher or parent.
        OR
    - Completing an appropriate notebook page.
  Either way, be sure to include the answers to the discussion questions and an overview of key people, places, dates, and events in your summary.
- You might enjoy singing along with the children the song inspired by Daniel's life found on your **ArtiosHCS** curriculum website.
- Be sure to visit your **ArtiosHCS** curriculum website for additional resources and any videos and websites assigned for this lesson.

Ancient: Elementary
Unit 12 : Great Kings and Prophets of Israel

Discussion Questions

1. Explain why King Nebuchadnezzar chose Daniel and his three friends.
2. Shadrach, Meshach, and Abednego chose not to obey one of King Nebuchadnezzar's commands. What was the command, and why did they not obey?
3. How did the King punish these men?
4. What miracle did God perform?
5. What happened to the Babylonian Empire after King Nebuchadnezzar died?

Adapted for Elementary School from the book:
The Wonder Book of Bible Stories
Arranged by Logan Marshall
The Story of the Fiery Furnace

After King Solomon died, the Kingdom of the Hebrews split in two. The tribes of Judah and Benjamin remained faithful to the descendants of David and Solomon. This group became known as the Kingdom of Judah. The other ten tribes rebelled and followed other leaders. They called themselves the Kingdom of Israel.

Now there was in Judah a wicked king named **Jehoiakim**, son of the good Josiah. While Jehoiakim ruled the land of Judah, **Nebuchadnezzar**, a great conqueror of the nations, came from Babylon with his army of Chaldean soldiers. He took the city of Jerusalem and made Jehoiakim promise to submit to him as his master. And when he returned to his own land he took with him all the gold and silver that he could find in the Temple, and he carried away as captives many of the princes and nobles, the best people in the land of Judah.

When these Jews were brought to the land of Babylon, King Nebuchadnezzar gave orders to the prince who had charge of his palace to choose among these Jewish captives some young men who were of noble rank, fine to look upon, and quick and bright in their minds—young men who would be able to learn readily. These young men were to be placed under the care of wise men, who should teach them and prepare them to stand before the King of Babylon so that they might be his helpers in carrying out his orders. The King wished them to be wise so they could advise him in ruling his people.

Among the young men thus chosen were four Jews who had been brought from Judah. By order of the King, the names of these men were changed. One of them, named **Daniel**, was to be called Belteshazzer. The other three young men were called **Shadrach**, **Meshach,** and **Abednego**. They were taught all the knowledge of the Chaldeans, and after three years of training, they were taken into the King's palace.

King Nebuchadnezzar was more pleased with them than any others who stood before him. He found them wise and faithful in the work given to them and able to rule over men under them. And these four men came to the highest places in the kingdom of the Chaldeans.

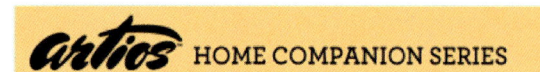

At one time, King Nebuchadnezzar ordered a great image of himself to be made and covered with gold. He set this image up as an idol to be worshiped, on the plain of Dura, near the city of Babylon. When it was finished, it stood upon its base or foundation almost a hundred feet high so that it could be seen from far away upon the plain. Then the King sent out a command for all the princes, rulers, and nobles in the land to come to a great gathering when the image was set apart for worship.

The great men of the kingdom came from far and near and stood around the image. Among them, by command of the King, were Daniel's three friends, the young Jews, Shadrach, Meshach, and Abednego. For some reason, Daniel himself was not there. He may have been busy with the work of the kingdom in some other place.

At one moment in the service, before the image, all the trumpets sounded, the drums were beaten, and music was made upon musical instruments of all kinds to signal all the people to kneel and worship the great golden image. But while the people were kneeling, three men remained standing and would not bow down to it. These were the three young Jews, Shadrach, Meshach, and Abednego. They would kneel only before the Lord God.

Many of the nobles had been jealous of these young men because they had been lifted to high places in the rule of the kingdom. These men who hated Daniel and his friends were glad to find that these three men had not obeyed the command of King Nebuchadnezzar. The King had declared that if anyone did not worship the golden image, he would be thrown into a furnace of fire.

These men who hated the Jews came to the King and said, "O King, may you live forever! You gave orders that when the music sounded, everyone must bow down and worship the golden image and that if any man did not worship it, he should be thrown into a furnace of fire. There are some Jews, whom you have made rulers in the land, who have not done as you commanded. Their names are Shadrach, Meshach, and Abednego. They do not serve your gods or worship the golden image you have set up."

Then Nebuchadnezzar was filled with rage and fury at hearing that anyone should dare to disobey his words. He sent for these three men and said to them, "O Shadrach, Meshach, and Abednego, was it by a purpose that you did not fall down and worship the image of gold? The music shall sound again; if you worship the image, all will be well. But if you will not, you shall be thrown into the furnace of fire to die."

These three young men were not afraid of the King. They replied, "O King Nebuchadnezzar, we will answer you immediately. The God we serve can save us from the fiery furnace, and we know He will save us. But if it is God's will that we should die, even then you may understand, O King, that we will not serve your gods nor worship the golden image."

This answer made the King more furious than before. He told his servants, "Make a fire in the furnace hotter than ever it has been before, as hot as fire can be made, and throw these three men into it."

Then the soldiers of the King's army seized the three young Jews as they stood in their loose robes, with their turbans on their heads. They tied them with ropes, dragged them to the mouth of the furnace, and threw them into the fire. The flames rushed from the open door with such fury that they burned to death, even the soldiers who were holding these men, while the Jews themselves fell, bound, into the middle of the fiery furnace.

King Nebuchadnezzar stood before the furnace and looked into the open door. As he looked, he was filled with wonder at what he saw, and he said to the nobles around him, "Did not we cast three men bound into the midst of the fire? Lo, I see four men loose, walking in the midst of the fire, and they have no hurt; the form of the fourth is like the Son of God."

And the nobles who stood by could scarcely speak, so great was their surprise.

"It is true, O King," at last, they said to Nebuchadnezzar, "that we cast these men into the flames, expecting them to be burned up, and we cannot understand how it happens that they have not been destroyed."

The King came near the furnace door as the fire lowered, and he called out to the three men within it, "Shadrach, Meshach, and Abednego, you who serve the Most High God, come out of the fire and come to me."

They came out and stood before King Nebuchadnezzar in the sight of all the princes, nobles, and rulers, and everyone could see they were alive.

Their garments had not been scorched, their hair singed, nor was there even the smell of fire upon them.

Then King Nebuchadnezzar said before all his rulers, "Blessed be the God of Shadrach, Meshach, and Abednego, who has sent His angel and has saved the lives of these men who trusted in Him. I now make a law that no man in all my kingdoms shall say a word against their God, for there is no other god who can save in this manner those who worship Him. And if any man speaks a word against their God, the Most High God, that man shall be cut in pieces, and his house shall be torn down."

After King Nebuchadnezzar died, his kingdom became weak, and the Medes and Persians took the city of Babylon under a mighty warrior named Cyrus the Great.

Shadrach, Meshach, and Abednego in the Fiery Furnace
CC0 1.0 Universal Public Domain Dedication

The Artios Home Companion Series
Unit 13: The Persian Empire

Teacher Overview

WHILE THE ISRAELITES were still in captivity in Babylon, the Medes and the Persians conquered the Babylonians. Daniel was still in the palace when this happened, faithfully serving God. Many years later, Esther and her uncle Mordecai were captives in the Persian captivity of Israel under King Ahasuerus, also known as Xerxes. Again, Esther is a prime example of someone who steps out in faith, stands by their beliefs, and is used by God as a light to those around them. We will also see how the Persian culture in which Esther lived differed from the Hebrew culture in which she grew up.

The days of the Persian Empire in which Esther lived were numbered, partly because they made the mistake of provoking the mighty Greeks. This unit will teach about the Persian Empire's history with Israel and Greece. We will see that whenever God uses an ungodly nation to punish His people, He punishes that nation for its wickedness afterward.

Key People, Places, and Events

Daniel
Darius "the Mede"
Battle of Marathon
Xerxes I
Battle of Thermopylae
Battle of Salamis
Battle of Plataea
Ahasuerus
Esther
Mordecai
Haman

Vocabulary

Lesson 1:
none

Lesson 2:
barrage
havoc
traitor

Lesson 3:
none

Emperor Cyrus the Great of Persia, by Jean Fouquet (c.1470)

Suggested Assignments

Based on your student's age and ability, the reading in this unit may be read aloud to the student, and journaling and notebook pages may be completed orally. Likewise, other assignments may be done with an appropriate combination of independent and guided study.

In this unit, students will:
- Complete three lessons in which they will learn about **Daniel in the Lion's Den**, the **Persian Wars**, and the **story of Esther**.
- Write a script or put together a play.
- Visit the **ArtiosHCS** curriculum website at **www.ArtiosHCS.com** for additional resources and any videos and websites assigned for this unit.

Heart Connections

God rewards faith.
> "For truly, I say to you, if you have faith like a grain of mustard seed, you will say to this mountain, 'Move from here to there,' and it will move, and nothing will be impossible for you."
> – Matthew 17:20

The testimony of each individual can make a difference in the lives of those around him.
> "You are the light of the world. A city set on a hill cannot be hidden. Nor do people light a lamp and put it under a basket, but on a stand, and it gives light to all in the house. In the same way, let your light shine before others, so that they may see your good works and give glory to your Father who is in heaven."
> – Matthew 5:14-16

God directs our lives according to His purposes.
> "And who knows whether you have not come to the kingdom for such a time as this?"
> – Esther 4:14b

Esther Crowned Queen of Persia, by Edwin Long (1878)

Lesson One

History Overview and Assignments
Hungry Lions

"They led Daniel to the mouth of the pit where the lions were kept, and they threw him in. Over the mouth, they placed a stone, and the King sealed it with his seal and with the seals of his nobles so that no one might take away the stone and let Daniel out of the den."

– from the adapted article below

Daniel in the Lions' Den, by David Teniers the Younger (1650)

Key People, Places, and Events

Daniel
Darius "the Mede"

Suggested Reading and Assignments

- Read the article: *The Story of Daniel in the Lions' Den.*
- After reading the article, summarize the story you read by either:
    - Retelling it out loud to your teacher or parent.
        OR
    - Completing an appropriate notebook page.
  Either way, be sure to include the answers to the discussion questions and an overview of key people, places, dates, and events in your summary.
- Be sure to visit your **ArtiosHCS** curriculum website for additional resources and any videos and websites assigned for this lesson.

Discussion Questions

1. Which nation conquered the Babylonian Empire?
2. What rule did the new king make that Daniel could not obey?
3. Why was the King sorry he had made the law?
4. How was Daniel punished?
5. How was God glorified in his deliverance of Daniel?

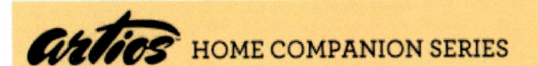

Ancient: Elementary
Unit 13: The Persian Empire

Adapted for Elementary School from the book:
The Wonder Book of Bible Stories
Arranged by Logan Marshall
The Story of Daniel in the Lions' Den

Daniel in the Service of King Darius

Daniel, the young Jewish man taken to Babylon in captivity, remained there through the Persian conquest of Babylon. When **Darius, "the Mede"** (which may have been another name for Cyrus the Great), became king, he gave to Daniel, who was now a very old man, a high place in honor and power. Daniel stood first among all the rulers over the land, for the King saw that he was wise and able to rule well. This made the other princes and rulers very jealous, and they tried to find something evil in Daniel to speak to the King against him.

These men saw that three times every day, Daniel went to his room and opened the window facing toward the city of Jerusalem, and looking toward Jerusalem, he prayed to God. Jerusalem was at that time in ruins, and the Temple was no longer standing, but Daniel prayed three times each day with his face facing toward the place where the house of God had once stood, although it was many hundreds of miles away.

Daniel and Cyrus Before the Idol Bel,
by Rembrandt (1633)

These nobles thought that in Daniel's prayers, they could find a chance to harm him and perhaps even cause him to be put to death. They came to the King and said to him: "All the rulers have agreed together to have a law made that for thirty days no one shall ask anything of any god or any man, except you, O King; and that if anyone shall pray to any god, or shall ask anything from any man during the thirty days, except from you, O King, he shall be thrown into the den where the lions are kept. Now, O King, make the law, and sign the writing so that it cannot be changed, for no law among the Medes and the Persians can be altered."

The King was not a wise man, and being foolish and vain, he was pleased with this law which would set him even above the gods. So without asking Daniel's advice, he signed the writing; the law was made, and the word was sent out through the kingdom that no one should pray to any god for thirty days.

Daniel learned that the law had been made, but every day he went to his room three times as usual, opened the window that looked toward Jerusalem, and offered his prayers to the Lord, just as he had prayed in other times. These rulers were watching nearby and saw Daniel kneeling in prayer to God. Then they rushed to the King and said:

"O King, have you not made a law that if anyone in thirty days offers a prayer, he shall be thrown into the den of lions?"

"It is true," said the King. "The law has been made, and it must stand."

Ancient: Elementary
Unit 13: The Persian Empire

They said to the King: "There is one man who does not obey the law you have made. It is Daniel, one of the captive Jews. Every day Daniel prays to his God three times, just as he did before you signed the writing of the law."

Then the King was very sorry for what he had done, for he loved Daniel and knew that no one could take his place in the kingdom. All day, until the sun went down, he tried in vain to find some way to save Daniel's life; but when evening came, these men again reminded him of the law that he had made and said to him that it must be kept. Very unwillingly, the King sent for Daniel and ordered that he be thrown into the lions' den. He told Daniel, "Perhaps your God, whom you serve faithfully, will save you from the lions."

They led Daniel to the mouth of the pit where the lions were kept, and they threw him in. Over the mouth, they placed a stone, and the King sealed it with his seal and with the seals of his nobles so that no one might take away the stone and let Daniel out of the den.

Then the King went again to his palace, but that night he was so sad that he could not eat or listen to music as usual. He could not sleep, for he was thinking of Daniel all through the night. Very early in the morning, he rose from his bed and hurried to the lions' den. He broke the seal and took away the stone, and in a voice full of sorrow, he called out, scarcely hoping to have an answer:

"O Daniel, servant of the living God, has your God been able to save you from the lions?"

And out of the darkness in the den came the voice of Daniel, saying:

"O King, may you live forever! My God has sent his angel and shut the lions' mouths. They have not hurt me because my God saw that I had done no wrong. And I have done no wrong toward you, O King!"

Then the King was glad. He gave his servants orders to take Daniel out of the den. Daniel was brought out safe and without harm because he trusted the Lord God fully. Then, by the King's command, they brought those men who had spoken against Daniel and their wives and children with them, for the King was exceedingly angry with them. They were all thrown into the den, and the hungry lions leaped upon them and tore them into pieces as soon as they fell upon the floor of the den.

After this, the King wrote to all the lands and the peoples in the many kingdoms under his rule:

"May peace be given to you all abundantly! I make a law that everywhere among my kingdoms men shall fear and worship the Lord God of Daniel, for He is the living God, above all other gods, who only can save men."

And Daniel served the King until the end of his reign.

Daniel's Answer to the King, (1892) After Briton Rivière

Lesson Two

History Overview and Assignments
The Persian Wars

"By the 6th century B.C., Cyrus the Great built Persia into an empire. When Persian armies reached the coast of Asia Minor, they insisted that the Greek colonies accept their rule and pay them a tax. The colonies objected. The Persians insisted. Then the Greek colonies asked the home country for help, and the stage was set for war."

– from the adapted article below

The Sea Battle at Salamis, by Wilhelm von Kaulbach (1868)

Suggested Reading and Assignments

- Read the article: *The Persian Wars*.
- After reading the article, summarize the story you read by either:
    - Retelling it out loud to your teacher or parent.
        OR
    - Completing an appropriate notebook page.
  Either way, be sure to include the answers to the discussion questions and an overview of key people, places, dates, and events in your summary.
- Define the vocabulary words in the context of the reading. Write the words and their definitions in the vocabulary section of your history notebook.
- Be sure to visit your **ArtiosHCS** curriculum website for additional resources and any videos and websites assigned for this lesson.

Vocabulary

barrage   havoc   traitor

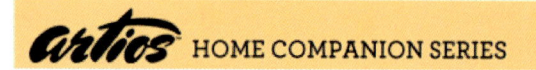

Ancient: Elementary
Unit 13: The Persian Empire

Key People, Places, and Events

Cyrus the Great
Battle of Marathon

Xerxes I
Battle of Thermopylae

Battle of Salamis
Battle of Plataea

Discussion Questions

1. Why did the Persians go to war against the Greeks?
2. Who won the Battle of Thermopylae?
3. How did the Greeks finally achieve victory over the Persians?

Adapted for Elementary School from the book:
The Story of Mankind
by Hendrik van Loon
The Persian Wars

Persia Grows

By the 6th century B.C., **Cyrus the Great** built Persia into an empire. When Persian armies reached the coast of Asia Minor, they insisted that the Greek colonies accept their rule and pay them a tax. The colonies objected. The Persians insisted. Then the Greek colonies asked the home country for help, and the stage was set for war.

Of course, the Greeks had some safety because their country lay hidden beyond the deep waters of the Aegean Sea. But here, their old enemies, the Phoenicians, stepped forward with offers of help and advice to the Persians. If the Persians provided the soldiers, the Phoenicians would guarantee to deliver the necessary ships to Europe. It was the year 492 B.C., and Asia made ready to destroy the rising power of Europe.

"Earth and Water"

According to an ancient historian, Greece sent messengers to Persia to seek peace, and the ruler demanded earth and water from Greece as a token of Greek submission. The messengers agreed to this, but when they arrived home, their countrymen promptly threw them into the nearest well where they would find both "earth and water" in great abundance. After that, of course, peace was impossible.

But the gods of High Olympus watch over their children, the Greeks say, so when the Phoenician fleet carrying the Persian troops neared Mount Athos, the storm god blew his cheeks until he almost burst the veins of his brow. A terrible hurricane destroyed the fleet, and the Persians were all drowned.

Painting of Cyrus the Great in battle
CC 3.0 by User Coyau on Wikimedia Commons

The First Persian War: Battle of Marathon

Two years later, the Persians returned. This time they sailed across the Aegean Sea and landed near the village of **Marathon**. When the Athenians heard this, they sent their army of ten thousand men to guard the hills surrounding the plain. At the same time, they sent a fast runner to Sparta to ask for help. But Sparta was envious of the fame of Athens and refused to come to her assistance. The other Greek cities followed her example—except tiny Plataea, which sent a thousand men.

On the 12th of September 490 B.C., the Athenian commander threw this little army against the hordes of the Persians. The Greeks broke through the Persian **barrage** of arrows, and their spears caused terrible **havoc** among the disorganized Persian troops, who had never been called upon to resist such an enemy.

The Battle of Marathon, illustration from *The Story of the Greatest Nations, From The Dawn Of History To The Twentieth Century,* by John Steeple Davis (1900)

That night the people of Athens watched the sky grow red with the flames of burning ships. Anxiously they waited for news. At last, a little cloud of dust appeared upon the road that led to the North. It was the runner. He stumbled and gasped, for his end was near. Only a few days before had he returned from his errand to Sparta. That morning he had taken part in the battle, and later he had volunteered to carry the news of victory to his beloved city. The people saw him fall and rushed forward to support him. "We have won," he whispered, and then he died, a glorious death which made him envied by all Greek warriors and which is remembered in modern times every time a *marathon* is run.

As for the Persians, they tried after this defeat to land near Athens, but they found the coast guarded and disappeared, and once more, Greece was at peace.

Eight years they waited, but during this time, the Greeks were not idle. They knew a final attack was to be expected, so they built a great fleet of ships.

In 481 B.C., a massive Persian army sent by Xerxes I (believed to be the king called Ahasuerus in the Biblical story of Esther) famously crossed the water between Asia and Europe on floating bridges. It appeared in Thessaly, a province of northern Greece.

In this hour of danger, Sparta, the great military city of Greece, was given command of the armies. But the Spartans cared little what happened to northern Greece, as long as their own country was not invaded—and they made a fatal error: they failed to strengthen the forces along the mountain passes that led into Greece.

Battle of Thermopylae

A small company of Spartans had been told to guard the narrow road between the high mountains and the sea which connected Thessaly with the southern provinces. The soldiers fought and held the pass with great bravery. But a **traitor** guided a regiment of Persians through the hills and made it possible for them to attack from the rear. Near the Warm Wells—called the **Thermopylae**—a fierce battle was fought, and the Greeks suffered a terrible loss.

Sea Battle of Salamis

So, the pass was lost, and most of Greece fell into the hands of the Persians. They marched upon Athens and burned the city. The people fled to the island of **Salamis**. All seemed lost. But on the 20th of September of the year 480 B.C., the Greeks forced the Persian fleet into a battle within the narrow waters that separated the island of Salamis from the mainland, and within a few hours, they destroyed three-quarters of the Persian ships.

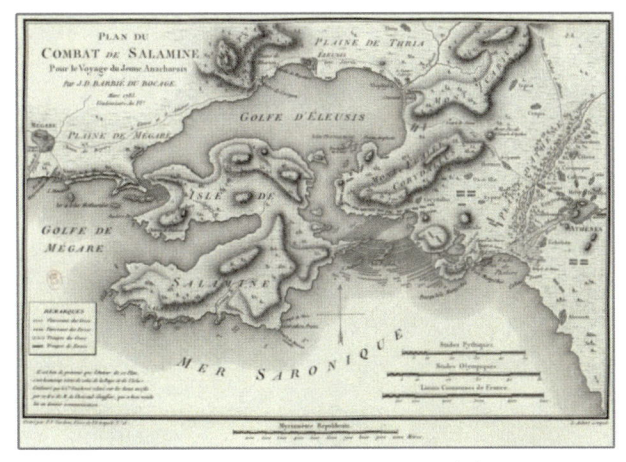

Battle of Salamis, engraving by Barthélémy (1798)

Xerxes was forced to retire from his assault upon Greece. The following year, he declared, would bring a final decision. He took his troops to Thessaly, and there he waited for spring.

Battle of Plataea

But this time, Sparta joined their countrymen and marched against the Persians. The united Greeks (some one hundred thousand men from a dozen different cities) attacked the three hundred thousand men of the enemy near **Plataea**. Once more, the heavy Greek army broke through the Persian barrage of arrows. The Persians were defeated, as they had been at Marathon, and this time, they left for good.

Thus did the first encounter between Asia and Europe end. Athens had covered herself with glory, and Sparta had fought bravely and well. If these two cities had come to an agreement and were willing to forget their little jealousies, they might have become the leaders of a strong and united Greece.

But alas, they allowed the hour of victory and enthusiasm to slip by, and the opportunity never returned. War would soon erupt between the different cities and sweep over the peninsula.

The Spartans at Plataea, depicted in *Cassell's Illustrated Universal History*, published in 1882

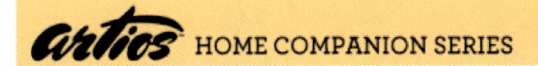

Lesson Three

History Overview and Assignments
A Brave Queen

> *"Then Mordecai went out from the presence of the king in royal robes of blue and white, with a great golden crown and a robe of fine linen and purple, and the city of Susa shouted and rejoiced. The Jews had light and gladness and joy and honor. And in every province and in every city, wherever the king's command and his edict reached, there was gladness and joy among the Jews, a feast and a holiday."*
> – Esther 8:15-17

Esther Denouncing Haman, by Ernest Normand (1888)

Suggested Reading and Assignments

- Read the book of Esther in your own Bible. Please read the KJV version or another translation, not a paraphrase such as *The Message* or *The Living Bible*.
- Write a script or put together a play that shows the events in the book of Esther. You may focus on one section of the story or include the entire story.
- Be sure to visit your **ArtiosHCS** curriculum website for additional resources and any videos and websites assigned for this lesson.

Key People, Places, and Events

Ahasuerus
Esther
Mordecai
Haman

Haman and Mordecai, by Paul Alexander Leroy (1884)

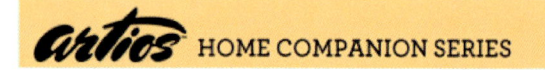

Ancient: Elementary
Unit 13: The Persian Empire

The Artios Home Companion Series
Unit 14: Ancient India – "Land of Spice and Wonder"

Teacher Overview

SCHOLARS ONCE THOUGHT civilization in India started later than in Egypt and Mesopotamia, but recent discoveries have uncovered remains of cities as old as some in the Middle East. The people of this early civilization didn't build huge monuments to glorify their rulers after death. Instead, they used their resources in practical ways to create a peaceful life in the Indus Valley. Kingdoms eventually rose and fell. Unfortunately, the religious beliefs of the Indian people led them to divide their people into a rigid caste system, which left many in severe poverty with no hope of a better life.

The Hindu demigod Garuda carries Vishnu, one of the principal deities, and his wife, Lakshmi, the goddess of wealth. The divine couple sits on a throne surrounded by a gold-covered frame (c.1820).

Suggested Assignments

Based on your student's age and ability, the reading in this unit may be read aloud to the student, and journaling and notebook pages may be completed orally. Likewise, other assignments may be done with an appropriate combination of independent and guided study.

In this unit, students will:
- Complete four lessons in which they will learn about ancient **India: its culture, history, and people**.
- Define vocabulary words.
- Work together as a class to produce and enjoy a sampling of Indian foods and ancient art.

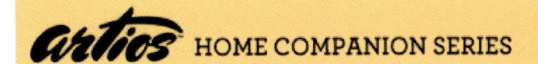

- Explore the website about the Indus Valley at the URL found on the **ArtiosHCS** curriculum website.
- Visit the **ArtiosHCS** curriculum website at **www.ArtiosHCS.com** for additional resources and any videos and websites assigned for this unit.

Heart Connections

God directs our lives according to His purposes.
"And who knows whether you have not come to the kingdom for such a time as this?"
– Esther 4:14b

Be wary of the untruthful teachings of false religions.
Jesus said to him, "I am the way, and the truth, and the life. No one comes to the Father except through me."
– John 14:6

It is appointed for man to die once, and after that comes judgment.
– Hebrews 9:27

Vocabulary

Lesson 1:
urban
excavate
complex
sewage
intricate
unearth
fertility

Lesson 2:
caste
role
patriarchal
patrilineal
stratification

Lesson 3:
reincarnation
karma
enlightenment
delusion
ignorance
nirvana
ultimate

Lesson 4:
none

Key People, Places, and Events

Indus Valley civilization
Harappa
Mohenjo-Daro
Rigveda
Mohandas Gandhi
Hinduism
Veda
Chandragupta I
Samudragupta
Chandragupta II

Vishnu seated in the lotus position on a lotus. Detail from a depiction of the poet Jayadeva bowing to Vishnu. The very picture of devotion, bare-bodied, head bowed, legs crossed, and hands folded, Jayadeva stands at left, with worship offerings placed before the lotus seat of Vishnu, who sits there, blessing the poet.

Lesson One

History Overview and Assignments
Early People Who Lived in the Indus Valley

THE SOCIETY that developed in the Indus Valley was a Bronze Age culture that developed remarkable ways of working with stone and metal. Ruins of the city of Harappa were discovered in 1921. Since then, more than a thousand cities and settlements of the Indus Valley civilization have been located.
– Adapted from *Boundless World History: The Indus River Valley Civilizations*

The archaeological site of Harappa (2013)
Photo by Smn121. CC BY-SA 3.0

Suggested Reading and Assignments

- Read the article: *The Indus River Valley Civilizations*.
- Define each vocabulary word in the context of the reading. Write the words and their definitions in the vocabulary section of your notebook.
- After reading the article, summarize the story you read by either:
    - Retelling it out loud to your teacher or parent.
      OR
    - Completing an appropriate notebook page.
  Either way, be sure to include the answer to the discussion question and an overview of key people, places, dates, and events in your summary.
- Begin working together as a class to produce and enjoy a sampling of Indian foods and ancient art.
- Explore the website about the Indus Valley at the URL found on your **ArtiosHCS** curriculum website.
- Be sure to visit your **ArtiosHCS** curriculum website for additional resources and any videos and websites assigned for this lesson.

Ancient: Elementary
Unit 14: Ancient India - "Land of Spice and Wonder"

Vocabulary

urban	complex	intricate	fertility
excavate	sewage	unearth	

Key People, Places, and Events

Indus Valley civilization   Harappa   Mohenjo-Daro

Discussion Questions

1. Did the societies of Harappa and Mohenjo-Daro seem to be peaceful or warlike? How can you tell?
2. What is surprising about their cities?
3. What can we tell about their craftsmanship?
4. What was their written language like?
5. List three possible reasons why the Indus Valley civilizations disappeared.

Adapted for Elementary School from:
Boundless World History
source: coursehero.com/study-guides/boundless-worldhistory
The Indus River Valley Civilizations
CC BY-SA: Attribution-ShareAlike

Indus Valley Civilization

The **Indus Valley civilization** was one of the earliest civilizations. At its peak, there were more than five million people in this society. The Indus Valley people worked very well with metals and gemstones, making intricate handicrafts and seal stamps that have been found in recent years. Their cities, which are still being **excavate**d, are surprising for their **urban** planning, with baked brick houses, **complex** drainage systems, water supply systems, and clusters of large buildings.

One of the first sites found in modern times was the city of **Harappa**, discovered in the 1920s. Soon afterward, another city was located called **Mohenjo-Daro**.

How the Cities Developed

Early villages in the Indus Valley gradually grew, and some became large cities by 2600 B.C. More than a thousand cities and settlements have been found.

These cities had well-ordered wastewater drainage, trash collection systems, and possibly grain storage buildings and public baths. Some modern communities in India and other places don't have such advanced techniques. Most Indus Valley city-dwellers were artisans and merchants grouped in distinct neighborhoods.

The Pashupati seal shows a seated and possibly three-headed figure surrounded by animals (c.2350-2000 B.C.). From the Mohenjo-Daro archaeological site

The people also built walls, probably protecting them from floods and enemies.

Unlike other early civilizations, such as ancient Egypt, the people of the Indus Valley did not make significant monuments. There is no evidence of palaces or temples (or even of kings, armies, or priests), and the most prominent buildings may be granaries.

The Indus Valley people developed new working methods with copper, bronze, lead, and tin, producing **intricate** handicrafts. Excavation sites have revealed many examples of the culture's art, including sculptures, seals, pottery, gold jewelry, and detailed terracotta, bronze, and stone figurines.

Miniature votive images or toy models from Harappa (c.2500 B.C.) CC BY

Trade and Transportation

The economy depended mainly on trade, which needed good transportation. The Indus Valley people may have been the first to use wheeled transport in the form of bull carts like those seen throughout South Asia today. It also appears they built boats—a claim supported by discoveries of a canal and docking facility at the coastal city of Lothal.

Trade focused on importing raw materials for workshops, including minerals from Iran and Afghanistan, lead and copper from other parts of India, jade from China, and cedar wood floated down rivers from the Himalayas and Kashmir. Other trade goods included clay pots, gold, silver, other metals, beads, flints for making tools, seashells, pearls, and colored gemstones.

It's believed that the Indus Valley people used a language of written symbols. A collection of written texts on clay and stone tablets **unearth**ed at Harappa contain markings that look like plants made them.

Religion

The Indus Valley religion remains a mystery. The people may have worshiped a mother goddess who symbolized **fertility**. Unlike other ancient societies, the Indus Valley civilization didn't seem to have any temples or palaces that would give clear evidence about religious rituals or deities.

Many Indus Valley seals also include the forms of animals, with some being carried in processions, leading scholars to wonder whether the Indus Valley religion involved animals. One seal from Mohenjo-Daro shows a half-human, half-buffalo monster attacking a tiger.

Disappearance of the Indus Valley Civilization

The great Indus Valley civilization began to decline around 1800 B.C. It eventually disappeared, along with its two great cities. Evidence indicates that trade with Mesopotamia, mainly located in modern Iraq, seemed to have ended around that time. The great cities' advanced drainage systems and baths were built over or blocked up. Writing began to disappear, and the weights and measures used for trade and taxation fell out of use.

Scholars have put forth differing theories to explain the disappearance of the Indus Valley people, including an invasion, an earthquake, and monsoons.

Lesson Two

History Overview and Assignments
The Caste System

AFTER THE INDUS VALLEY civilization disappeared, other groups came into the area, splitting their societies into groups called castes. The ruling castes insisted that lifestyles and occupations should be inherited. There were four classes of people in the resulting Indian caste system: Brahmins (priests and scholars), Kshatriyas (kings, governors, and warriors), Vaishyas (cattle herders, agriculturists, artisans, and merchants), and Shudras (laborers and service providers). A fifth group, Untouchables, was excluded from the caste system and performed all the jobs nobody else wanted to do.
– Adapted from *Boundless World History: Indo-European Civilizations*

A page from the manuscript *Seventy-two Specimens of Castes in India*, which consists of 72 full-color hand-painted images of men and women of the various castes and religious and ethnic groups found in Madura, India (1837)

Suggested Reading and Assignments

- Read the article: *The Indus River Valley Civilizations: The Caste System*.
- Define each vocabulary word in the context of the reading. Write the words and their definitions in the vocabulary section of your notebook.
- After reading the article, summarize the story you read by either:
    - Retelling it out loud to your teacher or parent.
       OR
    - Completing an appropriate notebook page.

  Either way, be sure to include the answer to the discussion question and an overview of key people, places, dates, and events in your summary.
- Be sure to visit your **ArtiosHCS** curriculum website for additional resources and any videos and websites assigned for this lesson.

Vocabulary

caste
role
patriarchal
patrilineal
stratification

Key People, Places, and Events

Rigveda
Mohandas Gandhi

Discussion Questions

1. Describe ancient India's caste system.
2. How do you think Jesus would respond to the idea of the caste system? Why?
3. What modern person worked to put an end to India's caste system?

Mohandas Gandhi

Adapted for Elementary School from:
Boundless World History
source: coursehero.com/study-guides/boundless-worldhistory
Indo-European Civilizations: The Caste System
CC BY-SA: Attribution-ShareAlike

After the Indus Valley civilization vanished, other people groups moved in. These groups, like many other ancient cultures, began splitting their societies into classes of people called **caste**s. The caste system in ancient India separated people based on their social positions, and the rulers assigned specific **role**s and occupations to each class. Stories of the deities in the Rigveda story influenced these roles and their importance.

In this story, the other gods sacrificed the god named Purusha. Afterward, Purusha's mind became the Moon; his eyes became the Sun, his head the Sky, and his feet the Earth.

The story says that people then came from Purusha's body. The *Brahmins*, or priests, came from Purusha's mouth. The *Kshatriyas*, or warrior rulers, came from Purusha's arms; the *Vaishyas*, or merchants, came from Purusha's thighs; and the *Shudras*, or laborers and servants, came from Purusha's feet. By around 1000 B.C., these caste distinctions were well set in Indian society.

Today the castes still exist in the form of varna, or class system, based on the original four castes described in the Vedas. A fifth group, Dalits, historically excluded from the varna system, are ostracized and called "Untouchables."

The castes maintained lifestyle, occupation, ritual status, and social status through generations of people.

Ancient India's caste system still survives today in parts of the country. Modern activists such as **Mohandas Gandhi**, the revered leader of the nonviolent Indian independence movement, have worked to rid the country of these ancient class divisions. Although modern India formally abolished the caste system in 1950, some parts of Indian society treat members of lower social classes poorly.

Lesson Three

History Overview and Assignments
Hinduism and Buddhism

HINDUISM GREW OUT OF TRADITIONS from India's various ancient cultures. Buddhism arose when a wealthy young man rejected the caste system and began teaching a way to spiritual happiness that he said came from avoiding pleasures and desires. He became known as the Buddha, and Buddhism has spread to become one of the world's major religions today.

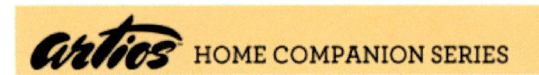

In a prominent Hindu myth, Matsaya, the fish form of the Hindu god Vishnu, rescued the first man, Manu, from a great deluge.

Vocabulary

reincarnation
karma
enlightenment
delusion
ignorance
nirvana
ultimate

Suggested Reading and Assignments

- Read the combined article: *The Rise of Hinduism* and *Buddhism*.
- Define each vocabulary word in the context of the reading. Write the words and their definitions in the vocabulary section of your notebook.
- After reading the article, summarize the story you read by either:
    - Retelling it out loud to your teacher or parent.
        OR
    - Completing an appropriate notebook page.

  Either way, be sure to include the answer to the discussion question and an overview of key people, places, dates, and events in your summary.
- Be sure to visit your **ArtiosHCS** curriculum website for additional resources and any videos and websites assigned for this lesson.

Key People, Places, and Events

Hinduism   Veda   Buddhism

Discussion Questions

1. What did ancient Hindus believe about life after death?
2. How did Siddhartha Gautama become known as the Buddha?
3. What does Buddhism teach is the way to gain happiness?
4. What does the Bible teach is the way to gain happiness?

Adapted for Elementary School from the book:
Boundless World History
source: coursehero.com/study-guides/boundless-worldhistory
Religion in the Indian Subcontinent: The Rise of Hinduism
and
Buddhism
CC BY-SA: Attribution-ShareAlike

Hinduism is one of the world's oldest religions. Modern scholars believe that it started as a blend of various ancient Indian religions and that it is more a way of life than a true religion. In ancient times, Hindus worshiped many gods and believed that people could die and be reborn into a new body. This belief, called **reincarnation**, says that people who live very good, unselfish lives are rewarded by being reborn into higher castes. This fate is called **karma**. Many modern Hindus don't believe in the gods or reincarnation but follow a way of life that keeps the religious traditions and rituals handed down for thousands of years.

The sacred writings called **Veda**s remain the oldest scriptures of the Hindu religion, which has grown through modern times to become one of the world's major religions.

Hinduism's Sacred Writings

The Vedas are a collection of writings. The Rigveda is the most important of the collection, made up of more than a thousand hymns.

Illustration of the Hindu deity Vishnu in *Mahabharata*, Hindi Gita Press

The Upanishads are a collection of texts that tell of the most important religious concepts of Hinduism and Buddhism. It discusses the nature of ultimate reality and the repeated cycle of birth, suffering, and death.

The first known Hindu temples were built during India's Golden Age, from the fourth through sixth centuries A.D. After that time, different types of Hinduism arose in other places. However, Hinduism endured through the ages to become the largest religion in India.

Adi Shankara, a famous 8th-century Hindu teacher, by Raja Ravi Varm (1904)

Buddhism

During the 5th or 6th century B.C., a wealthy young Indian named Siddhartha Gautama left behind the worldly comforts of his father's palace to seek spiritual **enlightenment**. Rejecting the caste system, he believed that all people could reach a state of perfect happiness. He began his quest by fasting to rid himself of desires. According to legend, he became so thin he could feel his hands if he placed one on his back and the other on his stomach. While sitting under a tree, he discovered what Buddhists call the Noble Eightfold Path and reached a state where he was utterly free of rage, hatred, and **delusion**.

He wanted to help people end their suffering by removing **ignorance** and cravings. He taught that this could be done by following the noble path, which he said was the way to achieve the blissful state of **nirvana**. Nirvana is the **ultimate** spiritual goal of **Buddhism**. It is said to mark the release from the cycle of rebirths.

Buddha image at Sarnath: The Buddha preached his first sermon here. He believed freedom from desires set people free from the cycle of death and rebirth.
Photo by Jean-Pierre Dalbéra. CC BY 2.0

Rise of Buddhism

Buddhists believe that after his death, the Buddha passed into nirvana. Over time Buddhism grew as more people became aware of its teachings, including those in western nations, eventually becoming one of the world's major religions.

A statue of the Hindu god Shiva, depicted as the cosmic dancer Nataraja, performing a joyful dance about the cycle of life, death, and rebirth.
Photographed by the LACMA. derivative work: Julia

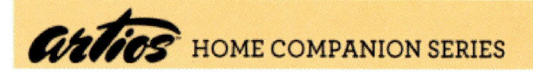

Lesson Four

History Overview and Assignments
The Gupta Empire

KINGDOMS ROSE AND FELL in Ancient India until one empire took shape, giving rise to India's Golden Age, known for its outstanding cultural and artistic achievements.

Kailash Temple, Ellora Caves
Photo by Sailko. CC BY 3.0

Suggested Reading and Assignments

- Review the discussion question and vocabulary, then read the combined article:
  The *Maurya Empire and The Gupta Empire.*
- Define each vocabulary word in the context of the reading. Write the words and their definitions in the vocabulary section of your notebook.
- After reading the article, summarize the story you read by either:
  - Retelling it out loud to your teacher or parent.
     OR
  - Completing an appropriate notebook page.
  Either way, be sure to include the answer to the discussion question and an overview of key people, places, dates, and events in your summary.
- Be sure to visit your **ArtiosHCS** curriculum website for additional resources and any videos and websites assigned for this lesson.

Key People, Places, and Events

| Gupta Empire | Chandragupta I | Samudragupta | Chandragupta II |

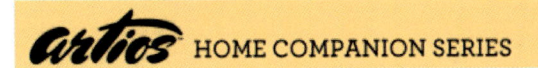

Discussion Questions

1. How did the Guptas come to rule much of India?
2. Describe India's Golden Age.
3. How did Indian culture spread to other regions during this time?
4. Why did the empire collapse?

Adapted for Elementary School from the book:
Boundless World History
source: coursehero.com/study-guides/boundless-worldhistory
Religion in the Indian Subcontinent:
The Maurya Empire and *the Gupta Empire*
CC BY-SA: Attribution-ShareAlike

The Gupta Empire: India's Golden Age

After several kingdoms rose and fell during India's ancient years, the **Gupta Empire** came to power. It spread over much of the Indian Subcontinent during the fourth through sixth centuries A.D. The rule of the Gupta emperors was a time of peace and prosperity marked by significant cultural progress.

One of the Gupta Empire's most notable rulers, **Chandragupta I**, came to the throne in the fourth century A.D. and soon had a realm stretching across much of India.

Coin of the Gupta emperor Samudragupta
Photo by PHGCOM. CC BY-SA 3.0

His son **Samudragupta** ruled for about 45 years, conquering kingdoms and attacking neighboring tribes. By the time he died, he had brought over 20 kingdoms into his realm and significantly extended the Gupta Empire's lands.

His son, **Chandragupta II**, also expanded the empire. By the end of the fourth century, his control over India extended coast-to-coast. Chandragupta II built a second capital city in central India at the high point of his rule.

Chandragupta II issued gold coin types of new types, notable for the designs on the face of each coin line, such as the Archer or the Tiger-Slayer. He was also the first Gupta king to issue silver coins.

Krishna Battling the Horse Demon, terracotta relief from the Gupta period
CC0 1.0 Universal

Although the Gupta rulers were warlike, there were many examples of cultural progress during the Gupta era, with buildings, sculptures, and paintings surviving as reminders of the creativity of the time, along with many written works of poetry and philosophy. This period is still remembered as the Golden Age of India.

Agni, the Indian god of fire from the ancient Vedic religion, shown riding a ram

The cultural creativity of the Golden Age of India produced stunning buildings, including palaces and temples, as well as sculptures and paintings of the highest quality. The walls of Buddhist shrines and monasteries were decorated with colorful wall paintings. These showed scenes from the life of the Buddha. Some temples were cut from the cliffs and decorated with sculptures and paintings.

The Gupta Dynasty promoted Hinduism but supported Buddhism as well. Gupta Buddhist art influenced East and Southeast Asia as trade increased. The Gupta Empire became an important cultural center and influenced nearby kingdoms and regions in Burma, Sri Lanka, and Southeast Asia. Classical forms of Indian music and dance, created under the Guptas, are still practiced throughout Asia today.

After many years of dominance, the Gupta Empire collapsed in 550 A.D. due to invasions and weak ruling leadership.

Ellora Caves (built 600–1000 A.D.). The Ajanta and Ellora caves were created during India's Golden Age and the Kailasanatha temple is carved out of one single rock.

Ancient: Elementary
Unit 14: Ancient India - "Land of Spice and Wonder"

The Artios Home Companion Series
Unit 15: Ancient China – "Land of Legends"

WHILE THE MIDDLE EASTERN civilizations were developing, other cultures were growing and expanding, too. China, a country of the Orient (which means "east"), developed somewhat apart from the rest of the world. That did not hinder the beauty of its culture. However, early on, they made up their own stories about the creation of the world and other history. God is particular about not worshiping any other gods. Keep that in mind as you learn about the myths and history of the Chinese people. It is important to see God's principles at work.

Key People, Places, and Events

Huangdi
Pwanku (or Pan-gu)
Yao
Shun
Yu the Great
Xia dynasty
Shang dynasty
Qin dynasty
Qin Chi Huang
Huns
Great Wall of China
Confucius
Han dynasty
Silk Road

Vocabulary

Lesson 1:
dike
defraud
gaudy
filial
piety
sly

Lessons 2 & 3:
none

King Cheng Tang of the Shang Dynasty, as imagined by Song Dynasty painter Ma Lin (c.1225)

Suggested Assignments

Based on your student's age and ability, the reading in this unit may be read aloud to the student, and journaling and notebook pages may be completed orally. Likewise, other assignments may be done with an appropriate combination of independent and guided study.

In this unit, students will:
- Complete three lessons in which they will learn about **ancient China**.
- Define vocabulary words.
- Illustrate a story.
- Explore websites about China and watch a video about a Chinese Creation Myth found at the ArtiosHCS curriculum website links.
- Visit the **ArtiosHCS** curriculum website at **www.ArtiosHCS.com** for additional resources and any videos and websites assigned for this unit.

Heart Connections

People tend to ignore what they know about God.

For even though they knew God, they did not honor Him as God or give thanks, but they became futile in their speculations, and their foolish heart was darkened. Professing to be wise, they became fools, and exchanged the glory of the incorruptible God for an image in the form of corruptible man and of birds and four-footed animals and crawling creatures.

– Romans 1:20-23

Additional Material for Parent or Teacher:

Links may be found on the **ArtiosHCS** curriculum website to several websites about China and one about Venn Diagrams. These may be shared with your student(s) as appropriate. Your student(s) may need the Venn Diagram in Lesson Six.

The mythical, three-legged money toad named Jin Chan. Jin Chan, a legendary animal of the Han people, is said to appear during the full moon near homes or businesses that will soon receive wealth.
Photo by Tristanb. CC BY-SA 3.0

Close-up of a baby 7-month-old panda cub in the Wolong Nature Reserve in Sichuan, China. Giant pandas lived for centuries in China's bamboo forests and were regarded as semi-divine during the Han dynasty. They are now an endangered species.
Photo by Sheila Lau

Oracle bone script: (from left) 馬/马 mǎ "horse", 虎 hǔ "tiger", 豕 shī "swine", 犬 quǎn "dog", 鼠 shǔ "rat and mouse", 象 xiàng "elephant", 豸 zhì "beasts of prey", 龜/龟 guī "turtle", 爿 qiáng "low table" (now 床 chuáng), 為/为 wèi "to lead" (now "do" or "for"), and 疾 jí "illness."

Ancient: Elementary
Unit 15: Ancient China – "Land of Legends"

Lesson One

History Overview and Assignments
Ancient Chinese Dynasties

CHINA, LAND OF WONDER: In 1974, some Chinese farmers digging a well struck some pieces of hardened clay with their shovels. It soon became apparent that they had made an unusual find—a collection of soldier statues made long ago from terracotta clay. Archeologists were brought in to excavate, and they found that more than 8,000 clay soldiers had been buried in the massive, magnificent tomb of Emperor Qin Shi Huang. The tomb was lined in bronze and contained an enormous model of the ruler's empire, complete with palaces, silver rivers made from mercury, and stars formed from gemstones.

Welcome to the wonder of China, a land of legend and mystery, in which more and more fascinating finds are being uncovered daily and whose creative and imaginative people have a rich and captivating history. Bounded by the world's tallest mountains, a massive desert, and the Pacific Ocean, China remained isolated from other civilizations. Hence, the ancient Chinese people developed a very different culture.

Key People, Places, and Events

Huangdi
Pwanku (or Pan-gu)
Yao
Shun
Yu the Great
Xia dynasty
Shang dynasty
Qin dynasty
Qin Chi Huang
Huns
Great Wall of China
Confucius
Han dynasty
Silk Road

Emperor Wu, one of the most influential rulers of the Han dynasty

Suggested Reading and Assignments

- Read the combined article: *Past and Present* and *Brief History of China*.
- After reading the article, summarize the story you read by either:
  - Retelling it out loud to your teacher or parent.
    OR
  - Completing an appropriate notebook page.

Either way, be sure to include the answers to the discussion questions and an overview of key people, places, dates, and events in your summary.

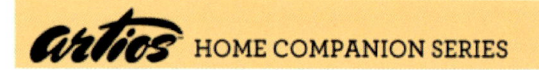

Ancient: Elementary
Unit 15: Ancient China – "Land of Legends"

- Define the vocabulary words in the context of the reading. Write the words and their definitions in the vocabulary section of your history notebook.
- Watch the YouTube video about the Chinese Creation Myth found on your **ArtiosHCS** curriculum website.
- Be sure to visit your **ArtiosHCS** curriculum website for additional resources and any videos and websites assigned for this lesson.

Vocabulary

dike	gaudy	piety
defraud	filial	sly

Discussion Questions

1. Why did Chinese culture develop differently from that of other countries?
2. How is China's flood story similar to the Biblical flood story? How is it different?
3. What character traits did King Shun display that earned him the praise and respect of the Chinese people?
4. Even though he was praised for his bravery, do you think it was wise of Shun to remain outside during a thundering rainstorm?
5. How did the Chinese way of choosing new rulers change during the country's early years?
6. List three things the Qin dynasty is known for.

Adapted for Elementary School from the book:
The Story of China
by Robert Van Bergen
Past and Present
and
Brief History of China

Ancient Legends of Heroes

Ancient Chinese legends tell of divine heroes named Fuxi and his wife Nuwa (or Nu Gua), who created people and taught them how to speak, use fire, and live as families. They say that much progress in civilization was made under another who came after them, named Shennong, that is, "the farmer." Then came rulers, beginning with **Huangdi** or the "Yellow Emperor." New inventions like writing, silk, and medicine helped the people and increased their comfort.

One Chinese Story About the World's Beginning: The Invisible Top

"The beginning of the world, as it is described to Chinese boys and girls, is stranger than a fairy tale. First of all, according to the story, there was something called 'khi' which could not be seen nor touched but was everywhere. After a time, this 'khi' began to turn around like a great invisible top. As it whirled round, the thicker part sank downwards and became the earth, whilst the thinner part rose upwards, growing clearer until it formed the sky, and so the heavens and the earth spun themselves into being. Presently, for the story changes like a dream, there came a giant named **Pwanku**. For thousands of years, the giant worked, splitting

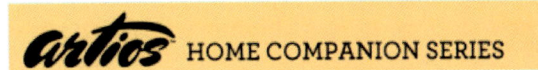

> *masses of rock with his mallet and chisel until the sun, moon, and stars could be seen through the openings which he had made. The heavens rose higher, the earth spread wider, and Pwanku himself grew six feet taller every day. When he died, his head became mountains, his breath wind, and his voice thunder; his veins changed into rivers, his body into the earth, his bones into rocks, and his beard into the stars that stream across the night sky."*
>
> – Source: *Children of China*, by Colin Campbell Brown

Another legend tells of another hero who saved the people from a great flood. The story goes like this:

At the time of the flood, the ruler of China was Emperor **Yao**. After the waters had gone down a bit, he called a meeting of his ministers and said to them, "A great many people are ruined because of this flood. What can we do to help them?"

The ministers answered: "Ask Gun!"

"No," replied the Emperor, " I cannot do so. Why, that man would not obey my orders but would do just as he pleased."

The ministers shook their heads and looked wise, but as they did not know any better advice to give, they all repeated, "Try him. Perhaps he may succeed."

So Emperor Yao consented and told his ministers to engage Gun but not to let him have things all his way. Gun worked hard for nine years but failed to bring help to the people. The ruler grew tired of waiting, and poor Gun was put to death.

Emperor Yao then sent for Gun's son, Yu, and asked him if he would try and do the work. Yu agreed, and he worked so hard that he succeeded. The story says that with the help of a dragon and a giant turtle, he built **dike**s, drained the land, and restored order in the empire.

When the Emperor heard of it, he sent for Yu, who came as quickly as possible. When he came before him, the Emperor began by making Yu feel at ease.

"You need not stand so far off!" he said to Yu. "By your looks, I should not be surprised if you had something interesting to tell me."

"Well, Your Majesty," replied Yu, "perhaps I have. The flood was very high, the water was well up on the high mountains, and the foothills could not be seen. When I could see the way, I took a boat; but the worst was when I had to climb on foot because of the brush. It was lucky that I had spiked shoes.

"I traveled from one mountain to another and made the people cut down trees. Sometimes I had a shot at some game and let them eat the meat raw, for there was no way to make a fire to cook it.

"Then, to make a passage for the water, I laid pipes, and we cut nine ditches. As soon as the ground was dry, I set the people plowing and sowing, and then they had a chance to cook their food. Sometimes a man would come and ask me for something, but when I found that he had something he did not need, I told him to trade it. So now, everybody is happy."

Emperor Yao was well pleased and would have spoken when he saw that Yu had not finished, so he smiled at him to go on.

"With Your Majesty's permission," said bold Yu, "I would say that you, too, have some work to do. Think how much mightier a ruler you would be if you looked after your ministers and observed what schemes they use to **defraud** the people. Then the people would admire and praise you."

Many rulers we have heard of would not have liked this sort of speech, but Emperor Yao was not a bad-hearted man. I suspect that is why the Chinese are so proud of him. He showed that he was not offended by calling a meeting of his ministers. When they had arrived, and the roll had been called, he said, "Gentlemen, do you know that you ought to be my legs and arms, my eyes and ears? Attend to your duties and help the people if they need any assistance. First, in every paper I want you to write, I am the Master. When you have done that, send for an artist, for I wish to have paintings made of the sun, moon, stars, mountains, dragons, insects, and flowers. Also, I need some new clothes. I do not care for **gaudy** colors; some embroidered cloth will do, with a neat mixture of blue, red, yellow, white, and black. Then the courts of law must be attended to, and don't forget the musicians, for I am fond of music. Pay the greatest attention to all these things. If I make a mistake, let me know it. Don't smile before my face and blame me when my back is turned! Now about the common people, you know what fools they are. If they do not attend to their business, gently remind them. Use the lash occasionally, make them learn their lessons, and see that they are kept at work. If any come and ask for work, let them have it; but if they are idle, stir them up."

When Yu heard of this speech to the ministers, he was pleased and said to the monarch, "The King is like a great light. Every man in this country may see it if he is not blind, even those near the Big Pond. But Your Majesty should hear what your ministers have to say. If you wish to promote them, let them show by their language that they are fit for the position and set a good example to the people. Have plenty of mounted police, and who will dare to raise any objection? Whenever a new law is made, have it published immediately, and keep a record of the criminals."

Emperor Yao died at the ripe age of one hundred and two. He did not leave the kingdom to his son but to a man named Shun.

Before I go on with my story, I shall tell you something about this Shun. His mother died when he was very young, and after some time, his father married again. Then the boy had a hard time of it. When his stepmother had children, his father loved them better than his oldest son. He began to beat poor Shun and, at last, tried to kill him. In China, a father can do what he pleases. His children must obey him and dare not even talk to him. This is called **filial piety**, and the child who neglects it is severely punished.

So Shun suffered in silence, more so because his stepmother was **sly** and his younger brother proud. But he bore it all and never once showed how much it hurt him. He was always obedient to his parents and kind to his brother. He decided to be respectful and quiet, and at last, his parents began to love him, and then he had his reward. But the neighbors had noticed all this, and when he was grown, they admired him so much for his conduct that they would have elected him to any position if only they had known what elections were.

When Emperor Yao first heard about Shun, he sent for him and gave him a government job so that he might see for himself. When he found Shun always the same—kind, just, polite, wise, and honest—he made him a general superintendent and afterward promoted him to be Master of Ceremonies, whose duty it was to introduce all the nobles who came to pay their respects to the Emperor.

One day, Shun was ordered to explore the vast forest's deepest parts and find out what was causing a flood. He was going about this work when a terrible thundering rainstorm overtook him, so people feared he might be killed. But he showed bravery by keeping calm and endured dangers that would have overwhelmed other men. Therefore, the Emperor could not help admiring Shun and thought of how to reward him.

Emperor Shun
Author: გიორგი ვარამაშვილი. CC BY-SA 4.0

You ought to know that rulers didn't leave the throne to their oldest sons during much of China's history, as in Europe. They were expected to study all their sons and choose the best one to be their heir. Earlier, a ruler could even appoint someone who wasn't a son, which is precisely what Emperor Yao did. Not only did he make Shun his heir, but he insisted that he should be emperor from that day. Shun obeyed and became another ruler of whom the Chinese are very proud. The legend says of him: "If you study the old Emperor Shun, you will find that he was wise, polite, kind, true, and honest."

Yu, who restored order after the great flood, was made prime minister. After reigning for thirty-three years, Shun resigned and made Yu his successor.

Yu the Great, as imagined by Song dynasty painter Ma Lin

The Xia and Shang Dynasties

According to legend, **Yu the Great**'s descendants ruled China for nearly 500 years in the Xia dynasty line until one became corrupt and cruel. Cheng Tang, a subject ruler, overthrew this king and founded a new Shang dynasty in the Huang River valley. The Shang dynasty is the earliest one we have reliable archaeological records about.

This first king of the Shang family is said to have worshiped a god named Shangdi, which means "Supreme Ruler." When no rain fell for seven years, legend says that Cheng Tang prayed earnestly: "Do not, on account of any neglect of mine, who am but a single man, destroy the lives of the people!" When his prayer was ended, it is said that rain began to fall plentifully.

The worship of images or idols began under Wuyi, the twenty-seventh Shang king. He is spoken of as one of the most wicked of all China's rulers. One history book tells that he ordered images of clay to be made in the shape of human beings and made the people worship them as gods. He grew tired of them, however, and cast them aside. Then he had leather bags made, filled with blood, which he threw up in the air. He shot at them with arrows, and when the blood was pouring down, he shouted: "I have killed the gods!" The people soon grew very tired of such a madman, and another dynasty succeeded to the throne.

When the 13-year-old King Zheng (who later renamed himself Qin Shi Huang, or "First Emperor" of the Qin) came to power in 221 B.C., one of his first acts was to begin preparing for his death. In addition to an army of over 8,000 clay soldiers, his tomb was lined in bronze and contained a vast wealth of jewels and artifacts beyond imagination.
CC BY-SA 3.0 Unported

The Qin Dynasty

After several more dynasties and periods of civil warfare, the **Qin dynasty**, from which comes the name of China, came to power under **Qin Chi Huang**. This dynasty existed only briefly, but it was the first dynasty that unified China.

Qin Chi Huang, whose name means "First Emperor," made his capital on the River Wei, where he built a splendid palace from the spoils of all the captive kings who had submitted to him, and he ordered that all the treasures of their palaces should be brought to him. He visited various parts of the empire, built public buildings, ordered canals and roads to be constructed, and drove the invading **Huns** back into Mongolia. It was he who much of the **Great Wall of China**, extending it from the sea to the desert, a distance of 1,250 miles.

This emperor was very vain. In his desire to be known as the first true emperor the country ever had, he ordered that every book in China should be burned. This order was carried out, and all the historical records of the country, as well as the works

First Emperor Qin Shi Huang is famed for having united the Warring States' walls to form The Great Wall of China. Most of the present structure, however, dates to the Ming dynasty.
Photo by Hao Wei. CC BY 2.0

of the famous philosopher **Confucius**, went up in flames. There is, however, no doubt that several copies of their works were saved.

Qin Chi Huang was also obsessed with immortality. He employed many sorcerers to make potions for him, and he ordered the construction of a massive tomb, complete with an army of soldiers made of terracotta clay.

The Han Dynasty: China's Golden Age

The Qin dynasty did not last long. The founder of the Han dynasty defeated Chi's successor. The Chinese say their modern history begins at this time and that this period was China's Golden Age. The government was reformed, science and inventions were encouraged, and the **Silk Road** was developed, which made a network for trading goods and ideas from Europe and the Middle East across Asia. Buddhism was brought from India into China during this time, and it grew to become one of China's major religions.

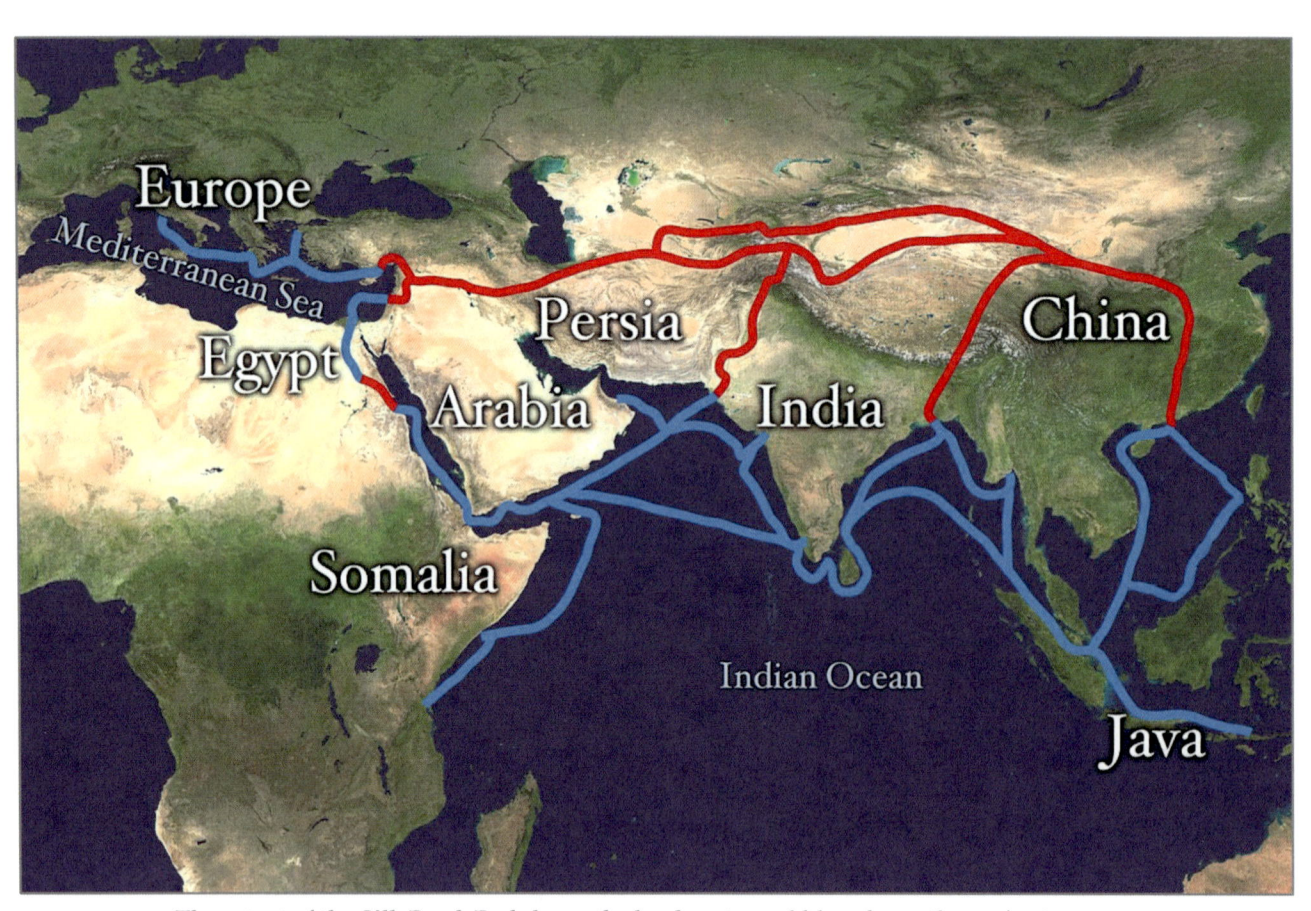

The extent of the Silk Road. Red shows the land route, and blue shows the sea/water route.
Courtesy NASA /Goddard Space Flight Center

Lesson Two

History Overview and Assignments
True Friends

THIS DELIGHTFUL TALE from China's early days portrays the value the Chinese culture places on trust and friendship.

Sound of Pines on a Mountain Path,
by Tang Yin (c.1516)

Suggested Reading and Assignments

- Read the article: *The Golden Nugget*.
- After reading the article, summarize the story you read by either:
    - Retelling it out loud to your teacher or parent.
      OR
    - Completing an appropriate notebook page.
  Either way, be sure to include an overview of key people, places, dates, and events in your summary.
- Illustrate this story and then be able to tell it back in your own words using your drawings.
- Be sure to visit your **ArtiosHCS** curriculum website for additional resources and any videos and websites assigned for this lesson.

Adapted for Elementary School from the book:
A Chinese Wonder Book
by Norman Hinsdale Pitman
The Golden Nugget

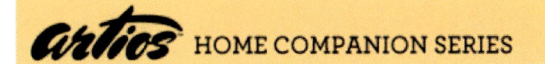

Once upon a time, many, many years ago, there lived in China two friends named Ki-wu and Pao-shu. These two young men were always together. No cross words passed between them, and no unkind thoughts marred their friendship. Many a fascinating tale might be told of their unselfishness and how the good fairies gave them the true reward of virtue. One story alone, however, will be enough to show how strong their affection and goodness were.

It was a bright, beautiful day in early spring when Ki-wu and Pao-shu set out for a stroll together, for they were tired of the city and its noises.

"Let us go into the heart of the pine forest," said Ki-wu lightly. "There we can forget the cares that worry us; there we can breathe the sweetness of the flowers and lie on the moss-covered ground."

"Good!" said Pao-shu, "I, too, am tired. The forest is the place for rest."

Happy as two travelers on a holiday, they passed along the winding road, their eyes turned in longing toward the distant treetops. Their hearts beat fast in youthful pleasure as they drew nearer and nearer to the woods.

They saw shining in the pathway, directly in front of them, a lump of gold.

"For thirty days, I have worked over my books," sighed Ki-wu. "For thirty days, I have not had a rest. My head is so full of wisdom that I fear it will burst. Oh, for a breath of the pure air blowing through the greenwood."

"And I," added Pao-shu sadly, "have worked like a slave at my counter and found it just as dull as you have found your books. My master mistreats me. It seems good, indeed, to get beyond his reach."

Now they came to the border of the grove, crossed a little stream, and plunged headlong among the trees and shrubs. They rambled on for many an hour, talking and laughing merrily; when suddenly on passing round a clump of flower-covered bushes, they saw a lump of gold shining in the pathway directly in front of them.

"See!" said both, speaking at the same time and pointing toward the treasure.

Ki-wu, stooping, picked up the nugget. It was nearly as large as a lemon and was very pretty. "It is yours, my dear friend," said he, at the same time handing it to Pao-shu. "Yours because you saw it first."

"No, no," answered Pao-shu, "You are wrong, my brother, for you were first to speak. Now, you can never say hereafter that the good fairies have not rewarded you for all your faithful hours of study."

"Repaid me for my study! Why, that is impossible. Are not the wise men always saying that study brings its reward? No, the gold is yours: I insist upon it. Think of your weeks of hard labor—of the masters that have ground you to the bone! Here is something far better. Take it," he insisted, laughing. "May it be the nest egg through which you may hatch out a great fortune."

Thus they joked for some minutes, each refusing to take the treasure for himself; each insisting that it belonged to the other. At last, the chunk of gold was dropped in the very spot where they had first spied it, and the two comrades went away, each happy because he loved his friend better than anything else in the world. Thus they turned their backs on any chance of quarreling.

"It was not for gold that we left the city," exclaimed Ki-wu warmly.

"No," replied his friend. "One day in this forest is worth a thousand nuggets."

"Let us go to the spring and sit on the rocks," suggested Ki-wu. "It is the coolest spot in the whole grove."

When they reached the spring, they were sorry to find the place already occupied. A countryman was stretched at full length on the ground.

"Wake up, fellow!" cried Pao-shu. "There is money for you nearby. Up yonder path, a golden apple is waiting for some man to go and pick it up."

Then they described the exact spot where the treasure was to the unwelcome stranger and were delighted to see him set out in eager search.

For an hour, the friends enjoyed each other's company, talking of all their hopes and ambitions for their future and listening to the music of the birds that hopped about on the branches overhead.

At last, they were startled by the angry voice of the man who had gone after the nugget. "What trick is this you have played on me, masters? Why do you make a poor man like me run his legs off for nothing on a hot day?"

"What do you mean, fellow?" asked Ki-wu, astonished. "Did you not find the fruit we told you about?"

"No," he answered, in a tone of half-hidden rage, "but in its place was a monster snake, which I cut in two with my blade. The gods will bring me bad luck for killing something in the woods. If you thought you could drive me from this place by such a trick, you'd soon find you were mistaken, for I was first upon this spot, and you have no right to give me orders."

"Stop your chatter, bumpkin, and take this copper for your trouble. We thought we were doing you a favor. If you are blind, there's no one but yourself to blame. Come, Pao-shu, let us go back and look at this wonderful snake hiding in a chunk of gold."

Laughing merrily, the two companions left the countryman and turned back in search of the nugget.

"If I am not mistaken," said the student, "the gold lies beyond that fallen tree."

"Quite true; we shall soon see the dead snake."

Quickly they crossed the remaining stretch of the pathway with their eyes fixed intently on the ground. Arriving at the spot where they had left the shining treasure, what was their surprise to see not the lump of gold, not the dead snake described by the idler, but two beautiful golden nuggets, each larger than the one they had seen at first.

Each friend picked up one of these treasures and handed it joyfully to his companion.

"At last, the fairies have rewarded you for your unselfishness!" said Ki-wu.

"Yes," answered Pao-shu, "by granting me a chance to give you your deserts."

Lesson Three

History Overview and Assignments
Ancient China

"The ancient Chinese believed that life carried on after death. People believed they would continue to do the things they had done in this life in the afterlife. Tombs were arranged with the objects people would need in the afterlife--weapons, ritual vessels, and personal ornaments."

– from http://www.ancientchina.co.uk/tombs/home_set.html

A Mandarin Chinese civil magistrate sitting on a cushion, smoking a pipe, and waiting for the arrival of a visitor, attended by a domestic servant. The Mandarin's rank and position are denoted by the bird embroidered on the badge on his breast, the red ball and peacock feather attached to his cap, and the beads of pearl and coral appending from his neck. The servant holds a purse with tobacco for his master; his girdle encloses a handkerchief and hangs his tobacco pouch and pipe. On the wall, Chinese characters are painted, signifying moral precepts. Drawing by William Alexander, draughtsman of the Macartney Embassy to China in 1793. Image taken from *The Costume of China* (1805)

Suggested Reading and Assignments

- There is no article to read for this lesson. Instead, visit the websites at the links found as suggested assignments for this lesson on your **ArtiosHCS** curriculum website to explore several areas of Chinese culture and history. Use your interest as a guide on what and how much to explore:
- Be sure to visit your **ArtiosHCS** curriculum website for additional resources and any videos and websites assigned for this lesson.

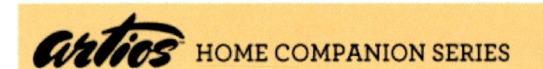

The Artios Home Companion Series
Unit 16: Ancient Japan – "Land of the Sunrise"

Teacher Overview

"Japan has been commonly viewed as an isolated island nation with a single language and culture shared by a uniform population. From ancient times, though, Japan has been home to more than one ethnic group. . . . From around the middle of the 11th century B.C. to 300 B.C., Japan was populated by a Neolithic civilization called the Jomon (rope pattern) culture. This group of hunters and gatherers decorated their pottery by twisting rope around the wet clay to produce a distinctive pattern. Remnants of their pit dwellings and enormous mounds of discarded shells mark the locations of their settlements, which were scattered throughout the islands. But it wasn't until the Yayoi period (300 B.C. to 250 A.D.) that Japan became a rice-loving culture. With the transmission of wet-field rice cultivation from the continent, the Yayoi people followed irrigation, planting, and harvesting techniques still used in modern agriculture."

– USHistory.org

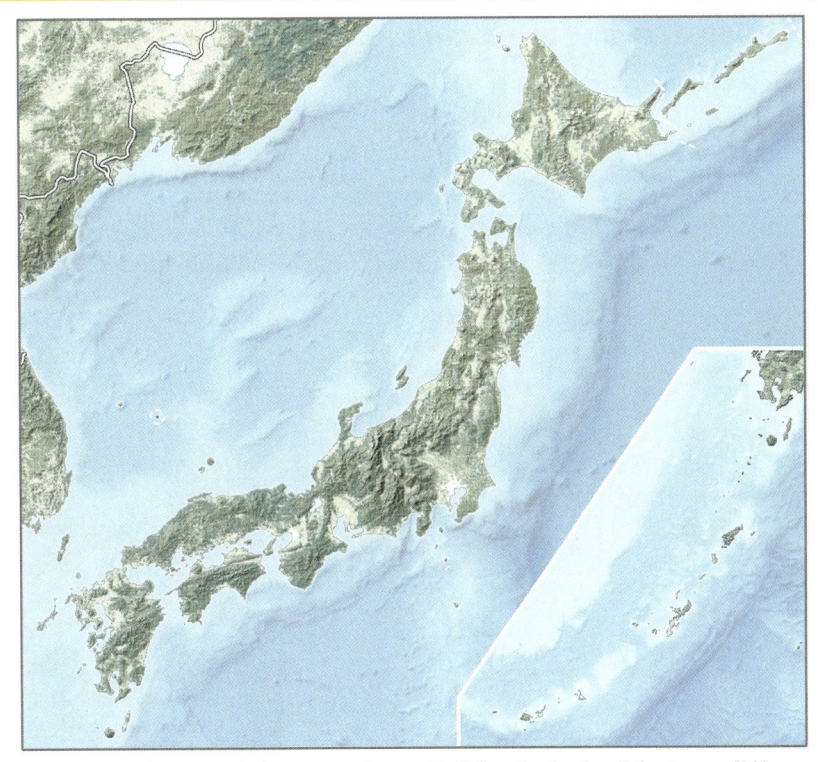

Although Japan is around the same size as California, its land features differ vastly.
The surrounding Sea of Japan and the Pacific Ocean made foreign invasion difficult,
so Japan developed a unique kind of culture.

Alexrk2, Japan location map with side map of the Ryukyu Islands.svg, (Chumwa) AVHRR Land Cover SRTM Data, ETOPO1 Natural Earth 1. CC BY-SA 3.0

Suggested Assignments

Based on your student's age and ability, the reading in this unit may be read aloud to the student, and journaling and notebook pages may be completed orally. Likewise, other assignments may be done with an appropriate combination of independent and guided study.

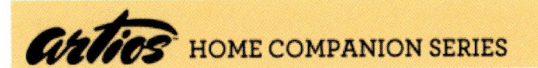

In this unit, students will:
- Complete three lessons in which they will learn about **ancient Japan**.
- Define vocabulary words.
- Learn about Japan using a website found at the links in the suggested assignments for this unit on the **ArtiosHCS** curriculum website and prepare to share what they learn.
- Illustrate a story.
- Watch the Creation Myth videos in the suggested assignments for this Unit on the **ArtiosHCS** curriculum. Create a Venn diagram and answer questions to compare and contrast the two creation myths.
- Visit the **ArtiosHCS** curriculum website at **www.ArtiosHCS.com** for additional resources and any videos and websites assigned for this unit.

Heart Connections

People tend to ignore what they know about God.

For even though they knew God, they did not honor Him as God or give thanks, but they became futile in their speculations, and their foolish heart was darkened. Professing to be wise, they became fools, and exchanged the glory of the incorruptible God for an image in the form of corruptible man and of birds and four-footed animals and crawling creatures.

– Romans 1:20-23

God despises idolatry.

"You shall have no other gods before me."

– Exodus 20:3

Additional Material for Parent or Teacher:

At the **ArtiosHCS** curriculum website, you will find a link to a website titled "What is a Venn Diagram?" You may use this to help your student(s) in Lesson Three.

A 19th-century depiction of the legendary Emperor Jimmu, aided in his conquests by a mythical three-legged crow. Woodblock print by Tsukioka Yoshitosh

Lesson One

History Overview and Assignments
Land of the Rising Sun

"Japan's location off the fringe of continental Asia made it an ideal place for its unique culture to develop. The islands are situated close enough to China and Korea to benefit from those great civilizations' cultural and technological innovations, but far enough removed across perilous seas to resist significant political and military domination from the two powers."

– from the adapted article below

The main gate to Fushimi Inari-Taisha in Kyoto, one of the oldest Shinto shrines in Japan
Photo by Chris Gladis. CC BY 2.0

Key People, Places, and Events

Ring of Fire
Jomon
Yayoi
Ainu
Nara period
Heian period
Shinto

Vocabulary

archipelago
tsunami
indigenous
tribute
inhabitant
misfortune

Suggested Reading and Assignments

- Read the article: *Ancient Japan*.
- Define the vocabulary words in the context of the reading. Write the words and their definitions in the vocabulary section of your history notebook.
- After reading the article, summarize the story you read by either:
    - Retelling it out loud to your teacher or parent.
        OR
    - Completing an appropriate notebook page.

  Either way, be sure to include the answers to the discussion questions and an overview of key people, places, dates, and events in your summary.
- Learn about the history and culture of Japan using the website found at the link on your **ArtiosHCS** curriculum website, and prepare to share what you have learned. Follow your interests in choosing what to read about.
- Be sure to visit your **ArtiosHCS** curriculum website for additional resources and any videos and websites assigned for this lesson.

Ancient: Elementary
Unit 16: Japan – "Land of the Sunrise"

Discussion Questions

1. What does the name "Nippon" mean?
2. What is the land like that makes up Japan?
3. What can we tell about Japan's earliest people?
4. What happened to the Ainu people?
5. Tell how Japan's imperial family rose to power.
6. Write down the four historical periods mentioned in today's reading and one thing each one is known for.
7. What two types of spirits do Shinto believers worship? What do the First and Second Commandments in the Bible say about who and how God wants people to worship?
8. What two other belief systems were later blended in with Shintoism?

Ancient Japan
by
Mary E. Hall

Japan's Creation Mythology

The Japanese creation story tells of spirits named Izanagi and Izanami who stood on heaven's rainbow bridge and dropped Japan's islands from the tip of a spear dipped in the ocean. The pair then came to live on the islands they had created, where they became the parents of the people of Japan and other spirits, such as the sun goddess Amaterasu, the most important supernatural being in Japan's **Shinto** religion.

An Island Nation

The Japanese call the long **archipelago** of islands that make up their nation *Nippon*, which means "Land of the Rising Sun." Japan has several large, mountainous islands and hundreds of smaller ones. Located on the volcanic **Ring of Fire** that encircles the Pacific Ocean, Japan is geologically active, with frequent volcanic eruptions, earthquakes, and **tsunami**s. Separated from the mainland by 200 miles of water, Japan was even more isolated than China from other civilizations in ancient times.

Cipangu on the 1453 *Fra Mauro Map*, the first known European description of the island. Marco Polo wrote the early Chinese word for Japan as Cipangu.

The Jomon Period

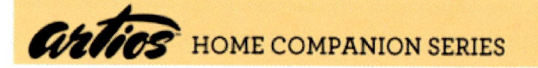

Unlike China, Japan kept no written records of its early history. Early Japanese society was made up of hunter-gatherer groups that had migrated from the Chinese mainland. These groups developed a common culture known today as **Jomon**, named for the rope designs pressed onto their pottery. Remains of many pit-dwellings and large mounds of discarded shells have been found, marking the locations of Jomon settlements throughout the islands.

An example of Jomon rope pottery from 10000–8000 B.C.

The Yayoi Period

The Jomon culture was followed by the **Yayoi**, which is named for the part of Tokyo in which early items have been found that look quite different from those of the Jomon.

The Yayoi people were probably primarily farmers from Korea. The Yayoi period was the time when the Japanese became a rice-loving people. In the northern part of Hokkaido's large island, the Yayoi conquered an **indigenous** group called the **Ainu**.

Large, square-shaped mound tombs built by the Yayoi give evidence of advanced Stone Age building ability, and artifacts indicate that alliances existed between local tribes. During the Yayoi period, rival family clans battled for supremacy over centuries throughout the mountainous islands.

A ceramic jar from the Yayoi period

Japan's Imperial Family

Legends say that a clan called the Yamato gained victory over the others in the seventh century B.C. Claiming they were descendants of the sun goddess, this clan, led by a chieftain named Jimmu, soon conquered all of Japan. The Yamato clan became Japan's imperial family, and it remains today the world's oldest hereditary monarchy.

The conquered clans were forced to pay **tribute** money to the Yamato clan, and their chieftains were forced to come to live at the royal court or send family hostages to make sure the clan remained loyal. Class distinctions structured Japanese society, built around maternal family groups and ruled by the warrior chieftains of the top clans.

Close relations developed between Japan and Korea during this time, making

Japan more familiar with the "world over the water." Buddhism was introduced to Japan in the year 552 by Chinese missionaries. The ruling class did not initially accept Buddhism, but gradually its values were blended into Japanese culture. Japan adopted the Chinese calendar, and Chinese governmental methods were implemented. Prince Shotoku encouraged building Buddhist temples and wrote a constitution based on the teachings of Confucius. After a group of scholars returned from China, a list of laws was made that declared authority of the monarch over clan chieftains. The governmental structure became a tightly controlled system over Japan's many provinces.

The Ainu are Hokkaido's indigenous people.

During the **Nara period** (710-84), a Japanese writing system was developed using Chinese characters. This allowed literature to flourish, and soon a collection of written poetry was gathered from across the islands.

During the **Heian period** from 794 to 1185, known as Japan's Golden Age, Japan's culture matured while Chinese influence declined. Imperial court life reached its splendor during this period, inspiring advancements in art, architecture, and literature.

The upper classes gathered armies of guards and soldiers to maintain power, which would later give rise to the *samurai* warrior class that fought battles for the rulers during Japan's feudal period.

Rebellions arose among various clans as the warrior class strengthened, but they couldn't take over the government for several more centuries.

Japan's samurai warriors had a strict code of conduct. They were the protectors of the Japanese people and the masters of the martial arts.

Shinto

Like all other cultures, the Japanese have wondered about how the world was created and how nature works. Ancient Japanese people believed the natural world was sacred and influenced by spirits, who sometimes took the form of animals residing in trees, mountains, waterfalls, or other elements of nature. The dazzling beauty of Japan's natural wonders has always stirred awe among her people.

These beliefs about spirits developed into a religion called **Shinto**, in which all-natural elements are believed to be good by nature and **inhabit**ed by spirits called *kami*. Shinto believes there is neither an all-powerful god nor a heaven for reward or hell for punishment. Instead, the many kami are believed to work together to oversee its events and connect everything.

Some kami are believed to be harmful, while others are helpful. As in other ancient religions, believers give worship offerings to man-made figures of the spirits in the hope of receiving blessings and avoiding **misfortune**. Shinto believers also worship the spirits of their ancestors.

Buddhism and Confucianism

During the sixth and seventh centuries A.D., Buddhism and Confucianism were brought in from China. Both became popular among Japan's upper classes and gradually blended into Shinto beliefs and practices. Buddhist and Confucian teachings about how to live and about life after death became deeply rooted in Japanese thought and are portrayed in much of the country's art and literature.

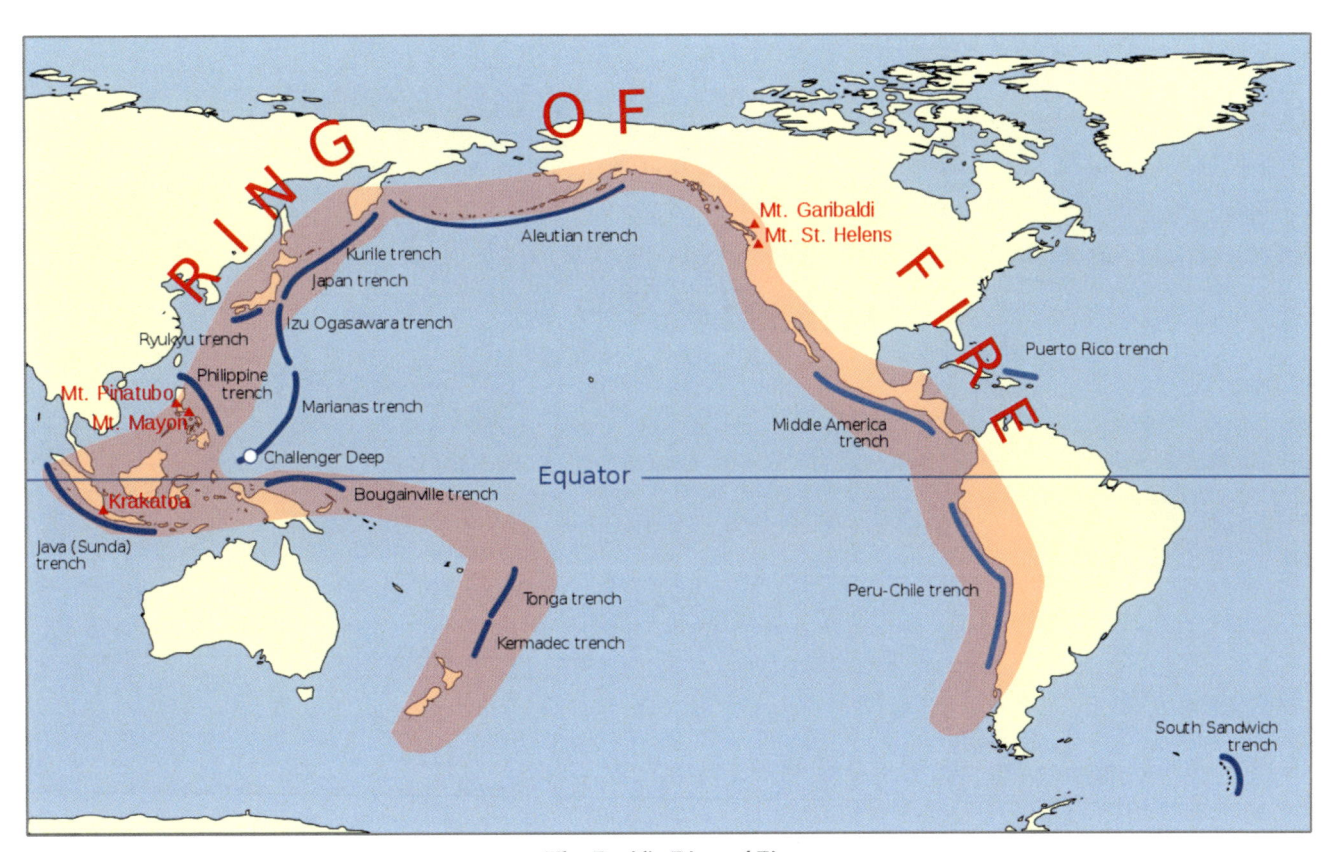

The Pacific Ring of Fire

Lesson Two

History Overview and Assignments
A Japanese Fairy Tale

THIS TALE FROM EARLY Japan warns against making hasty judgments, which can produce sad and harmful results.

"The Money began his Tale of Woe."
Image from *The Japanese Fairy Book*

Suggested Reading and Assignments

- Read the article: *The Sagacious Monkey and the Boar*.
- After reading the article, summarize the story you read by either:
    - Retelling it out loud to your teacher or parent.
        OR
    - Completing an appropriate notebook page.
  Either way, be sure to include an overview of key people, places, dates, and events in your summary.
- Illustrate this story and then be able to tell it back in your own words using your drawings.
- Be sure to visit your **ArtiosHCS** curriculum website for additional resources and any videos and websites assigned for this lesson.

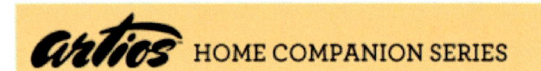

Ancient: Elementary
Unit 16: Japan – "Land of the Sunrise"

Adapted for Elementary School from the book:
Japanese Fairy Tales
by Yei Theodora Ozaki
The Sagacious Monkey and the Boar

Long, long ago, there lived in the province of Shinshin in Japan, a traveling monkey-man who earned his living by taking round a monkey and showing off the animal's tricks.

One evening the man came home in a terrible temper and told his wife to send for the butcher the next morning.

The wife was very bewildered and asked her husband, "Why do you wish me to send for the butcher?"

"It's no use taking that monkey around any longer; he's too old and forgets his tricks. I beat him with my stick all I know how, but he won't dance properly. I must now sell him to the butcher and make what money out of him I can. There is nothing else to be done."

The woman felt deeply sorry for the poor little animal and pleaded for her husband to spare the monkey, but her pleading was all in vain—the man was determined to sell him to the butcher.

Now the monkey was in the next room and overheard every conversation. He soon understood that he was to be killed and said, "Barbarous indeed is my master! Here I have served him faithfully for years, and instead of allowing me to end my days comfortably and in peace, he will let the butcher cut me up, and my poor body is to be roasted, stewed, and eaten? Woe is me! What am I to do? Ah! A bright thought has struck me! There is, I know, a wild bear living in the forest nearby. I have often heard tell of his wisdom. Perhaps if I go to him and tell him the strait I am in, he will give me his counsel. I will go and try."

There was no time to lose. The monkey slipped out of the house and ran as quickly as possible to the forest to find the boar. The boar was at home, and the monkey began his tale of woe at once.

"Good Mr. Boar, I have heard of your superior wisdom. I am in great trouble; you alone can help me. I have grown old in the service of my master, and because I cannot dance properly now, he intends to sell me to the butcher. What do you advise me to do? I know how clever you are!"

The boar was pleased with the flattery and determined to help the monkey. He thought briefly and then said, "Hasn't your master a baby?"

"Oh, yes," said the monkey, "he has one infant son."

"Doesn't it lie by the door in the morning when your mistress begins the work of the day? Well, I will come around early, and when I see my opportunity, I will seize the child and run off with it."

"What then?" said the monkey.

"Why the mother will be in a tremendous fright, and before your master and mistress know what to do, you must run after me and rescue the child and take it home safely to its parents, and you will see that when the butcher comes, they won't have the heart to sell you."

The monkey thanked the boar many times and then went home. As you may imagine, he did not sleep much that night for thinking of the morrow. His life depended on whether the boar's plan succeeded or not. He was the first up, waiting anxiously for what was to happen. It seemed to him an exceptionally long time before his master's wife moved about and opened the shutters to let in the light of day. Then all happened as the boar had planned. As usual, the mother placed her child near the porch while tidying up the house and getting her breakfast ready.

The child was crooning happily in the morning sunlight, dabbing on the mats at the play of light and shadow. Suddenly there was a noise on the porch and a loud cry from the child. The mother ran from the kitchen to the spot, just in time to see the boar disappearing through the gate with her child in its clutch. She flung out her hands with a loud cry of despair and rushed into the inner room where her husband was still sleeping soundly.

He sat up slowly, rubbed his eyes, and crossly demanded what his wife was making all that noise about. By the time the man was aware of what had happened, and they both got outside the gate, the boar had got far away, but they saw the monkey running after the thief as hard as his legs would carry him.

Both man and wife admired the sagacious monkey's plucky conduct, and their gratitude knew no bounds when the faithful monkey brought the child safely back into their arms.

"There!" said the wife. "This is the animal you want to kill—if the monkey hadn't been here, we should have lost our child forever."

"You are right, wife," said the man as he carried the child into the house. "You may send the butcher back when he comes, and now give us all a good breakfast—and the monkey too."

When the butcher arrived, he was sent away with an order for some boar's meat for the evening dinner, and the monkey was petted and lived the rest of his days in peace, nor did his master ever strike him again.

Japanese Fairy Tales
by Yei Theodora Ozaki

Free audiobooks from Lit2Go

The Sagacious Monkey and the Boar
Listen at: ETC.USF.EDU/LIT2GO/P/4849

Lesson Three

History Overview and Assignments
Ancient Creation Myths

"In the beginning, there was chaos long before heaven and earth even existed."
– from "Iznami and Iznagi: A Creation Myth from Japan."

Nuwa, also known as Nugua, is a goddess in ancient Chinese mythology, believed to have created mankind. Modern relief of Nuwa at the Ping Sien Si Temple in Perak, Malaysia
Photo by Anandajoti Bhikkhu. CC BY 2.0

Suggested Reading and Assignments

- There is no article to read for this lesson. Instead, watch the videos about the Japanese and Chinese creation myths found on your **ArtiosHCS** curriculum website for this Unit. Create a Venn diagram to compare and contrast the two myths. What do you find similar and different between the two? How do they differ from the Bible's account of creation? Why do you think the Japanese and Chinese each made their own story of creation?
- Be sure to visit your **ArtiosHCS** curriculum website for additional resources and any videos and websites assigned for this lesson.

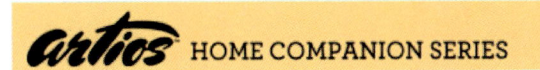

Ancient: Elementary
Unit 16: Japan – "Land of the Sunrise"

The Artios Home Companion Series
Unit 17: Ancient Africa – "Land of Kingdoms"

Teacher Overview

FURTHER SOUTH than all the other regions we've studied so far, the continent of Africa became home to a unique group of fascinating civilizations. Because there are few written records from the early years of these cultures, the whole story of early African history is challenging to unravel. But through ongoing archaeological research, a remarkable picture of the continent's first kingdoms is slowly emerging.

Satellite view of Africa, showing the Sahara Desert up north, and forests and grasslands further south
Photo by NASA

Suggested Assignments

Based on your student's age and ability, the reading in this unit may be read aloud to the student, and journaling and notebook pages may be completed orally. Likewise, other assignments may be done with an appropriate combination of independent and guided study.

In this unit, students will:
- Complete one lesson in which they will learn about **Africa's early people groups and kingdoms**.
- Make a page in their notebook for each early African culture they study. Be sure to include history, achievements, and more. Use the websites assigned for this lesson to add additional interesting details, such as African phrases, songs, events, etc. *Please be aware that some sites may be biased, so read through the material first.*
- Visit the **ArtiosHCS** curriculum website at **www.ArtiosHCS.com** for additional resources and any videos and websites assigned for this unit.

Heart Connections

People tend to ignore what they know about God.
For even though they knew God, they did not honor Him as God or give thanks, but they became futile in their speculations, and their foolish heart was darkened. Professing to be wise, they became fools, and exchanged the glory of the incorruptible God for an image in the form of corruptible man and of birds and four-footed animals and crawling creatures.
— Romans 1:20-23

God despises idolatry.
"You shall have no other gods before me."
— Exodus 20:3

God alone is to be worshiped.
"You shall not make idols for yourselves or erect an image or pillar, and you shall not set up a figured stone in your land to bow down to it, for I am the LORD your God."
— Leviticus 26:1

Additional Material for Parent or Teacher:

On the **ArtiosHCS** curriculum website, you will find links to some websites with supplemental ideas and material about Africa. Study them and share them with your student(s) as appropriate.

Ruins of ancient Carthage
Photo by Patrick Verdier, Free On Line Photos

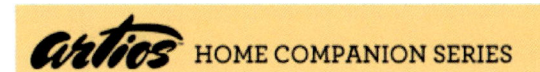

Lesson One

History Overview and Assignments
Early Kingdoms of Africa

"Upon Africa's soils, our prehistoric relatives have walked side by side. From its territories, great civilizations have risen to glory. Through its peoples, astounding cultures have grown and flourished. . . . Every day discoveries are made about Africa and new artifacts are displayed to enrich the community through their historical and cultural value."

– USHistory.org

Key People, Places, and Events

Nubia
Kush
Sao
Ghana Empire
Mali Empire
Carthage

Nok sculpture, terracotta, Louvre. The Nok people lived in what is now Nigeria for about two thousand years, starting around 1500 B.C.
Photo by Marie-Lan Nguyen

Suggested Reading and Assignments

- Read the article: *Ancient Africa*.
- After reading the article, summarize the story you read by either:
    - Retelling it out loud to your teacher or parent.
        OR
    - Completing an appropriate notebook page.
  Either way, be sure to include an overview of key people, places, dates, and events in your summary.
- Instead of answering discussion questions, make a page in your notebook for each of the African cultures you study. Be sure to include history, achievements, and more. Use the websites assigned for this lesson to add additional interesting details, such as African phrases, songs, events, etc. *Please be aware that some sites may have a bias, so be sure to have a parent or teacher read through the material first.*
- Be sure to visit your **ArtiosHCS** curriculum website for additional resources and any videos and websites assigned for this lesson.

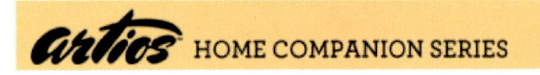

Ancient: Elementary
Unit 17: Ancient Africa – "Land of Kingdoms"

Adapted for Elementary School from the book:
Boundless World History
source: https://www.coursehero.com/study-guides/boundless-worldhistory
Ancient Africa
CC BY-SA: Attribution-ShareAlike

Nile Valley Cultures

*A few early people groups settled along the Nile River beside the Egyptians. One grew to become the kingdom of **Nubia**, which set up its line of pharaohs. These Nile Valley cultures developed over time into the country called Sudan. One group of Nubians formed the kingdom of **Kush**, which conquered all of Egypt and lasted nearly a thousand years. Kushites worshiped a number of the Egyptian deities and used some of their names for their throne names. The Kushites were known for their archery and stoneworking skills; hundreds of their ancient pyramids can still be seen today. The culture was also known for its ironworking, especially for making the weapons that let the Kushite kingdom last for so long.*

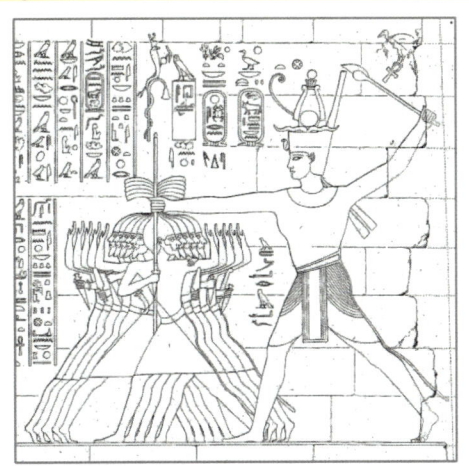

The Kushite king Senkamanisken slaying enemies

MIDDLE AFRICA

The Sao People

The region made up of the countries of Cameroon and Chad has been inhabited by many people groups. The earliest we know of was the **Sao** culture, known today only from artifacts and passed-down stories. The Sao left no written records. Little is known today about Sao culture or government. One theory believes that they descended from the Hyksos, who conquered Ancient Egypt and later moved south from the Nile valley into mid-Africa after fleeing from invaders.

Sao artifacts show they were skilled workers of metal. They made bronze sculptures, clay statues of human and animal figures, and decorated pottery.

The end of the Sao culture may have come about because of conquest. Today, several ethnic groups in the area believe they are descendants of the Sao.

Mali terracotta horseman figure
Photo by Franko Khoury

Other Early African Kingdoms

*Later, a kingdom emerged in Western Africa, developing into the wealthy **Ghana Empire**. This kingdom gained riches by transporting salt, gold, and slaves across the Sahara Desert. This kingdom, in time, became part of the **Mali Empire**. This kingdom reached its cultural height under the rule of a king named Mansa Musa, who made a journey to Mecca in Saudi Arabia. He displayed great riches and power, with hundreds of slaves and camels carrying vast amounts of gold.*

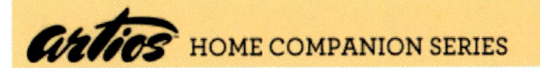

Ancient: Elementary
Unit 17: Ancient Africa – "Land of Kingdoms"

NORTH AFRICA

Ancient Carthage

Ancient **Carthage** was a North African city that grew into an empire lasting more than five hundred years before Rome conquered it. By the time of its defeat, the empire had spread across northern Africa and into the south of what is now Spain.

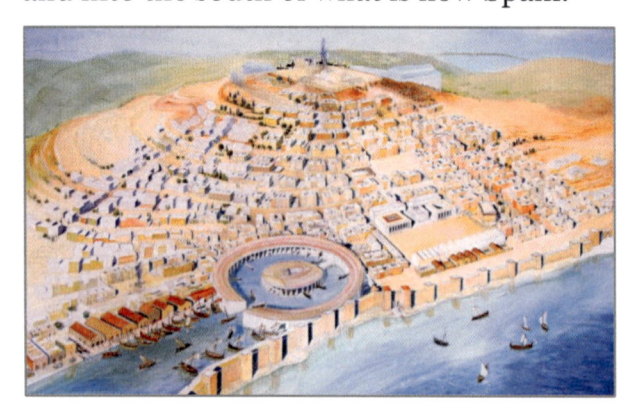

Modern reconstruction of ancient Carthage. The circular harbor at the front is the Cothon, the military port of Carthage, where all of the city's warships were anchored.
Photo by damian entwistle. CC BY-SA 2.0

One of the ancient world's wealthiest cities, Carthage produced embroidered silks, dyed cloth of many types, artistic pottery, and perfumes. Its craftsmen worked expertly with ivory, glassware, wood, metals, and precious stones. Carthage traded in salted Atlantic fish and bought and sold the products of almost every Mediterranean people group. The people of Carthage were also highly advanced and productive farmers who used iron plows, irrigation, and crop rotation.

Carthage was the Mediterranean's largest producer of silver goods. It sent trading caravans into many parts of Africa and Persia to trade in almost every product desired by the ancient world, including spices from Arabia, Africa, and India.

Military and Warfare

As Carthage developed into an empire, its military became one of the most significant forces in the ancient world. Carthage was almost constantly at war with the Greeks or the Romans. Ultimately, the Romans destroyed Carthage and became the most powerful state in the Western Mediterranean.

Salt caravan
Photo by Holger Reineccius. GNU Free Documentation License

The Artios Home Companion Series
Unit 18: Early People Groups of the Americas

Teacher Overview

THE ANCIENT CIVILIZATIONS of the American continents are fascinating to study. These cultures made many advances that we might think were found only on the other side of the world then. The religious beliefs of many of these people groups, though, were filled with darkness and violence as the people tried to please false gods. Human sacrifices were a part of life for these cultures, and sadly tens of thousands of people were slaughtered.

Buffalo Hunt, by George Catlin (1844)

Suggested Assignments

Based on your student's age and ability, the reading in this unit may be read aloud to the student, and journaling and notebook pages may be completed orally. Likewise, other assignments may be done with an appropriate combination of independent and guided study.

In this unit, students will:
- Complete three lessons in which they will learn about **ancient cultures in the Americas**.
- Define vocabulary words.
- Make a page in their notebook for each early culture they study in this unit.
- Visit the **ArtiosHCS** curriculum website at **www.ArtiosHCS.com** for additional resources and any videos and websites assigned for this unit.

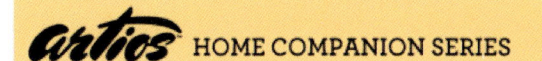

Heart Connections

People tend to ignore what they know about God.
For even though they knew God, they did not honor Him as God or give thanks, but they became futile in their speculations, and their foolish heart was darkened. Professing to be wise, they became fools, and exchanged the glory of the incorruptible God for an image in the form of corruptible man and of birds and four-footed animals and crawling creatures.
– Romans 1:20-23

God despises idolatry.
"You shall have no other gods before me."
– Exodus 20:3

God alone is to be worshiped.
"You shall not make idols for yourselves or erect an image or pillar, and you shall not set up a figured stone in your land to bow down to it, for I am the LORD your God."
– Leviticus 26:1

Key People, Places, and Events

Caral	Mesoamerica	First Nations
Andes Mountains	Olmec	Great Basin culture
Valdivia	Mixtec	Southwestern culture
Chavin	Teotihuacan	Eastern Woodland culture
Nazca	Maya	Mississippi culture
Nazca Lines	Pacific Coast culture	

Vocabulary

Lesson 1:
geoglyph
maize
apparent
merge
innovation

Lesson 2:
codex

Lesson 3:
leisure
lineage
potlatch
nomad
reservoir

Additional Material for Parent or Teacher:

Use the website at the link found on the **ArtiosHCS** curriculum website to enhance your student's knowledge of the Maya people based on your child's interest.

Lesson One

History Overview and Assignments
Early People Groups of South America

THE FIRST PEOPLE who came to the continents called the Americas probably migrated across a land bridge from Asia to Alaska thousands of years ago. They spread throughout the continents and developed unique cultures. Many groups hunted and gathered, so they moved from place to place to follow migrating herds of bison and other game animals. Some began farming, which let them stay in one place and form civilizations. One of the earliest of these people groups built a city called Caral in the Andes Mountains of South America.

Chavin de Huantar archeological site
Photo by Sharon odb. CC BY-SA 3.0

Suggested Reading and Assignments

- Read the article: *The Ancient Andes* and *Civilizations in the Americas*.
- After reading the article, summarize the story you read by either:
    - Retelling it out loud to your teacher or parent.
        OR
    - Completing an appropriate notebook page.
  Either way, be sure to include an overview of key people, places, dates, and events in your summary.
- Define the vocabulary words in the context of the reading. Write the words and their definitions in the vocabulary section of your history notebook.
- Instead of answering discussion questions, make a page in your notebook for each of the early cultures you study. Be sure to include history, achievements, and more.
- Be sure to visit your **ArtiosHCS** curriculum website for additional resources and any videos and websites assigned for this lesson.

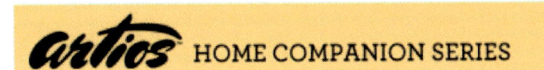

Ancient: Elementary
Unit 18: Early People Groups of the Americas

Key People, Places, and Events

Caral
Andes Mountains
Valdivia
Chavin
Nazca
Nazca Lines

Vocabulary

geoglyph
maize
apparent
merge
innovation

Aerial view of the Andes mountain range, between Santiago de Chile and Mendoza, Argentina
Photo by Jorge Morales Piderit

Adapted for Elementary School from the book:
Boundless World History
source: https://www.coursehero.com/study-guides/boundless-worldhistory
The Ancient Andes
and
Civilizations in the Americas
CC BY-SA: Attribution-ShareAlike

THE CARAL CULTURE

The **Caral** people, who built a city on the northern coast of Peru, near three rivers, about five thousand years ago, left some of the oldest signs of civilization in the Americas. The ancient city of Caral held plazas, homes, and a large temple. Later civilizations of the **Andes Mountains** built similar cities. At its peak, as many as 3,000 people may have lived in Caral.

One of the artifacts found at Caral is a knotted rope piece named a *quipu*, which archaeologists believe was a record-keeping device. Other artifacts include flutes made of condor and pelican bones and similar instruments made of deer and llama bones.

The Caral people were peaceful because no signs of warfare have been found. Perhaps they were the first people group that migrated to their part of the Andes Mountains.

An Inca quipu
Photo by Claus Ableiter. CC BY-SA 3.0

THE VALDIVIA CULTURE

The **Valdivia** built their civilization a little later on the coast of Ecuador. They set their homes in circles or ovals around open places. They farmed, fished, and sometimes hunted deer. From the remains found, we know that the Valdivia grew **maize**, beans, squash, chili peppers, and cotton plants for making clothing.

Valdivian pottery is the oldest found in the Americas.
Photo by Cristina Tolesano & Claudio Elias

The Valdivia were **apparent**ly the first Americans to make pottery. The crafters generally used red and gray colors, and polished dark red pottery was typical in the Valdivia period. Bowls, jars, and female statues were used in daily life and rituals. The Valdivia built rafts with sails and traded with tribes in the Andes and around the Amazon River.

Ancient Valdivian grinding mortars made in the shapes of a parrot and a jaguar
Photos by Germanam94

THE CHAVIN CIVILIZATION

The **Chavin** people lived in the northern mountains of Peru, in a valley where two rivers **merge**. The Chavin de Huantar temple was the religious and political center of the Chavin people. The temple's design shows remarkable **innovation** in adapting to the highland environment of Peru, including complex drainage systems to handle the area's frequent flooding.

Part of the Chavin de Huantar ruins
Photo by Martin St-Amant. CC BY 3.0

Chavin art was the first widespread, recognizable artistic style in the Andes. It was used to decorate the walls of their temple and included carvings, sculptures, and pottery. Artists made images of exotic creatures from other places, such as jaguars and eagles, rather than local plants and animals.

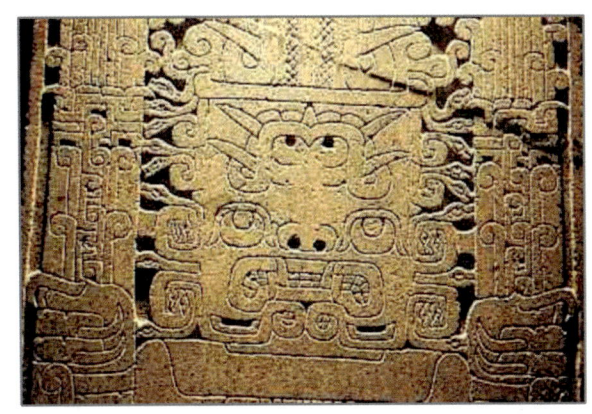

Detail of the Chavin stone engraving known as the *Raimondi Stela*

The Chavin people were skilled in metalworking and crafting with gold. They raised llamas, which were used as pack animals, and for wool fiber and meat. They also grew several crops, including potatoes and maize. They developed an irrigation system to help these crops grow.

THE NAZCA

The **Nazca** people lived near the dry southern coast of Peru. Early Nazca society was made up of local chiefdoms centered around ceremonial sites made up of mounds and plazas. People from across the Nazca region probably gathered there during certain times of the year to feast and make offerings.

Carving of nature deity in the form of an orca
Photo by Lyndsayruell. CC BY-SA 3.0

Nazca Lines

The **Nazca Lines** are a group of shapes and lines that run for miles and extensive drawings of animal figures made on the desert floor in the Nazca region. It may have taken many people many years to produce the lines. The lines may have been drawn by stretching a rope between two posts and removing the red pebbles on the desert surface along the rope. The contrast between the red desert pebbles and the lighter earth beneath would make the lines visible from high in the air. Rainfall would have easily eroded the drawings over time, but the desert air has preserved the lines for hundreds of years. The true meaning of the geoglyphs remains a mystery.

This Nazca line drawing is called *The Spider*.
Photo by Diego Delso. CC BY-SA 4.0

What the Nazca Ate and Grew

The Nazca grew most of what they ate. Ceramic art and artifacts show that the Nazca people ate a variety of crops, including maize, squash, sweet potatoes, beans, small amounts of fish, and peanuts. The Nazca also grew several non-food crops, such as cotton for cloth, and they raised llamas for food and used them as pack animals.

Lesson Two

History Overview and Assignments
Cultures of Mesoamerica

MESOAMERICA is the name archaeologists use for a part of Central America that stretches south from central Mexico into northern Costa Rica, where the earliest people groups lived. The first settlers in this region may have been hunter-gatherers, but they settled down and became farmers in time. Staying in one place to farm made civilization possible, allowing many fascinating cultures to rise.

The Maya ruins at Palenque are mysterious and beautiful.
Photo by Peter Andersen. CC BY-SA 3.0 Unported

Suggested Reading and Assignments

- Read the combined article:
  Early Civilizations of Mexico and Mesoamerica, *The Maya*, and *The Toltecs and the Aztecs*.
- After reading the article, summarize the story you read by either:
    - Retelling it out loud to your teacher or parent.
        OR
    - Completing an appropriate notebook page.
  Either way, be sure to include an overview of key people, places, dates, and events in your summary.
- Define the vocabulary word in the context of the reading. Write the word and its definition in the vocabulary section of your history notebook.
- Instead of answering discussion questions, make a page in your notebook for each of the early cultures you study. Be sure to include history, achievements, and more.
- Be sure to visit your **ArtiosHCS** curriculum website for additional resources and any videos and websites assigned for this lesson.

Vocabulary

codex

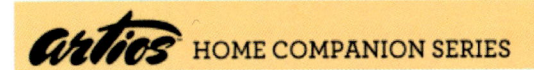

Ancient: Elementary
Unit 18: Early People Groups of the Americas

Key People, Places, and Events

Mesoamerica
Olmec
Mixtec
Teotihuacan
Maya

Mesoamerica and the people groups who lived there
Assumed author: GringoInChile. CC BY-SA 3.0

Adapted for Elementary School from the book:
Boundless World History
source: https://www.coursehero.com/study-guides/boundless-worldhistory
Early Civilizations of Mexico and Mesoamerica, The Maya,
and
The Toltecs and the Aztecs
CC BY-SA: Attribution-ShareAlike

THE OLMEC

The area called **Mesoamerica** stretches from central Mexico down into northern Costa Rica. The earliest large civilization in this region was the Olmec, which lived in the tropical lowlands of south-central Mexico. The Olmec laid the foundations for many of the civilizations that followed, and they probably invented the Mesoamerican ball game that later became what we know as soccer. They also had violent religious practices.

The area where the Olmec built their civilization was made up of swampy lands separated by low hills and volcanoes. They built temple cities, but most people lived in small villages.

Olmec artifacts have been found across Mesoamerica, showing that they traveled far to trade with distant cultures. Trading helped the Olmecs gain what they needed to build their temple cities. Homes usually had a storage pit nearby and gardens where people would grow herbs and small crops, such as sunflowers. Most farming for food was done in fields outside the villages, where they probably grew maize, beans, squash, sweet potatoes, and cotton.

Religion and Art

The art of the Olmec tells us about their religion. There were eight different Olmec deities and religious rituals probably involved the rulers and priests making offerings at their temples.

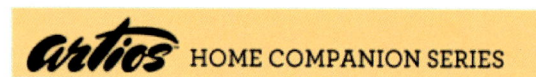

Olmec culture was defined and unified by a unique art style showing real animals and imaginary creatures. The most striking art left behind by the Olmec is colossal stone heads. Seventeen huge human heads sculpted from large boulders have been unearthed in the region. All portray mature men, possibly rulers, with fleshy cheeks, flat noses, and slightly crossed eyes. None of the heads are alike, which suggests they represent specific individuals.

A page from the *Codex Bodley*: This codex tells the story of the Tilantongo and Tiaxiaco dynasties.

TEOTIHUACAN

Near Mexico City sits the ancient Mesoamerican city of **Teotihuacan**. It is famous today for its pyramids and villages, but it was once a multicultural city with separate areas occupied by different people groups.

Teotihuacan
Photo by Ricardo David Sánchez. CC BY-SA 3.0

Colossal Head 4 from San Lorenzo Tenochtitlán, Veracruz, Mexico, one of the best-preserved examples. The head measures 6 feet 1 1/4 inches in height.
Photo by Marshall Astor. CC BY-SA 2.0

Evidence has been found of human sacrifices to honor the completion of buildings or at particular times of the year. Captives from wars were killed in brutal ways on special occasions.

The layout of Teotihuacan is aligned to a particular angle, the same angle at which the sun rose the same angle during one specific summer day each year. Settlers may have used the alignment as a marker for planting crops or performing certain rituals.

THE MIXTEC

The **Mixtec** people lived in a region known as La Mixteca, which covers part of Mexico's western coast. They are known for making **codices**, or picture documents, in which they wrote their history on deerskin. Codices can be read from right to left and often measure many feet long.

THE MAYA

The **Maya** began their civilization around four thousand years ago with farming villages. By around 1000 B.C., they had built a large, complex society with an elite class and established religious practices and armies.

Villages were built around open spaces and earthen mounds, sometimes enhanced by stonework. Warfare was fierce during this period, as shown by powerful weaponry, rulers beginning to be portrayed as warriors, and the appearance of mass graves and headless skeletons.

Some of the earliest remaining examples of the complex writing system of the Maya appear from the 3rd century B.C. The design represents complex concepts and often reflects the religious beliefs of the Maya, including jaguar worship, rulers practicing bloodletting rituals, and offerings to deities. The Maya also developed the concept of the number zero during this era. The number zero in their written records might be the first example of its numerical use worldwide. The appearance of this number also helped their architects and priests make exact calculations of the stars and buildings for religious and social purposes.

The Peak of the Maya

During the peak of the Maya civilization, the population numbered in the millions and spread throughout much of Mesoamerica. The Maya created many kingdoms and small empires, built monumental palaces and temples, held highly developed ceremonies, and developed an elaborate writing system.

The most notable monuments are the stepped pyramids the Maya built in their religious centers and the palaces of their rulers. Cities like Tikal and Copan show the wealth of architectural accomplishments during these productive centuries.

Chichen Itza, one of the largest Maya cities in the northern Maya lowlands, may have had the most diverse population in the Maya world.

Pyramid at Chichen Itza
Photo by Daniel Scjwem. CC BY-SA 4.0

Maya Math and Calendars

The Maya used complex math to build their monuments and portray the world of their religion. Each of the four directions represented specific deities, colors, and elements. The underworld, the cosmos, and a great tree of life at the center of the world all played their part in how buildings were built and when feasts or sacrifices were practiced.

A Maya calendar: Each symbol represents one day.
Photo by Matthew Bisanz. CC BY-SA 3.0

Lesson Three

History Overview and Assignments
Early People Groups of North America

IN NORTH AMERICA, some early people groups settled along the Pacific Coast, while others migrated throughout the Great Basin area, hunting animals and gathering plants for food. Still others spread through the dry Southwest region, building villages or settling in the woodlands further east, farming, making cloth, and crafting pottery.

Three Young Chinook Men, by George Catlin (c.1860)

Key People, Places, and Events

Pacific Coast culture
First Nations
Great Basin culture
Southwestern culture
Eastern Woodland culture
Mississippi culture

Vocabulary

leisure
lineage
potlatch
nomad
reservoir

Suggested Reading and Assignments

- Read the article: *Native American Cultures in North America*.
- After reading the article, summarize the story you read by either:
    - Retelling it out loud to your teacher or parent.
        OR
    - Completing an appropriate notebook page.
  Either way, be sure to include an overview of key people, places, dates, and events in your summary.
- Define the vocabulary words in the context of the reading. Write the words and their definitions in the vocabulary section of your history notebook.
- Instead of answering discussion questions, make a page in your notebook for each of the early cultures you study. Be sure to include history, achievements, and more.
- Be sure to visit your **ArtiosHCS** curriculum website for additional resources and any videos and websites assigned for this lesson.

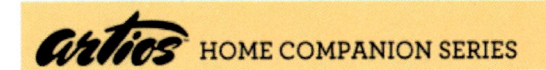

Adapted for Elementary School from the book:
Boundless World History
source: https://www.coursehero.com/study-guides/boundless-worldhistory
Native American Cultures in North America
CC BY-SA: Attribution-ShareAlike

PACIFIC COAST CULTURE

The mild climate and abundant natural resources of North America's northern Pacific coast, such as cedar trees and salmon, drew many early migrating people groups to settle there. The **Pacific Coast culture** that developed was made up of tribal groups that practiced various forms of forest gardening and advanced farming in the forests, grasslands, and wetlands of the region. Farmers burned small fires to prevent larger ones and rotated crops to nourish the soil. Ancient Pacific Coast people groups included the ancestors of today's Chinook Tlingit, Tillamook, and many other tribes and nations. Many of the indigenous groups of Canada are known as **First Nations** peoples.

Music and other arts flourished in this culture, and many songs were created for ceremonies, dancing, and festivities. Music was created to honor the Earth, the creator, ancestors, and all other parts of the supernatural world. Songs were also used to tell and pass down stories. As with music, art also served to pass down history, wisdom, and property from generation to generation.

Because food was abundant, most Northwest tribes had **leisure** time to create art. Many works of art served practical purposes, such as clothing, tools, weapons of war and hunting, transportation, cooking, and shelter. Art gave the people a tie to the land and constantly reminded them of their birthplaces, **lineage**s, and nations. One example is using symbols on *the Pacific Northwest coast's totem poles and plank houses.*

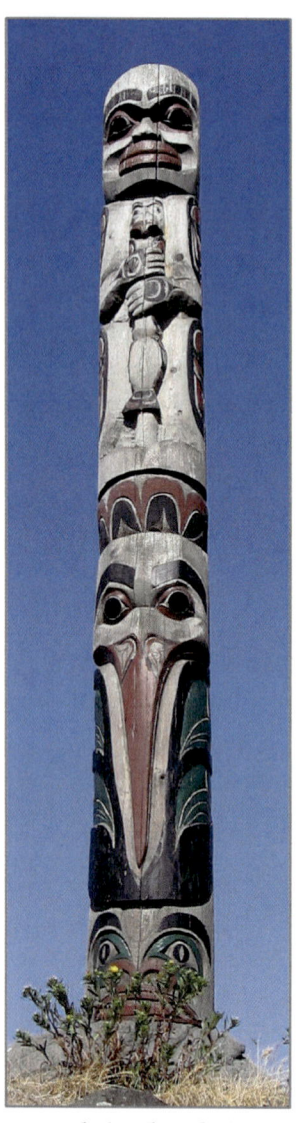

A totem pole in Thunderbird Park, Victoria, British Columbia, Canada

Nature and spiritualism played essential roles in day-to-day life. Therefore, it was not unusual for commonly used items to be adorned with symbols, crests, and totems representing important figures from both the seen and unseen worlds.

Pacific Coast Tribal art adorned plank houses and totem poles, serving as constant reminders of indigenous peoples' birth places, lineages, and nations.
Photo by HighInBC. CC BY-SA 2.5

Many of these religious or spiritual symbols would also be present during social ceremonies. The **potlatch**, a gift-giving feast, was one of Pacific Northwest groups' most critical social experiences. People would gather to celebrate a specific event, such as raising a totem pole or choosing a new chief. In the potlatch ceremony, the chief would give personal gifts to visitors to establish his power and prestige. By accepting these gifts, the visitors conveyed their approval of the chief. There were also great feasts and dance groups put on elaborate ceremonies. Watching these performances was considered an honor.

A *Kwakwaka'wakw* potlatch with dancers and singers.
Image from *The North American Indian*,
by Edward S. Curtis

GREAT BASIN CULTURE

The early peoples of the **Great Basin culture** lived west of the Rocky Mountains of North America. They lived in **nomad**ic groups that migrated to pursue game, mainly bison. Most traveled in small family groups for most of the year, returning yearly to the same springs. There they would camp for a few days, moving on after building a temporary shelter, making and/or repairing stone tools, or preparing meat for eating.

The climate in the Great Basin was and is very dry, and this affected the lifestyles and cultures of its inhabitants. The various groups lived peacefully and often shared common territories.

The use of pottery was rare among these nomadic peoples because it was usually heavy and hard to carry, but they wove baskets. Some of these were so carefully made that they could hold water and cook food.

Early peoples of the Great Basin did not farm because the area was too dry, and even modern farming in the Great Basin requires large mountain **reservoir**s or deep wells. Likewise, the Great Basin peoples had no permanent settlements, although the same groups of families might revisit winter villages year after year.

Ancient Great Basin peoples included the ancestors of today's Shoshone, Ute, Paiute, and many other tribes and nations.

SOUTHWESTERN CULTURE

Early tribes of the **Southwestern culture** probably began farming by cultivating wild grains, such as corn, with cobs measuring only one to two inches long. Better varieties were developed later or brought in from Mesoamerica. Cotton has been found in the Tucson basin, dating to about 1,200 B.C.

Traditional Navajo dwellings called *hogans* at Monument Valley Navajo Tribal Park
Photo by Dsdugan. CC BY-SA 4.0

Early Southwestern peoples built homes near water sources like rivers, swamps, and marshes, which had plenty of fish and drew birds and game animals. They hunted big game—bison, mammoths, and ground sloths—who were also attracted to these water sources. A relatively wet period allowed many cultures to flourish in the American Southwest. Extensive irrigation systems were developed and were among the largest in the ancient world. Elaborate adobe and sandstone buildings and complex cliff dwellings and communities were constructed, and highly decorative pottery was created.

Modern-day tribes and nations believed to have descended from the ancient Southwestern culture groups include the Navajo, Apache, Hopi, and many others.

The Ancestral Puebloans
The Ancestral Puebloans of North America's Southwest are known for building remarkable cliff cities at Mesa Verde in Colorado, Chaco Canyon and Taos Pueblo in New Mexico, and Canyon de Chelly, Arizona. They lived across parts of Utah, Arizona, New Mexico, and Colorado.

Cliff Palace, Mesa Verde National Park
Photo by Judson McCranie. CC BY-SA 3.0

EASTERN WOODLAND CULTURE

The **Eastern Woodland culture**, which flourished in the eastern part of North America between 1,000 B.C. and 1,000 A.D., spread across land stretching from southeastern Canada through the eastern United States, down to the Gulf of Mexico.

The Woodland people are known for making stone and bone tools, leather pieces and cloth, permanent settlements, mounds, and farms. Clan heads were buried along with goods received from their trading partners to symbolize their established relationships.

Early people groups of America's Eastern Woodland culture include the ancestors of today's Haudenosaunee (also known as Iroquois), Abenaki, Algonquin, and many others.

MISSISSIPPIAN CULTURE

People groups of the **Mississippian culture** flourished in the Mississippi Valley, building large earthwork mounds and practicing maize-based farming. Artifacts of differing styles show that they traveled far to trade. Mississippian cultures became known for their chiefdoms, in which one major center directly controlled several smaller communities.

Shell-tempered Mississippian ceramic effigy jug with swirls painted in clay slip, Rose Mound, Cross County, Arkansas, U.S., 1400-1600 CE, 8" (20 cm) high
Assumed author: Madman2001. CC BY 2.5

Some modern-day American Indian nations descended from the ancient Mississippian culture include the Choctaw, Cherokee, and Natchez.

What a mammoth hunt might have looked like
Frontispiece from *Children's Stories in American History*, by Henrietta Christian Wright (1885)

Mississippian cultures often built structures such as homes and burial buildings on platform mounds.

Ancient: Elementary
Unit 18: Early People Groups of the Americas

The Artios Home Companion Series
Unit 19: Ancient Greece

Teacher Overview

THIS WEEK WE WILL travel back across the ocean to learn about European history, beginning by spending a few weeks in ancient Greece. Much of Greece's early history was passed down by mouth from generation to generation until a writer named Homer wrote down many of the old stories, which were long, thrilling legends by then.

View of the Acropolis of Athens
Photo by Christophe Meneboeuf. CC BY-SA 3.0

Suggested Assignments

Based on your student's age and ability, the reading in this unit may be read aloud to the student, and journaling and notebook pages may be completed orally. Likewise, other assignments may be done with an appropriate combination of independent and guided study.

In this unit, students will:
- Complete three lessons in which they will learn about **ancient Greece**, its **people groups**, and its **city-states**.
- Define vocabulary words.
- Visit the **ArtiosHCS** curriculum website at **www.ArtiosHCS.com** for additional resources and any videos and websites assigned for this unit.

Key People, Places, and Events

Hellenes	Mycenaeans	Deucalion	Pyrrha	Thermopylae
Hellen	Aegean Sea	Thessaly	Delphi	

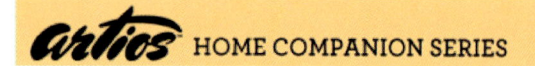

Heart Connections

People tend to ignore what they know about God.

For even though they knew God, they did not honor Him as God or give thanks, but they became futile in their speculations, and their foolish heart was darkened. Professing to be wise, they became fools, and exchanged the glory of the incorruptible God for an image in the form of corruptible man and of birds and four-footed animals and crawling creatures.

– Romans 1:20-23

God despises idolatry.

"You shall have no other gods before me."

– Exodus 20:3

God alone is to be worshiped.

"You shall not make idols for yourselves or erect an image or pillar, and you shall not set up a figured stone in your land to bow down to it, for I am the LORD your God."

– Leviticus 26:1

Christianity is the only way to eternal life.

Jesus said to him, "I am the way, and the truth, and the life. No one comes to the Father except through me."

– John 14:6

Additional Material for Parent or Teacher:

You will find a link for "Ancient Greece For Kids" at the **ArtiosHCS** curriculum website for this unit. Study it and share it with your student(s) as appropriate.

Vocabulary

Lesson 1:
none

Lesson 2:
recede
summons

Lesson 3:
none

Map of Greece, drawn in 1791 by William Faden, royal geographer to King George III

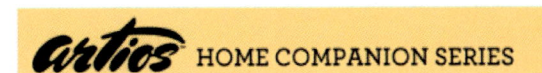

Lesson One

History Overview and Assignments
Wanderers With Bad Manners

"Ten centuries after their first appearance upon the scene, the Hellenes were the rulers of Greece, the Aegean, and the coastal regions of Asia Minor."

– from the adapted article below

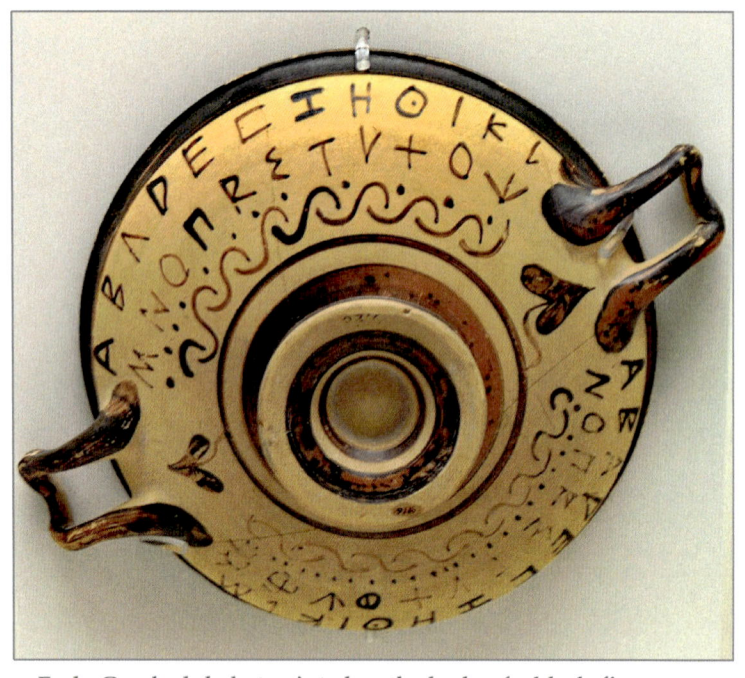

Early Greek alphabet painted on the body of a black-figure cup from Attica (c.8th century B.C.)
Photo by Marsyas. CC BY 2.5

Key People, Places, and Events

Hellenes
Hellen
Mycenaeans
Aegean Sea

Suggested Reading and Assignments

- Read the article: *The Hellenes*.
- After reading the article, summarize the story you read by either:
    - Retelling it out loud to your teacher or parent.
        OR
    - Completing an appropriate notebook page.
  Either way, be sure to include the answers to the discussion questions and an overview of key people, places, dates, and events in your summary.
- Be sure to visit your **ArtiosHCS** curriculum website for additional resources and any videos and websites assigned for this lesson.

Discussion Questions

1. What does the Greek flood story remind you of?
2. Describe the culture of the early Hellenes.
3. What did they learn from the mountain civilizations?
4. How did the Hellenes repay them for teaching them so many things?

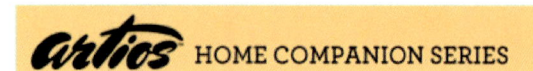

Adapted for Elementary School from the book:
The Story of Mankind
by Hendrik Willem van Loon
The Hellenes

About four thousand years ago, tribes of migrating people began forming a common culture in the land we now call Greece. They called themselves **Hellenes**, claiming they were descendants of **Hellen**, sons of Deucalion and Pyrrha. According to the old Greek stories, these were the only two who had escaped the great flood many years before and had destroyed all the world's people when they had grown so wicked that they disgusted Zeus, the mighty god who lived on Mount Olympus.

Of these early Hellenes, we know little. According to an ancient Greek historian, they had horrible manners. They lived like pigs and threw the bodies of their enemies to the wild dogs who guarded their sheep. They had very little respect for other people's rights and killed the natives they found when they came to Greece. They stole their farms, took their cows, and made their wives and daughters slaves.

But here and there, on the tops of high rocks, they saw castles made by more advanced people but did not attack them, for they feared the metal swords and spears of these soldiers and knew that they could not hope to defeat them with their clumsy stone axes.

For centuries, Hellenic tribes continued to wander from valley to valley and from mountainside to mountainside. In time they occupied the length and width of the land, and their migration ended. That moment was the beginning of Greek civilization.

The Hellenic farmers living near the mountain civilizations were finally driven by curiosity to visit their neighbors. They discovered they could learn many valuable things from the men who dwelt behind the high stone walls of Mycenae and Tiryns.

Within a short time, the Hellenes mastered the art of handling those strange iron weapons which the **Mycenaeans** and others had brought across the **Aegean Sea** from Babylon and Thebes. They learned how to build boats and find their way across the sea.

This gold burial mask is known famously as the *Mask of Agamemnon*, the heroic King of Mycenae in Homer's *Iliad*. Though mystery still surrounds the 16th-century B.C. Minoan and Mycenaean cultures, archaeologists have found fascinating artifacts, including frescoes, palaces, tombs, and other burial masks.

When they had learned everything those cultures could teach them, they turned upon their teachers and drove them away. Soon they ventured forth upon the sea and conquered cities on the Aegean. And ten centuries after their first appearance on the scene, the Hellenes were the rulers of Greece, the Aegean, and the coastal regions of Asia Minor.

Lesson Two

History Overview and Assignments
A Tale of a Flood and Stone Throwing

"Ten centuries after their first appearance upon the scene, the Hellenes were the rulers of Greece, the Aegean, and the coastal regions of Asia Minor."
– from the adapted article below

Deucalion was a son of Prometheus and Pronoia in Greek mythology.
Published by Guillaume Rouille in the 16-century book *Promptuarii Iconum Insigniorum*

Suggested Reading and Assignments

- Read the article: *The Story of Deucalion*.
- After reading the article, summarize the story you read by either:
    - Retelling it out loud to your teacher or parent.
      OR
    - Completing an appropriate notebook page.
  Either way, be sure to include an overview of key people, places, dates, and events in your summary.
- Be sure to visit your **ArtiosHCS** curriculum website for additional resources and any videos and websites assigned for this lesson.

Key People, Places, and Events

Deucalion
Thessaly
Pyrrha
Delphi
Thermopylae

Vocabulary

recede
summons

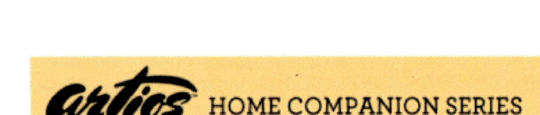

Ancient: Elementary
Unit 19: Ancient Greece

Adapted for Elementary School from the book:
Early Inhabitants of Greece
by H. A. Guerber
The Story of Deucalion

The Greeks used to tell their children that **Deucalion**, founder of the city of **Thessaly**, was a descendant of the gods, for each part of the country claimed that its first great man was the son of a god. They said that a great flood took place during the reign of Deucalion, and he and his wife, **Pyrrha,** were the only people left alive after the flood. When the waters had **recede**d, they went down the mountain and found that the temple at **Delphi**, where they worshiped their gods, was still unharmed. They entered and, kneeling before the altar, prayed for help.

A mysterious voice then bade them to travel further down the mountain, throwing their mother's bones behind them. They were very much troubled when they heard this until Deucalion said that a voice from heaven could not have meant them to do any harm. In thinking over the real meaning of the words he had heard, he told his wife that, since the Earth is the mother of all creatures, her "bones" must mean the stones.

Deucalion and Pyrrha, therefore, made their way slowly down the mountain, throwing stones behind them. The Greeks say that a sturdy race of men sprang up from the stones cast by Deucalion, while beautiful women came from those cast by Pyrrha.

The country was soon populated by the children of these two. They always proudly declared that the story was true and that they sprang from the race which owed its birth to this great miracle.

Deucalion reigned over these people as long as he lived, and when he died, his two sons, Amphictyon and Hellen, became kings in his stead. The former remained in Thessaly, and hearing that some people called Thracians were about to come over the mountains and drive his people away, he called the chiefs of all the different states to a council to ask their advice about the best means of defense. All the leaders obeyed the **summons** and met at a place in Thessaly where the mountains approach the sea so closely as to leave only a narrow pass between. In the pass are hot springs, and so it was called **Thermopylae**, or the "Hot Gateway."

Thermopylae derives part of its name from its hot springs. This river is formed by the steaming water, which smells of sulfur. In the background, you can see buildings of the modern baths. In ancient times the springs created a swamp.
Photo by Fkerasar. CC BY-SA 3.0

The chiefs thus gathered together called this assembly the Amphictyonic Council in honor of Amphictyon. After planning to drive back the Thracians, they decided to meet once a year, either at Thermopylae or at the temple at Delphi, to discuss all important matters.

Lesson Three

History Overview and Assignments
Life in Ancient Greek City-States

"In this hard school, the Greeks learned to excel in many things. They created new forms of government, new forms of literature, and new ideals in art, which we have never been able to surpass. They performed these miracles in little villages that covered less ground than four or five modern city blocks." — from the adapted article below

Ancient and modern Thermon, Aetolia, on the north coast of the Gulf of Corinth, Greece
Photo by Κώστας Κουκούλης

Suggested Reading and Assignments

- Read the article: *The Greek Cities*.
- After reading the article, summarize the story you read by either:
    - Retelling it out loud to your teacher or parent.
        OR
    - Completing an appropriate notebook page.
  Either way, be sure to include the answers to the discussion questions and an overview of key people, places, dates, and events in your summary.
- Be sure to visit your **ArtiosHCS** curriculum website for additional resources and any videos and websites assigned for this lesson.

Discussion Questions

1. How was life different in an ancient Greek city-state from life in ancient Egypt or Mesopotamia?
2. How did this change after Alexander the Great made his conquests?

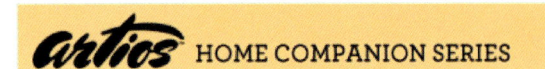

Adapted for Elementary School from the book:
The Story of Mankind
by Hendrik Willem van Loon
The Greek Cities

The Greek Cities, Which Were Really States

The people of ancient Egypt or Mesopotamia were subjects of mysterious rulers who probably lived miles and miles away in grand palaces and were rarely seen by the masses of the population. On the other hand, the Greeks were "free citizens" of hundreds of independent little "cities," the largest of which counted fewer inhabitants than a large modern village. When a peasant who lived in the Ur of the Chaldees said that he was a Babylonian, he meant that he was one of the millions of people who paid tribute to a king who, at that particular moment, happened to be the master of western Asia. But when a Greek proudly said he was an Athenian or a Theban, he spoke of a small town, which was both his home and his country and which recognized no master but the will of the people in the marketplace.

To the ancient Greek, his fatherland was the place where he was born, where he had spent his earliest years playing hide and seek amidst the rocks of the Acropolis, where he had grown into manhood with a thousand other boys and girls whose nicknames were as familiar to him as those of your schoolmates. His Fatherland was the soil where his father and mother lay buried. His wife and children lived safely in the small house within the high city walls. An entire world covered no more than a few hundred acres of rocky land.

Don't you see how these surroundings must have influenced a person in everything he did and said and thought? The people of Babylon and Assyria, and Egypt had been part of a vast mob. They had been lost in the multitude. On the other hand, the Greeks never lost touch with their immediate surroundings—even during Greece's great Classical period. He never ceased to be part of a town where everybody knew everyone else. He was always aware that his neighbors were watching him. Whatever he did, whether he wrote plays, made statues out of marble, or composed songs, he remembered that his efforts would be judged by all the citizens of his hometown who knew about such things. This knowledge forced him to strive for perfection.

In this hard school, the Greeks learned to excel in many things. They created new forms of government, new forms of literature, and new ideals in art, which we have never been able to surpass. They performed these miracles in villages covering less than four or five modern city blocks.

But look what happened!

In the 4th century B.C., Alexander the Great conquered the Mediterranean world and decided to give the benefits of the Greek genius to all mankind. He took Greek culture from the city-states and little villages and tried to make it blossom and bear fruit amidst the vast royal cities of his newly acquired empire. But the Greeks, removed from the familiar sight of their temples, removed from the well-known sounds and smells of their crooked streets, lost the festive joy and the marvelous sense of moderation that had inspired the work of their hands and brains while they labored for the glory of their old city-states. They became cheap artisans, content with second-rate work. The day the little city-states of ancient Greece lost their independence and were forced to become part of a big nation, the old Greek spirit died.

Ruins of Rhamnous, an ancient Greek city in Attica
Photo by Nefasdicere. CC Y 2.5

Acropolis of Athens, a noted *polis* (city) of classical Greece
Photo by A.Savin. CC BY-SA 3.0

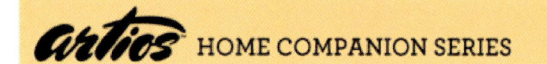

The Artios Home Companion Series
Unit 20: Classical Greek History

Teacher Overview

JUST LIKE MANY nations before them, the Greeks had a polytheistic society, meaning they worshiped many gods instead of the one true God. It is essential to heed Paul's warning in Romans 12:2 against being conformed to the world. It is easy to be influenced by the society around us rather than give attention and obedience to what God has revealed in Scripture. Paul warns against turning away from man's wisdom and instead encourages us to be transformed by renewing our minds through Scripture.

The Parthenon on the Athenian Acropolis, dedicated to Athena Parthenos
Photo by Steve Swayne. CC BY 2.0

Suggested Assignments

Based on your student's age and ability, the reading in this unit may be read aloud to the student, and journaling and notebook pages may be completed orally. Likewise, other assignments may be done with an appropriate combination of independent and guided study.

In this unit, students will:
- Complete three lessons in which they will start learning about **classical Greece**, including **Sparta and Athens**, and read a **Greek myth**.
- Define vocabulary words.
- Instead of answering discussion questions for the first two lessons, make a chart with two columns: one for **Sparta** and another for **Athens**, and list the unique characteristics of each city.
- Visit the **ArtiosHCS** curriculum website at **www.ArtiosHCS.com** for additional resources and any videos and websites assigned for this unit.

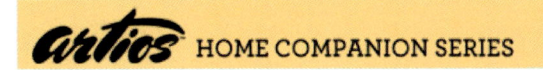

Heart Connections

Even though we live "in the world" we are not to be "of the world."

In Acts 17, Paul gives a sermon that makes it evident that he understood Greek philosophy. However, he did not stay there in his conversation. He presented the gospel to them. This is a great demonstration of not being "of the world" but being "sent into" the world.

– Acts 17 – Read or listen to this whole chapter in ESV at:
http://www.bible.is/ENGESV/Acts/17

To mature as Christians, we need to renew our minds.

Do not be conformed to this world, but be transformed by the renewal of your mind, that by testing you may discern what is the will of God, what is good and acceptable and perfect.

– Romans 12:2

Vocabulary

Lesson 1:
contempt
temperate
fatigue
strive

Lesson 2:
tyrant
jurisprudence
capital (offense)
humane
prosperity
gossip

Lesson 3:
dauntless
wimble
hoist
gale
pinion
cumber
portent

cleave
plumage
sheen
translucent
exquisite
dirge
pall
ecstasy

Key People, Places, and Events

Sparta
Lycurgus
Athens
Draco
Solon
Icarus
Daedalus
Minos

The ruins of the Temple of Olympian Zeus
Photo by A. Savin. CC BY-SA 3.0

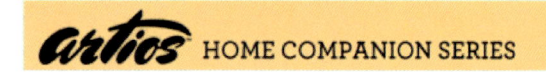

Lesson One

History Overview and Assignments
Military Life in Sparta

"Once a year, all the boys were brought to the Temple of Diana, where a severe flogging further tried their courage; and those who stood this whipping without a moan or whimper were duly praised. The little Spartan boys were so eager to be thought brave that it is said that some let themselves be flogged to death rather than complain."

– from the adapted article below

Key People, Places, and Events

Sparta
Lycurgus

Vocabulary

contempt
temperate
fatigue
strive

Ruins of Sparta as seen from the bank of the Eurotas River
Photo by ulrichstill. CC BY-SA 2.0 de

Suggested Reading and Assignments

- Read the combined article: *The Rise of Sparta, The Spartan Training, The Brave Spartan Boy*, and *Public Tables in Sparta*.
- Define the vocabulary words in the context of the reading. Write the words and their definitions in the vocabulary section of your history notebook.
- After reading the article, summarize the story you read by either:
    - Retelling it out loud to your teacher or parent.
        OR
    - Completing an appropriate notebook page.
  Either way, be sure to include an overview of key people, places, dates, and events in your summary.
- Instead of answering discussion questions for this lesson and the next, begin making a chart with two columns: Sparta and Athens. List the characteristics unique to each city.
- Be sure to visit your **ArtiosHCS** curriculum website for additional resources and any videos and websites assigned for this lesson.

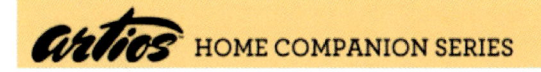

Ancient: Elementary
Unit 20: Classical Greek History

Adapted for Elementary School from the book:
The Story of the Greeks
by H. A. Guerber
The Rise of Sparta,
The Spartan Training,
The Brave Spartan Boy,
and
Public Tables in Sparta

The Rise of Sparta

The city of **Sparta**, founded by early peoples of Greece, was conquered by the Dorians, who came to call themselves Spartans. The old inhabitants of the surrounding land, called Laconia, went on living in the country, where they now had to sow and harvest for the benefit of the Spartans. All the prisoners of war, however, became slaves. They were forced to serve the Spartans in every way and were called *Helots*.

When the first king, Aristodemus, died, his twin sons were both made kings and as each of them left his throne to his descendants, Sparta went on to have two kings, instead of one, from this time forward.

Although he never bore the name of a king, one royal family member is the most noted man in Spartan history. This is **Lycurgus**, the son of one ruler, the brother of another, and the guardian of his nephew, the infant king named Charilaus.

According to legend, Lycurgus was known as a thoroughly good and upright man. We are told that the mother of the baby king offered to put her child to death so that Lycurgus might reign. Fearing for the babe's safety, Lycurgus pretended that he agreed to this plan and asked that the child be given to him to kill as he saw fit.

Lycurgus, given possession of the babe, carried him to the council hall. There he had the child named king, and Lycurgus promised to watch carefully over him, educate him well, and rule for him until he should be old and wise enough to reign alone.

While he was thus acting as ruler, Lycurgus used his power to bring many new customs into Sparta and change the laws. As he was one of the wisest men who ever lived, he knew very well that men must be good if they would be happy. He also knew that health is far better than riches, and, hoping to make the Spartans both good and healthy, he won them over little by little to obey a new set of laws, which he had made after visiting many of the neighboring countries, and learning all he could.

The Spartan philosopher Lycurgus, from a series of marble reliefs depicting the great lawgivers of history at the chamber of the US House of Representatives

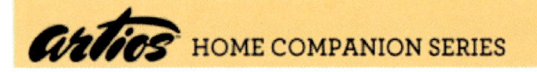

The Spartan Training

The laws which Lycurgus drew up for the Spartans were stringent. For instance, as soon as a babe came into the world, the law ordered that the father wrap it up in a cloak and carry it before a council of some of the oldest and wisest men.

They looked at the child carefully, and if it seemed strong and healthy and was neither crippled nor in any way deformed, they said it might live. Then they gave it back to the father and bade him to bring up the child for the honor of his country.

If the babe was sickly or deformed, it was carried off to a mountain nearby and left alone so that it soon died of hunger or thirst or was eaten up by the wild beasts.

The Spartan children remained under their father's roof and in their mother's care until they were seven. While in the nursery, they were taught all the beautiful old Greek legends and listened with delight to the stories of the ancient heroes, especially to the poems of Homer telling about the war of Troy and the adventures of Ulysses.

When the boys reached seven, they were given to the state's care and allowed to visit their parents only seldom. They were put in charge of chosen men, who trained them to become strong and brave; while the girls were taught not only all they needed to know to keep the house well but were also trained to be strong and fearless like their brothers.

All Spartan boys were allowed only one rough woolen garment, which served as their sole covering by night and day and was of the same material in summer as in winter. They were taught very little reading, writing, and arithmetic but were carefully trained to recite the poems of Homer, the patriotic songs and to accompany themselves skillfully on the lyre. They were also obliged to sing in the public chorus and to dance gracefully at all the religious feasts.

As the Spartans were very anxious that their boys should be strong and fearless, they were taught to endure pain and fatigue without a murmur, and, to make sure that they could do so, their teachers made them go through very severe training.

Led by one of the older boys, the little lads were often sent out for long tramps over rough and stony roads under the hot sun, and the best boy was the one who kept up longest despite bleeding feet, burning thirst, and great fatigue.

Spartan boys were allowed no beds to sleep in lest they should become lazy and hard to please. Their only couch was a heap of reeds, which they picked on the banks of the Eurotas River, and in winter, they were allowed to cover these with a layer of downy cat-tail fluff to make them softer and warmer.

Greek soldier fighting a Persian on a drinking cup from the 5th century B.C.

The Brave Spartan Boy

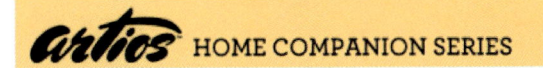

Since greedy and disobedient children were viewed at Sparta with the **contempt** they deserved, all the boys were trained to obey instantly whatever order was given and were allowed only the plainest and scantiest food.

Strange to relate, the Spartans also trained their boys to steal. They praised them when they succeeded without being found out and punished them only when caught in the act. The reason for this strange custom was this: the people were often engaged in war. As they had no baggage wagons following their army and no special officer to furnish food, they had to depend entirely upon the provisions they could get on their way.

Whenever an army came in sight, the people hid not only their wealth but also their food. If the Spartan soldiers had not been trained to steal, they would often have suffered much from hunger at war.

To test the courage of the Spartan boys, their teachers never allowed them to have a lantern and often sent them out alone in the middle of the night on errands which they had to complete as best they could.

Then, too, once a year, all the boys were brought to the Temple of Diana, where a severe flogging further tried their courage; and those who stood this whipping without a moan or whimper were duly praised. The little Spartan boys were so eager to be thought brave that it is said that some let themselves be flogged to death rather than complain.

The bravery of one of these boys was so astonishing that you would find it mentioned in nearly every Greek history you read. It is told that this little fellow stole a live fox and hid it in his garment on his way to school. The imprisoned fox, hoping to escape, began to gnaw a hole in the boy's chest and tear his flesh with his sharp claws, but, despite the pain, the lad sat still and let the fox bite him to death.

Only when he fell lifeless to the ground did the teachers find the fox and see how cruelly he had torn the brave little boy to pieces. Ever since then, boys have been called little Spartans in memory of this lad when they stand in pain bravely and without wincing.

So that the boys should be taught to behave well under all circumstances, they were never allowed to speak except when spoken to, and then their answers were expected to be as short and exact as possible.

This style of speaking, where much was said in few words, was so usual in the whole country of Laconia that it is still known as the laconic style.

To train them in this mode of speech, the elders made the boys pass an oral examination daily, asking them any questions they could think of. The boys had to answer promptly, briefly, and carefully; if they failed, it was considered a great disgrace.

These daily questions were meant to sharpen their wits, strengthen their memories, and teach them how to think and decide quickly and correctly.

The Spartan youths were further taught to treat all their elders with the greatest respect, and it must have been a pretty sight to see all these manly fellows respectfully saluting all the older people they met and even stopping their play to make way for them when they came on the street.

To strengthen their muscles, the boys were also carefully trained in gymnastics. They learned to handle weapons, throw heavy weights, wrestle, run with great speed, swim, jump, and ride, and became experts in all exercises which tended to make them strong, active, and well.

Public Tables in Sparta

The Spartan men prided themselves on living almost as plainly as the boys, and instead of eating their meals at home with their wives and children, they had a common table. Each man gave a certain amount of flour, oil, wine, vegetables, and money, just enough to provide for his share of food.

Instead of having varied and delicate dishes, they mainly ate the same things each day; and their favorite food was a thick dark stew or soup, which they called black broth. Rich and poor were treated alike, sat side by side, and ate the same food, intended to make them equally strong and able to serve their country.

The girls and women never came to these public tables, but the boys were given a seat there as soon as they had learned their first and most important lesson, obedience.

When the boys came into the public dining hall for the first time, the oldest man present called them to him and, pointing to the door, solemnly warned them that nothing said inside the walls was ever to be repeated without.

Then, while the boys took their places and ate without speaking a word, the older men talked freely of all they pleased, sure that Spartan lads would never be mean enough to repeat anything they said and trusting to their honor.

Although the Spartans had wine on their table, they were very temperate and drank only a little with each meal. To show the boys what a horrible thing drunkenness is and the sure result of too much drinking, the older men sometimes gave them an object lesson.

They sent for one of the meanest Helots or slaves and purposely gave him plenty of wine. He was encouraged to go on drinking until he sank to the floor in a drunken sleep. Then the older men would point him out to the boys and explain that a man who has drunk too much is unworthy of the love or esteem of his fellow creatures and is in many ways worse than a beast.

The Spartan boys, thus early warned of the evils of drinking, were careful to take only very little wine and to keep their heads quite clear so that they might always be considered worthy men and might never disgrace themselves as they had seen the Helots do.

When the boys had passed through the first training course, they, in turn, became the teachers and leaders of the smaller lads and thus served their country until they were old enough to go to war. When they left for their first campaign, all the people came out to see them off, and each mother gave her son his shield, saying:

"Come back with your shield or on it."

By this, she meant, "Come home honorably, bearing your shield, thus showing that you have never thrown it away to save yourself by flight; or die so bravely that your companions will return your body resting on your shield, giving you a glorious burial."

The Spartan girls, who the women brought up, were, like the boys, taught to wrestle, run, swim, and take part in gymnastics until they, too, became extraordinarily strong and supple and could stand almost any **fatigue**.

They were also taught to read, write, count, sing, play, dance, spin, weave, dye, and do all kinds of women's work. In short, they were expected to be strong, intelligent, and capable so that when they married, they might help their husbands govern the home and bring up their children sensibly. At some public festivals, the girls **strove** against one another in various games, which were witnessed only by their fathers and mothers and the other married people of the city. The winners in these contests were given fantastic prizes, which were much coveted.

Laws of Lycurgus

Lycurgus hoped to make the Spartans a strong and worthy people. To hinder the kings from doing anything wrong, he had the people choose five men, called *ephors*, to watch over and advise them.

Then, knowing that great wealth is not desirable, Lycurgus said that the Spartans should use only iron money. Therefore, all the Spartan coins were bars of iron, so heavy that a yoke of oxen and a strong cart were needed to carry a sum equal to one hundred dollars from one spot to another. Money was so bulky that it could neither be hidden nor stolen, and no one cared to make a fortune since it required a large space to stow away even a small sum.

When Charilaus, the infant king, had grown up, Lycurgus prepared to leave. Before he left the town, he called all the citizens together, reminded them of all he had done to make them great people and ended by asking every man present to swear to obey the laws until he came back.

The Spartans were incredibly grateful for all he had done for them, so they gladly took this oath, and Lycurgus left the place. Sometime after, he returned to Greece; but hearing that the Spartans were thriving under the rules he had laid down, he decided never to visit Sparta again.

Thus, the Spartans found themselves bound by a solemn oath to obey Lycurgus' laws forever; as long as they remembered this promise, they were a thriving and happy people.

Ancient Sparta
from *The Story of the Greatest Nations, from the Dawn of History to the Twentieth Century*,
by John Steeple Davis, published 1900

Lesson Two

History Overview and Assignments
Birth of Democracy in Athens

"After carefully studying the subject, Solon gave Athens a set of laws which bore testimony to that wonderful principle of moderation which was part of the Greek character."

– from the adapted article below

Reconstruction of the Acropolis and Areus Pagus in Athens, a depiction of what the Acropolis and Areopagus (in front) might have looked like, by Leo von Klenze (1846). This hilltop housed the famous Parthenon and included temples, theaters, and other public buildings important to Athenian culture.

Suggested Reading and Assignments

- Review the vocabulary, then read the article: *Greek Self-Government*.
- After reading the article, summarize the story you read by either:
    - Retelling it out loud to your teacher or parent.
        OR
    - Completing an appropriate notebook page.

  Either way, be sure to include an overview of key people, places, dates, and events in your summary.
- Define the vocabulary words in the context of the reading. Write the words and their definitions in the vocabulary section of your history notebook.
- Instead of answering discussion questions for this lesson, complete the chart you began in Lesson One.
- Be sure to visit your **ArtiosHCS** curriculum website for additional resources and any videos and websites assigned for this lesson.

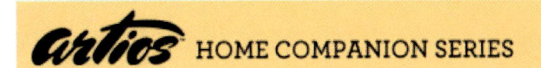

Key People, Places, and Events	Vocabulary
Athens Draco Solon	tyrant jurisprudence capital (offense) humane prosperity gossip

The contest of Athena and Poseidon, West Pediment of the Parthenon
Reconstruction of the west pediment of the Parthenon according to drawing by K. Schwerzek. CC BY-SA 2.0

Adapted for Elementary School from the book:
The Story of Mankind
by Hendrik Willem Van Loon
Greek Self-Government

Greek Self Government

In early Greek society, men were, for the most part, equally rich and equally poor. Every man owned a certain number of cows and sheep. His mud hut was his castle. He was free to come and go as he wished. Whenever it was necessary to discuss matters of public importance, all the citizens of a village would gather in the marketplace. One of the older men was elected chairman, and it was his duty to see that everybody had a chance to express his views. A particularly energetic and self-confident villager would be chosen commander in chief in war. Still, the same people who had given this man the right to be their leader claimed an equal right to deprive him of his job once the danger had been averted.

But gradually, the village would grow into a city. Some people worked hard, while others were lazy. A few were unlucky, and others were just plain dishonest in dealing with their neighbors and gathered great wealth. As a result, the city would no longer consist of equally well-off people. On the contrary, it was inhabited by a small class of extraordinarily wealthy people and a large class of extremely poor ones.

There was another change. The old commander-in-chief, who had been willingly recognized as "headman" or "king" because he knew how to lead his men to victory, disappeared from the scene. His place was taken by the nobles—a class of wealthy people who, over time, gained most of the farms and estates.

These nobles enjoyed many advantages over the common crowd of freemen. They could buy the best weapons to be found on the market of the eastern Mediterranean. They had much spare time to practice the art of fighting. They lived in strongly built homes and could hire soldiers to fight for them. They were constantly quarreling with each other to decide who should rule the city. The victorious nobleman then assumed a sort of kingship over all his neighbors. He governed the town until he, in turn, was killed or driven away by still another ambitious nobleman.

Such a king was called a **tyrant** by his soldiers, and during the 7th and 6th centuries B.C., every Greek city was, for a time, ruled by such tyrants, many of whom, by the way, happened to be exceedingly capable men. But in the long run, this state of affairs became unbearable. Then attempts were made to bring about reforms, and out of these reforms grew the first democratic government of which the world has a record.

It was early in the 7th century B.C. that the people of **Athens** decided to do some housecleaning and give the substantial number of freemen once more a voice in the government, such as they were supposed to have had in the days of their earliest ancestors. They asked a man named **Draco** to provide them with a set of laws that would protect the poor against the aggressions of the rich. Draco set to work. Unfortunately, he was a professional lawyer and very much out of touch with ordinary life. When he finished his code, the people of Athens discovered that these draconian laws were so severe that they could not be put into effect. There would not have been enough rope to hang all the criminals under their new jurisprudence system, which made stealing an apple a **capital** offense.

The Athenians looked about for a more **humane** reformer. At last, they found someone who could do that sort of thing better than anybody else. His name was **Solon**. He belonged to a noble family, traveled worldwide, and studied many other countries' government forms. After carefully studying the subject, Solon gave Athens a set of laws that benefited all citizens.

Photo of the *Draco Lawgiver* carving in the United States Supreme Court Library

Marble relief of Solon from the chamber of the US House of Representatives

Solon tried to improve the condition of the peasant without destroying the

prosperity of the nobles who were (or could be) of great service to the state as soldiers. To protect the poorer classes of citizens against abuse on the part of the judges (who were always elected from the class of the nobles because they received no salary), Solon made a provision whereby a citizen with a grievance had the right to state his case before a jury of thirty of his fellow Athenians.

Solon, depicted as a Medieval scholar in the *Nuremberg Chronicle*

Most importantly, Solon forced the average freeman to take a direct and personal interest in the city's affairs. He could no longer stay home and say, "Oh, I am too busy today," or, "It is raining, so I had better stay indoors." He was expected to do his share: to be at the town council meeting and carry part of the responsibility for the safety and prosperity of the state.

This government by the *demos*, or the people, was often far from successful. There was too much **gossip**. There were too many hateful and spiteful scenes between rivals for official honor. But it taught the Greek people to be independent and rely upon themselves, which was incredibly good.

Roman statuette of Athena, copy of the Phidias statue, created for the Parthenon in 447 B.C.
National Archaeological Museum, Athens
CC BY 2.5

Ancient: Elementary
Unit 20: Classical Greek History

Lesson Three

History Overview and Assignments
The Story of Icarus

"Beware, dear son of my heart," he said, "lest, in thy new-found power, thou seekest to soar even to the gates of Olympus. For as surely as the scorching rays from the burnished wheels of the chariot of Apollo smite thy wings, the wax that binds on thy feathers will melt, and then will come upon thee and on me woe unutterable."

– from the adapted article below

Jacob Peter Gowy's *The Flight of Icarus* (1635–1637), after Peter Paul Rubens

Suggested Reading and Assignments

- Review the vocabulary, then read the article: *Icarus*.
- After reading the article, summarize the story you read by either:
    - Retelling it out loud to your teacher or parent.
       OR
    - Completing an appropriate notebook page.

  Either way, be sure to include an overview of key people, places, dates, and events in your summary.
- Define the vocabulary words in the context of the reading. Write the words and their definitions in the vocabulary section of your history notebook.
- Be sure to visit your **ArtiosHCS** curriculum website for additional resources and any videos and websites assigned for this lesson.

Ancient: Elementary
Unit 20: Classical Greek History

Key People, Places, and Events

Icarus   Daedalus   Minos

Vocabulary

dauntless	gale	portent	sheen	dirge
wimble	pinion	cleave	translucent	pall
hoist	cumber	plumage	exquisite	ecstasy

Adapted for Elementary School from the book:
The Story of Mankind
by Hendrik Willem Van Loon
Icarus

Throughout history, how many fathers' and mothers' hearts have wept over the death of gallant sons, greatly promising and daring, who have sought to rule the skies by means of flight? With wings not well enough tried, they have soared **dauntless**ly aloft, only to add more names to the tragic list of those whose lives have been sacrificed so that the groping hands of science may become sure, so that in time the sons of men may sail through the heavens as fearlessly as their fathers sailed through the seas.

High overhead, we watch the airplane, the great, swooping thing, like a monster black-winged bird, and our minds travel back to the story of **Icarus**, who died so many years ago that some say that his story is but a foolish fable, an idle myth.

Daedalus, the grandson of the king of Athens, was the most outstanding craftsman of his day. Not only was he great as an architect, but as a sculptor he had the creative power to make men, women, and animals that looked alive, but to cause them to move and to be, to all appearances, endowed with life. To him, the craftsmen who followed him owed the invention of the axe, the wedge, the **wimble** for boring holes, and the carpenter's level, and his restless mind was ever-busy with new inventions. To his nephew Perdrix he taught all that he knew of all the mechanical arts. Soon it seemed that the nephew, though he might not excel his uncle, equaled Daedalus in his inventive power. As he walked by the seashore, the lad picked up the spine of a fish, and, having pondered its possibilities, he took it home, imitated it in iron, and so invented the saw. A still more fantastic invention followed this. While those who had always thought that there could be none more remarkable than Daedalus were still acclaiming the lad, there came to him the idea of putting two pieces of iron together, connecting them at one end with a rivet, and sharpening both ends, and a pair of compasses was made. Louder still were the acclamations of the people. Indeed one greater than Daedalus was here. Too much was this for the master craftsman's jealous spirit.

One day they stood together on the top of the Acropolis, and Daedalus, a murderer that comes from jealousy in his heart, threw his nephew down. Down, down he fell, knowing well that he would meet a cruel death, but Pallas Athena, the protectress of all clever craftsmen, came to his rescue. By her power, Perdrix was turned into the bird that still bears his name, and Daedalus beheld Perdrix, the partridge, rapidly winging his way to the far-off fields. Since then, no partridge has ever been built or roosted in a high place but has nestled in the hedge roots and amongst the standing corn, and as we mark it, we can see that its flight is always low.

Daedalus was banished from Athens for his crime, and in the court of **Minos**, king of Crete, he found refuge. He put all his mighty powers at the service of Minos and, for him, designed an intricate labyrinth which, like the river Meander, had neither beginning nor end but ever returned on itself in hopeless intricacy. Soon he stood high in favor of the king, but, ever greedy for power, he incurred Minos's wrath with one of his daring inventions. The angry monarch threw him into prison and imprisoned him with his son, Icarus. But prison bars and locks did not exist that were strong enough to baffle this master craftsman, and from the tower in which they were shut, Daedalus and his son were not long in making their escape.

To escape from Crete was a less easy matter. There were many places on that wild island where it was easy for the father and son to hide, but the subjects of Minos were mostly mariners. Daedalus knew well that they kept watching all along the shore lest he make himself a boat, **hoist** on it one of the sails of which he was part inventor, and speed away to safety like a sea bird driven before the **gale**. Then did there come to Daedalus, the pioneer of inventions, the great idea that by his skill, he might make a way for himself and his son through another element than the water. And he laughed aloud in his hiding place among the cypresses on the hillside at the thought of how he would baffle the simple sailormen who watched each creek and beach down on the shore. Mockingly, too, did he think of King Minos, who had dared to pit his power against the wits and skill of Daedalus, the mighty craftsman.

Many a Cretan bird was sacrificed before the task the inventor had set himself was accomplished. In a shady forest on the mountains, he fashioned light wooden frames and decked them with feathers until they looked like the pinions of a great eagle or of a swan that flapped its majestic way from lake to river. Each feather was bound on with wax, and the mechanism of the wings was such a perfect reproduction of that of the wings from which the feathers had been plucked that on the first day that he fastened them to his back and spread them out, Daedalus found that he could fly even as the bird flew. Two pairs he made; having tested one pair, a second pair was made for Icarus. Then, circling him like a mother bird that teaches her nestlings how to fly, Daedalus, his heart big with the pride of invention, showed Icarus how he might best soar upward to the sun or dive down to the blue sea far below and how he might conquer the winds and the air currents of the sky and make them his servants.

That was a joyous day for father and son, for the father had never drunk deeper of the intoxicating wine of the gods—Success—and for the lad, it was all pure joy. Never before had he known freedom and power so utterly glorious. As a little child, he had watched the birds fly far away over the blue hills to where the sun was setting and longed for wings that he might follow in their flight. At times, in his dreams, he had known the power, and in his dreaming, fancy had risen from the **cumber**ing earth and soared high above the trees and fields on strong pinions that bore him away to the fair land of heart's desire—to the Islands of the Blessed. But when sleep left him, and the dreams silently slipped out before the coming of the light of day, and the boy sprang from his couch and eagerly spread his arms as, in his dreams, he had done, he could no longer fly. Disappointment and unsatisfied longing ever came with his waking hours. Now all that had come to an end, and Daedalus was glad and proud as well to watch his son's joy and his fearless daring. One word of counsel only did he give him.

"Beware, dear son of my heart," he said, "lest, in thy new-found power, thou seekest to soar even to the gates of Olympus. For as surely as the scorching rays from the burnished wheels of the chariot of Apollo smite thy wings, the wax that binds on thy feathers will melt, and then will come upon thee and on me woe unutterable."

In his dreams that night, Icarus flew. When he awoke, fearing to find only the haunting remembrance of a dream, he found his father standing by the side of his bed of soft leaves under the shadowy cypresses, ready to bind on his willing shoulders the great pinions that he had made.

Gentle dawn, the rosy-fingered, was slowly making her way up from the East when Daedalus and Icarus began their flight. Slowly they glided at first, and the goatherds who tended their flocks on the slopes of Mount Ida looked up in fear when they saw the dark shadows of their wings and marked the monster birds making their way out to sea. From the riverbeds, the waterfowl arose from the reeds and, with a great outcry, flew swiftly to escape them. And down by the seashore, the mariners' hearts sank within them as they watched, believing that a sight so strange must be a **portent** of disaster. Homeward, they hastened to offer sacrifices on the altars of Poseidon, ruler of the deep.

Samos and Delos were passed on the left and Lebynthos on the right, long ere the sun god had started on his daily course, and as the mighty wings of Icarus **cleft** the cold air, the boy's slim body grew chilled. He longed for the sun's rays to turn the waters of the Aegean Sea over which he flew from green-grey into limpid sapphire, emerald, and burning gold. Toward Sicily, he and his father bent their course, and when they saw the beautiful island afar off lying like a gem in the sea, Apollo made the waves in which it lay a fitting setting for it.

With a cry of joy, Icarus marked the sun's rays painting the chill water. Apollo looked down at the tremendous white-winged bird, a snowy swan with the face and form of a beautiful boy, who sped exulting onward, while a clumsier thing, with wings of a darker hue, followed less quickly, in the same line of flight. As the god looked, the warmth that radiated from his chariot touched the icy limbs of Icarus as with the caressing touch of gentle, life-giving hands.

Not long before, his flight had lagged, but now it seemed like new life was his. Like a bird that wheels and soars and dives as if for the lightness of heart, so did Icarus until each feather of his **plumage** had a **silver and gold sheen**. Down, down, he darted, so near the water that the white-tipped waves almost caught his wings as he skimmed over them. Then up, up, up he soared, ever higher, higher still, and when he saw the radiant sun god smiling down on him, the warning of Daedalus was forgotten. As he had excelled with other lads in foot races, Icarus wished to excel with the birds.

Daedalus he left far behind, and still upwards, he mounted. So strong he felt, so fearless was he, that to him it seemed that he could storm Olympus, that he could call to Apollo as he swept past him in his flight and dare him to race for a wager from the Aegean Sea to where the sun god's horses took their nightly rest by the trackless seas of the unknown West.

The Fall of Icarus (1819) by Merry-Joseph Blondel, in the Rotunda of Apollo at the Louvre

In terror, his father watched him, and as he called to him in a voice of anguished warning that was drowned by the whistling rush of the air currents through the wings of Icarus and the moist whisper of the clouds as through them, he cleft a way for himself, there occurred the dreaded thing. It seemed as though the strong wings had begun to lose their power. Like a wounded bird, Icarus fluttered, lunged sidewise from the straight, clean line of his flight, recovered himself, and fluttered again. And then, like the bird into whose soft chest the sure hand of a mighty archer has driven an arrow, downward he fell, turning over and yet turning again, downward, ever downward, until he fell with a plunge into the sea that still was radiant in shining emerald and **translucent** blue.

Then did the chariot of Apollo drive on. His rays had slain one who was too greatly daring, and now they stroked the little white feathers that had fallen from the broken wings and floated on the water like the petals of a torn flower.

On the dead, still face of Icarus, they shone, spangled as if with diamonds, the wet plumage that still, widespread, bore him up on the waves.

Stricken at heart was Daedalus, but there was no time to lament his son's untimely end, for even now, the black-prowed ships of Minos might be in pursuit. Onward he flew to safety and, in Sicily, built a temple to Apollo, and there hung up his wings as an apologetic offering to the god who had slain his son.

The Lament for Icarus by Herbert James Draper (1898)

And when gray night came down on that part of the sea that bears the name of Icarus to this day, still there floated the body of the boy whose dreams had come true. For only a little while had he known the **exquisite** realization of dreamed-of possibilities, for only a few hours tasted the sweetness of perfect pleasure, and then, by an over-daring flight, had lost it all forever.

The sorrowing Nereids sang a **dirge** over him as he was swayed gently hither and thither by the tide. When the silver stars came out from the dark dome of heaven and were reflected in the blackness of the sea at night, it was as though a velvet **pall**, silver-decked in his honor, was spread around the slim white body with its outstretched snowy wings.

So much had he dared—so little accomplished.

Is it not the oft-told tale of those who have followed Icarus? Yet who can say that gallant youth has lived in vain when, as Icarus did, he has breasted the very skies, has flown with fearless heart and soul to the provinces of the deathless gods?—when, even for the space of a few of the heartbeats of Time, he has tasted supreme power—the **ecstasy** of limitless happiness?

The Fall of Icarus, a 17th-century relief with a Cretan labyrinth bottom right

In Bruegel's *Landscape with the Fall of Icarus*, the fallen Icarus is a small detail at the lower right.
by Pieter Brueghel the Elder (c.1558)

The Artios Home Companion Series
Unit 21: Classical Greek Culture

Teacher Overview

THE ARTS ARE SAID to reflect the society that creates them. Nowhere is this truer than in the case of the ancient Greeks. The Greeks portrayed their lives, culture, and beliefs through their temples, art, and literature. They also showed their eagerness to worship false gods to gain blessings. The apostle Paul warns us in today's Leading Idea against following the ways of our societies, but instead to become wise by studying God's Word.

Bazaar of Athens, by Edward Dodwell (1821)

Suggested Assignments

Based on your student's age and ability, the reading in this unit may be read aloud to the student, and journaling and notebook pages may be completed orally. Likewise, other assignments may be done with an appropriate combination of independent and guided study.

In this unit, students will:
- Complete three lessons in which they will learn about **Greek culture during the classical era**.
- Explore websites about Greek culture and prepare to talk about what they learn. The LINKs for the sites to explore may be found on the **ArtiosHCS** curriculum website.
- Make a descriptive list.
- Illustrate one or more Greek myths.
- Visit the **ArtiosHCS** curriculum website at **www.ArtiosHCS.com** for additional resources and any videos and websites assigned for this unit.

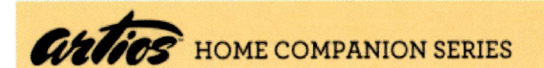

Heart Connections

To mature as Christians, we need to renew our minds.

Do not be conformed to this world, but be transformed by the renewal of your mind, that by testing you may discern what is the will of God, what is good and acceptable and perfect.

– Romans 12:2

Initially used in religious rituals, Greek masks became an essential part of every Greek theater performance.
Photo by Carole Raddato. CCA

Key People, Places, and Events

Mount Olympus
Zeus
Kronos
Poseidon
Hades
Hephaestus
Athena
Hera
Hermes
Vesta
Apollo
Artemis
Niobe
Helios
Eos
Phaeton
Aphrodite
Eros
Adonis
Pluto
Demeter
Persephone
Charon
The Fates

What the Temple of Olympian Zeus in Athens may have once looked like
Valentin Fiumefreddo. CC BY-SA 4.0

Lesson One

History Overview and Assignments
The Culture and Religion of Classical Greece

"The Greeks thought twelve ruling gods and goddesses lived on a mountain called Olympus. There is such a mountain in Greece, and the people thought the gods lived on the top of it."
– from the adapted article below

Hera and Prometheus shown on a 5th-century B.C. cup from Vulci, Etruria
Photo by Jastrow

Suggested Reading and Assignments

- Read the article: *Olympus*.
- After reading the article, summarize the story you read by either:
    - Retelling it out loud to your teacher or parent.
        OR
    - Completing an appropriate notebook page.
  Either way, be sure to include an overview of key people, places, dates, and events in your summary.
- Instead of answering discussion questions, make a list of the deities whose names are written in bold letters in today's reading, and write what each is known for.
- Explore the websites at the links in the suggested assignments for this lesson on your **ArtiosHCS** curriculum website, and prepare to talk about what you learn about classical Greek culture.
- Be sure to visit your **ArtiosHCS** curriculum website for additional resources and any videos and websites assigned for this lesson.

Ancient: Elementary
Unit 21: Classical Greek Culture

Key People, Places, and Events

Mount Olympus	Poseidon	Athena	Hermes
Zeus	Hades	Hera	Vesta
Kronos	Hephaestus		

Adapted for Elementary School from the book:
Aunt Charlotte's Stories of Greek History
by Charlotte M. Yonge
Olympus

The Greek Gods of Olympus

I am going to tell you the history of some of the most wondrous people who ever lived. But I have to begin with a good deal that is not true; for the people who descended from Noah's grandson Javan and lived in the beautiful islands and peninsulas called Greece were not trained in the knowledge of God like the Israelites but had to guess for themselves. They made up strange stories, partly from the old beliefs they brought from the East, partly from their ways of speaking about the powers of nature—sky, sun, moon, stars, and clouds—as if they were living beings, and so again of good or bad qualities as beings also, and partly from old stories about their forefathers.

These stories got mixed up with their beliefs and became part of their religion and history; they authored beautiful poems about them and made such lovely statues in their honor that nobody can understand anything about art or learning who has not learned these stories. I must begin by trying to tell you a few of them.

In the first place, the Greeks thought twelve ruling gods and goddesses lived on a mountain called **Olympus**. There is such a mountain in Greece, and the people thought the gods lived on top of it. The one they considered the chief of all, the father of gods and men, was the sky god, **Zeus**, as the Greeks called him, or Jupiter, as he was called in Latin.

However, as they believed all things are born of Time, the sky or Jupiter was said to have a father, Time, whose Greek name was **Kronos**. His other name was Saturn, and just as Time devoured his offspring, Saturn was said to have had the bad habit of eating up his children as fast as they were born till his wife Rhea contrived to give him a stone in swaddling clothes. While he was biting this hard morsel, Jupiter was saved from him, and afterward, two other sons, Neptune (**Poseidon**) and Pluto (**Hades**), became lords of the ocean and of the world of the spirits of the dead; for over the sea and on death Time has no power.

Greek God Kronos/Saturnus with a sickle, from *Dr. Vollmers Wörterbuch der Mythologie aller Völker*, by Stuttgart (1874)

However, Saturn's reign was thought to be very peaceful and happy. For as people always think of the days of Paradise in Eden and believe that the days of old were better than their times, so the Greeks thought there had been four ages—the Golden Age, the Silver Age, the Bronze Age, and the Iron age—and that people had been getting worse in each of them. Poor old Saturn, after the Silver age, had had to retire, with only his star, the planet Saturn, left to him.

Jupiter was now reigning on his throne atop Olympus, at the head of the twelve greater gods and goddesses, and it was the Iron Age below. His star, the planet we still call by his name, was much larger and brighter than Saturn.

The Greeks always thought of Jupiter as a majestic-looking man with full strength, thick hair and beard, bolts of lightning in his hand, and an eagle by his side. These bolts of lightning or thunderbolts were forged by his lame son Vulcan (**Hephaestus**), the god of fire and the smith and armorer of Olympus, whose smithies were inside the volcanoes (so called from his name), and whose workmen were the Cyclops or Round Eyes—giants, each with one eye in the middle of his forehead.

Once, indeed, Jupiter had needed his bolts, for the Titans, a horrible race of monstrous giants, of whom the worst was Briareus (who had a hundred hands), had tried, by piling up mountains one upon the other, to reach heaven and throw him down. Still, when Jupiter was hardest pressed, a dreadful pain in his head caused him to beg Vulcan to strike it with his hammer. Then out from his head darted Heavenly Wisdom, his beautiful daughter **Athena**, fully armed, with piercing, shining eyes, and by her counsels, he cast down the Titans and heaped their mountains, Etna and Ossa and Pelion, on them to keep them down; and whenever there was an earthquake, it was thought to be caused by one of these giants struggling to get free, though perhaps there was some remembrance of the tower of Babel in the story. Athena, this glorious daughter of Jupiter, was wise, brave, and strong, and she was also the goddess of women's works—of all spinning, weaving, and sewing.

Jupiter's wife, the queen of heaven and the air was Juno—in Greek, **Hera**—the white-armed, ox-eyed, stately lady whose bird was the peacock. Do you know how the peacock got the eyes in his tail? They once belonged to Argus, a shepherd with a hundred eyes, whom Juno had set to watch a cow named Io, who was really a lady, much hated by her. Argus watched until Mercury (Hermes) came, lulled him to sleep with soft music, and then drove Io away. Juno was so angry that she caused all the eyes to be taken from Argus and put into her peacock's tail.

Mercury has a planet named after him, too, a very small one, so close to the sun that we see it only just after sunset or before sunrise. I believe Mercury or Hermes means "the morning breeze." The story says that he was born early in the morning in a cave, and after he had slept a little while in his cradle, he came forth and, finding the shell of a tortoise with some strings of the innards stretched across it, he at once began to play on it and thus formed the first lyre. He was so swift that he was the messenger of Jupiter, and he is always represented with wings on his cap and sandals. Still, as the wind not only makes music but blows things away unawares, Mercury came to be viewed not only as the god of fair speech, but as a terrible thief, the god of thieves. You see, as long as these Greek stories are parables, they are grand and beautiful, but when the beings are looked on as like men, they are absurd and often horrid.

The gods had another messenger, Iris, the rainbow, who always carried messages of mercy, a recollection of the bow in the clouds, but she chiefly belonged to Juno.

All the twelve significant gods had palaces on Olympus and met every day in Jupiter's hall to feast on *ambrosia*, a sort of food of life that made them immortal. Their drink was nectar, which was poured into their golden cups at first by Vulcan, but he stumbled and hobbled so severely with his lame leg that they chose instead the fresh and graceful Hebe, the goddess of youth, till she was careless and one day fell, cup and nectar and all. The gods thought they must find another cupbearer, and, looking down, they saw a beautiful youth named Ganymede watching his flocks upon Mount Ida. So, they sent Jupiter's eagle down to fly away with him and bring him to Olympus. They gave him some ambrosia to make him immortal and let him become their cupbearer.

Besides ambrosia and nectar, the gods were thought to feed on the smoke and smell of the sacrifices people offered on earth and consistently help those who offered them the most sacrifices of animals and incense.

The familiar names of these twelve were Jupiter, Neptune, Juno, Latona, Apollo, Diana, Pallas, Venus, Vulcan, Mercury, Vesta, and Ceres, but there were multitudes of minor deities. Every river had its god, every mountain and wood was full of *nymphs* (female nature deities), and there was a great god of all nature called Pan, which in Greek means All.

Neptune was only a visitor on Olympus, though he had a right to be there. His kingdom was the sea, which he ruled with his trident, and where he had an entire world of lesser gods and nymphs, tritons, and sea horses to attend upon his chariot.

And the quietest and best of all the goddesses was **Vesta**, the goddess of the household hearth—of home, that is to say. There are no stories to be told about her, but a fire was always kept burning in her honor in each city, and no one might tend it who was not good and pure.

Lesson Two

History Overview and Assignments
Greek Tales of Wonder

"Apollo was lord of the day and Artemis queen of the night. They were as bright and pure as man's imagination could make them and always young."

– from the adapted article below

The Return of Persephone, by Frederic Leighton (1891)

Key People, Places, and Events

Apollo
Artemis
Niobe
Helios
Eos
Phaeton
Zeus
Aphrodite
Eros
Hephaestus
Hermes
Adonis
Pluto
Demeter
Persephone
Charon
The Fates

Suggested Reading and Assignments

- Read the article: *Light and Dark*.
- After reading the article, summarize the story you read by either:
    - Retelling it out loud to your teacher or parent.
        OR
    - Completing an appropriate notebook page.
  Either way, be sure to include an overview of key people, places, dates, and events in your summary.
- Instead of answering discussion questions, add to your list from Lesson One with any new names written in bold in today's reading, and tell what each is known for.
- Continue exploring the websites at the links in the suggested assignments for this lesson on your **ArtiosHCS** curriculum website. Prepare to talk about what you learn about classical Greek culture.
- Read some more Greek myths at the link in the suggested assignments for this lesson on your **ArtiosHCS** curriculum website.
- Be sure to visit your **ArtiosHCS** curriculum website for additional resources and any videos and websites assigned for this lesson.

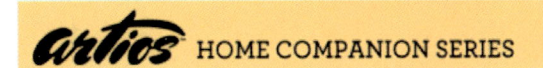

Ancient: Elementary
Unit 21: Classical Greek Culture

Adapted for Elementary School from the book:
Aunt Charlotte's Stories of Greek History
by Charlotte M. Yonge
Light and Dark

Light and Dark

The god and goddess of light were the glorious twin brother and sister **Apollo** and **Artemis**. They were born on the Greek isle of Delos, which was made to rise out of the sea to save their mother, Latona, from the horrid serpent, Python, who wanted to devour her. Gods were born strong and mighty; the first thing Apollo did was slay the serpent at Delphi with his arrows.

Here was a dim remembrance of the promise in Genesis 3 that the Seed of the woman should bruise the serpent's head and also a thought of the way Light slays the dragon of darkness with his beams.

Apollo was lord of the day and Artemis queen of the night. They were as bright and pure as man's imagination could make them and always young. The beams or rays were their arrows, so Artemis was a huntress, always in the woods with her nymphs. She was so modest that once when an unfortunate wanderer named Actaeon came across her with her nymphs by chance when they were bathing in a stream, she splashed some water in his face and turned him into a stag so that his dogs gave chase to him and killed him.

I am afraid Apollo and Artemis were rather cruel, and the darting rays of the sun and moon sometimes kill and bless, so they were the senders of all sharp, sudden heat strokes.

There was a queen called **Niobe**, who had six sons and daughters so bright and fair that she boasted that they were equal to Apollo and Artemis, which made Latona so angry that she sent her son and daughter to slay them all with their darts. The unhappy Niobe, thus punished for her boastful pride, wept a river of tears till she was turned into stone.

SUPPOSED TEMPLE OF JUPITER PANHELLENIUS IN AEGINA.

The moon belonged to Artemis and was her chariot; the sun, in like manner, to Apollo; though he did not drive the chariot himself, **Helios**, the sun god, did. The world was considered a flat plate, with Delphi in the middle and the ocean all around. In the far east, the lady dawn, **Eos**, opened the gates with her rosy fingers, and out came the golden chariot of the sun, with glorious white horses driven by Helios, attended by the Hours strewing dew and flowers. It passed over the arch of the heavens to the ocean again on the west, and there Eos met it again in golden colors, unfastened the horses, and let them feed.

Eos had married a man named Tithonus. She gave him ambrosia, which made him immortal, but she could not keep him from growing old, so he became smaller and smaller until he dwindled into a grasshopper, and at last, only his voice was to be heard chirping at sunrise and sunset.

Helios had an earthly wife too, and a son named Phaeton, who once begged to be allowed to drive the chariot of the sun for just one day. Helios yielded, but poor Phaeton had no strength nor skill to guide the horses in the correct curve. At one moment, they rushed to the earth and scorched the trees; at another, they flew up to heaven and would have burned Olympus if Zeus had not cast his thunderbolts at the rash driver and hurled him down into a river, where he was drowned. His sisters wept till they were changed into poplar trees, and their tears hardened into amber drops.

Hermes gave his lyre to Apollo, who was the true god of music and poetry, and under him were nine nymphs—the Muses, daughters of memory—who dwelt on Mount Parnassus and were thought to inspire all noble and heroic song, all poems in praise to or of the gods or of brave men, and the graceful music and dancing at their feasts, also the knowledge of the stars of earth and heaven.

There was also a goddess of beauty called Aphrodite. Such beauty was hers as is the mere prettiness and charm of pleasure—nothing high or fine. She was said to have risen out of the sea as the sunshine touched the waves, her golden hair dripping with the spray, and her favorite home was in myrtle groves. There she drove her chariot, drawn by doves, attended by the three Graces, and by multitudes of little winged children called Loves. Still, there was generally said to be one special son of hers, Love (Eros in Greek, Cupid in Latin), whose arrows, when tipped with gold, made people fall in love and, when tipped with lead, made them hate one another. Her husband was the ugly, stooping smith named Hephaestus. Perhaps she wed him because pretty ornaments came from the demanding work of the smith, but she never behaved well toward him and only coaxed him when she wanted something that his clever hands could make.

She was much fonder of amusing herself with Hermes, the god of war, another of the evil gods, for he was fierce, cruel, and violent, and wherever he went, slaughter and blood were sure to follow him and his horrid daughter Bellona. His star was the red planet Mars, but Aphrodite (Venus in Latin) had the beautiful clear one, which, depending on whether it is seen at sunrise or sunset, is called the morning or evening star. Aphrodite also loved a handsome young earthly youth called Adonis, who died of a thrust from a wild boar's tusk, while his blood stained crimson the pretty flower known as pheasant's eye, which is still called Adonis.

Aphrodite was so sorrowful that she persuaded Zeus to decree that Adonis should come back and live for one-half of the year, but he was to go down to Pluto's underground kingdom the other half. This was because plants and flowers are beautiful for one year, die down, and rise again.

But there is a much prettier story, with something of the same meaning, about Demeter, the grave, motherly goddess of corn and all the fruits of the earth. She had one fair daughter, Persephone, who was playing with her companions near Mount Etna, gathering flowers in the meadows when grim old Pluto pounced upon her and carried her off into his underground world to be his bride. Poor Demeter did not know what had become of her darling and wandered up and down the world seeking for her, tasting no food or drink, till at last, entirely spent, she was taken in as a poor woman by Celeus, king of Eleusis. She became a nurse to his infant child Triptolemus.

All Eleusis was made rich with corn, while no rain fell and no crops grew on the rest of the earth; and though first Iris and then all the gods came to beg Demeter to relent, she would grant nothing unless she had her daughter back. So Zeus sent Hermes to bring Persephone home, but she was only allowed to stay on earth because she had eaten nothing while in the underworld. Knowing this, Pluto had coaxed her to eat half a pomegranate, so she could not stay with her mother; but Demeter's tears prevailed so far that she was allowed to spend the summers above ground and the winters below, for she was the flowers and fruit.

Demeter had grown so fond of little Triptolemus that she wanted to make him immortal, but, as she had no ambrosia, this could only be done by putting him on the fire night after night to burn away his mortal part. His mother looked in one night during the operation and shrieked so that she prevented it so that all Demeter could do for him was to give him grains of wheat and a dragon chariot, with which he traveled all about the world, teaching men to sow corn and reap harvests.

Persephone seems contented in her underground kingdom, where she ruled with Pluto. This was said to be located below the volcanic grounds in southern Italy, near Lake Avernus. The entrance was guarded by a three-headed dog named Cerberus, and the River Styx barred the way to the lake. Every evening Hermes brought all the spirits of the people who had died during the day to the shore of the Styx, and if their funeral rites had been properly performed, and they had a little coin on the tongue to pay the fare, **Charon**, the ferryman, took them across; but if their corpses were in the sea, or on battle-fields, unburied, the poor spirits had to flit about, vainly begging to be ferried over.

After the dead had crossed, they were judged by three judges, and if they were wicked, they were sent over the river of fire to be tormented by the three Furies—Alecto, Megara, and Tisiphone, who had snakes as whips and in their hair. If the dead had been brave and virtuous, they would have been allowed to live among beautiful trees and flowers in the Elysian fields, where Pluto reigned. However, they seem always to have longed after the life they had lost, and these Greek notions of bliss seem sad, besides what we know to be the truth about death and the afterlife.

Here lived the three **Fates**, constantly spinning the threads of men's lives; Clotho held the distaff, Lachesis drew out the thread, and Atropos, with her shears, cut it off when the man was to die. And, though Zeus was mighty, nothing could happen but by the Fates, stronger than he.

MARS AND VICTORY.

Lesson Three

History Overview and Assignments
On Your Own: Picture Project

Triptolemus, Demeter, and Persephone, by a Triptolemus-painter (c.470 B.C.)

Suggested Assignment

- Illustrate three myths described in the previous lesson, drawing or painting at least one picture to accompany each story.
- Be sure to visit your **ArtiosHCS** curriculum website for additional resources and any videos and websites assigned for this lesson.

Fall of Phaeton, by Johann Michael Franz

The Artios Home Companion Series
Unit 22: Alexander the Great

Teacher Overview

ALEXANDER THE GREAT, son of Philip of Macedonia, conquered much of the ancient world. He is responsible for the final demise of the Persian Empire. His greed finally led to his downfall, and he died of fever in 323 B.C. After his death, his generals fought over control of his empire, leading to wars and division into a number of separate kingdoms. Greek culture was spread to these kingdoms, bringing many advances, but the Romans eventually conquered them.

Alexander the Great Founding Alexandria, by Placido Costanzi (c.1736).
In conquests from Greece and Egypt to Afghanistan, the Macedonian ruler, Alexander the Great, founded cities, often naming them for himself in crucial military and trading locations. Alexandria in Egypt is the only one still thriving today. Alexander was often involved in the planning. Here he gives instructions to the Greek architect Dinocrates. Behind them, massive walls are under construction.

Suggested Assignments

Based on your student's age and ability, the reading in this unit may be read aloud to the student, and journaling and notebook pages may be completed orally. Likewise, other assignments may be done with an appropriate combination of independent and guided study.

In this unit, students will:
- Complete one lesson in which they will learn about **Alexander the Great** and **his conquests**.
- Define vocabulary words.
- Visit the **ArtiosHCS** curriculum website at **www.ArtiosHCS.com** for additional resources and any videos and websites assigned for this unit.

Ancient: Elementary
Unit 22: Alexander the Great

Heart Connections

Learning to work well is important.
For even when we were with you, we would give you this command: If anyone is not willing to work, let him not eat.
– 2 Thessalonians 3:10

It is important to do our best.
Whatever you do, work heartily, as for the Lord and not for men,
– Colossians 3:23

This medallion of Alexander was produced in Imperial Rome, showing the conqueror's enduring influence.

A map of Alexander the Great's empire at its largest extent c.323 B.C., including details of key roads, locations, and battles
CC BY-SA 3.0

Lesson One

History Overview and Assignments
Alexander the Great and His Conquests

IN THE SPRING of 334 B.C., a young ruler named Alexander left Europe as the head of a large army. Seven years later, he reached India. In the meantime, he had conquered Phoenicia, Egypt, and the Persian Empire. After conquering part of India, he stopped and announced even more ambitious plans.

The Battle of Gaugamela (detail). Ivory relief by an anonymous artist (18th century) depicting Alexander fighting atop his horse, named Bucephalus
Photo by Luis Garcia. CC BY-SA 3.0

Suggested Reading and Assignments

- Review the discussion questions and vocabulary, then read the article: *Alexander the Great*.
- After reading the article, summarize the story you read by either:
    - Retelling it out loud to your teacher or parent.
        OR
    - Completing an appropriate notebook page.

  Either way, be sure to include an overview of key people, places, dates, and events in your summary.
- Define the vocabulary words in the context of the reading. Write the words and their definitions in the vocabulary section of your history notebook.
- Be sure to visit your **ArtiosHCS** curriculum website for additional resources and any videos and websites assigned for this lesson.

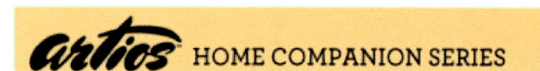

Ancient: Elementary
Unit 22: Alexander the Great

Key People, Places, and Events

Philip of Macedonia
Alexander the Great

Vocabulary

fruitless
ambitious
influence
domain

Discussion Questions

1. What did Philip of Macedonia like about the Greeks?
2. What did Philip of Macedonia despise about the Greeks?
3. How did Philip die?
4. Who was Philip's son?
5. Who was his son's teacher?
6. Describe Alexander the Great's travels and battles.
7. How did Alexander envision the new empire, and what steps did he take to change things?
8. How did Alexander die?
9. What happened to his empire after his death?
10. By the time the Romans took over, Greek culture had become a blend of what civilizations?
11. If you had been alive when Alexander the Great lived and had been captured by his army, what is one part of Greek culture you know you would have had to reject if you were a Christian?

Detail of Alexander on the *Alexander Sarcophagus* in Lebanon

Adapted for Elementary School from the book:
The Story of Mankind
by Hendrik Willem Van Loon
Alexander the Great

When people first started migrating from the north into Greece, some settled in the mountains of Macedonia. Now it happened that just when Sparta and Athens finished their disastrous war against each other, Macedonia was ruled by a clever king named **Philip**. He admired the Greek culture but despised the Greeks' lack of self-control in warring among themselves. Seeing perfectly good people waste their men and money upon fruitless quarrels annoyed him. So he settled the difficulty by invading and making himself the ruler of all Greece. Then he asked his new subjects to join him on a voyage in which he meant to pay Persia back for the invading visit Xerxes had paid the Greeks one hundred and fifty years before.

Aristotle Tutoring Alexander,
by Jean Leon Gerome Ferris (1895)

Niketerion (victory medallion) bearing the effigy of King Philip II of Macedon, 3rd century A.D.

Sadly for Philip, he was murdered before he could start this well-prepared expedition. The task of avenging the destruction of Athens was left to Philip's son **Alexander**, a pupil of Aristotle, the wisest of all Greek teachers.

Alexander said farewell to Europe in the spring of the year 334 B.C. Seven years later, he reached India. In the meantime, he had destroyed Phoenicia, the old rival of the Greek merchants. He had conquered Egypt and had been worshiped by the people of the Nile Valley as a pharaoh. He had defeated the last Persian king, had overthrown the Persian Empire, and had given orders to rebuild Babylon. He had led his troops into the Himalayan Mountains' heart and made the entire world a Macedonian province and dependency. Then he stopped and announced even more **ambitious** plans.

Ancient: Elementary
Unit 22: Alexander the Great

3rd century B.C. bust of Alexander the Great

He declared that the newly formed empire must be taught to live like the Greeks. The people must be taught the Greek language, live in cities built after a Greek model, and worship the Greek gods. The soldier now turned schoolmaster. The military camps of yesterday became the peaceful centers of the newly imported Greek culture. Higher and higher did the flood of Greek **influence** rise—when suddenly Alexander was stricken with a fever and died in the old Persian palace.

Alexander's new empire did not remain whole for long. A number of his ambitious generals divided the territory among themselves. But they, too, remained faithful to the dream of a great world brotherhood of Greek and Asiatic ideas and knowledge. Many advances in science, art, and literature were made during this era.

Ptolemaic coin showing Alexander the Great wearing an elephant scalp, a symbol of his conquest in India
Photo by Marie-Lan Nguyen. CC BY 2.5

Eventually, the Romans added these new kingdoms to their other **domain**s. This new civilization, part Greek, part Persian, part Egyptian, and Babylonian, fell to the Roman conquerors. During the following centuries, it gained such a firm hold upon the Roman world that we feel its influence in our lives today.

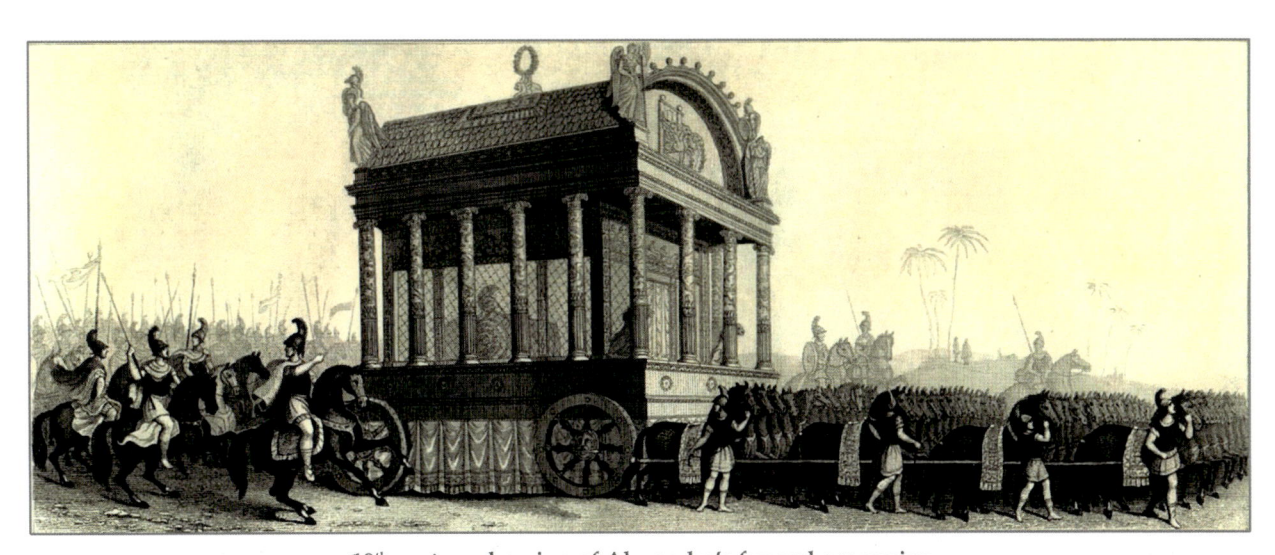

19th century drawing of Alexander's funeral procession

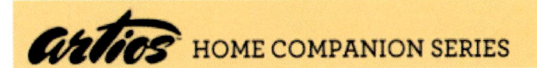

Ancient: Elementary
Unit 22: Alexander the Great

The Artios Home Companion Series
Unit 23: The Founding of Rome

Teacher Overview

AFTER THE CLASSICAL PERIOD in Greece came to an end with Alexander the Great, another country stepped into the spotlight. When she was attacked, she fought back, and in time she became ruler of lands all around the Mediterranean Sea.

Circus Maximus, where chariot races were held in ancient Rome
Photo by Rabax63. CC BY-SA 4.0

Suggested Assignments

Based on your student's age and ability, the reading in this unit may be read aloud to the student, and journaling and notebook pages may be completed orally. Likewise, other assignments may be done with an appropriate combination of independent and guided study.

In this unit, students will:
- Complete four lessons in which they will learn about **ancient Rome**.
- Define vocabulary words.
- Explore a website about Ancient Rome. The URL will be found on the **ArtiosHCS** curriculum website.
- Visit the **ArtiosHCS** curriculum website at **www.ArtiosHCS.com** for additional resources and any videos and websites assigned for this unit.

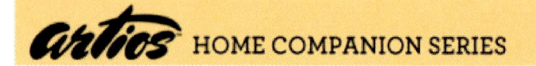

Heart Connections

God detests pride and honors humility.
> One's pride will bring him low, but he who is lowly in spirit will obtain honor.
> – Proverbs 29:23

There is only one God.
> There is one God, the Father, from whom are all things and for whom we exist, and one Lord, Jesus Christ, through whom are all things and through whom we exist.
> – 1 Corinthians 8:6

Key People, Places, and Events

Mediterranean Sea	Romulus	First Punic War	Second Punic War
Italy	Remus	Hannibal	Third Punic War
Rome	Tiber River	Alps	Gracchi brothers
	Carthage	Scipio	

Vocabulary

Lesson 1:
scheme

Lesson 2:
none

Lesson 3:
chariot
gladiator
bloodshed
extravagance

Lesson 4:
none

The Eiger (on the left, beside the Mönch and the Jungfrau) has the tallest north face in the Alps, making it one of the best-known sites of the mountain range.
Photo by Cable1

Ancient: Elementary
Unit 23: The Founding of Rome

Lesson One

History Overview and Assignments
The Legend of Romulus and Remus

"The children of Aeneas and Lavinia ruled over the land, and they had children, and their children had children, and their children had children until at last boy twins were born. These twins were named Romulus and Remus. Here ends the first part of the story, and the trouble begins, for they did not live happily ever after."

– from the adapted article below

Altar to Mars (who, according to Roman myth, was the divine father of Romulus and Remus) and Venus (another divine ancestor of the twins) depicting elements of their legend. Tiberinus (divine father of the Tiber River) and the infant twins being suckled by a she-wolf in the Lupercal are below. A vulture of omen and the Palatine Hill are to the left.

Suggested Reading and Assignments

- Read the article: *A Bad Beginning*.
- Define the vocabulary word in the context of the reading. Write the word and its definition in the vocabulary section of your history notebook.
- After reading the article, summarize the story you read by either:
    - Retelling it out loud to your teacher or parent.
      OR
    - Completing an appropriate notebook page.

  Either way, be sure to include the answers to the discussion questions and an overview of key people, places, dates, and events in your summary.
- Be sure to visit your **ArtiosHCS** curriculum website for additional resources and any videos and websites assigned for this lesson.

Vocabulary

scheme

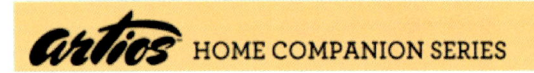

Ancient: Elementary
Unit 23: The Founding of Rome

Key People, Places, and Events

Mediterranean Sea
Italy
Rome
Romulus
Remus
Tiber River

Discussion Questions

1. Who was Aeneas in Roman legend?
2. What is the legend about the founding of Rome?
3. Why does the author consider this story a bad beginning for Rome?

Adapted for Elementary School from the book:
A Child's History of the World
by V.M. Hillyer
A Bad Beginning

A Bad Beginning

Have you ever heard of the Seven-League Boots, the boots in which one could walk many miles in a single step? Well, there is a still bigger boot, over five hundred miles long and in the **Mediterranean Sea**. No, it's not an actual boot, but it would look like one if you were miles high in an airplane and looking down upon it.

It is called **Italy**.

Map of the Italian peninsula by Eric Gaba and NordNordWest
CC BY-SA 3.0

Something significant happened in Italy not long after the First Olympiad in Greece. It was so important that it was called the Year 1, and for a thousand years, people counted from it as the Greeks did from the First Olympiad and as we do now from the birth of Christ. This thing that happened was not the birth of a man, however. It was the birth of a city, and this city was called **Rome**.

The history of Rome starts with stories that we know are fairy tales or myths, in the same way, that the history of Greece does. Homer told about the wanderings of the Greek named Odysseus. Many years later, a poet named Virgil told about the wanderings of a Trojan named Aeneas.

Aeneas fled from Troy when that city was burning down and started off to find a new home. Finally, after several years he came to Italy and the mouth of a river called the Tiber. There Aeneas met the daughter of the man ruling over that country, a girl named Lavinia, and married her, and they lived happily ever after. So, the children of Aeneas and Lavinia ruled over the land, and they had children, and their children had children, and their children had children until, at last, boy twins were born. These twins were named **Romulus** and **Remus**. Here ends the first part of the story, and the trouble begins, for they did not live happily ever after.

Before the twins were born, a man had stolen the kingdom, and he feared that these two boys might grow up and take his stolen kingdom away from him. So, he put the twins in a basket and set them afloat on the **Tiber River** like Baby Moses, but he was hoping that they might be carried out to sea or upset and drowned. He thought this might be all right, as long as he didn't kill them with his hands. But the basket drifted ashore instead of going out to sea or turning over, and a mother wolf found the twins and cared for them as if they were her babies. And a woodpecker also helped and fed them berries. At last, a shepherd found them and brought them up as if they were his sons until they grew up and became men. This sounds like the stories of Heracles and Cyrus, who were left out to die but were found and brought up by shepherds.

Romulus and Remus with the wolf

Each of the twins then wished to build a city. But they could not agree on which to do, and Romulus killed his twin brother Remus in quarreling over the matter. Romulus then built the city by the Tiber River on the spot where he and his brother had been saved and nursed by the mother wolf. Here there were seven hills. This was in 753 BC. He named the city Roma after his name, and the people who lived there were called Romans. So that is why, ever afterward, the Roman kings always said they were descended from the Trojan hero, Aeneas, the great-great-great-grandfather of Romulus.

Romulus and his brother Remus, from a 15th century frieze in Certosa di Pavia

Do you believe this story? Neither do I. But it is such an old story that everyone seems to think of it as history, even though it is only a legend.

To get people for the city he had started, it is said that Romulus invited all the thieves and evil men who had escaped from jail to come and live in Rome, promising them they would be safe there.

Then since none of the men had wives, and there were no women in his new city, Romulus thought up a **scheme** to get the men wives. He invited some people called Sabines, who lived nearby, both men and women, to come to Rome for a big party.

They accepted, and a great feast was spread. In the middle of the feast, when everyone was eating and drinking, a signal was given, and each of the Romans seized a

Sabine woman for his wife and ran off with her.

The Sabine husbands immediately prepared for war against the Romans who had stolen their wives. When the battle began between the two armies, the Sabine women ran out during the fighting between their new and old husbands and begged them both to stop. They said they had come to love their new husbands and would not return to their old homes.

What do you think of that?

It sounds like a pretty sorry beginning for a new city, doesn't it? And you may wonder how Rome turned out—a city that started with Romulus killing his brother and was settled by escaped prisoners who stole their neighbors' wives. Well, they believed in the same gods as the Greeks, and we have heard how their gods did all sorts of wicked things themselves. This was long before Christ was born, and they did not know anything about the Christian religion or what we call right and wrong.

You can see that I have tried to think of some good excuses for the actions of these first Romans. But after Rome's bad start, she had one king after another, and while some of these kings were pretty good, many were pretty bad.

The Rape of the Sabine Women, detail, by Giovanni Francesco Romanelli. One of a series of ceiling frescoes about the feats performed by Roman warriors (1655–1658)

Lesson Two

History Overview and Assignments
The Punic Wars

"Carthage did not like to see Rome getting so strong and growing so big and becoming so powerful. In other words, Carthage was jealous of Rome. On her side, Rome was jealous of Carthage's wealth and trade. So, Rome anxiously looked around for some excuse to get into a fight with her."

– from the adapted article below

Hannibal's celebrated feat of crossing the Alps with war elephants passed into European legend.
Detail of a fresco by Jacopo Ripanda (1510)
Upload by José Luiz Bernardes Ribeiro. CC BY-SA 4.0

Suggested Reading and Assignments

- Read the combined article: *Picking a Fight* and *The Boot Kicks and Stamps*.
- After reading the article, summarize the story you read by either:
    - Retelling it out loud to your teacher or parent.
       OR
    - Completing an appropriate notebook page.

  Either way, be sure to include the answers to the discussion questions and an overview of key people, places, dates, and events in your summary.
- Be sure to visit your **ArtiosHCS** curriculum website for additional resources and any videos and websites assigned for this lesson.

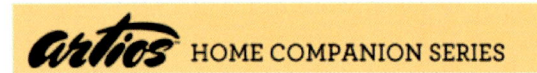

Ancient: Elementary
Unit 23: The Founding of Rome

Key People, Places, and Events

Carthage
First Punic War
Hannibal
Alps
Scipio
Second Punic War
Third Punic War

Discussion Questions

1. What was the First Punic War about?
2. What were the battles like during this war?
3. Who won?
4. What did Hannibal do during the Second Punic War to get into Italy, and what type of animal did he use to do it?
5. Who won this war?
6. What happened during the Third Punic War?

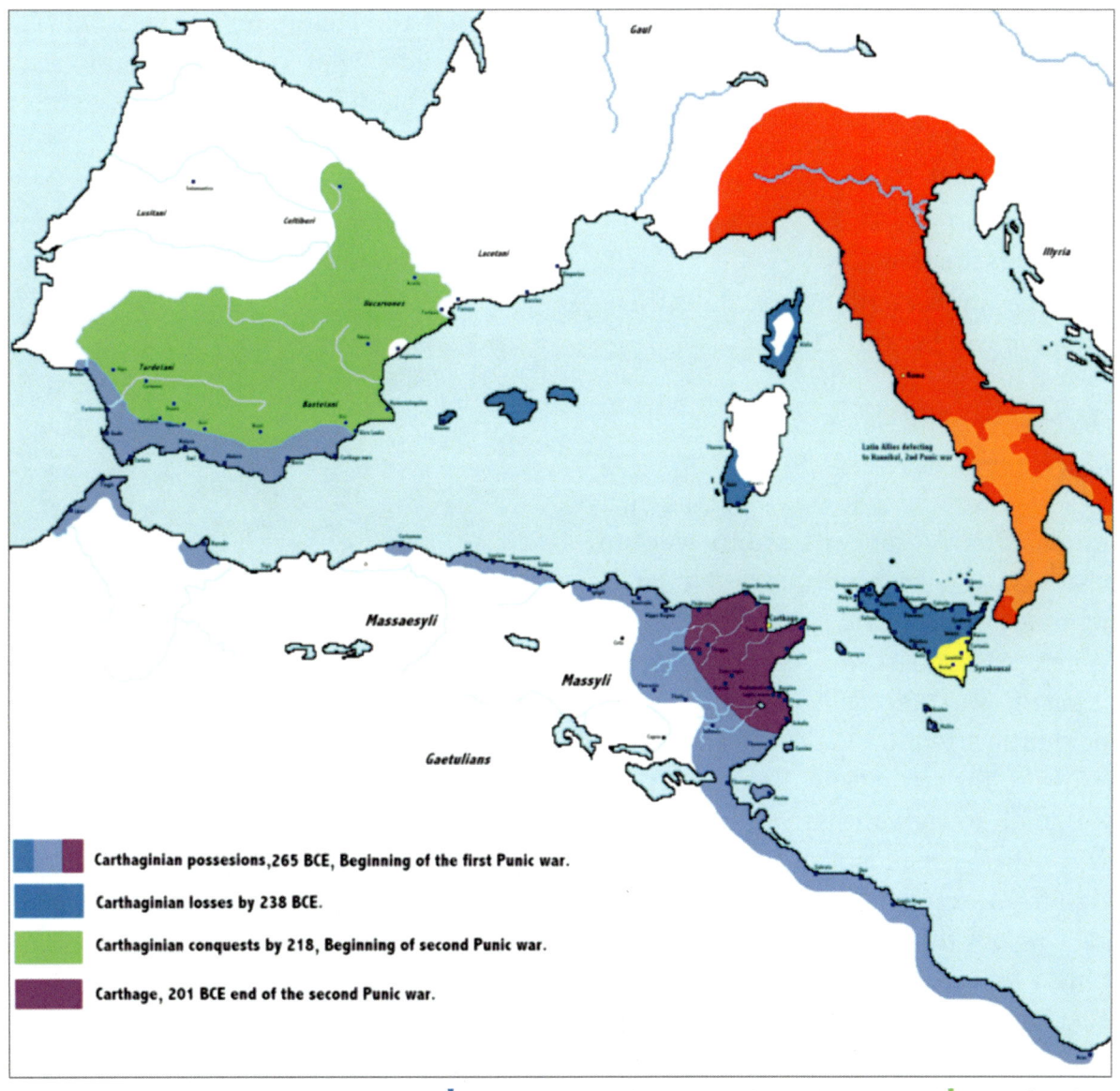

The downfall of the Carthaginian Empire | Lost to Rome in the First Punic War (264–241 BC) | Won after the First Punic War, lost in the Second Punic War | Lost in the Second Punic War (218–201 BC) | Conquered by Rome in the Third Punic War (149–146 BC). Map by Javierfv1212

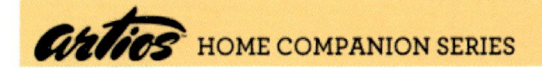

Adapted for Elementary School from the book:
A Child's History of the World
by V.M. Hillyer
Picking a Fight
and
The Boot Kicks and Stamps

Picking a Fight

"Every dog has his day."

A tennis or golf champion may win over the one who was champion before him and then have a few years during which they are unbeaten. Sooner or later, however, some younger and better player wins, taking the championship.

It seems almost the same way with countries as with people. One country wins the championship from another, holds it for a few years, and finally loses it to some newcomer.

We have seen that:

Nineveh was champion for a while; then.
Babylon had her turn, then.
Persia had her turn, then.
Greece; and, lastly,
Macedonia.

You may wonder who was to be the next champion after Alexander's empire went to pieces—who was to have the next turn of ruling much of the world.

When Alexander was conquering, he went east toward the rising sun and south. He paid little attention to the country to the west toward the setting sun. Rome was then only a small town with narrow streets and frame houses. It was not nearly important enough for Alexander to think much about. Rome was not thinking of anything except keeping the neighboring towns from beating her.

It is usual to speak of a city as "her" or "she" as if a city were a girl, but Rome was more like a small boy whom all the other boys were "picking" on. Over time, however, Rome began to grow up and was not only able to take care of herself but could put up a very stiff fight. She was then no longer satisfied with just defending herself. So she fought and won battles with most of the other towns in Italy until, at last, she found herself the champion of the whole "boot." Then she began to look around to see what other countries outside of Italy she might conquer.

Perhaps you have noticed that Italy, the "boot," seems about to kick a little island like a football. This island is Sicily, and just opposite Sicily was a city called **Carthage**.

Idealized depiction of Carthage from the 1493 *Nuremberg Chronicle*

The Phoenicians had founded Carthage many years before, and had become a very rich and powerful city. As she was by the sea, she had built many ships and traded with all the other seaports along the Mediterranean, just as the old Phoenician cities of Tyre and Sidon had done.

Carthage did not like seeing Rome

getting so strong, growing so big, and becoming so powerful. In other words, Carthage was jealous of Rome.

On her side, Rome was jealous of Carthage's wealth and trade. So, Rome anxiously looked around for some excuse to get into a fight with her.

You know how easy it is to pick a quarrel and start a fight when you are "looking for trouble." One boy sticks out his tongue, the other kicks him, and the fight is on.

The two countries are sometimes just like little boys; they start a fight with just as little excuse, and though they call the conflict "war," it is nothing but a "scrap." Only there are no fathers to come along, give them both a spanking, and send them to bed without any supper.

So, Rome and Carthage didn't take long to find an excuse, and a war was started between them. The Romans called this fight a Punic War, for "Punic" was their name for Phoenicians, and the Carthaginians were Phoenicians.

Since Carthage was across the water, the Romans could not get to her except by boat. But Rome had no boats. The city was not on the seashore, and she knew nothing about making or sailing boats.

On the other hand, the Carthaginians had many boats and, like all the Phoenicians, were old and experienced sailors.

But Rome happened to find the wreck of a Carthaginian ship that had been cast ashore, and she at once set to work to make a copy of it. In a remarkably short time, she had built one ship, then another, and another, until she had many ships. Then, though she was new at the game, she attacked the Carthaginian fleet.

It would seem that the Carthaginians could easily have won, for the Romans knew so little about boats. But in sea battles, before this, the fighting had been done by running into the enemy and ramming and sinking their ships.

Detail from the Ahenobarbus relief showing two Roman foot-soldiers from the second century B.C.

The Romans knew they were no match for the Carthaginians in this fighting. So they thought up a way to fight them as if on land.

To do this, they invented a big hook called a "crow." The idea was for a ship to run close alongside a Carthaginian ship and, instead of trying to sink her, to throw out this big hook or "crow," catch hold of the other ship, and pull both boats close together. The Roman soldiers would scramble over the sides into the enemy's boat and fight them like they would on land.

The scheme worked.

This new kind of fighting surprised the Carthaginians, who were no match for the Romans initially.

But Rome did not have things all her way

by any means. The Carthaginians soon learned how to fight in this fashion, too. So Rome lost, as well as won, battles both on land and at sea. But at last, she did win, and the Carthaginians were beaten. Thus ended the **First Punic War**.

The Boot Kicks and Stamps

But the Carthaginians were not beaten for good. They were only waiting for another chance to get even. Since they had been unsuccessful in attacking Italy from in front, they decided to attack her from the back. They planned to go a long way through Spain and down into Italy from the north.

To do this, they had, first of all, to conquer Spain to get through. They did this relatively quickly, for the Carthaginians had a great general named **Hannibal**. But then came the great difficulty of getting into Italy by this back way.

Illustration of Hannibal and his army crossing the Alps, by Heinrich Leutemann (1866)

Across the top of the "boot," in the north of Italy, are the great mountains called the **Alps**. They are miles high and covered even in summer with ice and snow. There are crags and cliffs along which anyone passing who made a single misstep would be dashed to death thousands of feet below.

It was the Alps, therefore, that formed a bigger and better wall than any city or country could possibly build. Of course, the Romans thought it impossible for any army to climb over such a high and dangerous wall.

Time and again, there have been things that people call impossible to do, and then someone has come along and done them.

People said it was impossible to fly.

Then someone did it.

People said it was impossible to cross the Alps with an army.

Then Hannibal came along, and he had done it before the Romans knew what had happened. He had crossed the Alps with his army—using elephants!—and was at the back door!

The Romans could not keep him from marching toward their city, winning battle after battle as he came along. They could not prevent him from marching up and down Italy, conquering other towns in Italy, and doing pretty much as he pleased. It seemed as if Rome were beaten, and she was to lose all of Italy.

In some games, if you can't defend your goal, it may be a good plan to try attacking your opponent's goal.

Rome thought she would try this plan. While Hannibal attacked her, she attacked Carthage while its general was away, and there was no strong goalkeeper to defend that city.

So, the Romans sent a young man named **Scipio** with an army to do this.

First, however, Scipio went to Spain to cut Hannibal off from how he had come, and this country Scipio reconquered for Rome.

Then he went over to Africa to attack Carthage itself.

The Carthaginians, frightened at being attacked with their general and his army far off in Italy, sent an order as fast as they could for Hannibal to come home. When at last he arrived, it was too late. Scipio fought a famous battle at Zama near Carthage, and the Romans beat the Carthaginians a second time. Thus ended the **Second Punic War** in 202 BC. This is another easy name and easy date—just like an old-style telephone number:

Zama—two-O-two.

Drawing of Carthaginian war elephants engaging Roman infantry at the Battle of Zama (202 B.C.), by Henri-Paul Motte (c.1890)

The Romans had won two wars against Carthage; you would think they would now be satisfied. But they weren't. They felt they had not beaten Carthage badly enough. They feared she was not quite dead or might come to life. They thought there might be a little spark left that might start a fire if it weren't trampled out.

Now, it is poor sport to punch your opponent after he is beaten, and Carthage was beaten—beaten, black and blue—there was no hope of her "coming back." And yet a few years later, the Romans attacked her again for the third and last time—in the **Third Punic War**.

Carthage could not defend herself, and the Romans viciously burned the city to the ground. It is said they even plowed over the land so that no trace of the city should remain and sowed it with salt, which prevented anything from growing there. After that, Carthage was never rebuilt, and now it is hard to tell even where the old city once was.

The *Hellenistic Prince*, tentatively identified as Scipio Aemilianus
Photo by Carole Raddato. CC BY-SA 2.0

Lesson Three

History Overview and Assignments
Rome Wasn't Built in a Day

"The New Champion of the World, who was to be champion for many years, was very businesslike and practical. The Greeks loved beautiful things, buildings, sculptures, and poems. The Romans copied the Greeks and learned from them how to make many beautiful things, but the Romans were most interested in practical and useful things."

– from the adapted article below

The multiple arches of the Pont du Gard in Roman Gaul (modern-day southern France). The upper tier encloses an aqueduct that carried water in Roman times; its lower tier was expanded in the 1740s to carry a wide road across the river.
Photo by Benh LIEU SONG. CC BY-SA 3.0

Suggested Reading and Assignments

- Read the article: *The New Champion of the World*.
- Define the vocabulary word in the context of the reading. Write the word and its definition in the vocabulary section of your notebook.
- After reading the article, summarize the story you read by either:
    - Retelling it out loud to your teacher or parent.
        OR
    - Completing an appropriate notebook page.
  Either way, be sure to include the answers to the discussion questions and an overview of key people, places, dates, and events in your summary.
- Be sure to visit your **ArtiosHCS** curriculum website for additional resources and any videos and websites assigned for this lesson.

Key People, Places, and Events

Gracchi brothers

Vocabulary

Chariot
Gladiator
bloodshed
extravagance

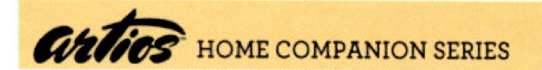

Discussion Questions

1. How were the Roman roads built?
2. How does an aqueduct work?
3. What happened at gladiator fights?
4. Who were the Gracchi brothers, and for what are they known?
5. What happened to them?

Adapted for Elementary School from the book:
A Child's History of the World
by V.M. Hillyer
The New Champion of the World

The New Champion of the World

You can well imagine how proud all the Romans now were that they were Romans, for Rome was the champion fighter of the world. If a man could toss his head and say, "I am a Roman citizen," people were always ready to do something for him, afraid to do him any harm, fearful of what might happen to them if they did. Rome was the ruler not only of Italy but of Spain and Africa. Like other nations before her, once she had started conquering, she kept on conquering until, by 100 BC, she, in her turn, was the ruler of almost all the countries bordering the Mediterranean Sea—all except Egypt.

The New Champion of the World was to be champion for many years and was very businesslike and practical.

The Greeks loved beautiful things, buildings, sculptures, and poems. The Romans copied the Greeks and learned from them how to make many beautiful things, but the Romans were most interested in practical and useful things.

For example, now that Rome ruled much of the world, she had to be able to send messengers and armies easily and quickly in every direction to the end of her empire and back again. So, she needed roads, for there were no railroads then. Now, an ordinary road made by simply clearing away the ground gets full of deep ruts and, in rainy weather, becomes so muddy that it can hardly be used at all.

So, Rome set to work and built better roads. These roads were like paved streets. Large rocks were placed at the bottom for a foundation, smaller stones were placed on top, and large, flat paving stones were laid over all.

A Roman street in Pompeii, with steppingstones for crossing during times of heavy rain
Photo by Ad Meskens. CC BY-SA 4.0

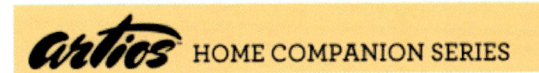

She built thousands of miles of roads to all parts of her empire. One could go from almost anywhere to Rome on paved roads. We still have an expression, "All roads lead to Rome." So well were these roads made that many still exist today, two thousand years after they were built.

Road construction shown on Trajan's Column in Rome
Photo by Romanian National History Museum Cast. CC BY-SA 3.0

The Romans also showed their practical minds by making significant city improvements. If you live in a city today, you turn on a faucet and get plenty of clean water whenever you want it. However, the people in cities at that time usually had to get their water for drinking and washing from wells or springs nearby. These springs and wells often became dirty and made the people very sick. And so every once in a while, because of such dirty water, there were terrible plagues, terribly contagious diseases.

The Romans wanted pure water, so they worked to find lakes from which they could get pure water. As often these lakes were many miles away, they built long pipes to carry the water to the city. Such a pipe was not made of iron or terracotta as nowadays but of stone and concrete and was called an "aqueduct," which in Latin means "water carrier." If this aqueduct had to cross a river or a valley, they built a bridge to hold it up. Many of these Roman aqueducts are still standing and in use today.

Now, up to this time, wastewater and other dirt and trash were dumped into the street after using it. This naturally made the city or town filthy and unhealthy and was another cause of plagues. But the Romans built great underground sewers to carry off this dirt and wastewater and empty it into the river or into some other place where it would do no harm and cause no sickness. Nowadays, every large city has aqueducts and sewers, but the Romans were the first to build them on a large scale.

Roman aqueduct: The water would travel slightly downhill in a pipe along the top.

One of the most essential things that Rome did was to make rules that everyone had to obey—or laws, as we call them. Many of these laws were so fair and just that some of our laws today are copied from them.

All the cities and towns of the Roman Empire had to pay money or taxes to Rome. So, Rome became the wealthiest city in the world. Millions of this money were spent on putting up beautiful buildings in the city, temples to the gods, splendid palaces for the rulers, public baths, and substantial open-air places called amphitheaters where the people could be amused.

The amphitheaters were something like our football and baseball fields or stadiums. They did not have football or baseball, however. They had **chariot** races and deadly fights between men or between men and animals. Chariots were small carts with large wheels drawn by two or four horses and driven by a man standing up. Perhaps you have seen chariot races in the circus.

A reconstructed Roman chariot drawn by horses
Photo by Álvaro Pérez Vilariño. CC BY-SA 2.0

But the sport that the Romans enjoyed most was the fight of **gladiator**s. Gladiators were powerful men who had been captured in battle by the Romans. They were made to fight with one another or wild animals for the crowd's amusement. These gladiatorial fights were fierce, but the Romans enjoyed seeing **bloodshed**. They liked to see one man kill another or a wild animal. It was so amusing. The movies would not have interested them half so much. Usually, the gladiators fought until one or the other was killed, for the people were not, as a rule, satisfied until this was done.

Sometimes, however, if a gladiator who had been knocked out had shown himself particularly brave and a good fighter or a good sport, the people around the arena would turn their thumbs up as a sign that his life was to be spared by the other gladiator. So, before killing his opponent whom he had down, the winning gladiator would wait to see what the people wished. He would finish the fight by killing his man if they turned their thumbs down.

But although Rome had become such a fine, beautiful, and healthy city in which to live, the rich people were getting most of the money from all over the Empire. They were getting richer and richer all the time, while the poor people, who got nothing, were getting poorer and poorer all the time. The Romans brought the people they conquered in battle to Rome and made them work for them without pay. These were slaves, and they did all the work. It is said that there were more than twice as many enslaved people as Romans—two slaves for every Roman citizen.

Scipio, who had conquered Hannibal in the Punic Wars, had a daughter named Cornelia Graccha, and she had two sons. They were wonderful boys, and Cornelia was naturally very proud of them.

One day a wealthy Roman woman was visiting Cornelia and showing off all her rings, necklaces, and other ornaments, which she had many and was very proud of.

Engraving after Vincenzo Camuccini, Cornelia, Mother of the Gracchi, Presents Her Children to a Capuana Woman (1870)

She asked to see Cornelia's jewels when she had shown off all she had.

Cornelia called to her two boys who were playing outside, and when they came into their mother, she put her arms around them and said, "These are my jewels."

But boys who are jewels when they are young do not always turn out to be jewels when they grow up. So, you may wonder how Cornelia's jewels turned out.

When they grew up, the **Gracchi brothers**, as they were called, saw such great **extravagance** among the rich and such great misery among the poor that they wanted to do something about it. They saw that people experiencing poverty had hardly anything to eat and no place to live. This did not seem fair. So, they tried to lower the price of food so that the poor could buy enough to eat. Then they tried to find some way to give the poor at least a small piece of land where they might raise vegetables. They were partly successful in bringing this about. But the rich people didn't like giving up anything to the poor, and they killed one of the Gracchi brothers and later killed the other. These were Cornelia's jewels."

Depiction of the two Gracchi brothers made during the 19th century by Eugene Guillaume, today located at the Musée d'Orsay in Paris. The brothers lay their hands on a document titled "property," consistent with then-current interpretations of their lives.

Gladiator tournament: part of the *Zliten* mosaic from Libya (Leptis Magna), about 2nd century A.D., showing (left to right) a *thraex* fighting a *murmillo*, a *hoplomachus* standing with another murmillo (who is signaling his defeat to the referee), and one of a matched pair
Photo courtesy Livius.org

Lesson Four

History Overview and Assignments
Exploring Ancient Rome

"The Romans spread across Europe, Southwest Asia, and North Africa bringing their traditions and their language."
— from http://rome.mrdonn.org/achievements.html

Reconstruction of the Amphitheater of Statilius Taurus, Rome, Italy (1663)

Suggested Reading and Assignments

- There is no article to read for this lesson; instead, visit the website at the URL on your **ArtiosHCS** curriculum website about Ancient Rome and explore one or more areas you are interested in. Be prepared to share what you learn with the class.
- Be sure to visit your **ArtiosHCS** curriculum website for additional resources and any videos and websites assigned for this lesson.

The Artios Home Companion Series
Unit 24: Making of an Empire

Teacher Overview

JULIUS CAESAR is the most famous of the Roman rulers. Many Roman rulers were assassinated when others became jealous of their power. Julius Caesar was assassinated in the Roman Senate and stabbed twenty-three times by senators, including his close friend Brutus. Shakespeare wrote about these events in his play *Julius Caesar*. Although Caesar's murderers succeeded in stopping a man they saw as a dictator who held too much power, they also sent the republic back into chaos. This paved the way for the rise of the Roman Empire.

Julius Caesar (44-30 B.C.)

The Imperial Aquila (eagle) of the Roman Empire
File extraction by Mattia332. CC BY-SA 4.0

Augustus of Prima Porta, 1st century A.D., depicting Octavian, titled Augustus Caesar, the first Roman emperor
Photo by Till Niermann

Suggested Assignments

Based on your student's age and ability, the reading in this unit may be read aloud to the student, and journaling and notebook pages may be completed orally. Likewise, other assignments may be done with an appropriate combination of independent and guided study.

In this unit, students will:
- Complete three lessons in which they will learn about **Julius Caesar** and the **rise of the Roman Empire**.
- Explore a website about **Julius Caesar** found at a URL on the **ArtiosHCS** curriculum website.
- Visit the ArtiosHCS curriculum website at www.ArtiosHCS.com for additional resources and any videos and websites assigned for this unit.

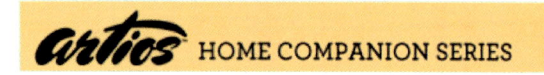

Heart Connections

God detests pride and honors humility.
> *One's pride will bring him low, but he who is lowly in spirit will obtain honor.*
> – Proverbs 29:23

There is only one God.
> *There is one God, the Father, from whom are all things and for whom we exist, and one Lord, Jesus Christ, through whom are all things and through whom we exist.*
> – 1 Corinthians 8:6

The Messiah would be born in Bethlehem.
> *"But you, O Bethlehem Ephrathah, who are too little to be among the clans of Judah, from you shall come forth for me one who is to be ruler in Israel, whose coming forth is from of old, from ancient days."*
> – Micah 5:1-2

Key People, Places, and Events

Julius Caesar	Mark Antony	Colosseum	Caligula
Pompey	Octavian/Augustus	Virgil	Tiberius
Rubicon River	Caesar	Horace	Claudius
Cleopatra	Pantheon	Pax Romana	Nero
Brutus	Roman Forum		

Additional Material for Parent or Teacher:

The **ArtiosHCS** curriculum website has URLs in the Additional Material section. Study the sites and share with your student(s) as you see fit.

Flag of Roman Empire: The *vexillum* of the Roman Empire was a red banner with the letters SPQR (meaning "The Senate and People of Rome") in gold surrounded by a gold wreath, hung on a military standard topped by a Roman eagle or an image of the goddess Victoria.
Image by Ssolbergj. CC BY 3.0

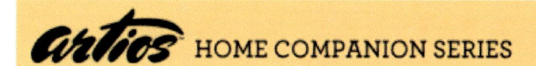

Lesson One

History Overview and Assignments
Death of the Republic

"In a few days, Caesar had made himself head not only of Rome but of all Italy. Caesar then went after Pompey in Greece and beat him badly in a battle with his army. Now that Pompey was out of the way, Caesar was the chief ruler of the whole Roman world."

– from the adapted article below

In this cropped image from *The Death of Julius Caesar* (1806) by Vincenzo Camuccini, Caesar can be seen staring at his friend Brutus, who is looking away from Caesar's gaze.

Suggested Reading and Assignments

- Read the article: *The Noblest Roman of Them All*.
- After reading the article, summarize the story you read by either:
    - Retelling it out loud to your teacher or parent.
       OR
    - Completing an appropriate notebook page.

  Either way, be sure to include the answers to the discussion questions and an overview of key people, places, dates, and events in your summary.
- Be sure to visit your **ArtiosHCS** curriculum website for additional resources and any videos and websites assigned for this lesson.

Key People, Places, and Events

Julius Caesar
Pompey
Rubicon River
Cleopatra
Brutus

Ancient: Elementary
Unit 24: Making of an Empire

Discussion Questions

1. Why was Julius Caesar given an army?
2. Why did he decide to cross the Rubicon?
3. How did he become chief ruler of the whole of the Roman world?
4. Why did he make Cleopatra queen of Egypt?
5. What close friend of Caesar's was involved in his murder?
6. Why did the senators murder Caesar?
7. What famous writer wrote a play about Julius Caesar?
8. Which month is named for him?

Adapted for Elementary School from the book:
A Child's History of the World
by V.M. Hillyer
The Noblest Roman of Them All

Julius Caesar's military might, political knowledge, and diplomatic genius made him supremely popular among the Roman citizenry.

Here's a puzzle for you:

A man once found an incredibly old piece of money that had on it the date "100 B. C."

That couldn't be so. Why not? See if you can tell without looking at the answer at the end of this article.[1]

In the year 100 B. C., a boy named Julius Caesar was born in Rome.

If you had asked him when he was born, he would have said in the Year 653.

Why do you suppose?

Because Roman boys counted time from the founding of Rome in 753 B.C., and Caesar was born 653 years after the city was founded. That makes it 100 years before Christ, doesn't it?

Pirates seemed to be everywhere in the Mediterranean Sea at that time. And now that Rome was the ruler of the world, many ships carried gold from different parts of the Empire to Rome. So, the pirates sailed up and down, lying in wait to capture and rob these ships laden with gold.

When Caesar grew to be a young man, he was sent off to sea to fight these pirates, and they captured him. The pirates kept Caesar a prisoner and sent word to Rome, saying they would not let him go unless Rome sent them a great deal of money. Caesar knew that he would be killed if the money was not sent. He knew, too, that he might be killed, anyway. But he was not only not afraid, but he told the pirates that if he lived to get back home, he would return with a fleet and punish every one of them. When at last, the money came, they let him go anyway. They thought Caesar would not dare to do what he said. They thought he was "talking big." At any rate, they did not believe he could catch them. Caesar, however, kept his word, came back after them as he said he would, and took them prisoner. Then he had them all put to death on crosses, the Roman way of punishing thieves.

The far-off places of the Roman Empire were always fighting against Rome, trying to get rid of her rule, and had to be kept in order by generals with armies. Since Caesar had shown such bravery in fighting the pirates, he was given an army and sent to fight two of these far-off places—Spain and a country north of Spain, then known as Gaul, which is now France.

Caesar conquered these countries, and then he wrote a history of his battles in Latin, which of course, was his language. Nowadays, this book, called *Caesar's Commentaries*, is usually the first book that those who study Latin read.

In 55 B.C., Caesar crossed over in ships to the island of Britain, conquered it, and returned the following year in 54 B.C.

Caesar was becoming famous for how he conquered and ruled the western part of the Roman Empire. Besides this, he was very popular with his soldiers.

Now there was in Rome at this time another general named **Pompey**. Pompey fought successfully in the eastern part of the Roman Empire, while Caesar fought in the west. Pompey had been a great friend of Caesar, but when he saw how much land Caesar had conquered and how popular he was with his soldiers, he became very jealous of him. Notice how many quarrels and wars are caused simply by jealousy.

So, while Caesar was away with his army, Pompey went to the Roman Senate and persuaded the senators to order Caesar to give up the command of his army and return to Rome.

Roman bust of General Pompey

When Caesar received the order from the Senate to give up his command and return to Rome, he thought over the matter for some time. Then, at last, he decided to return to Rome but would not give up his command. Instead, he decided that he and his army would take command of Rome itself.

Now, there was a river called the **Rubicon** which separated the part of the country over which Caesar was given charge from that of Rome. The Roman law forbade any general to cross this stream with an army ready to fight—this was the line beyond which he must not pass, for the Romans were afraid that if a general with an army got too close to Rome, he might make himself king.

When Caesar decided not to obey the Senate, he crossed the Rubicon River with his army and marched to Rome.

People now speak of any dividing line from danger as "the Rubicon" and say that a person "crosses the Rubicon" when he takes a step from which there is no turning back when he starts something difficult or dangerous which he must finish.

When Pompey heard that Caesar was coming, he took to his heels and fled to

Greece. In a few days, Caesar had made himself head not only of Rome but of all Italy. Caesar then went after Pompey in Greece and beat him badly in a battle with his army.

Now that Pompey was out of the way, Caesar was the chief ruler of the whole of the Roman world.

Egypt did not yet belong to Rome. So, Caesar next went there and conquered that country. Now, in Egypt, there was ruling a beautiful queen named **Cleopatra**. Cleopatra was so charming and powerful that she seemed able to make everyone fall in love with her. Cleopatra so fascinated Caesar that he almost forgot everything except being with her. So, although he had won Egypt, he made Cleopatra the queen of that country.

Cleopatra dressed as a pharaoh presenting offerings to the goddess Isis

Just at this time, some people in the far eastern part of the Empire started a war to get rid of the rule of Rome. Caesar left Egypt, traveled rapidly to where the enemy was, made quick work of conquering them, then sent back the news of his victory to Rome in the shortest description of a battle. There were only three words in the message. Although the messenger could have carried three thousand as quickly as three words, Caesar sent a message that would have been short even for a telegram. He wrote, "*Veni, vidi, vici,*" which means, "I came, I saw, I conquered."

When Caesar finally returned to Rome, the people wanted to make him king or said they did. Caesar was already more than a king, for he was head of the Roman world. But he wasn't called king, for most Romans did not like the idea of a king.

A few senators thought Caesar was gaining too much power and believed it would be terrible to make him a king. They, therefore, decided on a plot to prevent such a thing from happening. One of these plotters was a man named **Brutus,** who had been Caesar's best friend.

One day in 44 B.C., when Caesar was expected to visit the Roman Senate, they lay in wait for him until he should appear—in the same way I have seen boys hide around the corner for some schoolmate against whom they had a grudge until he should come out of school.

Caesar came along, and just as he was about to enter the Senate, the plotters crowded around him, and one after another, they stabbed him.

Caesar, taken by surprise, tried to defend himself; but all he had was his *stylus*, a kind of pen he used for writing, and he could not do much with that, despite a famous saying, "The pen is mightier than the sword."

In this 19th-century painting by Abel de Pujol, Caesar leaves his wife on March 15, called the "Ides of March," the day of his murder.

William Shakespeare wrote a play called "Julius Caesar," in which, when at last Caesar saw Brutus—his best friend—strike at him, his heart seemed broken, and he gave up. Then, exclaiming in Latin, "*Et tu, Brute!*" which means, "You as well, Brutus!" he fell dead.

Mark Antony, one of Caesar's true friends, spoke over Caesar's dead body, and his words so stirred the crowd of people that gathered round that they would have torn the murderers to pieces if they could have caught them.

Now whom do you suppose Mark Antony called "The Noblest Roman of Them All"?

Julius Caesar?

No, you're mistaken. Brutus, the friend who stabbed Caesar, was called "The Noblest Roman of Them All."

Why, do you suppose?

You'll have to read Antony's speech at the end of Shakespeare's play to find out.

The month of July is named after Julius Caesar. Also, Caesar was pronounced in Latin "kaiser." In later years, the rulers of Germany were called this, and those of another country by the shortened form, "czar."

The Standard Bearer of the Tenth Legion jumps from his ship and marches up the shores of England, leading the Roman invasion, from *The Britons in A Chronicle of England: B.C. 55 – A.D. 1485*, by James William Edmund Doyle (1864)

1. People living 100 years before Christ could not have known when He was to be born and would not have put such a date on the coins they made.

Ancient: Elementary
Unit 24: Making of an Empire

Lesson Two

History Overview and Assignments
Rise of the Roman Empire

"Although Rome had gotten rid of her kings hundreds of years before, she would have emperors from now on. They were more than kings, for they ruled over many countries."
– from the adapted article below

Interior of the Pantheon in Rome
Photo by Macrons. CC BY-SA 4.0

Suggested Reading and Assignments

- Read the combined article:
  An Emperor Who Was Made a God and *The Roman Empire, Part One*.
- After reading the article, summarize the story you read by either:
  - Retelling it out loud to your teacher or parent.
      OR
  - Completing an appropriate notebook page.

  Either way, be sure to include the answers to the discussion questions and an overview of key people, places, dates, and events in your summary.
- Be sure to visit your **ArtiosHCS** curriculum website for additional resources and any videos and websites assigned for this lesson.

Key People, Places, and Events

Mark Antony	Colosseum	Caligula
Octavian/Augustus Caesar	Virgil	Tiberius
Pantheon	Horace	Claudius
Roman Forum	Pax Romana	Nero

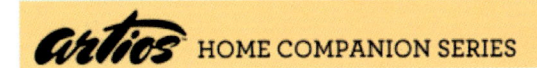

Ancient: Elementary
Unit 24: Making of an Empire

Discussion Questions

1. How did Octavius become known as Augustus, and what does that title mean?
2. Why was he revered as a god after his death?
3. List some of the ways Augustus Caesar made Rome better than he found it.
4. Name three ways you can help make your community better than you found it.
5. Who was born in a stable in Bethlehem while Octavian was emperor?
6. What were the emperors like who came after Octavian?

Adapted for Elementary School from the book:
A Child's History of the World
by V.M. Hillyer
An Emperor Who Was Made a God
and from the book:
The Story of Mankind
by Hendrik van Loon
The Roman Empire, Part One

Anyone with a town or a major street named after him is probably famous.

Will you ever do anything significant enough to have even an alley named after you?

But suppose a month, one of the twelve months of the year, was given your name!

Millions upon millions of people would then write and speak your name forever!

But I'm going to tell you about a man who not only had a month named after him but was worshiped as a god!

After Julius Caesar was killed, three men ruled the Roman Empire. One of these three men was **Mark Antony**, the friend of Caesar who made the famous speech over his dead body. The second was Caesar's adopted son, who was named **Octavius**. The name of the third you don't need to know now, for Antony and Octavius soon got rid of him. Then no sooner had they forced him out than each of these two began to plot to get a share of the other.

Mark Antony's share, over which he ruled, was the eastern part of the Empire. The capital of this part was Alexandria in Egypt, so Antony went there to live.

In Egypt, he fell in love with Cleopatra, as Caesar had before him, and he finally married her.

The Meeting of Antony and Cleopatra (1885), by Lawrence Alma-Tadema

Octavius, in the west, which was his share, then made war on Antony and Cleopatra together, and in the end, beat them both. Antony felt so bad at being beaten by Octavius that he killed himself.

His widow, Cleopatra, hoped to make Octavius fall in love with her and win him that way.

Ancient: Elementary
Unit 24: Making of an Empire

But it was no use. Octavius was a different kind of man from both Julius Caesar and Mark Antony. He was cold-blooded and businesslike. He would not let a woman charm him or turn him aside from his plan to be the most powerful man in the world!

Cleopatra saw that it was no use trying her tricks on him. Then she heard she would be taken back to Rome and paraded through the streets, as with any other prisoners in battle. She could not stand such shame as that, so she decided she would not be taken back to Rome.

In Egypt, there is a kind of snake called an asp, which is deadly poisonous. Taking one of these asps in her hand, she uncovered her chest and let it bite her, so she died.

Octavius was now ruler over all the countries that belonged to Rome, and when he returned home to that city, the people hailed him "Emperor." He then gave up the name Octavius and was called "**Augustus Caesar**," like saying, "His Majesty, Caesar." This was in 27 B.C. Although Rome had gotten rid of her kings hundreds of years before, she would have emperors from now on. They were more than kings, for they ruled over many countries.

Octavius, now with his name changed to Augustus Caesar, was only thirty-six years old when he became the sole master of the Roman world, and Rome was the grand capital of this vast empire.

Augustus set to work to make Rome a beautiful city. He tore down many old brick buildings and built many new, handsome marble ones. And so, Augustus always bragged that he found Rome made of brick and left it made of marble.

One of the finest buildings in Rome, the **Pantheon**, was built. The Pantheon was the temple of all the gods. Do not mix this with the Parthenon in Athens. The two buildings are quite different, and though the names look something alike and sound something alike, they mean entirely different things. Parthenon is named for the goddess Athena Parthenos; Pantheon is from the two words "*Pan theon*," which means "all gods."

The Pantheon in Rome
Photo by ParsonsPhotographyNL. Cropped. CCBY-SA 4.0

The Pantheon has a dome built of concrete that is shaped like a bowl turned upside down. At the top of the dome is a round opening called an *oculus*, which means "eye." Though this eye is uncovered, the height is so great above the floor (43 meters) some people believe that rain coming through the eye does not wet the floor below but evaporates before reaching it. (Actually, the floor was built on a slight incline to let water run into drains constructed beneath it.)

So magnificent did the city become with all these beautiful buildings, and so permanently did it seem to be built that it was known as The Eternal City and is still so spoken of.

There was a public square called the **Roman Forum**. Here markets were held, and the people came together for various activities. Around the Forum were built temples to the gods, courthouses, and other public buildings. These courthouses were like the temples the Greeks built but with columns on the inside instead of the outside.

How the Roman Forum may have looked during the Late Empire, in a derivative work of a 3D model by Lasha Tskhondia
Derivation by Mark Miller. CC BY-SA 3.0

Triumphal arches were also built to celebrate great victories. When a conquering hero returned from the war, he and his army passed through this arch in a triumphal parade.

There had been in Rome a great amphitheater that is supposed to have held more people than any structure that has ever been built—two hundred thousand, it is said, or more than all the people who live in some good-sized cities. This was called the Circus Maximus. It was at last torn down to make room for other buildings.

Another amphitheater was the **Colosseum**, which was not built until after Augustus died. It held about the same number as large stadiums do today. Here were held those fights between men called gladiators and wild animals that I have already told you about. It is still standing, and, though it is in ruins, you can sit in the same seats where the old Roman emperors did, see the dens where the wild animals were kept, the doors where they were let into the arena, and even bloody marks that are said to be the stains made by the slain men and beasts.

The Colosseum in Rome
Photo by FeaturedPics. CC BY-SA 4.0

So many famous writers lived during the time of Augustus that it was called the Augustan Age. After finishing *Caesar's Commentaries*, two of the best-known Latin poets, whom every Latin student now reads, lived at this time. These poets were **Virgil** and **Horace**. Virgil wrote the *Aeneid*, which tells of the wanderings of Aeneas, the Trojan who settled in Italy and was fabled to be the great-great-great-grandfather of Romulus and Remus. Horace authored many short poems called odes. They were love songs of shepherds, shepherdesses, and songs of the farm and country life. People liked his songs, and many still name their sons after him.

When Augustus Caesar died, he was revered as a god because he had done so much for Rome. Temples were built in which he was worshiped, and the month of August was named after him.

Lesson Three

History Overview and Assignments
"You, Too, My Child?"

"The statesman and general Julius Caesar (100-44 B.C.) expanded the Roman Republic through a series of battles across Europe before declaring himself dictator for life. He died famously on the steps of the Senate at the hands of political rivals. Julius Caesar is often remembered as one of the greatest military minds in history and credited with laying the foundation for the Roman Empire."
– Source: http://www.history.com/topics/ancient-history/julius-caesar

Brutus and the Ghost of Caesar, from Shakespeare's play *Julius Caesar*. Copperplate engraving by Edward Scriven from a painting by Richard Westall (1802). A caption reads: "XXX. JULIUS CAESAR. ACT IV. SCENE III. BRUTUS'S TENT, IN THE CAMP NEAR SARDIS"

Suggested Reading and Assignments

- There is no article to read for this lesson; instead, visit the website at the URL on your **ArtiosHCS** curriculum website and explore to learn more about Julius Caesar. Be prepared to share what you learn with the class:
- Be sure to visit your **ArtiosHCS** curriculum website for additional resources and any videos and websites assigned for this lesson.

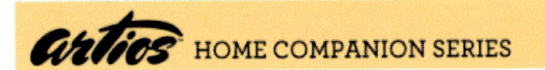

The Artios Home Companion Series
Unit 25: The Culture of Ancient Rome

Teacher Overview

THE CULTURE AND lifestyle of the ancient Romans were remarkably similar to those of the Greeks. Different social classes lived and worked near each other. Still, during the Pax Romana, the wealthy lived lavishly; the average citizen lived comfortably, while the largest group lived in poverty.

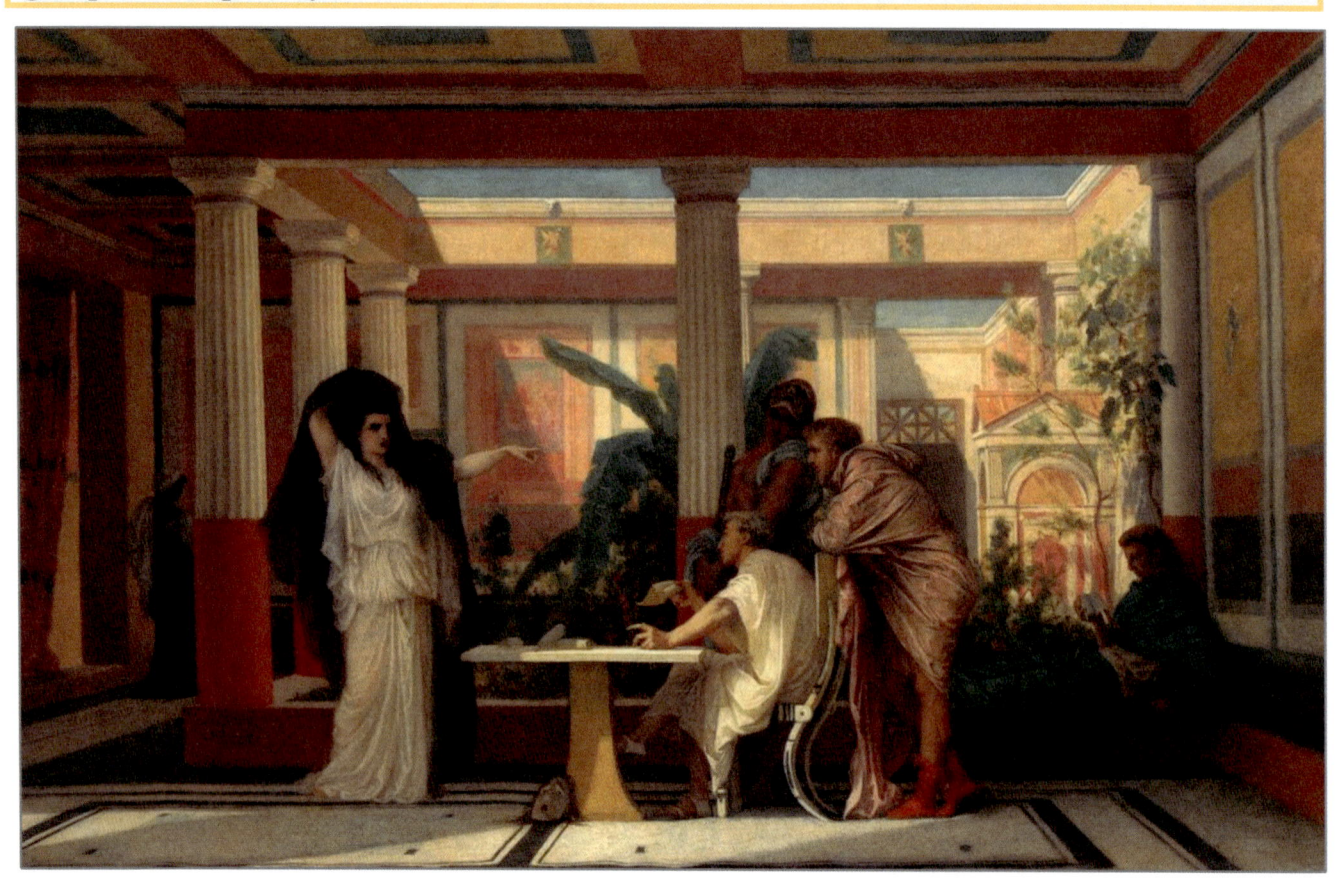

Theatrical Rehearsal in the House of an Ancient Rome Poet, by Gustave Boulanger (1855)

Suggested Assignments

Based on your student's age and ability, the reading in this unit may be read aloud to the student, and journaling and notebook pages may be completed orally. Likewise, other assignments may be done with an appropriate combination of independent and guided study.

In this unit, students will:
- Complete two lessons in which they will learn about **life and culture in Ancient Rome**.
- Define vocabulary words.
- Make a comparison list using two websites.
- Visit the **ArtiosHCS** curriculum website at **www.ArtiosHCS.com** for additional resources and any videos and websites assigned for this unit.

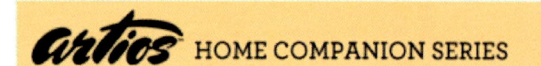

Heart Connections

God detests pride and honors humility.
One's pride will bring him low, but he who is lowly in spirit will obtain honor.
— Proverbs 29:23

There is only one God.
There is one God, the Father, from whom are all things and for whom we exist, and one Lord, Jesus Christ, through whom are all things and through whom we exist.
— 1 Corinthians 8:6

The Messiah would be born in Bethlehem.
"But you, O Bethlehem Ephrathah, who are too little to be among the clans of Judah, from you shall come forth for me one who is to be ruler in Israel, whose coming forth is from of old, from ancient days."
— Micah 5:1-2

Bloodthirstiness is not Christian.
Bloodthirsty men hate one who is blameless and seek the life of the upright.
— Proverbs 29:10

Vocabulary

Lesson 1:
acquire

Lesson 2:
oration
exhibit
derive
patriarch

Artist's idea of life in a Roman *cardo* (a north-south market street running through the *cardia* or heart of Ancient Roman cities) of Jerusalem during the Aelia Capitolina period
Carole Raddato. CC BY-SA 2.0

Lesson One

History Overview and Assignments
Life in Ancient Rome

"The ancient Romans believed it was important to start their day with breakfast. Lower-class Romans would breakfast on bread with maybe some cheese or olives added. The bread was dipped in wine to soften it. If a workman was in a hurry or running late, he might stop at a bread shop to grab a loaf to eat on the way. Bread was so important to the ancient Romans that they gave bread away free of charge to unemployed Roman people."

– from http://rome.mrdonn.org/breakfast.html

Villa of the Mysteries in Pompeii, seen from above
Photo by ElfQrin. CC BY-SA 4.0

Suggested Reading and Assignments

- Read the article: *The Houses, Customs, Institutions, Etc.*
- Define the vocabulary word in the context of the reading. Write the word and its definition in the vocabulary section of your notebook.
- On paper or posterboard, make two columns. Label one **Ancient Roman Life** and label the other **Modern Life**. As you read today's article, write the **article headings** in each column, and make a list of differences between modern life and ancient Roman life. Across from each item you list in the Ancient Roman Life column, write about the same area in the column labeled Modern Life. Use the websites found at the links on your **ArtiosHCS** curriculum website to add more information about those and any other areas that interest you.

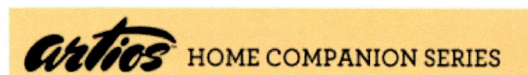

artios HOME COMPANION SERIES

Ancient: Elementary
Unit 25: The Culture of Ancient Rome

- Keep this paper or posterboard for the next lesson as well.
- Be sure to visit your **ArtiosHCS** curriculum website for additional resources.

Vocabulary

acquire

Adapted for Elementary School from the book:
Ancient Rome From the Earliest Times Down to 476 A.D.
by Robert F. Pennell
The Houses, Customs, Institutions, Etc.

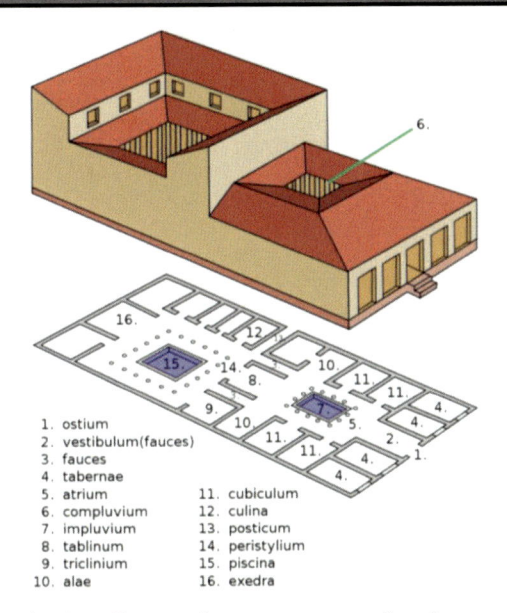

Ancient Roman *domus*, or upper-class home

1. ostium
2. vestibulum(fauces)
3. fauces
4. tabernae
5. atrium
6. compluvium
7. impluvium
8. tablinum
9. triclinium
10. alae
11. cubiculum
12. culina
13. posticum
14. peristylium
15. piscina
16. exedra

Homes

The private houses of the Romans were small and rude until after the Roman armies conquered the East when money began to pour into Rome. Many huge houses were then built and decorated with columns, paintings, statues, and costly works of art.

The main parts of a Roman house were the *Vestibulum, Ostium, Atrium, Alae, Tablínum, Fauces,* and *Peristylium*. The VESTIBULUM was a court surrounded by the house on three sides and open on the fourth to the street. The OSTIUM was like our front hall. From it, a door opened into the ATRIUM, a large room with an opening in the center of its roof, through which the rainwater was carried into a container sunk into the floor beneath the opening. To the right and left of the Atrium were side rooms called the ALAE, and the TABLINUM was a balcony attached to it. The passages from the Atrium to the house's interior were called FAUCES. The PERISTYLIUM, towards which these passages ran, was an open court surrounded by columns decorated with flowers and shrubs. It was somewhat larger than the Atrium.

Roman portraiture fresco from Pompeii (1st century A.D.) depicting a man wearing a laurel wreath and holding a *volumen*

The floors were covered with stone, marble, or mosaics. The walls were lined with marble slabs, or painted with *frescoes*, while the ceilings were either bare, exposing the beams, or, in the finer houses, covered with ivory, gold, and frescoing.

The main rooms were lit from above; the side rooms received light from these, not through windows looking into the street. The windows of rooms on the upper stories were not supplied with glass until the time of the Empire. They were merely openings in the wall, covered with latticework. To heat a room, portable stoves were generally

Ancient: Elementary
Unit 25: The Culture of Ancient Rome

used, in which charcoal was burned. There were no chimneys, and the smoke passed through the windows or the openings in the roofs.

The rooms of the wealthy were furnished with great splendor. The walls were frescoed with scenes from Greek mythology, landscapes, etc. The vestibules included fine sculptures, costly marble walls, and doors ornamented with gold, silver, and rare shells. There were expensive rugs from the East and, in fact, everything that could be obtained that might add to the room's attractiveness.

A late 19th-century artist's reimagining of an atrium in a Pompeian domus, by Luigi Bazzani (1882)

Candles were used in early times, but later the wealthy used lamps made of terracotta or bronze. They were primarily oval, flat on the top, often with figures in relief. In them were one or more round holes for the wick. They either rested on tables or were suspended by chains from the ceiling.

Meals

The meals were the *Jentaculum*, *Prandium*, and *Coena*. The first was our breakfast, though served early, sometimes as early as four o'clock. It consisted of bread, cheese, and dried fruits. The PRANDIUM was a lunch served at about noon. The COENA, or dinner, served between three and sunset, was usually of three courses. The first course consisted of eggs, or lettuce, and olives; the second, which was the main course, consisted of meats, fowl, or fish with condiments; the third course was made up of fruits, nuts, sweetmeats, and cakes.

At elaborate dinners, the guests assembled, each with his napkin and full dress of bright colors. The shoes were removed so as not to soil the couches. These couches usually were adapted for three guests, who reclined, resting their head on the left hand, with the elbow supported by pillows. The Romans took the food with their fingers. Dinner was served in a room called the TRICLINIUM. In Nero's "Golden House," the dining room was constructed like a theater, with shifting scenes to change with every course.

Reproduction of a Roman triclinium. The couches would have been covered with cushions.
Photo by Mattes

Clothing

The Roman men usually wore two garments, the *Tunic* and *Toga*. The former was a short woolen undergarment with short sleeves. The TUNIC was girded around the waist with a belt. The TOGA was peculiarly a Roman garment, and none but citizens were allowed to wear it. It was also the garment of peace, in distinction from the *Sagum*, which soldiers wore. The toga was of white wool and was nearly semicircular, but being a heavy garment, it became customary in later times to wear it only on state occasions. The poor wore only the tunic; others wore, in place of the toga, the *Lacerna*, which was an open cloak fastened to the right shoulder by a buckle. Boys, until about sixteen, wore a toga with a purple hem.

A toga *praetexta*, a white toga with a broad purple stripe on its border, worn over a tunic with two broad, vertical purple stripes by magistrates, freeborn boys, and some priests

The women wore a *Tunic*, *Stola*, and *Pallium*. The STOLA was a loose garment, gathered in and girdled at the waist with a deep flounce extending to the feet. The PALLIUM was a sort of shawl to throw over the whole figure and to be worn out of doors. The ladies indulged their fancy for ornaments as freely as their purses would allow.

Footgear mainly was of two kinds, the *Calceus* and the *Soleae*. The former was much like our shoes and was worn in the street. The latter were sandals strapped to the bare feet and worn in the house. The poor used wooden shoes.

Statue of Livia Drusilla wearing a stola and pallium
Photo by Ángel M. Felicísimo. CC BY-SA 4.0

Bathing

Bathing was a popular pastime among the wealthy. Fine buildings were erected, with elegant decorations and all conveniences for cold, warm, hot, and vapor baths. These bathhouses were numerous and were places of popular resort. Attached to many of them were rooms for exercise, with seats for spectators. The usual time for bathing was just before dinner. Upon leaving the bath, it was customary to anoint the body with oil.

Festivals, Games, Etc.

The SATURNALIA was the festival of Saturn, who was credited with introducing agriculture and the arts of civilized life. It was celebrated near the end of December, corresponding to our Christmas holidays, and under the Empire, it lasted seven days. No public business was transacted during the festival, the law courts were closed, the schools had a holiday, and slaves were relieved from all ordinary toil. All classes devoted themselves to pleasure, and presents were exchanged among friends.

Partly rebuilt Roman bath in England
Photo by Diliff. CC BY 2.5

The LUPERCALIA: a festival in honor of Lupercus, the god of fertility, was celebrated on the 15th of February. It was one of the most ancient festivals and was held in the Lupercal, where Romulus and Remus were said to have been nursed by the she-wolf *(lupa)*. The priests of Lupercus were called LUPERCI. On the day of the festival, these priests met at the Lupercal, offered sacrifices of goats, and took a meal with plenty of wine. They then cut up the skins of the goats which they had sacrificed. With some of these, they covered parts of their bodies, and with others, they made thongs and, holding them in their hands, ran through the streets of Rome, striking with them all whom they met, especially women, as it was believed this would make them fruitful.

The QUIRINALIA was celebrated on the 17th of February when Quirínus (Romulus) was said to have been carried up to heaven.

Gladiator Contests

Gladiators were men who fought with swords in the amphitheater and other places for the people's amusement. These shows were first confined to public funerals; afterward, gladiators were to be seen at the funerals of most men of rank. Under the Empire, the passion for this kind of amusement increased to such an extent that gladiators were kept and trained in special schools, and their trainers were called *Lanistae*.

In the show, the fights began with wooden swords. At the sound of the trumpet, these were exchanged for steel weapons. When a combatant was wounded, if the spectators wished him spared, they held their thumbs down but turned them up if they wanted him killed.

Saturnalia (1783), by Antoine-François Callet, showing his interpretation of what the Saturnalia might have looked like
Photo by Themadchopper. CC0

Musicians playing a Roman tuba, a water organ (*hydraulis*), and a pair of *cornua*, detail from the *Zliten Mosaic*, 2nd century A.D. The complete mosaic portrayed them as accompanying gladiator combat and wild-animal events in the arena.
Photo by Nacéra Benseddik. CC BY-SA 1.0

The Amphitheater, Theater, and Circus

The AMPHITHEATER was a place for the exhibition of gladiatorial shows, combats of wild beasts, and sometimes even naval engagements. Its shape was that of an ellipse, surrounded by seats for the spectators. The word Amphitheater was first applied to a wooden building erected by Caesar. Augustus built one of stone in the Campus Martius. However, the most celebrated amphitheater was built by Vespasian and Titus and dedicated in 80 A. D. It is still standing, though partly in ruins, covers nearly six acres, and could seat ninety thousand people. The name given to it today is the COLOSSEUM. The open space in the center was called the ARENA and was surrounded by a wall about fifteen feet high to protect the spectators from the wild beasts. Before the time of Caesar, the shows were held in the Forum and the Circus.

The THEATER was never as popular with the Romans as with the Greeks. Pompey built the first stone Roman theater in 55 B. C., near the Campus Martius. It was a fine building with a seating capacity of forty thousand. The seats were arranged in a semicircle, as at present, the orchestra being reserved for the Senators and other distinguished persons. Then came fourteen rows of seats for the Equites, and behind these sat the usual crowd.

The CIRCUS MAXIMUS, between the Palatine and Aventine Hills, was built for chariot races, boxing, and gymnastic contests. It was an immense structure, with galleries three stories high, and it sat one hundred thousand spectators. Its seats were arranged as in the theater. Six kinds of games were celebrated: chariot racing, a sham-fight between young men on horseback, a sham-fight between infantry and cavalry, athletic sports of all kinds, fights with wild beasts such as lions, boars, etc., and even sea fights, in which water was let into a canal to float ships. The combatants were captives, or criminals condemned to death, who fought until one party was killed unless saved by the kindness of the Emperor.

Panel from a representation of the triumph of Emperor Marcus Aurelius; a winged *genius* (protective spirit) hovers above his head.
Photo by MatthiasKabel. CC BY-SA 3.0

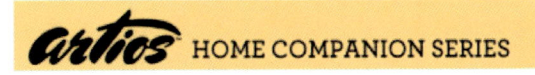

A Triumphal Procession

When he returned from a successful war, the Imperator was sometimes allowed to enjoy a triumphal procession. The temples were all thrown open, garlands of flowers decorated every shrine and image, and incense was smoked on every altar. The Imperator ascended the triumphal chariot and entered a city gate, where he was met by the whole body of the Senate, headed by the magistrates. The Imperator was attired in a gold-embroidered robe and a flowered tunic; he held a laurel bough in his right hand, a scepter in his left, and his brow was encircled with a laurel wreath.

The OVATION was a sort of smaller triumph. The commander entered the city on foot, in later times, on horseback. He was clothed in a purple-bordered robe. His head was crowned with laurel, and a sheep was sacrificed instead of a bull, as in the case of a triumph.

Names

Every man in Rome had three names. The given name *(praenomen)* is Lucius, Marcus, and Gaius. The names of the gens (nomen) are Cornelius, Tullius, and Julius. The name of the *family (cognómen)* is Scipio, Cicero, Caesar. To these names was sometimes added another, the *agnomen*, given for some exploit, or to show that the person was adopted from some other gens. Thus, Scipio the elder was called AFRICANUS, and all his descendants had the right to the name. Africanus the younger was adopted from the Cornelian gens into the Aemilian gens; therefore, he added to his other name AEMILIANUS.

The women were called only by the name of their gens. The daughter of Scipio was called, for example, CORNELIA, and to distinguish her from others of the Cornelian gens, she was called Cornelia, daughter of Scipio. If there were more than one daughter, to the eldest's name was added *prima* (first), to that of the next, *secunda* (second), etc.

Ancient Romans making their wedding vows
Photo by Ad Meskens. CC BY-SA 3.0

Marriage

Intermarriage between patricians and plebeians was forbidden before 445; after that, the offspring of such marriages took the rank of the father. After the parties had agreed to marry, and the consent of the parents or persons in authority was given, the marriage contract was drawn up and signed by both parties. The wedding day was then fixed upon.

The bride was dressed in a long white robe, with a bridal veil and shoes of bright yellow color. She was conducted in the evening to her future husband's home by three boys, one of whom carried before her a torch, the other two supporting her by the arm. Friends of both parties accompanied them. The groom received the bride at the door, which she entered with distaff and spindle (for spinning cloth) in hand. The keys to the house were then delivered to her, and the day ended with a feast given by the husband.

On the following day, another feast was given by the husband, and the wife performed certain religious rites.

The position of the Roman woman after marriage was quite different from that of the Greek. She presided over the whole household, educated her children, watched over and preserved the honor of the house, and shared the honors and respect shown to her husband.

Roman memorial stone (2nd century A.D.) The translated inscription reads, "Valeria Prisca, daughter of Marcus, who lived as a great delight for 23 years. Her mother made this for her daughter."
Source: http://reptonix.awardspace.co.uk/photos/2012-02-19.htm. CCY 3.0

Funerals

When a Roman was at the point of death, his nearest relative present tried to catch his last breath with his mouth. The ring was removed from the dying person's hand, and as soon as he was dead, his eyes and mouth were closed by the nearest relative, who called upon the deceased by name, exclaiming, "Farewell!" The body was then washed and anointed with oil and perfumes by slaves or undertakers. A small coin was placed in the mouth of the body to pay the ferryman (Charon) in Hades, and the body was laid out on a couch in the vestibulum, with its feet toward the door.

The funeral held the ninth day after the death, was headed by musicians playing mournful strains and mourning women hired to lament and sing the funeral song. These were sometimes followed by players and buffoons, one of whom represented the character of the deceased and imitated his words and actions.

Images of his ancestors and any crown and military rewards he had gained were carried before the body. The couch on which the body was carried was sometimes made of ivory and covered with gold and purple. Following it were the relatives in mourning, often uttering loud lamentations, the women beating their breasts and tearing their hair.

The procession of the most highly admired dead passed through the Forum and stopped before the *Rostra*, where a funeral oration was delivered. From here, the body was carried to its place of burial, which had to be outside the city.

Relief found in Neumagen near Trier of a teacher with two students, as a third arrives with his *loculus*, a writing case containing pens, an ink pot, and a sponge to correct errors (c.180–185 A.D.)
Photo: Wikipedia / Shakko. CC BY-SA 3.0

Education

In early times the education of the Romans was confined to reading, writing, and arithmetic, but as they came in contact with the Greeks, a taste for higher education was **acquire**d. Greek slaves were employed by wealthy families to watch over the children and to teach them to converse in Greek.

An entire course of instruction included

the elementary branches mentioned above, and a careful study of the best Greek and Latin writers, besides a course in philosophy and rhetoric, under some well-known professors abroad, usually at Athens or Rhodes.

Books and Letter Writing

The most common material on which books were written was the thin rind of the Egyptian papyrus tree. Besides papyrus, parchment was often used. The paper or parchment was joined together to form one sheet and was rolled on a staff, from which we get the word "volume" (from *volvere,* to roll).

Letter writing was widespread among the educated. Letters were usually written with a *stylus*, an iron instrument like a pencil in size and shape, on thin slips of wood or ivory covered with wax and folded together with the writing on the inside. A string tied the slips together, and the knot was sealed with wax and stamped with a signet ring. Letters were also written on parchment with ink. Special messengers were employed to carry letters, as no regular mail service existed. Roman letters differed from ours chiefly in the opening and closing. The writer always began by sending a "greeting" to the person addressed and closed with a simple "farewell" without any signature. Thus "Cicero S.D. Pompeio" (S.D.=sends greeting) would be the usual opening of a letter from Cicero to Pompey.

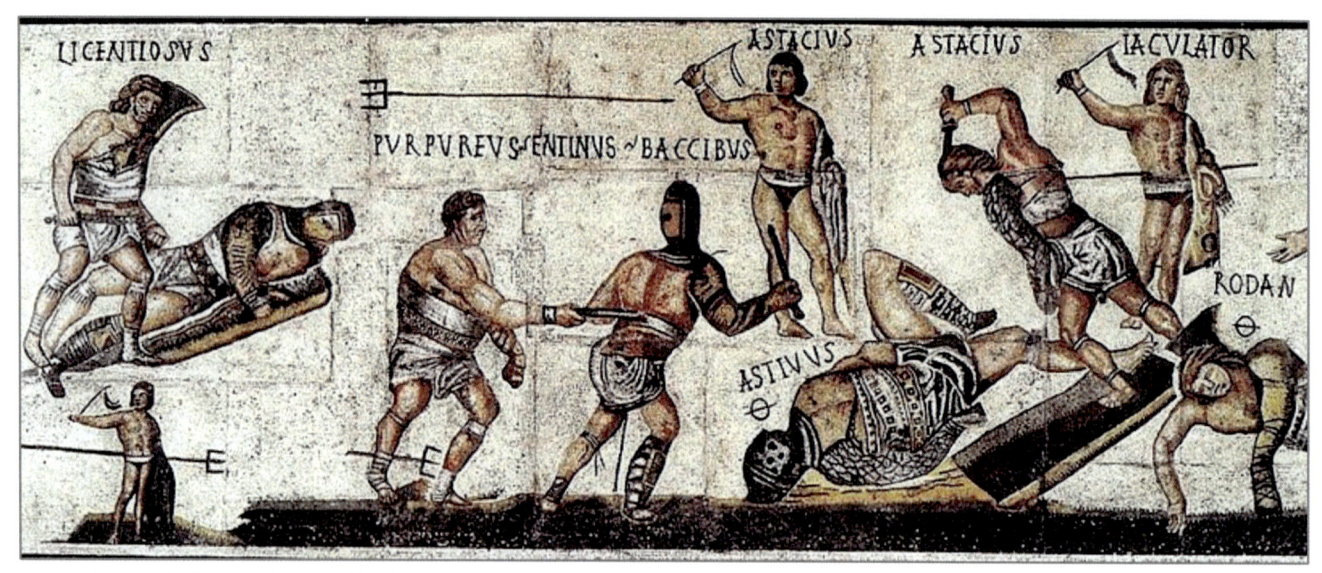

Part of the *Gladiator Mosaic*, displayed at the Galleria Borghese. It dates from approximately 320 A.D. The Ø symbol is the *theta nigrum* ("black theta") or *theta infelix* ("unlucky theta"), a symbol of death in Greek and Latin epigraphy.

Lesson Two

History Overview and Assignments
Arts and Sciences in Ancient Rome

"During the Pax Romana, the wealthy built huge, lavishly decorated houses and usually had servants or slaves to tend to their every need. The average citizen worked hard and lived reasonably comfortably in modest housing. Despite the riches of the Roman Empire, the largest class lived in what can only be described as poverty."

– from the adapted article below

Photochrome print of the ancient "Circular Bath" plunge pool at the Roman Baths in Bath, England
Reproduction number: LC-DIG-ppmsc-07999 from Library of Congress, Prints and Photographs Division

Suggested Reading and Assignments

- Read the article: *The Arts and Sciences in Rome*.
- Define the vocabulary words in the context of the reading. Write the words and their definitions in the vocabulary section of your history notebook.
- Continue the comparison list you began in Lesson One using the same websites.
- Be sure to visit your **HCS Class pages** for additional resources.

Vocabulary

oration
exhibit
derive
patriarch

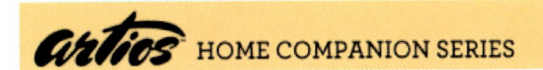

Adapted for Elementary School from the book:
History of Ancient Civilization
by Charles Seignobos
The Arts and Sciences in Rome

WRITERS AND ORATORS

The Age of Augustus

The reign of Emperor Augustus is considered the most brilliant period in Latin literature. It was the time of **Virgil**, **Horace**, and **Ovid**. The Emperor paid some of these poets, especially Horace and Virgil, who sang of Augustus's glory and his time. But this Augustan Age was preceded and followed by two centuries that perhaps equaled it. In the century before it (sometimes called the Age of Cicero), the first before Christ, the most original Roman poet **Lucretius** appeared, and **Cicero**, the greatest orator.

Marcus Tullius Cicero, by Visconti

Famous Speakers

The actual national art of the Roman Republic was **oration** because educated ancient Romans loved to speak in public and because the policy was determined through persuasiveness and popularity. The greatest orator of all was Cicero, the only orator whose works have come down to us in anything but fragments, and yet we have his speeches only as he left them and not as they were delivered.

Gaius Gracchus, Tribune of the People, Presiding Over the Plebeian Council, by Silvestre David Mirys, in *Figures de l'histoire de la république romaine accompagnées d'un précis historique* (1799)

With the fall of the republic, the assemblies and the great political trials ceased. Then came the mania for public lectures. Pollio, a favorite of Augustus, had set the example. For a century, it was the fashion to read poems, praises, and even tragedies before an audience of friends assembled to applaud them. The taste for eloquence that had once produced great orators **exhibit**ed in the later centuries only pre-written declarations.

Popularity of Latin Literature and Language

Latin literature profited from the conquests of Rome since the Romans carried it with their language to their conquered subjects of the West. Most of the peoples of Italy, Gaul, Spain, Africa, and Europe discarded their languages and switched to Latin. Having no national literature, they adopted that of their masters.

The Empire was thus divided between the two languages of the two great peoples of antiquity: the East continued to speak Greek, while almost the entire West spoke Latin. Latin was not only the official language of the state officials and great men, but the common people also spoke it so well that today, many centuries after the conquest, five of the major languages of Europe are **derive**d from the Latin—Italian, Spanish, Portuguese, French, and Romanian.

With the Latin language, Latin literature spread over the West. Acts, laws, history, and science books were written in Latin throughout Medieval times. In the convents and the schools, they read, copied, and appreciated only works written in Latin; other than books of piety, only the Latin authors were known—Virgil, Horace, Cicero, and Pliny the Younger. The Renaissance of the 15th and 16th centuries consisted partly in reviving the forgotten Latin writers. More than ever, it was the fashion to know and to imitate them.

As the Romans built a body of literature imitating the Greeks, the moderns have taken Latin writers as their models. Our romance languages are daughters of Latin, and our literature is full of the Romans' ideas and literary methods. The whole Western world is steeped in Latin literature.

THE ARTS

Sculpture and Painting

Significant numbers of Roman statues and *bas-reliefs* of the time of the Empire have come to light. Some are reproductions, and almost all are imitations of Greek words. The most original productions of this form of art are the bas-reliefs and the busts.

Mosaic depicting a theatrical troupe preparing for a performance in the House of the Tragic Poet, Pompeii
Photo by Marie-Lan Nguyen

Bas-reliefs, or carvings on flat panels, adorned the monuments, temples, columns, triumphal arches, and tombs. Many depict natural scenes, such as processions, sacrifices, combats, and funeral ceremonies, giving us information about ancient life. The bas-reliefs surrounding Trajan and Marcus Aurelius columns bring us into the presence of the great scenes of their wars. One may see the soldiers fighting against their enemies, besieging their fortresses, leading away the captives, the solemn sacrifices, and the Emperor commanding the troops.

The busts are primarily of the emperors and their families. Since they were made throughout the Empire, so many have been found that today all the great museums of Europe have collections of Roman imperial busts. They are actual portraits and probably remarkably close resemblances, for each emperor had a recognizable face.

In general, Roman sculpture holds itself much closer to reality than Greek; it may be said that the artist is less concerned with representing things beautifully than exactly.

A woman fixing her hair in the mirror, fresco from the Villa of Arianna at Stabiae (1st century A.D.)

Of Roman painting, we know only the frescoes painted on the walls of the wealthy houses of Pompeii and the house of Livy in Rome. These may be the work of Greek painters; they bear a close resemblance to the paintings on Greek vases, having the same simple and elegant grace.

Still life in the Second Style of Pompeiian wall painting. Fresco from the home of Julia Felix, Pompeii (c.70 A.D.)

Architecture

The Roman art that most met a practical need was architecture. In this, the Romans imitated the Greeks, especially in making columns. But they had a form that the Greeks never employed—the arch, that is to say, the art of arranging cut stones in the arc of a circle so that they support one another. The arch allowed them to construct larger and more varied buildings than the Greeks.

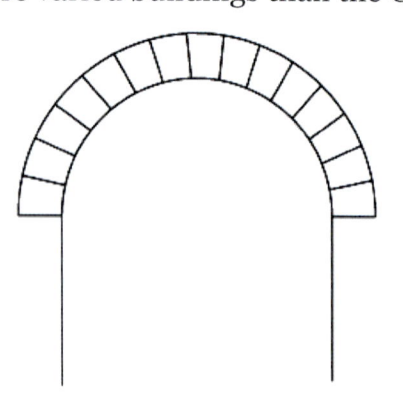

Round or semicircular arch
Illustration by Rundbåge. CC BY-SA 3.0

The following are the principal varieties of Roman monuments:

1) The *temple* was sometimes similar to a Greek temple with a broad vestibule, sometimes vaster and topped with a dome. Of this sort is the Pantheon built in Rome under Augustus.

Maison Carrée at Nîmes in France, one of the best preserved Roman temples
Photo by Aoudot25. CC BY-SA 3.0

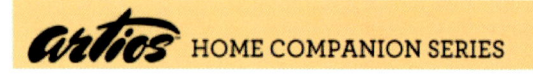

2) The basilica was a long low building surrounded by porticos. The judge sat with his assistants about him while traders discussed the price of goods nearby. The place was at once a market and a tribunal.

3) The amphitheater and the circus were built of several stories of arcades surrounding an arena; each range of arcades supported many rows of seats. Such were the Colosseum at Rome and the arenas at Arles and Nîmes.

Roman Theater of Mérida, Spain
Photo by Benjamín Núñez González. CC BY-SA 4.0

4) The arch of triumph was a gate of honor, adorned with columns and surmounted by a group of sculptures and wide enough for the passage of a chariot. The Arch of Titus is an example.

Arch of Titus, Upper Via Sacra, Rome
Photo by Carole Raddato. CC BY-SA 2.0

5) The baths were composed of bathing halls furnished with basins. A furnace placed in an underground chamber provided the heat for some rooms.

Cross-section of the Baths of Diocletian, as imagined by French architect Edmond Jean-Baptiste (1880)

6) The bridge and the aqueduct were supported by a line of arches built over a river or a valley.

7) The house of a wealthy Roman was a work of art. Unlike our modern houses, the ancient house had no outside decoration; it was turned entirely toward the inside; on the outside, it showed only bare walls.

Character of the Roman Architecture

The Romans, unlike the Greeks, did not always build in marble. Usually, they used the stone they found in the country, binding this with a strong mortar that has resisted even dampness for many hundreds of years. Their monuments do not have the extraordinary grace of the Greek monuments, but they are large, strong, and solid—like the Roman power. We are astonished to find monuments almost intact, as remotely as the deserts of Africa. When it was planned to furnish a water system for the city of Tunis, all that had to be done was to repair an ancient Roman aqueduct.

Marble relief of Mithras slaying a bull (2nd century). Iconic scenes of Mithras show him being born from a rock, slaughtering a bull, and sharing a banquet with the sun god, Sol. Mithraism was among the most widespread "mystery cult" religions of the Roman Empire.
Photo by Jean-Pol GRANDMOT. CC BY 3.0

Rome and its Monuments

At the time of the emperors, Rome was a city of 2,000,000 inhabitants. The general population was crowded into houses of five and six stories, poorly built and clustered together. The crowded quarters were a maze of steep and poorly paved angled paths. At **Pompeii**, a city of luxury, it may be seen how narrow the streets were of a Roman city. Amid the hovels, monuments by the hundred would be erected.

Theaters of Pompeii seen from above with a drone, with Mount Vesuvius in the background
Photo by ElfQrin. CC BY-SA 4.0

SCIENCES

The sciences of ancient Rome were a combination of advancements adopted from conquered territories and original discoveries and inventions.

Egyptian astronomers had written about mathematics, the movements of heavenly bodies, and about geology and geography. The Romans learned much of the math required to study astronomy from the Egyptians, although the Roman numbering system was awkward to use in complex calculations. **Ptolemy** in Alexandria was known as a geographer, an astronomer, and a mathematician. His astronomical writing, called the *Almagest,* put forth the earth-centered view of the universe that was accepted until the 16th century.

The Phoenicians were great shipbuilders and glass workers, and it was from them that the Romans learned much of their crafts in these areas.

The Romans themselves were masters of mine- and stone-working, as well as of civil engineering, which they used to build arched and domed structures as well as durable, adequate roads, sewers, water-heating systems, and aqueducts.

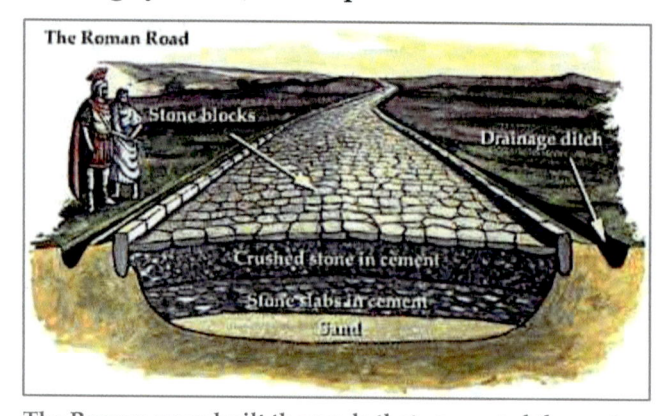

The Roman army built the roads that connected the vast Roman Empire. By layering sand, cement, and stone, they created durable roads that lasted long after the fall of Rome.

Public health was of great concern to the Romans, who employed physicians in infirmaries where all could receive medical care without personal cost. **Galen**, a doctor for a gladiator training center, was brought to Rome to be the physician for Emperor Marcus Aurelius. Galen became renowned for significant advances in the field of medicine, producing a medical encyclopedia that remained in everyday use until the Renaissance.

Model of Imperial Rome depicting the Temple of Claudius to the south (left) of the Colosseum (right)
Photo by Jean-Pierre Dalbéra. CC BY 2.0

Portrait of Galen, by Georg Paul Busch, in *The Lancet* (18th century)

Ancient Romans also developed major learning centers throughout Italy and parts of Europe. Pliny the Elder conducted outstanding research to compile his *Natural History*, a fascinating work of science widely read through the early Medieval period.

ROMAN ENTERTAINMENTS

The Roman Baths

Much of ancient Roman social life revolved around entertainment. The *thermae* in a Roman city was what the gymnasium was in a Greek city—a gathering place for the wealthy. Much more than the gymnasium, it was filled with halls of many types: there was a cool hall, warm apartments, a robing-room, a hall where the body was anointed with oil, parlors, halls for exercise, gardens, and the whole surrounded by an enormous wall. Public baths, available for both rich and poor, provided a place for exercise, relaxation, and conversation. Gardens, libraries, art galleries, and gymnasiums were contained within the larger public bathhouses, which became centers for political interaction. Patrons moved through a series of cleansing rooms and baths, often spending much of the day enjoying their luxuries.

Games

Romans loved their games, including wrestling, boxing, and foot races. Spectacular chariot races were highly popular on tracks called *circuses*, and their victors were hailed as heroes, much like sports celebrities are today.

Model of Rome in the 4th century A.D., by Paul Bigot. The Circus Maximus lies between the Aventine Hill (left) and Palatine (right); the oval structure to the far right is the Colosseum.
Photo by Pascal Radigue. CC BY-SA 3.0

The largest of these chariot tracks, called the **Circus Maximus**, seated about 150,000. As many as two dozen daily races were conducted there, presided over by the Emperor or one of his chosen representatives.

Gladiator contests held equal or even greater popularity among the people—these brutal competitions in arenas and pitted combatants against each other or ferocious animals. Sometimes the fighters were armed, sometimes not. Defeated gladiators who had gained the people's affection were sometimes spared final execution.

The largest of the gladiatorial arenas was the Roman **Colosseum**—which was watertight to allow for the occasional staging of sea battles. Gladiatorial contests were popular until the 5th century, when Christianity stopped the barbaric practice.

This 5th-century mosaic in the Great Palace of Constantinople depicts two venatores fighting a tiger.

The Artios Home Companion Series
Unit 26: Early Christian Life in the Roman World

Teacher Overview

FOR TWO HUNDRED YEARS, the Roman Empire experienced a period of relative peace and prosperity. This time became known as the *Pax Romana,* or "Roman Peace." The Empire, which had spread from Britain in the north to Northern Africa in the south, now contained millions of people. During this time, God's son Jesus Christ was born in Israel. His life and message changed the world forever, and the Christian Church was born.

An Eastern icon depicting the Descent of the Holy Spirit. The date of Pentecost on which this took place is considered the birthday of the Christian Church. You can read about this beautiful event in the Book of Acts in your Bible.

Suggested Assignments

Based on your student's age and ability, the reading in this unit may be read aloud to the student, and journaling and notebook pages may be completed orally. Likewise, other assignments may be done with an appropriate combination of independent and guided study.

In this unit, students will:
- Complete two lessons in which they will learn about the **years of Roman peace** and the **early years of the Christian Church**.
- Define a vocabulary word.
- Read a Bible passage to answer a question.
- Write a character description.
- Visit the **ArtiosHCS** curriculum website at **www.ArtiosHCS.com** for additional resources and any videos and websites assigned for this unit.

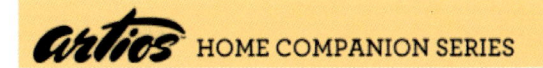

Ancient: Elementary
Unit 26: Early Christian Life in the Roman World

Heart Connections

The Messiah would be born in Bethlehem.
"But you, O Bethlehem Ephrathah, who are too little to be among the clans of Judah, from you shall come forth for me one who is to be ruler in Israel, whose coming forth is from of old, from ancient days."
— Micah 5:1-2

The Messiah would be a descendant of Abraham.
"In your offspring shall all the nations of the earth be blessed, because you have obeyed my voice."
— Genesis 22:18

Nothing can separate us from God's love.
Who shall separate us from the love of Christ? Shall tribulation, or distress, or persecution, or famine, or nakedness, or danger, or sword?
— Romans 8:35

Key People, Places, and Events

Pax Romana
Tiberius
Caligula
Claudius
Nero
Jesus of Nazareth
Pontius Pilate
Stephen
Saul of Tarsus/Paul
Peter

Vocabulary

Lesson 1:
none

Lesson 2:
conceited

The Fire of Rome, by Hubert Robert (1785)

Lesson One

History Overview and Assignments
Worldly and Spiritual Peace

"When Augustus Caesar was emperor, he was the ruler of the world. He had found Rome made of brick and left it remade of gleaming marble. He had had a month named after him, and he had been made a god! Surely no one could ever be greater than he! Yet a greater One was living at the very same time—a greater Ruler of a greater kingdom with greater power and greater glory. However, Augustus knew nothing about Him and lived and died without ever having heard of Him. This One was born in the eastern part of the Empire in a tiny little village called Bethlehem, and His name was Jesus of Nazareth."

– from the adapted article below

St. Peter Preaching the Gospel in the Catacombs, by Jan Styka

Suggested Reading and Assignments

- Read the combined article:
  The Roman Empire, Part Two and *"Thine is the Kingdom, the Power, and the Glory."*
- After reading the article, summarize the story you read by either:
  - Retelling it out loud to your teacher or parent.
    OR
  - Completing an appropriate notebook page.

  Either way, be sure to include the answers to the discussion questions and an overview of key people, places, dates, and events in your summary.
- Be sure to visit your **ArtiosHCS** curriculum website for additional resources and any videos and websites assigned for this lesson.

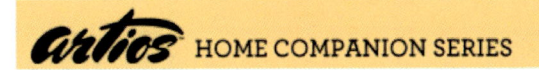

Ancient: Elementary
Unit 26: Early Christian Life in the Roman World

Key People, Places, and Events

Pax Romana
Tiberius
Caligula
Claudius
Nero
Jesus of Nazareth
Pontius Pilate
Stephen
Saul of Tarsus/Paul
Peter

The execution of the patriarch Peter of Alexandria under Emperor Maximinus Daia, depicted in the Menologion of Basil II

Discussion Questions

1. Why was the Pax Romana called that?
2. Which two of the first four rulers after Octavian were especially cruel and brutal?
3. How far did the Roman Empire spread during the Pax Romana?
4. What was the life of Jesus like when He was a young man?
5. List five truths that Jesus taught.
6. Why did the Jewish teachers despise Him?
7. How did they arrange to get Him killed?
8. Read Mark 16 in your Bible and describe what happened after Jesus was killed.
9. Why were Christians willing to die rather than turn from their faith?
10. How did Saul become a believer?
11. How did Peter honor Jesus in his death?
12. What do B.C. and A.D. mean?

Adapted for Elementary School from the book:
The Story of Mankind
by Hendrik van Loon
The Roman Empire, Part Two
and from the book:
A Child's History of the World
by V.M. Hillyer
"Thine is the Kingdom, the Power, and the Glory"

The Pax Romana

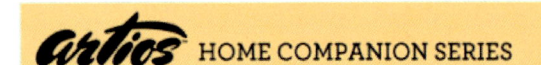

Augustus Octavian's successors were true "emperors"—absolute rulers of the largest empire the world had ever seen. The period they ushered in became known as the **Pax Romana**, or "Roman peace," because there weren't as many wars as usual during those years. Peace came at a price because the emperors who ruled during those years held firm control over the people, and most were cruel and brutal.

Emperor Augustus didn't leave instructions for the choice of a successor, and the first four emperors who followed him were men of the Caesar family line. The first and third proved reasonably capable rulers, but the second and fourth were especially vicious.

The first of this family line, **Tiberius**, was a bad-tempered man. Ordered by Augustus to divorce the wife he loved and marry the unpleasant daughter of Augustus to become his heir, so he became bitter. Although Tiberius was a capable ruler at first, the end of his reign was marked by suspicion and inexcusable executions.

Caligula, who ruled after Tiberius and was described as a madman known for delighting in sickening cruelty, insisted on being worshiped as a deity. His mental instability became known to all when he promoted his favorite horse to the rank of a Roman consul and began forcing senators to participate in gladiator competitions! Caligula was murdered in the end by a group of senators and members of his guard.

Claudius, an uncle of Caligula and the only remaining man in the family was declared emperor by Caligula's assassins. Afflicted with a limp and partial deafness, these rivals viewed Claudius as unthreatening and controllable. However, he proved to be a good administrator, and the Empire was well maintained during his reign. Many roads and aqueducts were built by his orders, and the Roman conquest of Britain began. However, Claudius died after ruling for only thirteen years. He was believed to be poisoned by his fourth wife so that her son **Nero** could rise to the throne.

Nero, the murderous tyrant who succeeded Claudius at 16, was notorious for his immoral behavior, the murders of his mother and wife, his vicious persecution of Christians, and his seeming lack of concern during the great fire that ravaged Rome in A.D. 64.

His reign was marked by oppression and extravagance, along with excessive cruelty, demonstrated, for example, by his burning Christians to provide light for banquets.

Sculpture of Agrippina crowning her young son Nero (c.54–59 A.D.) with a laurel wreath. She carries a *cornucopia* (a symbol of fortune and plenty), and Nero wears the armor and cloak of a Roman commander, with a helmet on the ground at his feet. The scene refers to Nero becoming emperor in 54 A.D. and belongs before 59 A.D. when Nero had Agrippina murdered.
Photo by Carlos Delgado. CC BY-SA 3.0

Spread of Roman Control

Despite poor leadership, the Roman Empire reached the height of its glory during the years of the Pax Romana. During those years, Roman control spread from the

British Isles to the Euphrates River and included much of Western Europe. Prosperous trade brought wealth to the capital city of Rome, roads were improved to facilitate that trade, and culture developed and thrived. But this prosperity was enjoyed only by the rich. Underneath this glory lived millions of poor and tired human beings, toiling like ants who have built a nest underneath a heavy stone.

"Thine is the Kingdom, the Power, and the Glory"

When Augustus Caesar was emperor, he was the ruler of the world. He had found Rome made of brick and left it remade of gleaming marble. He had had a month named after him, and he had been made a god!

Adoration of the Shepherds,
by Gerard van Honthorst (c.1622)

Surely no one could ever be greater than he! Yet a greater One was living at the same time—a more significant Ruler of a greater kingdom with greater power and greater glory, although Augustus knew nothing about Him and lived and died without ever having heard of Him. This One was born in the eastern part of the Empire in a tiny little village called Bethlehem, and His name was **Jesus of Nazareth**.

For many years after Jesus was born, no one except His family and friends knew or cared anything about His birth or paid the slightest attention to it.

Jesus was a Jew, the son of a builder. As a boy and young man, He led a very simple and quiet life working in His father's shop. Jesus did not preach until He was over thirty years old. Then He taught the people what we know today as the Christian religion.

He taught that there was one God over all.

He taught brotherly love, that one should love one's neighbor as oneself, and that they should turn from their selfish, sinful ways and love God with all their hearts.

He taught the Golden Rule—"Treat others as you would want them to treat you."

The Sermon on the Mount,
by Carl Bloch (1877)

He taught that there was a life after death for which this short life on earth was only a preparation; that, therefore, you should "lay up your treasures in heaven" by doing good works here and earning rewards from God.

The poorer Jews listened to Jesus and believed what He taught them. But they thought He would set them free from the rule of the Romans, which they hated. The Jewish priests, however, were afraid of what Jesus taught. He was teaching some things just the opposite of what they taught because He taught about God's way of living and not about all the rules the teachers had added to that way to make themselves powerful over the people. So, they plotted to have Him put to death.

Ecce Homo ("Behold the Man"), Antonio Ciseri's depiction of Pilate presenting a scourged Jesus to the people of Jerusalem (c.1860-1880)

Now, the Jews could not put Jesus to death without the permission of the Roman ruler of that part of the Empire where Jesus lived. This ruler was named **Pontius Pilate**. So, they went to Pilate and told him Jesus was trying to make himself king. Jesus meant and always said He was a heavenly ruler, not an earthly king. The Jews knew Pilate would not care what religion Jesus taught. There were all sorts of religions in the Roman Empire—those that worshiped mythological gods and those that worshiped idols, and those that even worshiped the sun, moon, and so on—one more new religion made slight difference to the Romans. Jesus would not be put to death simply for teaching another. But the Jews knew if they could make Pilate believe that Jesus was trying to make himself a king, that was a thing He could be crucified for. Pilate did not believe much in what the Jews said against Jesus. It was a small matter to him, one way or the other, however. But he wanted to please the Jews, so he told them to go ahead and put Jesus to death if they wanted to. So, He was crucified.

The Death of Jesus, by James Tissot (c.1890)

But on the third day, something incredible happened! You can read about it in the Bible. There is a good description in the Gospel of Mark, chapter 16.

Jesus had chosen twelve men to teach what He told them. These twelve men were called *apostles*, which means "sent ones." After Jesus was crucified, these apostles went through the land, teaching the people what Jesus had taught them. Those who believed in and followed His teachings were called *disciples* of Jesus Christ or Christians. The apostles were teachers, and the disciples were pupils. The name Christ means "Messiah"—the One the Jewish prophets had taught about, who would deliver the people from their sins.

The Romans thought these disciples of Jesus were trying to start a new world empire and that they were against Rome and the Emperor and should be arrested and imprisoned. They also didn't like being told they needed to turn from their sinful ways. So, the Christians usually held their meetings in secret places, sometimes even underground, so they would not be found and arrested.

But after a while, the leaders of the Christians became bolder. They came out of their secret places, taught, and preached openly, although they knew they would eventually be imprisoned and perhaps killed for refusing to turn from their faith and worship the Emperor. Indeed, so strongly did they believe in the teachings of Jesus that they seemed even glad to die for His sake, just as He had been killed on a wooden cross for them.

Good Shepherd, drawn by Christians in the underground Catacomb of Priscilla (250–300 A.D.)

> Jesus had said, "If anyone is ashamed of Me and My words, the Son of Man will be ashamed of him when He comes in His glory and the glory of the Father and the holy angels," so His people refused to turn away from honoring Him. If you are ever faced with a terrible choice like those faced by the early Christians in the Roman Empire, will you remember His words as they did?

In the first hundred years after Christ, there were a great many Christians put to death because they were thought to be traitors. Christians who died for Jesus' sake were called *martyrs*. The first martyr was named **Stephen**. He was stoned to death about 33 A.D.

The Stoning of St. Stephen, by Rembrandt (1625). This is the first signed painting by the Dutch artist Rembrandt, made when he was 19.

One of the men who helped in putting Stephen to death was a man named **Saul of Tarsus**. Saul was a Roman citizen and, like other Roman citizens, was very proud of that fact. He thought the Christians were enemies of his country, and he did everything he could to have the Christians punished. Then, after a remarkable encounter with the risen Jesus, Saul had a change of heart and came to believe in the religion of the very people against whom he had been fighting. Whatever Saul did or whatever he believed, he always did or believed with his whole soul. Though he had never heard Jesus teach before His death, Saul became one of the chief Christians and then was made an apostle and was called by his Roman name, **Paul**.

Paul preached the new religion far and wide just as earnestly as he had initially fought against it. Then he, too, was condemned to death. As I have said, Paul, however, was a Roman citizen. A Roman citizen could not be put to death by ordinary judges who were not Roman citizens, nor in a usual way by crucifying. So, Paul appealed to the Emperor. Nevertheless, he was put in prison in Rome and afterward beheaded. So, we remember him with honor.

Saint Paul arrested, early 1900s Bible illustration

Peter was another of the chief apostles. Peter was also thrown into prison and sentenced to be crucified. But he asked to be crucified with his head downward. He thought it too great an honor to die in the same way as his Lord. On the spot in Rome where Peter was put to death, the largest church in the world was built long afterward, the Cathedral of St. Peter.

The Crucifixion of Saint Peter, by Caravaggio (1601)

As everything before Christ's birth is called B.C. (which means "Before Christ") and everything since His birth is called A.D. (which means Anno Domini, or "In the year of our Lord," marking the years since His inception), you would naturally suppose that the year 0 would mark the date of His birth. But it was not until some five hundred years later that people began to count the dates this way. And when they did this, they made a mistake. It was found out later that Jesus was born about four years before He was supposed to have been born—that is, around 4 B.C.—but when the mistake was discovered, it was too late to change.

Lesson Two

History Overview and Assignments
Blood and Thunder, Part One

"Nero built an immense palace and overlaid it extravagantly with gold and mother-of-pearl. It was known as Nero's House of Gold. At its front door, he put up a colossal statue of himself in bronze fifty feet high. The House of Gold and the statue were later destroyed, but the Colosseum, built a few years later, was named Colosseum from this 'coloss-al' statue of Nero that was once there."

– from the adapted article below

The Fire of Rome, by Karl von Piloty (1861). According to Tacitus, Nero blamed Christians for the fire.

Suggested Reading and Assignments

- Read the article: *Blood and Thunder, Part One*.
- After reading the article, summarize the story you read by either:
  - Retelling it out loud to your teacher or parent.
    OR
  - Completing an appropriate notebook page.
- Define the vocabulary word in the context of the reading. Write the word and its definition in the vocabulary section of your history notebook.
- Instead of answering discussion questions, describe what Emperor Nero's character was like—and what you want your character to be like.
- Be sure to visit your **ArtiosHCS** curriculum website for additional resources and any videos and websites assigned for this lesson.

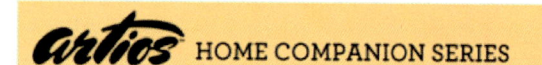

Ancient: Elementary
Unit 26: Early Christian Life in the Roman World

Key People, Places, and Events

conceited

Triumph of Faith, by Eugene Thirion (19th century), depicting Christian martyrs in the time of Nero

Adapted for Elementary School from the book:
A Child's History of the World
by V.M. Hillyer
Blood and Thunder, Part One

A gold coin showing Nero and his mother (c.54 A.D.)

I once had a big Newfoundland dog, and he was one of the best friends a boy ever had. I don't know who named him; he was named before I got him, but whomever it was must either have been ignorant of history or a bad chooser of names. He was called Nero, and even a dog would have hated such a name had he known whose it once was.

Every good story usually has a villain to make it interesting. Nero is the prize villain of history. He was a Roman emperor who lived not long after Christ and is considered the most terribly cruel and wicked ruler that ever lived.

He killed his mother.

He killed his wife.

He killed his teacher, who was named Seneca. He was not a bad teacher, either.

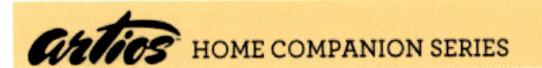

Ancient: Elementary
Unit 26: Early Christian Life in the Roman World

We think that Nero ordered both St. Peter and St. Paul put to death, for they were executed at this same time.

Nero seemed to take immense pleasure in making others suffer. He loved to see men torn to pieces by wild beasts; it amused him greatly. I have seen boys who liked to throw stones at dogs to hear them yelp or pull the wings off of butterflies. Such boys must have some Nero in them, don't you think?

If a man was a Christian, that gave Nero an excuse to torture him horribly. Nero had some of the Christians wrapped in tar and pitch, then placed them around the garden of his palace and set them on fire as if they were torches.

It is even said that Nero set Rome on fire just for the fun of seeing the city burn. Then he sat in a tower and played on a harp while watching the blaze spread. It is sometimes said that "Nero fiddled while Rome burned," but there were no fiddles then, so we know it must have been a harp. The fire burned day and night for a week, destroying over half of the city. Then Nero blamed the Christians, who, he said, started the fire. Did you ever blame another for something you had done?

Some think Nero was crazy, and we hope he was, for it is hard to believe any person who was not crazy could act as he did.

Nero built an immense palace and overlaid it extravagantly with gold and mother-of-pearl. It was known as Nero's House of Gold. At its front door, he put up a colossal statue of himself in bronze fifty feet high. Both the House of Gold and that statue were later destroyed, but the Colosseum built a few years later, was named Colosseum after another "coloss-al" statue of Nero that was once there.

Medallion showing a bullfighting an elephant inside the Colosseum, seen from above; the Colossus of Nero and Meta Sudans, and the Temple of Venus and Rome, or the Ludus Magnus on either side
Classical Numismatic Group. CC BY-SA 2.5

Nero was very **conceited**. He thought he could write poetry and sing beautifully. Although he did both very badly, Nero liked to show off, and no one dared to laugh at him. Had anyone been so bold as to make fun of him or even to smile, he would have had that person put to death instantly.

Even the Roman people who were not Christians feared and hated Nero. So, they voted to have him put out of the way. But before they had a chance to do anything, Nero heard what they were planning, and to save himself from the disgrace of being put to death by his own people, he decided to kill himself. However, he was such a coward that he couldn't quite bring himself to plunge the sword into his heart. But as he hesitated, holding the sword to his breast and whimpering, his slave, impatient to finish the job, shoved the blade in. Thus Rome was rid of its worst ruler. So much for the first part of this "blood and thunder" story.

The Artios Home Companion Series
Unit 27: The Later Empire and the Christian Church

Teacher Overview

AFTER EMPEROR NERO'S DEATH, the Pax Romana continued with a year of chaos, followed by the Flavian dynasty, known for making reforms. The Nerva-Antonine dynasty followed, known for its "Five Good Emperors." The death of Marcus Aurelius in 180 A.D. marked the end of the Pax Romana.

After a century of chaos, Diocletian divided the Empire to create the Tetrarchy of four rulers, which stabilized the government for a time. After Constantine defeated his rivals in the Tetrarchy and proclaimed himself emperor, he founded a new Rome in the East called Constantinople.

Constantine made Christianity the religion of Rome, but he did not understand that a government cannot dictate what a person honestly believes within their heart. True Christianity involves a turning from sin with a heart of repentance. Many people claiming to be Christians in the Roman Empire at this time continued to worship their pagan gods and idols, and immorality continued.

Depiction of the grand palace of Emperor Diocletian in its imagined original appearance,
by Ernest Hébrard (1912)

Suggested Assignments

Based on your student's age and ability, the reading in this unit may be read aloud to the student, and journaling and notebook pages may be completed orally. Likewise, other assignments may be done with an appropriate combination of independent and guided study.

In this unit, students will:
- Complete two lessons in which they will learn about the **later years of the Roman Empire** and the **growth of the Christian Church**.

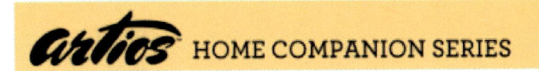

- Define vocabulary words.
- Write a summary.
- Visit the **ArtiosHCS** curriculum website at **www.ArtiosHCS.com** for additional resources and any videos and websites assigned for this unit.

Heart Connections

The Messiah would be born in Bethlehem.
"But you, O Bethlehem Ephrathah, who are too little to be among the clans of Judah, from you shall come forth for me one who is to be ruler in Israel, whose coming forth is from of old, from ancient days."
– Micah 5:1-2

The Messiah would be a descendant of Abraham.
"In your offspring shall all the nations of the earth be blessed, because you have obeyed my voice."
– Genesis 22:18

Nothing can separate us from God's love.
Who shall separate us from the love of Christ? Shall tribulation, or distress, or persecution, or famine, or nakedness, or danger, or sword?
– Romans 8:35

Key People, Places, and Events

Titus	Stoic	Commodus
Destruction of Jerusalem	Zeno	Epicurus
Mount Vesuvius	Nero	Constantine
Pompeii	Marcus Aurelius	Constantinople

Vocabulary

Lesson 1:
garrison
vestibule
previous
pious

Lesson 2:
none

The Eruption of Vesuvius (1821), by Johan Christian Dahl

Lesson One

History Overview and Assignments
Blood and Thunder, Part Two

"Though Marcus Aurelius was not a Christian, he was more Christian in the way he acted than some of the later emperors who were supposed to be Christians. But like many people who are very good themselves, Marcus Aurelius was unable to bring up his son to be so. His son was named Commodus, and Commodus was just as bad as his father was good."
– from the adapted article below

Siege and Destruction of Jerusalem (c.1504)
CC0

Key People, Places, and Events

Titus
Destruction of Jerusalem
Mount Vesuvius
Pompeii
Stoic
Zeno
Nero
Marcus Aurelius
Commodus
Epicurus

Vocabulary

garrison
vestibule
previous
pious

Suggested Reading and Assignments

- Read the combined article:
  Blood and Thunder, Part Two and *A Good Emperor and a Bad Son*.
- Define the vocabulary words in the context of the reading. Write the words and their definitions in the vocabulary section of your history notebook.
- After reading the article, summarize the story you read by either:
  - Retelling it out loud to your teacher or parent.
    OR
  - Completing an appropriate notebook page.

  Either way, be sure to include the answers to the discussion questions and an overview of key people, places, dates, and events in your summary.
- Be sure to visit your **ArtiosHCS** curriculum website for additional resources and any videos and websites assigned for this lesson.

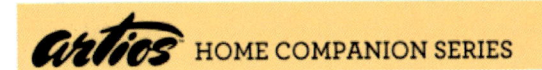

Discussion Questions

1. Why did the Jews in Jerusalem rebel against the Romans?
2. What did Titus do in response?
3. Where does the word "volcano" come from?
4. What happened to the town of Pompeii in the year A.D. 79?
5. What can you tell about the character of Marcus Aurelius?
6. In what ways was his son different from him?

Adapted for Elementary School from the book:
A Child's History of the World
by V.M. Hillyer
Blood and Thunder, Part Two
and
A Good Emperor and a Bad Son

Destruction of Jerusalem

Here is the second part of the Blood and Thunder story.

The Jews in Jerusalem didn't like to have Rome rule over them. They never had. They were afraid to do much about it but finally rebelled in the Year 70 A.D. That is, they said they would no longer obey Rome or pay money in tribute. And they attacked and captured a Roman **garrison**. The Emperor ordered his son, who was named **Titus**, to end the rebellion and punish the Jews as if they were disobedient children.

The Jews crowded into their city of Jerusalem to make a last stand against the Romans. But Titus destroyed that city and the Jews in it, a million of them, it is believed. Then he robbed the great Jewish Temple of all its valuable ornaments and brought them to Rome.

To celebrate this **Destruction of Jerusalem**, an arch was built in the Forum at Rome, and through this arch Titus and his army marched in triumph. On this arch was carved a procession showing Titus leaving the city of Jerusalem with these ornaments. Chief among the sacred items was a golden seven-branched candlestick he had taken from the temple. Today we see many copies in brass of this famous seven-branched candlestick called a *menorah*. Perhaps you may have one in your home.

The south inner panel of the triumphal Arch of Titus showing spoils carried back to Rome after the Destruction of Jerusalem
Photo by Carole Raddato. CC BY-SA 2.0

The city was rebuilt later, but most Jews who left have ever since been living in all the other countries of the earth.

In time Titus became emperor. In spite of how he had massacred so many Jews, he was not such a bad emperor as you might suppose. He thought he had done right in killing these people because they had rebelled against Rome. But Titus had a rule of life, much like that the Boy Scouts now have. This rule was, "Do at least one good turn daily."

The third part of this story is about the "thunder."

Eruption of Mount Vesuvius

In Italy, there is a volcano named **Mount Vesuvius**. You may remember that the word "volcano" comes from the name "Vulcan," the blacksmith god, and people imagined that his forge in the heart of a volcano made the smoke, flame, and ashes. From time to time, this volcano, Vesuvius, thunders and quakes, spouts forth fire, throws up stones and gas, and boils over with red-hot melted rock called lava. It is the hot inside of the earth exploding. Yet people build houses and towns nearby and live even on the volcano's sides. Every once in a while, their homes are destroyed when the volcano quakes or pours forth fire. Yet the same people often go right back and build again in the same place!

At the time of Titus, there was a small town named **Pompeii** near the base of Vesuvius. Wealthy Romans used to go there to spend the summer. One day in the year 79 A.D., just after Titus had become emperor, Vesuvius began to spout fire. The people living in Pompeii ran for their lives, but they hadn't time to escape. They were smothered with the gases from the volcano and, falling dead, were buried deep in a boiling rain of fire and ashes, just where they happened to be when the eruption occurred.

The people and their houses lay buried beneath the ashes for nearly two thousand years, and over time everyone forgot there ever had been such a place. People came back as they had before and built houses over the spot where everyone had forgotten there once was a city. Then one day, a man was digging a well over where Pompeii had once been. He dug up a man's hand—no, not a real hand, but the hand of a statue. He told others, and they set to work and dug and dug to see what else they could find until the whole town was dug out. And now, one can see Pompeii very much as it was in 79 A.D. before it was ever destroyed.

Reconstructed peristyle garden based on the House of the Vettii, Pompeii
Photo by Sailko. CC BY 2.5

There are houses of the Romans who went there to spend their vacations. There are shops, temples, palaces, public baths, the theater, and the marketplace or forum. The streets were paved with blocks of lava, once melted stone. They still show ruts worn into them by the wheels of the chariots the Romans used to drive. Stepping stones were placed at some crossings so that in case of heavy rains when the streets were full of water, one could cross on them from curb to curb. These stepping stones are still there. The floors of the houses were made of bits of colored stone to form pictures. They are still there. In the **vestibule** of one house, there is a mosaic picture on the floor of a dog. Under it are the Latin words "*Cave Canem*." What does that mean? Can you guess? It means "Beware of the dog!" That was a Roman's idea of a joke two thousand years ago!

The bones of the people caught and

buried alive in the ashes were also found. There were also found bronze ornaments worn by the women, vases that decorated the home, lamps used to light the houses, pots, pans, and dishes. Beds and chairs were found just as they had been buried. Still more remarkable, cakes were found on the table, a loaf of bread half eaten, meat ready to be cooked, a kettle on the fire with the ashes still underneath it—beans and peas and one egg unbroken—probably the oldest egg in the world!

Cave Canem Roman mosaic inside the entrance to the House of the Tragic Poet in Pompeii, Italy, 2nd century B.C. Photo by Sailko. CC BY-SA 4.0

A Good Emperor and a Bad Son

Have you ever said, "I don't care," when you really did care?

I have. Everyone has, at least in their heart.

Perhaps you have been naughty and told you could have no dessert or must go to bed early, and you tossed your head proudly and retorted, "I don't care."

Well, once upon a time, a society or club formed of grown-up people who said they wouldn't ever care what happened to them; whether it was good or bad would make no difference. I should call them the "Don't Care Club," but they called themselves "**Stoics**," and they thought the way to be good was "not to care."

If a Stoic's house burned down, he would say to himself and try to make himself believe, "I don't care; it doesn't matter."

If someone gave him a million dollars, he would say, "I don't care; it doesn't matter."

If he were told by the doctor he was going to die next week, he would say, "I don't care; it doesn't matter."

This Society of Stoics was started by a Greek philosopher named **Zeno**.

Zeno lived in Athens later than those philosophers named Socrates and Plato, whom you have already heard about. Zeno said that the only way to be happy was not to care for pleasure and not to mind pain or suffering but calmly to put up with everything, no matter how unpleasant or disagreeable, and the Stoics believed him. Even today, people who bear troubles and pain and hardships without a murmur are called stoics.

One of the chief members of the society was a Roman emperor.

Rome's worst emperor, Nero, had been dead a hundred years when this new emperor came to the throne, who was just as good as Nero was evil. This emperor was named **Marcus Aurelius**. Although he was very good and pious, he was not a Christian. Indeed, Marcus Aurelius treated the Christians terribly, as the previous emperors had treated them terribly, for he thought them traitors to the Empire.

At this time, most of the Romans had very little religion. They were not Christians but did not put much faith in their gods, Jupiter and Juno and the rest. They honored them because they were brought up to honor them and because they thought if they didn't honor them, they might have bad luck, so they took no chances. But instead of believing in such gods, people usually accepted the teachings of some wise man or philosopher and obeyed more or less the rules he made. Zeno was one of these philosophers, and the Stoics were the members of this society.

Marcus Aurelius
Photo by Daniel Martin. CC BY-SA 4.0

Although Marcus Aurelius was an emperor, he would rather have been a Stoic philosopher or a priest. Although he had to be a soldier and a general, he would rather have been a writer. When he was off fighting with his army, he carried his writing materials with him, and he would go to his tent at night and write out his thoughts. These thoughts he called his *Meditations*. Here is one of the things he wrote:

"When you find you do not want to get up early in the morning, make this short speech to yourself. I am getting up now to do the business of a man. Was I made to do nothing but doze and keep warm under the covers?"

That was written long years ago, yet your mother or father might have told you something similar this morning.

People read this book of Marcus Aurelius today, either in the Greek in which it was written or translated into English.

A great many of Marcus Aurelius' sayings seem almost as if they might have been in the Bible. Indeed, some people keep his book by their bedside as if it were a Bible.

One of his rules was, "Forgive your enemies," and he seemed almost glad to have enemies so that he might have a chance to forgive them. Indeed, he took such a particular delight in forgiving his enemies that he even went out of his way to do so. Though Marcus Aurelius was not a Christian, he was more Christian in his actions than some of the later emperors who claimed to be Christians.

But like many people who are very good themselves, Marcus Aurelius was unable to bring up his son to be so. His son was named **Commodus**, and Commodus was just as bad as his father was good. He may have been bored by too many of his father's instructions as a child. When he grew up and could choose for himself and do as he pleased, instead of following Zeno and joining the Stoics, he joined the society of another philosopher called **Epicurus**.

Epicurus lived about the same time as Zeno. But he had taught what at first seemed almost the opposite of what Zeno taught. Epicurus said that man's chief end and aim and the only good in the world was pleasure. But, said he, the pleasure must be of the right kind. Nowadays, people who are very fond of eating pleasant things, whose whole thought is the pleasure of eating, are sometimes called "epicureans."

Commodus's one thought was pleasure and the worst kind of pleasure at that. A friend of mine thought Marcus Aurelius was such a fine man that he named his son after him, but when the son grew up, he was not at all like his namesake. The name "Commodus" would have suited him much better, for instead of being good and **pious**, he thought of nothing but pleasure, and he was so bad that he ended up in jail.

Commodus thought nothing about giving his people a good government. He only thought of giving himself a good time. He was an athlete and had beautiful muscles and a handsome figure, of which he was so proud that he had a statue made of himself. The statue showed him as the strong and muscular god Hercules. Commodus made the people worship him as if he were this god. He participated in prize fights to show off his muscles and athletic ability—quite bad taste for an emperor. He poisoned or killed anyone who found fault with or criticized him. He led a wild and dissipated life but finally met the end he deserved. He was strangled to death by a wrestler.

Lycurgus would have repeated: "I told you so."

Emperor Commodus dressed as Hercules (c.191 A.D.)
Photo by Jofrey Rudel Marie-Lan Nguyen (Jastrow). CC0

Restored version of John Martin's *Destruction of Pompeii and Herculaneum*

Lesson Two

History Overview and Assignments
In This Sign You Shall Conquer

> *"Once upon a time, Constantine was fighting with an enemy when he dreamed one night that he saw in the sky a flaming cross. Beneath this cross were written the Latin words: 'In hoc signo vinces.' In English, this means: 'In this sign you shall conquer.' Constantine thought this meant he would conquer if he carried the Christian cross into battle. He thought it would at least be worthwhile to give the Christian God a trial. So, he had his soldiers carry the cross, and he did win the battle. Then immediately, he declared himself a Christian and expected everyone in the Roman Empire to become a Christian. From that time on, all the Roman emperors who came after Constantine, all except one, were Christians."*
>
> – from the adapted article below

An icon depicting Emperor Constantine, accompanied by the bishops of the First Council of Nicaea (325 A.D.) and holding the Niceno–Constantinopolitan Creed of 381 A.D.

Suggested Reading and Assignments

- Read the article: *I — H — — S — — — — — V — — — — —*.
- After reading the article, summarize the story you read by either:
  - Retelling it out loud to your teacher or parent.
    OR
  - Completing an appropriate notebook page.

  Either way, be sure to include the answers to the discussion questions and an overview of key people, places, dates, and events in your summary.

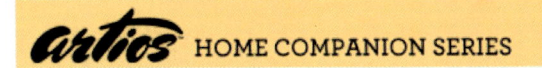

Ancient: Elementary
Unit 27: The Later Empire and the Christian Church

- Instead of answering discussion questions, summarize the story of how **Emperor Constantine** made Christianity the state religion of the Roman Empire.
- Be sure to visit your **ArtiosHCS** curriculum website for additional resources and any videos and websites assigned for this lesson.

Key People, Places, and Events

Constantine
Constantinople

Adapted for Elementary School from the book:
A Child's History of the World
by V.M. Hillyer
I – H – – S – – – – V – – – – –

A coin of Constantine (c.337 A.D.) showing a depiction of his labarum *spearing a serpent on the reverse; the inscription reads SPES PVBLICA, or "hope of the public." The scene has powerful Christian imagery portraying the power of Christianity over evil.*

I'm going to put the name of this story at the end, for you wouldn't know what it means, anyway, until you have heard the story, so it's no use looking ahead.

Through many years since Jesus was crucified, those who said they believed in Him had been treated terribly—"persecuted," we call it—because they were Christians. They had been flogged; they had been stoned; they had been torn with iron hooks; they had been roasted and burned to death. Yet, strange as it may seem, despite this terrible treatment, more and more people became Christians daily. They believed so strongly in life after death and would be so much happier if they died for Christ's sake that they seemed even glad to suffer and be killed. But at last, the Emperor himself stopped all these persecutions. This is how it happened.

About the year 300 A.D., Rome had an emperor by the name of **Constantine**. Constantine was not a Christian. His gods were the old Roman gods. He probably did not put much faith in them, however.

Well, once upon a time, Constantine was fighting with an enemy when he dreamed one night that he saw in the sky a flaming cross. Beneath this cross were written the Latin words: *"In hoc signo vinces."* In English, this means: "In this sign you shall conquer." Constantine thought this meant he would conquer if he carried the Christian cross into battle. He thought it would at least be worthwhile to give the Christian God a trial. So, he had his soldiers carry the cross, and he did win the battle. Then immediately, he declared himself a Christian and expected everyone in the Roman Empire to become a Christian. From that time on, all the Roman emperors who came after Constantine, except one, were Christians.

To celebrate Constantine's victory, the Roman Senate built a triumphal arch in the Forum of Rome called the Arch of Constantine.

The Arch of Constantine
Photo by Alexander Z. CC BY-SA 3.0

Constantine's mother was named Helena. She was among the very first to become a Christian and be baptized. Then she gave up her life to Christian works and built churches at Bethlehem and on the Mount of Olives. It is said that she went to Palestine and found the actual cross on which Christ had been crucified three hundred years before and sent part of it to Rome. She was declared a saint when she died and is now called St. Helena.

Constantine built a church over where St. Peter was supposed to have been crucified. This church was torn down many years later, so a much larger and grander church to St. Peter might be built there.

But Constantine did not care for Rome. He preferred to live in another city in the Eastern part of the Roman Empire. This city was called Byzantium. So, he moved from Rome to Byzantium and made that city his capital. Byzantium was called New Rome, and the name was changed to Constantine's City. In Greek, the word for "city" is "polis." We see the term used in Annapolis and Indianapolis. So, Constantine's City became *Constantinepolis* and later was shortened to **Constantinople**.

Saint Helena With the Cross,
by Lucas Cranach the Elder (1525)

Hardly had the Roman Empire become Christian before a quarrel arose between those Christians who believed one thing and those who thought another. The chief thing they quarreled about was whether Christ was equal to God the Father or not equal to Him. Constantine called the two disagreeing sides together at Nicaea to settle the question. There the leaders of each side argued the matter hotly. Finally, it was decided that the Christian Church should believe that God the Son and God the Father were equal. Then they agreed to put what they believed in words. The statement was called a *creed*, which means "believe," and because it was made at Nicaea, it was known as the Nicene Creed, which many Christians still recite every Sunday.

Before the time of Constantine, there were no weekly holidays. Sunday was no different from any other day. People worked or did the same things on Sunday as on other days. Constantine thought Christians should have one day a week to worship God—a "holy day," or holiday, as we call it—so he made Sunday the Christian day of rest, a "holy day" such as Saturday was for the Jews.

But although Constantine was head of the Roman Empire, there was another man all Christians worldwide looked to as their spiritual head. This man was the Bishop of Rome. In Latin, he was called *papa*, which means the same thing in Latin that it does in English: "father." So, the bishop of Rome was called "papa," and this became "pope." St. Peter was believed to have been the first Bishop of Rome. For many centuries, the pope was the spiritual ruler of all Christians everywhere, no matter in what country they lived.

As now you know what the name of this story means, I'm putting it here:

In Hoc Signo Vinces.

Detail from *The Vision of the Cross*, by assistants of Raphael, depicting the vision of the cross and the Greek writing "Εν τούτω νίκα" (*"In Hoc Signo Vinces,"* or "In this sign you shall conquer") in the sky before the Battle of the Milvian Bridge, in which Constantine defeated his rival Maxentius to become emperor in 312 A.D.

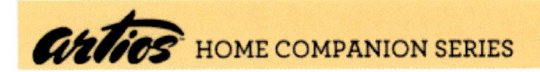

The Artios Home Companion Series
Unit 28: The Fall of Rome

Teacher Overview

THE GREAT ROMAN EMPIRE had conquered many lands and spread around the Mediterranean Sea. Still, its corrupt rulers could not maintain control over the people and keep out invaders forever. During the fifth century A.D., conquering tribes from the north overran the Italian peninsula and then conquered Rome. In 476, the Roman Emperor was forced to give up his throne. While this conquest spelled doom for the Empire, it also opened doors for Christianity to spread worldwide.

Invasion of the Huns Approaching Rome, by Ulpiano Checa (1887)

Suggested Assignments

Based on your student's age and ability, the reading in this unit may be read aloud to the student, and journaling and notebook pages may be completed orally. Likewise, other assignments may be done with an appropriate combination of independent and guided study.

In this unit, students will:
- Complete two lessons in which they will learn about the **Fall of the Roman Empire**.
- Make two lists.
- Visit the **ArtiosHCS** curriculum website at **www.ArtiosHCS.com** for additional resources and any videos and websites assigned for this unit.

Heart Connections

> *Blessed is the nation whose God is the LORD, the people whom he has chosen as his heritage!*
> – Psalm 33:12

Key People, Places, and Events

Teutons
Woden
Thor
Tiw
Freya
Saturn
Angles
Saxons
Anglo-Saxons
Vandals
Franks
Goths
Alaric
Huns
Attila
Battle of Châlons
Leo I
Romulus Augustulus

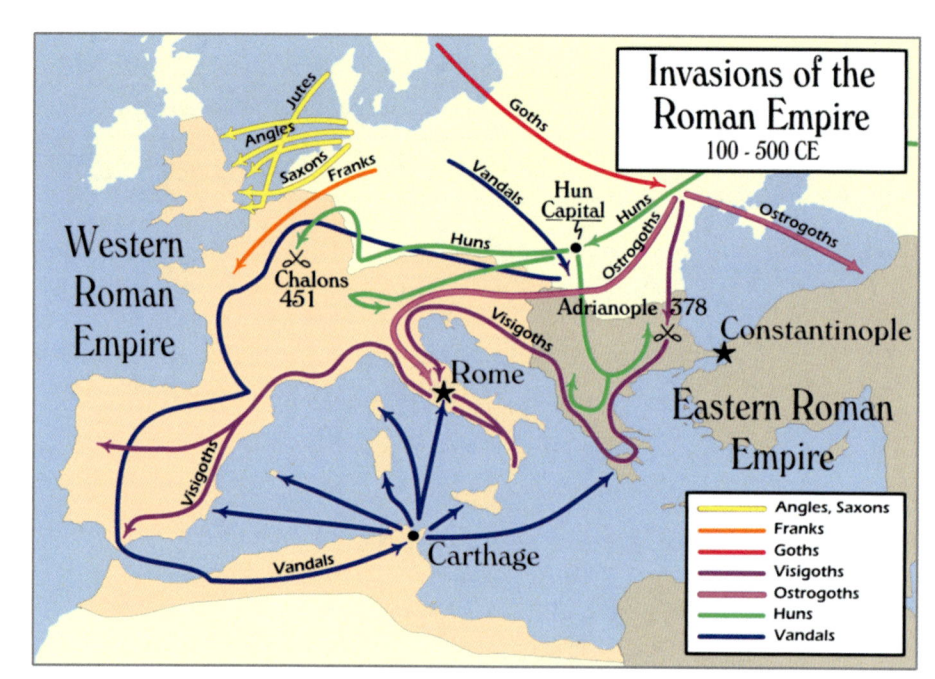

Invasions of the Roman Empire between 100 and 500 A.D.
Map by MapMaster. CC BY-SA 2.5

Romulus Augustus giving up his crown to Odoacer

Lesson One

History Overview and Assignments
Divided We Fall

"Alaric and his Goths crossed over the mountains into Italy and robbed or destroyed everything of value they could lay their hands on. They then entered Rome and carried away whatever they wanted, and the Romans could not stop them. But the worst was yet to come."
— from the adapted article below

The 3rd-century Great Ludovisi sarcophagus frieze depicts a battle between the Goths and Romans (251 A.D).

Suggested Reading and Assignments

- Read the article: *Our Tough Ancestors*.
- After reading the article, summarize the story you read by either:
    - Retelling it out loud to your teacher or parent.
         OR
    - Completing an appropriate notebook page.

  Either way, be sure to include an overview of key people, places, dates, and events in your summary.
- Instead of answering discussion questions, make one list of the Teutonic deities and what each is known for and another list of the Teutonic people groups mentioned in today's reading and where they each migrated.
- Be sure to visit your **ArtiosHCS** curriculum website for additional resources and any videos and websites assigned for this lesson.

Key People, Places, and Events

Teutons	Tiw	Angles	Vandals	Goths
Woden	Freya	Saxons	Franks	Alaric
Thor	Saturn	Anglo-Saxons		

Ancient: Elementary
Unit 28: The Fall of Rome

Adapted for Elementary School from the book:
A Child's History of the World
by V.M. Hillyer
Our Tough Ancestors

Rome, with the Roman Empire, had had her day. She had risen as high as she could. It was her turn to fall. She had become as large as she ever was to be. It was her turn to be conquered. But you cannot guess what people would do the conquering and be next in power.

When I was a boy, a tough gang lived by the railroad tracks. They were ragged, unwashed, unschooled, but terrible fighters. Their leader was known to us as Mug Mike, and the very mention of him and his gang struck terror in our souls. Now and then, they visited our neighborhood. One time we offered defense, but with such terrible results that the alarm would be sounded ever after at word of their approach, and we would hide indoors.

Teuton warrior

For ages, there had been such a gang of half-civilized toughs living on the northern borders of the Roman Empire. Now and then, they tried to cross the border into the Roman lands, and the Romans had to fight them to keep them back where they belonged constantly. Julius Caesar had fought against them. So had Marcus Aurelius, and so had Constantine. These wild and warlike people were called **Teutons,** and—you may be shocked to hear it, but—they are the ancestors of most of us!

They had light hair and blue eyes. The Greeks, Romans, and other people living around the Mediterranean Sea had black hair and dark eyes. If you have light or brown hair, you are probably a Teuton. If you have black hair, you are probably not. But don't think your ancestors weren't tough bullies because many probably were.

The Teutons were uneducated toughs and could neither read nor write.

They wore the skins of animals instead of clothes made of cloth. They lived in huts made of wood, sometimes of branches woven together—like a large basket. The women raised vegetables and took care of the cows and horses. The men did the hunting and fighting and blacksmithing. Blacksmithing was especially important, for the blacksmith made the swords and spears with which they fought and the tools with which they worked. That is why the name "Smith" was so honored among them.

When the men went to battle, they wore the heads of animals they had killed, an ox's head, horns and all, or the head of a wolf, bear, or fox. This was to make themselves look fierce and to frighten the enemy.

Bravery was the chief thing the Teutons thought was good. A man might lie, steal, or even commit murder, but he was called a "good" man if he was a brave warrior.

The Teutons did not have a king. They elected their chiefs, and of course, they always chose the bravest and strongest man. But he could not make his son ruler after him. So, in that way, he was more like a president than a king.

The Teutons had an entirely distinct set of gods from those of Greece and Rome. As you might guess, their chief god was the god of war, and they called him **Woden** (or Odin). Woden was also the god of the sky. He was like the two Roman gods, Jupiter and Mars. Woden was believed to live in a wonderful palace in the sky called Valhalla, and many tales are told of the wonderful things he did and his adventures. Wednesday, which was once "Wodensday," is named after him. That is why there is a letter "d" in this word, although we don't pronounce it.

Valhalla, by Max Brückner (1896)

After Woden, **Thor** was the next most important god. He was the god of thunder and lightning. He carried a hammer, with which he fought great giants who lived in the far-off cold lands and were called "ice giants." Thursday, which was once "Thorsday," is named after him.

Another god was named **Tiw,** and from his name we get Tuesday, and a goddess named **Freya**, from whom we get Friday, so that four out of seven of our days are named after Teuton gods, although we are—most of us—Christians and no longer believe in these gods.

Thor's Fight with the Giants (*Tors strid med jättarna*), by Mårten Eskil Winge (1872)

Of the other three days of the week, Sunday and Monday are named after the sun and moon, and Saturday is named after a Greek god, **Saturn**.

From these wild people, all fair-haired people today are said to be descended: the English, French, German, and such of us whose ancestors are English or French or German.

About the Year 400 A.D., these Teuton toughs started becoming particularly troublesome to the Romans. They began to push their way down into the northern part of the Roman Empire, and after a few years, the Romans could hold them back no longer. Two of these Teuton gangs, or tribes, as they were called, went over into Britain, and the Romans living there found it wisest to get out, go back to Rome, and leave the country to the Teutons.

These tribes who settled in Britain were known as **Angles** and **Saxons**. So, the country came to be called the land of the Angles, or, for short, "Angle-land." After the words "Angle-land" were said for many years, they became "England," which we call the country today. The people of England are still known by the full name "**Anglo-Saxons**." This is the name we call everyone descended from these old Teuton tribes of Angles and Saxons who settled in Britain about 400 A.D.

Another gang or tribe called the **Vandals** went into Gaul. Gaul is where France is now. Then they continued into Spain, stealing, smashing, and burning like Mug Mike's gang of toughs on Halloween. They crossed over by boat into Africa. They injured or destroyed everything they came upon. So, today when anyone damages or destroys property wickedly, we call him a vandal. If you cut up your desk, tear your books, or scratch names on walls or fences, you, too, are a vandal.

A tribe called the **Franks** followed the Vandals into Gaul, where they stayed, giving the name "France" to that country.

The Teutons north of Italy were the **Goths**. Their leader was **Alaric**. He was the "Mug Mike" of the gang of Goths. Alaric and his Goths crossed over the mountains into Italy and robbed or destroyed everything of value they could lay their hands on. They then entered Rome and carried away whatever they wanted, and the Romans could not stop them. But the worst was yet to come.

A 16th-century perception of the Vandals, painted by Lucas de Heere in the second half of the 16th century and preserved in the Ghent University Library

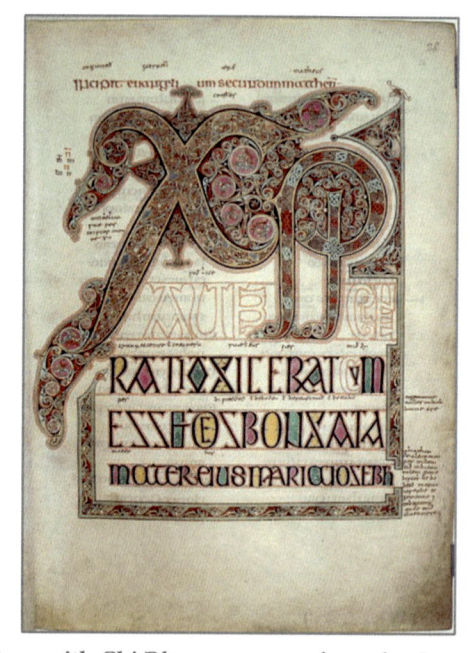

Page with Chi Rho monogram from the Gospel of Matthew in the *Lindisfarne Gospels* (c.700), possibly created by Eadfrith of Lindisfarne

Lesson Two

History Overview and Assignments
The Fallen Champion

"Poor old Rome! She was at last beaten! She had been the Champion for a great many years. But now all her strength was gone. She was old and weak and could no longer defend herself against these gangs of toughs."

– from the adapted article below

Raphael's *The Meeting between Leo the Great and Attila* depicts Leo, escorted by Saint Peter and Saint Paul, meeting with the Hun king outside Rome.

Suggested Reading and Assignments

- Read the article: *White Toughs and Yellow Toughs Meet the Champions of the World.*
- After reading the article, summarize the story you read by either:
    - Retelling it out loud to your teacher or parent.
        OR
    - Completing an appropriate notebook page.
  Either way, be sure to include the answers to the discussion questions and an overview of key people, places, dates, and events in your summary.
- Be sure to visit your **ArtiosHCS** curriculum website for additional resources and any videos and websites assigned for this lesson.

Key People, Places, and Events

Huns	Battle of Châlons	Romulus Augustulus
Attila	Leo I	Odoacer

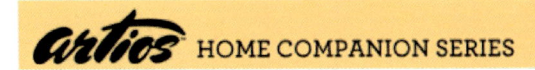

Discussion Questions

1. In what year did the Teutons beat the Huns in battle outside Paris?
2. Why does the author say this victory was important to history?
3. Who stopped Attila and his Huns from attacking Rome?
4. Who finally forced the last Roman emperor to give up his crown?
5. Why is the year 476 considered the end of Ancient history?
6. How were the Italian, French, and Spanish languages formed?
7. How was Christianity brought to England?

Sack of Rome by Alaric, by Maître François (c.1475), showing sacred vessels carried to a church for safety

Adapted for Elementary School from the book:
A Child's History of the World
by V.M. Hillyer
White Toughs and Yellow Toughs Meet the Champions of the World

Farther north of the Teutons and to the east was a tribe of people who were even more savage and fierce. They were called **Huns**. They lived far off in the forests and wilds way beyond the Teutons, in a part of the country that no one then knew much about.

Even the Teutons themselves, fierce fighters though they were, feared the Huns, and it was chiefly because they were afraid of them and wanted to get as far as they could from them that the Teutons migrated over the borders into the Roman Empire. It was much easier to fight the Romans than it was to fight the Huns.

The Huns seemed more like wild beasts than human beings. Their leader was a dreadful man named **Attila**. He boasted that nothing ever grew again where his horse had trod. He and his Huns had conquered and laid waste the country from the East almost to Paris. At last, the Teutons stood against them and fought a great battle at a place not so far from Paris called Châlons.

The Teutons fought desperately; they fought madly, and finally, the Huns were beaten. It was lucky they were beaten, for if they had won, these dreadful, wild bullies might have conquered and ruled the world. So the **Battle of Châlons**, 451 A.D., is written in history in capital letters and large figures—CHÂLONS 451.

After Attila and his Huns had been beaten at Châlons, they left the Teutons alone and went after the Romans. Turning back, the Huns entered Italy, where no one could stop them. They destroyed everything as they moved on. The people of the country didn't even attempt to fight. They thought the Huns were monsters and fled before them. So on to Rome, the Huns went.

Saint Leo Magnus ("Pope Leo I"), by Francisco de Herrera el Mozo (17th century)

There was a pope in Rome at this time named **Leo I**, which means "Lion." Leo was neither a soldier nor a fighting man, but he and his cardinals and bishops went out from Rome to meet Attila. They were not clad in armor, and none of them carried any weapons with which to fight. The Pope and those with him wore gorgeous robes and richly colored garments. It seemed as if they would surely be slaughtered by Attila and his Huns, like lambs before wolves.

But something strange happened when Attila and the Pope met—precisely what no one knows. Perhaps Attila was awed by the pomp and splendor of those Christians. Perhaps he feared what Heaven might do to him if he destroyed those holy beings who had come out to meet him as if from Heaven. At any rate, he did not destroy them, nor did he enter Rome, but turned about and left Italy, left it for good and all, and he and his Huns returned to the unknown land to the north from which they had come.

Now that the dreaded Attila was out of the way, the Vandals in Africa saw their chance to attack Rome. Attila had barely left Italy before the Vandals crossed over from a kingdom they'd made in Africa and sailed up the Tiber to Rome. They captured the city easily, helped themselves to everything they wanted, and carried away all Rome's treasures.

Poor old Rome! She was at last beaten! She had been the Champion for a great many years. But now all her strength was gone. She was old and weak and could no longer defend herself against these gangs of toughs. Rome's last emperor had the high-sounding name "**Romulus Augustulus**," the same name as the first king, Romulus, with the addition of Augustulus, which means "the little Augustus." But despite his high-sounding name, Romulus Augustulus could do nothing. He was like the little boy living in the marble house on the avenue, the little boy with curls and a velvet suit, who Mug Mike caught out one day and—you can guess the rest.

It was in the Year 476 that Rome was finally conquered, and the Teuton named **Odoacer** forced Romulus Augustulus to give up his crown. The western half of the Empire, of which Rome had been the capital, broke into pieces, and Teutons ruled over the parts. Like Humpty Dumpty, Rome had had a great fall, and all the king's horses and all the king's men couldn't put it together again. Only the eastern part, of which Constantinople was the capital, remained. The barbarians did not conquer this eastern half, and it kept going for nearly a thousand years longer until—but wait till we come to that time in history.

People speak of this year, 476, as the end of Ancient History. After Ancient History, there was a time over five hundred years long known as the Dark Ages—the Nighttime of History. The Dark Ages lasted from 476 to about 1000 A.D. These centuries are called the Dark Ages because during that long time, the Teutons, those uneducated toughs who were unable even to read and write, were the chief people in Europe, and they ruled over those who had once been the educated and cultured people.

The Teutons, though such rough toughs, barbarians as they were called, were, strange to say, quick to learn many things from the Romans whom they had conquered. Even before they had conquered Rome, most of the Teutons had already become Christians.

Of course, they had to learn Latin to talk to their subjects. But they changed Latin a lot and mixed it with their language. At last, this mixture of their language with Latin became Italian. The Teutons who went to Spain in a like way mixed their language with Latin, and this mixture became Spanish. In France, the mix of the two languages became French.

In Britain, however, the Anglo-Saxons would have nothing to do with the Romans and would not use the Roman language but kept their language. After a while, this language of the Anglo-Saxons was called English. The Anglo-Saxons also kept their religion and worshiped Thor and Woden and their other gods until about one hundred years later, or about 600 A.D.

At that time, some English slaves were being sold in the slave market in Rome. They were very handsome. The Pope saw them and asked who they were.

"They are Angles," he was told.

"Angles!" exclaimed he; "they are handsome enough to be angels, and they should certainly be Christians."

So, he sent some missionaries to England to convert the English; to change Angles into Angels. So, at last, the English, too, became Christians.

Augustine of Canterbury, on his mission to Anglo-Saxon England

Made in the USA
Middletown, DE
23 August 2023